THE PRAEGER HANDBOOK OF PLAY ACROSS THE LIFE CYCLE

THE PRAEGER HANDBOOK OF PLAY ACROSS THE LIFE CYCLE

Fun from Infancy to Old Age

Luciano L'Abate

Foreword by
Arthur M. Horne

PRAEGER

An Imprint of ABC-CLIO, LLC

A B C CLIO

Santa Barbara, California • Denver, Colorado • Oxford, England

James A. Dimmock and J. Robert Grove, "Indentification with Sports Teams as a Function of the Search for Certainty," *Journal of Sports Sciences*, Vol. 24, Issue 11. Copyright © 2006 by Taylor and Francis Group. Reprinted by permission of the publisher, Taylor and Francis Group, http://www.informaworld.com.

Hilary Aydt and William A. Corsaro, "Differences in Children's Construction of Gender Across Culture: An Interpretive Approach," *American Behavioral Scientist*, Vol. 46, Issue 10. Copyright © 2003 by SAGE Publications. Reprinted by Permission of SAGE Publications.

Ann-Carita Evaldsson and William A. Corsaro, "Play and Games in the Peer Cultures of Preschool and Preadolescent Children: An Interpretative Approach," *Childhood*, Vol. 5, Issue 4. Copyright © 1998 by SAGE Publications. Reprinted by Permission of SAGE Publications

Library of Congress Cataloging-in-Publication Data

L'Abate, Luciano, 1928-
 The Praeger handbook of play across the life cycle : fun from infancy to old age / Luciano L'Abate ; Foreword by Arthur M. Horne.
     p. cm.
 Includes bibliographical references and index.
 ISBN 978-0-313-35929-3 (hard copy : alk. paper) — ISBN 978-0-313-35930-9 (ebook)
 1. Play—Psychological aspects. 2. Play—Social aspects. 3. Symbolic play. I. Title.
 BF717.L33 2009
 155—dc22   2009016698

13 12 11 10 9 1 2 3 4 5

This book is also available on the World Wide Web as an eBook.
Visit www.abc-clio.com for details.

ABC-CLIO, LLC
130 Cremona Drive, P.O. Box 1911
Santa Barbara, California 93116-1911

This book is printed on acid-free paper ∞
Manufactured in the United States of America

60.00

To Brian Sutton-Smith who contributed more about play and playing than anyone else I know, and to my two beloved grandchildren, Alessandra and Ian, who may value play just as much as work.

CONTENTS

FOREWORD

What a delight to be involved with Luciano L'Abate and his book on play, *The Praeger Handbook of Play across the Life Cycle: Fun from Infancy to Old Age.*

As a family therapy teacher, researcher, and practitioner for more than three decades, I had long been familiar with Lu's writing—everyone in the field has been influenced by his scholarship and originality of thinking on families, therapy, and the world of mental health. But although I knew much of his writing, I did not know Lu personally until about a decade ago, when we met at an international conference on family psychology. Our first evening together I became acquainted with a Dr. L'Abate I had not known from his writing: one who was quick of wit, mischievously engaging, and eager to finish the night with singing, dancing, and robust stories of Italy. In short, in addition to being a scholar and academic, he was a fun person and a delight to be with. So when Lu informed me he was writing a book on play, I knew it would represent great integrity of scholarship and thoroughness of the literature review, but more importantly, would also be fun to read and experience. Thus, long before having the manuscript to read, I anticipated a most enjoyable experience—one that would educate, inform, and even entertain. Having now read the material, my anticipations have been fulfilled. It is a L'Abate book, with exceptional scholarship and also very personal and engaging material that will have readers learning about Lu's extensive life experiences related to play and fun, and reflecting on their own experiences and how those events have shaped their lives and influenced their world view. This is a book on play that is fun to read.

The Praeger Handbook of Play across the Life Cycle: Fun from Infancy to old Age provides the reader with an in-depth review of what play is and how it influences all stages of life development, certainly in a positive manner when done well, and with sad results when play does not occur or is thwarted. Fun is such an integral component of life that the psychiatrist William Glasser includes the concept as one of his five essential components to life. Glasser (2001) explains that when people are having fun, when they play and engage, they are learning, and that continued learning provides the health and growth necessary to be fully functioning people; without play, we are not fully experiencing life. Play in childhood allows children to experience, learn, and be engaged. These characteristics are necessary through all developmental stages of life and are particularly essential for providing balance and perspective.

Dr. L'Abate is a natural storyteller, and throughout the book he provides wonderful and moving anecdotes, illustrations, and descriptions of play. In doing so, he illustrates how important play is. The humanness of his examples brings to life the way that play can impact and connect. By telling tales of poker groups that continue for decades, or travel that expands knowledge, or sewing circles that bring people out to share together, he illustrates how very differently we can find ways to play and how we can experience others in many enjoyable and engaging ways.

A characteristic of modern times is that we have accumulated greater wealth, which allows us to create lifestyles that are more isolated than in the past. For example, many families fear for the safety of their children, so the children are not allowed to wander around neighborhoods or have unsupervised time with friends; instead, their time becomes more circumscribed, and they are often provided with gadgets rather than people to serve as their companions: game boxes, televisions, computer monitors. Although children can play with these devices, they lose the interactional and relational aspects that were generated in the past through friendships and neighborhood gatherings, and thus their lives are stunted from what they could be.

Play has taken a different form for adults as well, as Dr. L'Abate so clearly illustrates. As adults have become aware of the need for physical activity to stay healthy, they have often moved to more isolated forms of exercise than previously. Rather than participating in neighborhood projects, city ball clubs, and energetic family picnics, many adults today gain their exercise through isolated machinery in the form of treadmills and home gyms or through solitary or isolated workouts at fitness centers, where the object is serious exercise rather than play and fun. Others ignore the importance of exercise and define their entertainment through television and computers, experiencing the engagement of the devices, but losing out on the relational and friendship characteristics that arise from team sports, neighborhood clubs, and family gatherings.

Another characteristic of our modern society is that we have less visiting than previously. In decades gone by, "drop-in" visits, weekly family gatherings, and church or work groups that visited and shared, often with storytelling, card games, jokes, and shared memories, were common and represented a way to play, to engage, and to have fun. Today's loneliness of cubicles at work, isolated living conditions, and an abundance of solitary entertainment equipment have made opportunities for fun, playing, and relationships more difficult to create and maintain.

Tied to the concern of isolated living circumstances, free time is less available than it has been for years, and rather than reducing the number of hours we work, we have been steadily increasing them. In 2000, for example, we worked 36 more hours in the year than in 1990 (CNN.com, 2001), in essence adding a full week of work to the average yearly workload over a ten-year period. In the 1970s, as machinery and computers became more sophisticated, there were predictions of enormous leisure, and there was concern that people would be unprepared for their extra time. Universities even created programs called health and leisure studies, or recreation and leisure training. And yet, as the CNN report indicates, we are working more with less leisure time. It is important that we establish a better understanding of the role of play and the effective use of leisure time in our lives to gain the balance and perspective that provides for healthy aging. Addressing the means of being engaged, having fun, playing, and being athletic will require a national focus that moves toward relationships and away from the level of consumerism that has been so prevalent in our lives recently.

An area of concern some have had is that play and relational competition can lead to aggression and violence. L'Abate addresses the concern, emphasizing that just the opposite is likely to happen with effective play: that, through the interactions and the learning of play rules, people can develop an appreciation of others and learn empathy, cooperation, and team building—all essential characteristics. In our own studying of bullying over the past decades, we have learned that effective learning and play interactions result in reduced aggression and greater cooperation, essential characteristics in our busy and isolated worlds today (Orpinas & Horne, 2006).

I can see this book being an essential addition to libraries of all people involved in helping foster healthy development and fulfilling lives. Psychologists, psychiatrists, social workers, counselors, and all other mental health workers will benefit from the knowledge provided by L'Abate in this text. Yet this book is more than an informative call to play; it is an awareness-developing experience for the reader to recognize the importance of making personal, family, community, and cultural changes to endorse the value and role of play in our lives. Dr. L'Abate has provided a scholarly review that provides policymakers and program leaders with the information necessary to find ways to incorporate play and fun into the lives of our citizens, thus providing information about the role of prevention through fun, play, and engagement. This is important, the message is essential, and the book will be a great find for so many people.

Arthur M. Horne
Dean and Distinguished Research Professor
The University of Georgia

PREFACE

One purpose of this book is to overview the evolution of play, summarizing current research and theory, showing how we play at various ages and stages of the chronological life cycle, through the interplay of development and socialization. Do play and playing help us develop into healthy people—physically, intellectually, emotionally, and spiritually? In spite of the vast literature on this topic emphasizing the importance of play in relational competence and socialization, there is very little written about the life cycle aspects of play. We still subscribe to the notion that play is for children; adults have "leisure time," but if they play, it is for competition, from sports to card games, bridge, poker, or board games such as Scrabble. Otherwise, in old age, leisure time may mean sitting passively watching someone else play on television or listening to numbers called in Bingo.

Trying to include all the information available about play would require an unending and encyclopedic effort (and one beyond the contractual limit of pages set for this work), so I will indicate, where needed, where the interested reader can find further information. There is no need for me to repeat information that is available in finer and greater detail elsewhere. Therefore, the information included in this volume is by necessity selective and, oftentimes, condensed.

A PsychINFO search of relevant research and publications failed to find any references to "play" cross-referenced with "life cycle." However, cross-referencing "play" with "personality development" yielded 5,291 references. A more restricted search substituting "socialization" for "development" yielded 291 references. In other words, there is plenty of literature to mine. When this search was restricted to stages of development, "infancy" included 516 references, "preschool" and "pre-kindergarten" over 2,000, "kindergarten" 185, "elementary school" 264, "puberty" 148, "adolescent youth" 147, "adulthood" 505, "middle age" 39, and "old age" 13. Cross-referencing for "play," "games," and "health" yielded 120 references. Of course, there are at least sixteen additional academic search engines under psychology that can be used in a review of the relevant literature. This shows how selective I had to be in writing this book.

For specific games in old age, the numbers of references were as follows: "bowling" 12, "cards" 123, "golf" 26, and "tennis" 35. There is substantial literature on adulthood and beyond when, instead of "play," "leisure" is cross-indexed with "age." Hence, there is a vast reserve of additional information that can be included at each stage of the life cycle for preventive and psychotherapeutic purposes. When "play therapy" was included in this search, literally thousands of entries were found; for that reason I asked Dr. Lauren Wynne to help on Chapter 15, dedicated to that topic. There is no question in my mind, therefore, that play throughout the life span is an important aspect of any health promotional, preventive, psychotherapeutic, and rehabilitative interventions because play, in its various forms, has been and still is an important part of my life. It is also the best form of self-help (Harwood & L'Abate, 2009).

I must confess regretfully, and warn the reader from the outset about, four major gaps present in this book because of space and time limitations. First, I kept my focus on human beings, and by necessity I neglected the important topic of play in nonhumans. I am sorry for this failure, but I must admit to my personal and editorial limitations. To include this literature would require more time and space that can or should be devoted to it. Readers who are interested in this topic can consult excellent introductions on the topic of play in the great apes (Gomez & Martin-Andrade, 2005; Pellegrini & Smith, 2005), monkeys (Bolig, Price, O'Neill-Wagner, & Suomi, 1998; New, Cunningham, & Sughrue, 1998), and other animals (Biben & Champoux, 1999; Champoux, Shannon, Airoso, & Suomi, 1999; De Long, 1999).

The second unfortunate gap that I had to leave has to do with the exciting and extremely promising literature of neurological and cerebral functioning on play (Burghardt, 2004; Greenberg, 2004; Rike, 2004; Wilkinson, 2004). With the advent of neuroimaging and other technological breakthroughs, it is relatively easy to predict that this specialty field in the study of play has a brilliant future.

Another gap lies in my skimpy historical and theoretical coverage of play advocates ("Children should play"), apologists ("Play is good for you because . . ."), and theorists ("This is how, what, when, and why play is"). I must also admit my inability to interpret and integrate a variety of conclusions and data that were obtained by a frustrating diversity of methods and participants, which make it a stretch to arrive at definite conclusions. I have attempted to make up for both of these deficiencies by interpreting and integrating play within a theory of relational competence (L'Abate, 2005; L'Abate & Cusinato, 2007), as presented in Chapter 19 here.

As Americans and people in other developed societies worldwide focus more and more of their time and energy on work, "playtime" has plummeted, and playful activities have too often become been equated with "idleness," "laziness," or at least "pointlessness." Even with children—now being overscheduled, trained, and prepared for college as early as elementary and middle school—play is sometimes seen as a dispensable draw on time, with schools reducing or altogether cutting recess and classes in physical education (Linder, 1970). But are we losing anything vital with these ideas and actions? Play, as one scholar puts it, "is not a luxury but rather a crucial dynamic of healthy physical, intellectual, social and emotional development at all age levels." (Elkind, 2007, p. 5). This conclusion is so strong that there has been one attempt to reclaim "childhood and letting children be children in our achievement-oriented society" (Crain, 2003) and a strongly worded 1977 Declaration of the Child's Right to Play by the International Play Association (2004).

In other words, play seems a necessary component for healthy body and healthy mind. Play and playful activities have developed and changed across past and recent history, and their necessity has been the subject of changing cultural and educational views and controversies. Disgracefully, there are still undeveloped countries, such as Egypt among many others, where children are exploited to work from an early age, as early as 10 years old (*Atlanta Journal and Constitution,* Sunday April 6, 2008).

Supposedly, the more leisure time people have the greater the possibilities are of engaging in play and playful activities. Unfortunately, that is not the case (Linder, 1970). In spite of the many technological advances that should save time both at home and at work, leisure time available to us has not increased. Why? It is indeed true that we are not only achievement oriented but also performance and production oriented (Pershing, 2006), to the point that we do not know how to be together unless there is a special reason, such as refreshments, a football game, or, at best, a book club (Spiegel, 1971). Doing and Having are more important than Being together with family and friends just for the pleasure of being together.

I will never forget the experience of being a tourist in the major square of Salamanca, Spain, toward the evening hours, and observing a ritual that I have never seen anywhere else. Individuals lined up arm in arm, up to six or seven abreast, talking and laughing with each other, were walking together around the center fountain, like the moving spokes of a wheel. At the same time, on another part of the square, there were two elderly men, talking with each other while walking back and forth from a predetermined spot to another predetermined spot. Apparently, these pursuits were performed for the pleasure of being together and nothing else! To make sure about the reliability of this phenomenon, in a second visit to Spain, I went to the same square in the same town at dusk. Sure enough, the same phenomenon was occurring as a natural happening, though I did not see the two old men.

When I discussed this phenomenon with my graduate class on personality theory in the family, I asked the students whether they had seen anything resembling this phenomenon in the United States. One student commented that if people walk, often they do it for exercise and not for being together, because while walking they are not talking with each other, as senior citizens do inside malls during the cold or bad weather. Another student recalled the same scene about two elderly men talking with each other while walking back and forth from set places. However, this instance did not happen in a public square. It happened in a state hospital!

The issue here is how and how much play occupies our lives and what effects, if any, it has on personal, interpersonal, intimate, and family relationships throughout the life cycle. Furthermore, it is crucial to find whether play is beneficial, as asserted by various authorities. Consequently, a review of the professional and research literature at each stage of the life cycle should concentrate on the supposedly beneficial, immediate and long-term outcomes of play, using studies, if available, that include experimental (play activities) and control (no play or other no play activities) groups.

Play behavior and play therapy were the subject of a great deal of attention and speculation during the last third of the past century (Avedon & Sutton-Smith, 1971; Ellis, 1973; Herron & Sutton-Smith, 1971; Lieberman, 1977; Millar, 1968; Piers, 1972; Schaefer, 1979; and Slovenko & Knight, 1967). There is no question that play and playfulness are important activities supposedly related to personality development and functionality (Brown & Gottfried, 1985; Caplan & Caplan, 1973; Cohen, 1987; Hein, 1969; Herron & Sutton-Smith, 1982; Levy, 1978; Lieberman, 1977; Norbeck, 1969; Piers, 1972; Sadler, 1969; Schwartzman, 1978; Sutton-Smith, 1986), in spite of environmental constraints (Barnett & Kane, 1985a, b).

This handbook is a follow-up to a recently edited work (L'Abate, 2007) and another on self-help in mental health (Harwood & L'Abate, 2009). Even though a variety of verbal, nonverbal, relational, and nonrelational activities were included in those volumes, the specific topic of play as a low-cost approach to promote physical and mental health was not included, in spite of the fact that here there is a great deal of advocacy about play and play therapy. This literature recognizes the importance of play in personality socialization in the early years, supposedly fostering creativity and imagination in health promotion, prevention, psychotherapy, and rehabilitation in older years. However, the literature is bare about play during the rest of the life cycle. Why? Because play in the later stages of life is conceived as leisure and, supposedly, there is lots of it for some people after retirement but not before (Wade, 1985).

I call the sustained but unsystematic advocacy about the goodness of play "regressive advocacy" that laments the way children play now (with computers) versus the way we used to play as children when we had more time to play and we were not as overscheduled, as many children are today. Of course, the ways children play now are completely different from the ways we used to play. We did not have as many toys and games as there are available, and easily obtainable, today. We operated our toys or we made them. I remember making my own kites with inexpensive materials. Now toys operate themselves with microchips, batteries, and self-operating mechanisms. They operate us. There is little group-play at close physical face-to-face contact; children now play at a distance from each other through the Internet (Ciofi & Graziano, 2003; Elkind, 2007; Goldstein, Buckingham, & Brougere, 2004).

What are the profound consequences to personality socialization of these dramatic changes? How will they affect children growing up in a cyberspace technology who, when grown, will need professional help at whatever stage of the life cycle? Will they seek face-to-face talk-based psychotherapy, or will they seek help online from mental health professionals or others? In spite of the vast literature on this topic cited above, emphasizing the importance of play in personality competence and socialization, there is very little written about the life cycle aspects of play in their applications to health promotion, prevention, psychotherapy, and rehabilitation. Furthermore, a superficial perusal of the contents of major personality psychology treatises fails to find any references to play, with the sole exception of Erikson's theory about developmental stages in the life cycle (Ewen, 1988). Even more relevant, an important treatise on adult development (Demick & Andreoletti, 2003) did not make any reference to play. This is a very important gap. Personality theorists do not acknowledge the importance of play or are unable to extend their theories to play. By the same token, play theorists rarely refer to personality theories, because they seem irrelevant to the whole enterprise of play.

INTERESTED AUDIENCES FOR THIS HANDBOOK

Despite the gaps in academic interest just described, play in its various forms occupies a great part of our lives from infancy to old age (Orthner, Barnett-Morris, & Mancini, 1994; Wade, 1985; Witt & Goodale, 1985). What, then, are the empirical bases for recommending play activities across the life cycle? Who is interested in play? Likely, buyers/readers of this Handbook would be mental health professionals working with children in the usual disciplines of medicine, psychology, social work, school counseling, teaching, and educational psychology, as well as pediatricians. One would guess that there are approximately 1,000,000+ mental health professionals working with children, not including students wanting to work with children, even including undergraduates.

More specifically, who should read this book? Informed and interested adults, of course, but who in particular? If play is an important activity throughout the life cycle, a great number of lay, nonprofessional people might be interested in reading about this topic. Additionally, since to my knowledge, there might not be a resource of this type available professionally, there are at least four potential professions that could be interested in play across the life cycle: (1) play therapists as a secondary audience who would be interested in this topic; (2) leisure time and recreation specialists, health promoters, and prevention advocates, including child specialists; (3) psychotherapists in the various specializations (individuals, couples, and families); and (4) developmental and personality scholars and researchers who could use this volume as a base for courses in child and personality development and socialization.

ORGANIZATION OF THIS HANDBOOK

This Handbook is organized into five Parts. Part I concentrates on definitions, history, theoretical, and empirical backgrounds of play from Chapters 1 through 6. Part II is organized chronologically, according to various stages of play across the life cycle, from Chapters 7 through 13. Part III is concerned with the benefits of play and its applications in play therapy and rehabilitation, from Chapters 14 through 16. Part IV concentrates on various controversies that have existed throughout the evolution of play, including the technology of play and of media, and especially how play fits, does not fit, or should not fit into educational pursuits, Chapters 17 and 18. Finally, Part IV concludes with Chapter 19, devoted to answer questions such as: "Why is there no contemporary theory to describe and explain play? Is there one that can?" I shall attempt to answer both questions to the best of my knowledge and wits in that concluding chapter.

Luciano L'Abate
Atlanta, Georgia
April 21, 2009

ACKNOWLEDGMENTS

This book would not have been written if it were not for the absolute dedication to this topic by Debora Carvalko, Senior Acquisitions Editor at Praeger, and for her belief in my being able to carry out my original proposal. Her idea that I should write for accessibility to nonpsychologists in addition to professional readers was a challenge. However, the topic has long been of interest to me; especially intriguing since I started to conduct play therapy more than half a century ago. I started play therapy with my first child participant at the Wichita Child Guidance Clinic, and that child started to destroy practically the whole playroom, while I helplessly and nondirectively was mumbling "Hum, hum," à la Carl Rogers. Then, I became aware of the importance of play for a much larger audience than professionals. I hope I have fulfilled and satisfied in some measure Debora Carvalko's trust in me and her continuous support throughout the writing of this book. I am also indebted to Jerome Colburn, Theresa Lawrence, and Lisa Connery for their superb copyediting and project management, and to Dr. Laura Sweeney for drawing Figure 6.1 and to Raj Bojambi for retouching Figure 6.2. I am grateful to Andy Horne for his willingness to write a Foreword to this book in spite of his many important commitments. I am very grateful to Dr. Lauren Wynne for writing the major part of Chapter 15. I would not have been able to accomplish this task without her competent help and professional expertise.

I am also grateful for Sarah Steiner, Learning Commons Librarian at Georgia State University for her help and expertise in finding, within minutes, references that would have taken me hours to locate.

Part 1

DEFINITIONS AND A BIRD'S EYE VIEW OF PLAY

This introductory part attempts to give the reader a systematic and historical background for understanding how play has been part of life since times immemorial.

1

COME, LET'S PLAY

Play is not a luxury but rather a crucial dynamic of healthy, physical, intellectual and social emotional development at all age levels (p. 4). Play, love, and work are operative throughout the human life cycle.

(Elkind, 2007, p. 5)

Play is a voluntary activity which permits freedom of action, diversion from routines, and an imaginary world to master. Play has unique power for building body control and interpersonal relations. Play provides a base for language learning and investigation. Play is the most dynamic childhood learning method.

(Caplan & Caplan, 1973, p. xi)

Alessandra

When my beloved granddaughter was about two years old, after almost random use of toys, which I would define as exploration, between infancy and toddlerhood, Alessandra and I built more Lego-blocks castles than I can remember. She had great fun building one and then laughing, with a quick swift of her hand, broke it into pieces. From castles we progressed to simple card games. From 2 to 3 years, she was an ardent viewer of *Teletubbies* on TV, graduating then to *Barney*. Now she watches the Cartoon Network and *Hannah Montana,* joining the craze about this program, including the *American Girl* on the Internet. At about three years of age, Alessandra entered a pretend phase where she would insist in serving us (her maternal grandmother and grandfather, who are absolutely gaga over her) elaborate, multi-course meals complete with an appetizer, main entrée, and dessert. This pretend phase lasted until she was about five years old, when her play was diverted to other children in her neighborhood and she started kindergarten. At this stage she began to be interested in dolls and computers, discovering on the Internet the *American Girl* web pages, which offer a whole colorful panoply of solo-parallel, or multi-player games, puzzles, and creative opportunities for girls from kindergarten to puberty. At seven years of age Alessandra has no problem in searching and surfing the Internet and becoming proficient in playing many of the competitive games produced by the *American Girl*. Indeed, she has shown me on my Mac how to use bookmarks and such that I was not familiar with after 25 years of computer use.

Her pretend play still exists and is present when she plays with her dolls, making them converse with each other and, with a boy doll and a girl doll, even kissing each other. She attends an International School that integrates children from forty-three different countries. Ethnically, even though she knows the Italian background of her grandfather, she defines herself as being American-Greek, after her maternal grandmother, who is of the same ethnic background. In a recent United Nations Day Parade at her International School where the children wore ethnic clothing and carried the flags of their respective countries, Alessandra wore traditional Greek clothes and carried the Greek flag and a corresponding sign. She also attends regular lessons of Greek dancing and now is starting to learn Greek at the same church her grandmother is attending. To even out things, she informed her grandparents that in the next United Nation celebration at school she will wear Italian clothes and carry a corresponding flag and sign.

She lives with her single mother in a gated co-op community where parking is completely separate from condominiums. The streets, free of car traffic, are a veritable, consistently used playground for children of any age, including an open-air playground with swings, parallel bars, and a sandbox. Next to this playground there is a large lawn for soccer and volleyball, and in another section of the community there is a court for basketball. Quite a few toys are found right on the street, for almost any child to use freely.

Consequently, when she is not in school, Alessandra uses the streets as common playgrounds with other children, and she also plays in the homes of children her own age and they in hers. In the common house of this community, there is also a playroom full of toys and games at whatever age level from toddlerhood up to elementary school age. I spent quite a few hours in that playroom while baby-sitting Alessandra. Now, however, as far as I know, she no longer goes there to play. Since first grade, she has participated in a local soccer league for elementary school children, playing once a week with competing teams during the fall season. Recently, a few months from her eighth birthday, when I gave her my cell phone to call her mother, she found games on it and started playing them as if she were a veteran. I would not know how to access those games, let alone play them.

Ian

My beloved grandson, Ian, who is six years old and in the first grade as of this writing, has had completely different sets of toys and games from his cousin. He lives with his father and mother in a house in an open subdivision chosen for the excellence of its school system in a well-to-do section of a northern suburb of Atlanta. His major toys, among many others, consist mainly of model cars, trucks of all kinds, and, in the last two years, Lego Bionicles. To my amazement, these Bionicles are extremely threatening-looking, warrior-type figures, but can be configured in thousands of ways. We started playing by throwing balls at each other and building forts with Lego blocks between two and four years of age, but since four years of age, Ian became more interested in building incredible-looking Bionicles that raged wars with each other. We played one group of Bionicles against each other, and my grandson always won.

He is also interested in why the world spins around, and in the nature of the solar system. He has stated clearly his goal to become a "scientist." He plays at home with selected friends from kindergarten and neighborhood by invitation only. He is not allowed to go on the street, and his outdoor playing is limited to the school playground and the house's backyard. Last year he was enrolled in a kindergarten soccer league, uniform and all. This year he has switched to T-ball, where he has shown excellent eye-hand coordination.

An interesting development took place for Ian in his kindergarten class of twelve children, almost equally divided by gender. The girls apparently expressed a uniform liking for him. Ian, by the same token, has expressed his reciprocal liking for one specific girl. This apparently obvious liking has produced extreme jealousy in another boy, who lives also in the same neighborhood where Ian lives. This boy has become cruel and mean toward Ian to the point that Ian would come home and, crying, would relate to his mother how mean that boy had been to him. The teacher confirmed the validity of this rivalry and after the boy's mother was informed about it and became "horrified" to hear about her son's behavior, she had him apologize profusely to Ian. Five years old and already involved in a love triangle!

The North Georgia Lego Train Club

The *Atlanta Journal-Constitution* (March 15, 2008) reported about a family whose father founded the North Georgia Lego Train Club after he started using Lego Bricks as a hobby that spawned into a fun family activity. Now, the father's two children, a 5-year-old girl and an 11 year old boy, are helping him build train sets. With the help of a friend, the older boy created a Lego robot that plays tic-tac-toe.

Lu

Writing this vignette was fraught with many qualms about writing what could be interpreted as a self-serving narrative. On the other hand, I needed something to link the youth of my two grandchildren and the play of the preceding family with the narratives that follow, dedicated to playing cards in old age. Consequently, I hope readers will forgive me for this personal exposition of my "play history." I remember very little about my playing in the preschool years. I do remember, however, my seventh birthday. That was a watershed year because we moved from Florence, Italy, to my mother's hometown, Brindisi, where I was born.

We lived in my maternal grandfather's palace, which had ample room for us and for some of his children and grandchildren when they came to visit him. Calling it a palace may sound pompous. However, it was certainly not a house and it was not a castle. Whatever it could be called, however, it was large enough to accommodate adult children comfortably and allow many children and grandchildren to live, come, go, and visit. More importantly, this building had a garden where my brother, our cousins, and I could play hide-and-seek. Its attic was enormous, contained all sorts of old junk that we used to play with in the adjoining large terrace, where we practiced "flying" from the steps of the turret, using "wings" made out of the junk in the attic. For my birthday, I was given a mechanic set that, I guess, was the predecessor of plastic games. Apparently, I was able to work on it and built a bell that somehow matched the sound of the house bell. Therefore, my game consisted of playing this bell and enjoying seeing the amazement in the face of whoever opened the door and found no one was there. After one year in Brindisi, we went back to Florence, where I lived until I came to the United States, after attending the School of Architecture at the University of Florence for one year.

In late elementary school years, my leisure time consisted of playing with little clay balls that correspond to marbles in the United States, in either one of four garden or square playgrounds in Florence, a group game that includes two to four players. Weather permitting, after school I would go, with my little satchel of clay balls, to play in any of the playgrounds where the "action" was, all within blocks of our condominium. If there was no action in one playground, by word of mouth, my buddies and I would move to another playground where the action might be taking place. As I reached middle school, this clay ball game no longer interested me because it was for smaller children. With the help of my mother's scaffolding (a concept discussed in Chapter 5 of this volume), I graduated to Monopoly and spent most of middle school playing that game in a friend's house.

However, two important happenings occurred when we spent two wonderful summers (1941–1942) on the beautiful island of Lussino, a small island off the coast of Croatia that used to belong to Italy between the two world wars, where my father was commander of the naval base. Lussino was, and apparently still is, an old Austro-Hungarian resort with lots of pines and many small coves for bathing and swimming. During the summer of 1941 our hotel (otherwise empty of guests because of the war) was close to the seashore, and I therefore obtained a bamboo pole, to which I attached a line and a hook to start fishing. On my first attempt in the afternoon, I went to fish at the pier of a nearby cannery that threw all its fish entrails right in the sea. Consequently, the pier brimmed with thousands of fish that came to feast on the entrails. While I was trying to hook fish, my parents and my younger brother, Alberto, came by as they were taking a leisurely afternoon stroll. Predictably, my brother asked me to let him use my fishing pole. I had not caught any fish yet. Very reluctantly, due to the insistence of my parents, I gave my fishing pole to my brother, who proceeded to catch thirty-four fish in as many minutes or less time. To add insult to injury, my brother took the fish to the hotel and we had them for supper. I have never used that pole nor fished ever since.

The next summer (1942) my father rented a relatively isolated house next to a cove that was, however, within walking distance of town and other summer homes. This time, I asked my parents for a BB gun to go hunting. Once I received it, my brother tagged along in our first hunting expedition into the nearby woods. After I had tried unsuccessfully to bring down birds perched on trees, my brother asked me to let him try shooting the gun. I did let him have it, and in just a few minutes he shot three birds. That was the end of my first and last hunting expedition. The irony of this episode is that my brother, years later, became one of the most nonviolent pacifists of Italy.

After we came back to Florence, while I was still in middle school, after much begging from my parents, I received a bicycle, which enabled me to join my buddies as they went to visit in each other's home in less time than walking, also competing in how fast we could go from one part of town to the other. That bicycle came in handy during the war, when I could go into the country outside Florence and buy bread from farmers. What had initially been a source of enjoyment became a means of survival. In high school I graduated to sports, where, in addition to playing volleyball and practicing gymnastics intramurally, I was involved also in Greco-Roman wrestling extramurally, and dabbled in skiing and mountain climbing.

During this war time (1944–1945), after American forces liberated Florence, my bicycle buddies and I discovered the American Big Band music from records belonging to American officers who rented part of an apartment where one of my buddies lived. With the help of the first movie imported from the United States that we saw, *Sun Valley Serenade*, with music by Glenn Miller and his Orchestra, and with the help of various girlfriends, we learned to dance American style, a skill that I have been able to retain over the years with occasional practice, whenever possible, with my wife. I still love to "cut a rug" whenever I can.

In my senior high school year, because of my wrestling record, I was invited to join the University of Florence rugby team even though I had not yet graduated. By American standards, I guess I could have been called a jock. In addition, I became a volunteer, part-time director of sports for the Florence YMCA, where soccer was the major sport, because soccer was and still is the most popular game in Italy, followed by bicycle racing.

One day at the YMCA office, we were visited by three Italian American representatives who were offering to give us uniforms and equipment to play baseball, a game unknown to Italians at that time (1947). When I asked for soccer balls and shoes instead, these representatives emphasized their investment in *baseball* equipment. When I raised the question about who would coach this game, they drew a blank, but nonetheless, supplying this equipment was their primary mission. Talk about cultural attunement even at a game level! Consequently, I resigned from my position. Now baseball is an accepted but secondary sport in Italy.

Fifty years later, during a visit with my family, I took a ride around the playgrounds of my elementary school years with my brother, who has lived in Florence all his life. I remarked to him that I could not see any children playing there. Why? He answered: "They are all at home, playing with their computers."

After I moved to the United States, I was not able to spend too much time in any leisure activity until after completing my studies and starting to work. During my first job, while I was still a bachelor in Greenville, North Carolina, I joined the local theater club to break the monotony of what was then a rather small but very hospitable Southern college town. To amuse myself, I played the parts of the Greek landowner in *My Sister Eileen* and the Italian smuggler in Agatha Christie's *Three Blind Mice*. I also joined a pottery club, whose members either were so ashamed of my production or else felt so sorry for me that they each gave me one of their pieces when we progressed to a final show of our "masterpieces."

While working in St. Louis during my second job, I picked up tennis, a sport that I continued to pursue in Atlanta until I could no longer play because of an arthritic spine and neck, which also prevented me from walking for an extended period of time. After retirement from GSU, I picked up tai chi, but I became bored with it, and I quit after four years of practice. However, I continue to exercise 30 minutes almost every day on a foam mattress with ankle and hand weights. During the summer months I also swim for the same length of time. I hope to continue both activities as I reach my eightieth birthday and beyond. Over the years I have been collecting art stamps, but I have not yet had time to arrange them. Perhaps, when I really retire, I may be able to really enjoy working on them.

When Pigs Play

Too many people reach a point in life where they feel that being silly or childlike and indulging in activities usually associated with people several decades younger is unbecoming. How sad for them. For our group of women, play is a major factor. We have been friends over a period of about 30 years. We became a "serious" group in 1991, when we had our First Annual Triathlon Summer Outing (FATSO). We wore shirts printed with pigs, and we became Pigs. We decided that we liked the FATSO acronym so much that we became Friends Acquired Through Spiritual Organizations because we had met at church. Since then we have gone on a cruise (Fat Asses Tour Southern Oceans) and celebrated Festivals Acknowledging The Significant Occasion. We take "pigtures," and we go on "pignics." Our children are "piglets," and our grandchildren are "grandpiglets." The great thing about "Pigness" is that none of us is embarrassed or ashamed of the word.

The joy of reaching a certain age is accepting that there is little to be embarrassed about. We have nothing to prove, other than that we can adapt as circumstances allow. If an activity becomes too strenuous, we adjust. If we like the game pieces, but not the rules, we change them. There is no need to conform to what has been laid out as structure. We have wisdom and experience at our beck and call, and we enjoy the opportunity to make play more appropriate to our capacities, physical and mental.

In the past few years a number of us had turned 60. So for such a significant event we "forked" each other's lawns on that special day. Forking is sticking plastic forks in the ground in the shape of a large 60. Since we are getting older, we've decided that forking takes too much energy, so we are looking for other options, since some of us are now getting ready to turn 70, and obviously we must celebrate.

Once a year, in February, as many of us as possible take off for the North Georgia Mountains. This gives us an opportunity to spend time together, be silly, and just enjoy ourselves. Over time the weekend has evolved into an actual schedule of events. The first night, Thursday, is for those who can get away early. By Friday night everyone has arrived. We have dinner and relax. At some point someone brings out some game, perhaps Trivial Pursuit or Taboo. It depends on what games anyone has had the foresight to bring. The rule is that there are no rules. A game of Balderdash becomes an opportunity to use rarely encountered words in a new and totally inappropriate way. Each game has its own set of challenges, and we adapt the rules. The flexibility of reaching a certain age is having the confidence to know when the rules apply and when they don't. One of the women is extraordinarily talented artistically, and each year she brings materials for a "project." These projects frequently involve some simple skill, but, amazingly, there is always someone who doesn't "get it." Does this hinder anyone? Not at all. It's like being in kindergarten, where there are those children who get the concept and those who don't. There is always someone who is willing and patient enough to show the unskilled what to do. Over the years a pattern of "teacher" and "student" has evolved. The beauty of it is that the talents of the group shift, so that each person's strength has become evident.

So when one thinks about old people and how they play, think about this, that no matter what the chronological age, it's not the years that count, but what you have in you. It's one's ability to look at all sides of the matter and then approach it with the logic of experience. It's having the wisdom to accept one's limitations, live within them, and be generous with the gifts one has been given. We are at an age when fighting on principle is not necessary. We learn to laugh at ourselves and with our world. We know who has what talents and respect each other's privacy when it's needed. And, above all, we love to play.

Contributed by Mary Costa with the permission of her Pig friends.

Poker Games

Even before my family and I settled in Atlanta in 1965, I used to belong to a poker group in Florence during my late school years and in St. Louis. Since moving to Atlanta then, I have been a member of a poker group that meets on a monthly basis in each of its members' homes in rotation. There are now only three members remaining from the original group of six or seven. Over the years we have lost members to moves, death, or loss of interest. We play dealer's choice with nickel-dime bets up to a quarter (against my will) but no more than three raises. Chips in the amount of five dollars are used as exchange currency to play. At the end of the game, the host collects from the losers and pays off the winners. In addition to beer and soft drinks, the host is responsible for providing munchies such as peanuts or potato chips for while we are playing and the makings of sandwiches for when we are not. In our younger days, when we started playing in our thirties or forties, it was not uncommon for us to drink an average of two to three beers per member. The average age now is about 80 plus or minus a couple of years, and we may drink a couple of beers among all six players, otherwise sticking with soft drinks or water. We used to smoke cigarettes and cigars, but no one smokes anymore.

At the present, this group is composed of one child psychiatrist, two clinical psychologists, a former head of a specialty department in a medical school, a former executive from the Centers for Disease Control (CDC), and a retired construction and real estate owner who fought in the Battle of the Bulge during World War II. In addition to our reduced drinking, age is beginning to show in the increasing number of errors we make while playing, to the point that we spend a great deal of time correcting each other as we play. Now we use a mechanical shuffler to mix cards after each hand because some members have arthritic hands and find it difficult to shuffle cards by hand. Frequently some members are absent on leisure travels with their wives or families or because of sickness. Consequently, to reach a suitable quorum of five to six players, we sometimes invite occasional fill-ins. We are all completely or partly retired, living within 20 or 30 minutes from each other. In this group, travel seems to be the most prevalent leisure-time activity in addition to poker. I am not aware of any other leisure or recreational activities in this group, except for attending symphonic music concerts or operas.

Thirty years ago, I was invited to become a member of another neighborhood poker group that is still going on at the present. This group meets every two weeks and plays only nickels and dimes, with 15 cents on a pair of cards showing on the table, but no more than three raises. This group plays with real change instead of chips, so we all carry satchels with our change in them. This group originally offered only beer and munchies. More recently, it has begun to offer candies, chocolates, and sometimes fruit as well. Again, our beer intake has decreased considerably over the years, at the same rate as the other group. However, this group has suffered more serious illness recently than the other group, with five knee replacements and occasional hospitalizations for sundry medical problems, with forgetfulness and errors increasing from one meeting to the next. However, we still shuffle cards with our hands. Two members in this group attend movie theaters regularly.

Occupationally, this group is composed of two retired members of the CDC, a former successful operator of beauty salons, a former representative of a pharmaceutical company, and a retired Air Force colonel with a second career as treasurer of a county mental health clinic. Some members do have other play interests. One gambles in casinos in nearby states or Las Vegas and, in the fall, goes hunting for deer or quail. Another member plays golf regularly and takes a cruise with his wife practically three or four times a year. We are all retired from our previous jobs and live within 5 to 10 minutes' distance of each other. When we are sick or in hospital, sometimes we visit each other at bedside or call at home.

There are some similarities between these two groups. They are composed exclusively of men. Some wives sometimes greet members when they come into the house, but they make themselves scarce after meeting the guests. In the second group, two wives used to play bridge with two other women friends in a different house from the host. That group, however, came to an end because of sickness and because some of them were no longer able to drive at night.

La Societa Italiana of Atlanta, Georgia

Early in 2008, I became informed of the existence of this club, composed of middle-aged individuals and couples of Italian origin that are members of a Catholic church in the northwest part of Atlanta. This group meets on a regular basis in their members' homes except for formal occasions, when they celebrate religious or patriotic holidays such as Columbus Day. Otherwise, there are potluck dinners in the homes of members on an almost regular monthly basis. What is relevant to play in this group is the fact that at least three members of this club built bocce courts in the backyards of their homes. This game is the Italian equivalent of bowling, and the equipment consists of one small ball (the pallino), which serves as a target, and eight larger balls, which either two or four players try to get as close as possible to the small ball. Whichever side (individual or pair) throws a large ball closest to the small ball wins. As a result of playing with this group, during the summer months I was able to compete in two bocce tournaments, complete with referees (with a measuring stick to judge distances between balls) and scorekeepers.

In addition, every year in February there is a formal Masked Ball in a local country club complete with dance band, raffle of prizes, King and Queen of the Ball, and announcements about forthcoming officers of the organization. That was the first time I got together with this club, and I had so much fun dancing and meeting so many men and women from my home country, feeling very much at home, that I joined this club and I have had fun ever since, looking forward to many other joyous occasions in the future. Maria Costa, who wrote the earlier segment "When Pigs Play," was my official sponsor and made sure that I would be taken care of at whatever meeting I attended.

WHAT IS PLAY?

Play was been studied scientifically mainly in the first half of the last century, even though play (as discussed in Chapter 2) has existed since the beginning of time (Caplan & Caplan, 1987). For a complete list of definitions by many educators, philosophers, and advocates of play, the interested reader is referred to the work of Saracho and Spodek (1998a, pp. 3–4). In spite of this growth in studies and theories of play, there are still some critics who look at play as Utopia (Fingarette, 1969), to the point that there is no such a thing as "pure play" because there are so many factors entering into it, such as sensuality (according to Sigmund Freud) and power (according to Herbert Marcuse):

> What might be termed pure play is an ideal, an ideal which is more and more approachable only as one has learned to master anxieties, learned technical skills, learned the complex forms and arts of civilized existence. Then, as culmination, a person may engage, at last, in activities for their own sake ... to satisfy ... communion.... The ability to play, in this sense, is an ideal trait of personality. We aspire to it. We partially achieve it (Fingarette, 1969, pp. 18–19).

Play could also be considered a "primitive form of communication" (Sutton-Smith, 1986, p. 137).

One of the major criticisms of play, especially for the mature years, lies in its being for the rich and not for the poor. Rather than attempt to counter this criticism, I will consider differences in socioeconomic status (SES) as an important factor in the study of play throughout the rest of this book.

Interviewing 103 children aged 2 to 6 years and surveying 73 parents and 60 preschool teachers about their perceptions of play, Rothlein (1987) found that most parents defined play as something for fun or amusement, while teachers saw it as fun and as an opportunity for cognitive and social development. The majority of teachers did not view play as an integral part of the curriculum but instead described a learn–play dichotomy. Parents did not support having their children spend a large amount of time in play during preschool. Children's favorite play activities according to all three sources of information were outdoor play, dramatic play, and art activities.

In pragmatic, strictly mechanistic circles, play could be considered a complete waste of time. More specifically, there are certain driven personalities, such as Type A, workaholics, and addictive personalities, who are unable to play, because, in their drivenness, play and leisure do seem to them a "waste of time." To play one needs to be relaxed, with a minimum of need to impress anybody, including the self. This is why play represents an intrinsic pleasure that is self-reinforcing and self-propagating. In the extreme, especially in adulthood, it may be such a pleasure that it becomes an addiction, to the point that it occupies more and more time that could and should be used for more useful pursuits, including sleep.

In addition to the foregoing considerations, there are other characteristics of play:

1. Play involves exaggeration and repetition of motor acts and the reordering of behavioral sequences following tacit or stated rules and regulations.

2. Play is initiated by play signals (Bateson, 1986).

3. Play occurs when basic needs are met and the individual is in a relaxed state.

This latter characteristic is important because it essentially states what has not been affirmed clearly in the extant literature on play: that play occurs when the individual has time and inclination to play, a state that may not be available to troubled individuals.

4. Sequences of motor acts may start as incomplete and fragmented, but with time and practice they may become more differentiated and integrated within a total personality functioning (see Chapter 19 this volume).

5. Role reversal and self-handicapping occur, to the extent that role-play in pretend games is quite fluid and flexible, so that players feel free to assume a variety of roles at the same time.

6. Play is simply fun (Cotter, 2004, p. 330).

THE STRUCTURE OF PLAYING

What is the composition of playing, and what are its component characteristics? The preceding definition referred to processes of playing. However, how does play happen? How is it or should it be conducted as a process, regardless of its contents? Play consists of two fundamental characteristics: (1) objects that are used and called toys, when (2) those objects are manipulated for a variety of supposedly pleasurable purposes, such as manipulation, exploration, aggression, and construction. This is an important distinction, because toys in and of themselves are statically inert. They are unmovable and do not move unless they are played with. Moving and manipulating them for pleasurable purposes makes them enter into a game. Games, therefore, imply movement and manipulation of toys. Therefore, the process of play is determined by the following contents that constitute a structure:

1. What types and numbers of toys and games are used? Of what are they made: wood, plastic, metal, or other materials? Does a toy represent a bond with or obligation to someone, such as gifts at birthdays, celebrating holidays such as Christmas, or special occasions? (Sutton-Smith, 1986)

2. What is the context of the game? Does it occur in the home, in a playground, on the streets, in a field? Is the game solitary or social? Games like Nintendo may be solitary, but there are many games on the Internet that require socializing with someone else, even if unknown.

3. What are the natures, ages, genders, and backgrounds of the players involved? Are they of different ages and different physical sizes? Are they a mix of both genders or mostly of one gender? Do they have different cultural backgrounds? These factors need consideration, even though players often self-select other players on the basis of these characteristics.

4. What is the particular sequence followed in the game? A sequence means that there is a structure to a game, and how that sequence should be followed in each game implies some kind of order. It is important to consider what process the game follows. For instance, if playing Cowboys and Indians, does the game involve a necessary fight?

5. How much space is needed to play with the toy or game, and how is that space managed? This issue reverts to the contextual nature of a game, such as a hand held Nintendo or elaborate electronic games found in some restaurants or airports.

6. Is the style of play involved mental or physical? Competitive or cooperative? Aggressive or constructive? As we shall see, the style of play is very important, especially when there are characteristics that may be unacceptable to some players, such as aggression and even violence.

7. How much energy or effort is necessary to play with the toy or participate in a particular game? This characteristic may vary from very little effort, such as playing an Internet game, to the great deal of effort and energy expended in a soccer or football game.

8. Is the play solitary, parallel, or in groups? Is there one sole player with toys, two players alongside each other, or a multiplayer group? "Social play is a complex entity that carries with it a variety of psychological meanings. And, *nonsocial* play is even more complex and multidimensional" (Rubin & Coplan, 1998, p. 144).

Each of these possibilities has its pros and cons. For instance, solitary play may be necessary at certain stages of the life cycle. However, over-reliance on that kind of play may indicate the need for the child to learn to play with other children. By the same token, a child who wants to play only with other children and consistently avoids playing alone may need to be helped in learning to entertain himself or herself without the necessary company of others.

Smilansky (1968) elaborated on Piaget's (1972) distinction (discussed in Chapter 3, this volume) among practice, symbolic, and rules-governed games by distinguishing the following types of play activity:

- *Functional* and repetitious movements, involving manipulation and exploration of toys (if present) and game-related actions

- *Constructive* building or creating a non-preexisting structure out of sand, blocks, or other materials, which represents a progression from exploration to building or making something, as when my granddaughter and I built block castles and my grandson built Bionicles

- *Dramatic* involvement in a nonliteral production of something imaginary out of the immediate context, as in role-playing, pretending, and making something out of imagination and fantasy

- *Rule-governed* games, in which players have to follow a given format or process based on some plan, set, or regulation that sets the boundaries of how a game is to be conducted; the plan is either developed by the players themselves or imported from outside and agreed to by the players

Furthermore, *sensorimotor* play involves jumping, climbing, and balancing. *Construction* play may provide an opportunity to produce a product. *Symbolic* play could involve pretending and dramatic enactments, assuming roles such as kings and queens, cowboys and Indians (Phelps, 1984). Another way to classify play consists of looking at playing as: (1) pretending, (2) mastery, (3) exploration, and (4) imagination (Sutton-Smith, 1986, p. 205).

These types of play may develop in a linear sequence, one after another, with functional playing being present in infancy as exploration, followed by constructive and dramatic play, with rule-governed playing beginning around kindergarten and proceeding into adulthood.

On the basis of quantitative evidence, Fagot (1984) characterized play by six factors: (1) cognitive, (2) social cooperation, (3) active, (4) make-believe, (5) passive-nontask, and (6) female-typical. From all possibilities from different sources, the reader can pick whatever characteristic repeats itself from one source to another.

Through participant observations and intensive interviews of adult participants, the Daily Occupational Experience Survey (DOES) obtained characteristics of play and corresponding measurement dimensions in the following order of importance (adapted from Blanche, 2002, p. 252):

1. Spontaneity: from spontaneous to planned
2. Arousal seeking: from exciting to boring
3. Use and release of energy: from stressful to relaxing and from energized to depleted
4. Pleasure: from pleasurable to miserable
5. Necessity for survival: from a frill to necessity
6. Creativity: from creative to customary
7. Clarity of objectives: from clear purpose to unclear
8. Physical activity: from active to nonactive
9. Mental activity: from active to nonactive
10. Freedom: from free to restrained
11. Intrinsic motivation: for the player's own sake to for someone else's
12. Fantasy: from true to imagined

From the data collected from adult participants the following patterns of experience about leisure and play resulted: (1) restoration of energy, (2) momentary high, (3) heightened self-awareness, (4) mastery, (5) adventure, and (6) creation (Blanche, 2002, p. 258). An analysis of these six patterns yielded two basic dimensions of play: *novelty* along a continuum from mastery through adventure to creation and *intensity of involvement* along a continuum of involvement from restoration to a momentary high and heightened self-awareness. These two dimensions suggest two circular models: intensity of involvement, defined by the poles of heightened self-awareness and restoration, and novelty, defined by the poles of creativity-mastery and adventure. From these models a conceptual map of process-oriented experiences can be drawn consisting of two orthogonal (independent) dimensions: (1) horizontally, mastery–adventure–creativity, (2) vertically, heightened self-awareness–restoration (Blanche, 2002, pp. 273–274).

The Processes of Playing

The relative resurgence of the study of play is largely due to the therapeutic applications of play as part of child treatment after World War I in Europe (O'Connor, 2000). Despite the different approaches just described, there is considerable agreement that play has some if not all of the following characteristics:

1. Play is an action or activity pursued and performed for its own sake, for the intrinsic pleasure it produces on the player. This pleasure provides the motivation for the prolongation and repetition of that activity over time.

2. The process of playing is more important than the outcome of playing. Even though there may be competition, it is still considered play if the outcome is secondary to the process.

3. The focus of the action is specific, related to manipulation and exploration of a particular behavior, object, or relationship with a certain person or with another or many other players.

4. The endeavor is not serious and does not or should not leave unpleasant after-effects, because it is understood from the process and outcome that play is not work, is not study, and is not subject to the same evaluations as work or study. It should be pleasurable.

5. The rules of the game dictate how the play should be conducted by tacit agreement or mutual understanding on the part of all involved players.

6. All players are actively engaged in the process, and, unless defined beforehand, the status of the players involved is equal for everybody. No one is more important than others, unless the status is attributed by all players involved, as in a team or a group game where the status and function of a leader is clearly allocated by all players.

7. Spontaneity is or should be present to ensure that the process does not become onerous and inflexible and so resemble work or study.

8. Play is proactive rather than just reactive, in the sense that play does not start as a response to someone else unless that someone does indicate in some way, verbal or nonverbal, that "this is play, do you care to join me?" Of course, throughout play there are reactions and counter-reactions. However, they occur within the context of playing rather than any other context, domestic or business.

To summarize some of the above into an acceptable definition: *Play consists of an* Active *(rather than passive),* Spontaneous *(natural rather than demanded, guided, or requested), and* Voluntary *(rather than forced or involuntary)* Involvement *(rather than uninvolvement) that is* Pleasurable *and relatively* Prolonged. *It consists of interactions with oneself and/or with selected others through games and toys for the sake of the interactions themselves rather than for anything else.*

KINDS OF PLAY

Play needs to be classified to understand it in its complexity. In the following paragraphs a list of play dimensions is presented and discussed in some detail. Some dimensions of this classification may overlap with each other as well as with the dimensions discussed at the end of "The Structure of Playing" earlier in this chapter. Each dimension is described in terms of its extremes. The reader should understand that the word "versus" between these terms is used here as a connection between the extremes of each dimension. Any given play activity is to be located somewhere on a continuum between these extremes rather than defined as either one or the other. Naturally, there are stages of chronological age when different points on these continua are preferred, such as when, from being solitary, playing becomes more and more social or socialized (Sutton-Smith, 1986, p. 38).

Structured versus unstructured: The structure, as discussed below, can be found in the kind of toys and games available, or in the nature of the playground, or in the presence or absence of others in addition to peers, teachers, supervisors, parents, or observers. More of this dimension will be discussed in Part 2 of this book.

Miniature versus gross motor: Nowadays, electronic games like Nintendo, for instance, are portable and require fine eye-hand coordination. Many children carry them in their backpacks or in their pockets. At the other end of this dimension there are toys that are so voluminous that it is impossible to carry them. Either they are stationary, such as the swings and parallel bars in public playgrounds, or, if they are movable at all, they are too bulky to carry, such as many electronic machines. A more nuanced classification of gross motor activities, derived from Brazilian rain forest cultures, is described in Chapter 4 of this volume.

Fantasy versus reality: Make-believe comprises a great deal of what children, especially preschoolers, tend to fantasize, impersonating legendary heroes, such as (in my days) Batman, Mandrake, Spider-Man, or Flash Gordon, and more up-to-date similar heroes, too many to count. Make-believe fantasy is similar to other kinds of play but it includes many other aspects, such as (1) practice, (2) improvised drama, (3) traditional drama, (4) games with rules, (5) imitation, (6) symbolization, (7) pretense in the sense of "false appearance," (8) storytelling, (9) imagination, (10) delusions in disturbed individuals, and (11) holiday rituals and celebrations (Ariel, 2002, pp. 8–14).

Mental versus physical: Solving crossword puzzles is clearly a mental activity, whereas playing ball with someone else is a physical activity.

Solitary versus social: Playing by oneself is just as important as playing with others (Sutton-Smith, 1986, p. 38). Playing with others is another way to learn how to interact, get along, and solve problems that inevitably arise from any social activity. Socially, play can be (1) asymmetrical, meaning dyads of parent with child or older sibs with younger sibs, as in playing house; (2) asymmetrical in groups, such as children and teachers, older and younger children, such as playing school, witch, trains; (3) symmetrical dyads or groups, such as friend with friend, in any one of a number of games; (4) meta-complementary relationships, in which play may be called symmetrical but confused with asymmetrical, where parents and children play as equals but they are not equal; (5) group confrontations, such as cops and robbers (Schwartzman, 1978, p. 244).

Within this dimension, there is a category where solitary play is mixed with other aspects taking place together, as children assembling by themselves parts of a puzzle that must be then put together by the group of children (Beckman & Kohl, 1984). Parten (1932) pioneered a classification of play roles according to: (1) *unoccupied* without focus or direction, such as staring into space or wondering aimlessly, (2) *onlooker,* when the child watches other children play but does not become involved, (3) *solitary,* when the child plays alone at a distance from other children, (4) *parallel,* when a child plays on a separate game alongside another child who is also playing on another separate game, (5) *group,* when the child plays with other children around a mutually agreed-upon game. To this classification, Rubin and Coplan (1998, p. 146) added an important distinction between play *content* and play *context.* This distinction could be elaborated in terms of play *structure* versus play *process,* as discussed earlier in this chapter and throughout various chapters of this volume, to the extent that the structure of play may determine its process. Solitary play could also be conceived as one stage of development, progressing later to parallel and group play (Wall & Pickert, 1982).

Spontaneous versus directed or guided: Even though earlier play was defined as a spontaneous activity, that is not necessarily so. Many team sports played as games are under the direction of coaches. When children are playing in a school playground during recess, they are usually supervised by a teacher, who sometimes directs children toward specific games, depending on what equipment is available on the playground. Another variation on this kind of play is a *preferred* versus *nonpreferred* play partner. Preferred partners may generate more relevant and irrelevant utterances and approximately twice as many relevant response-generating utterances than nonpreferred partners, suggesting that playing with a preferred partner may lead toward a more effective use of language (George & Krantz, 1981).

Physical contact versus noncontact: Wrestling, boxing, and a great many team sports, such as football or hockey, involve inevitable physical contact between players. On the other hand, golf, tennis, and racquetball require no physical contact at all, with baseball, soccer, and volleyball somewhere in the middle of this dimension.

Cooperative versus competitive: Cooperation is a relative term, because members of a team may work cooperatively to compete with and defeat an adversary team.

Dangerous versus safe: Climbing mountains is dangerous. Playing cards is not dangerous. Skateboarding and skiing are somewhere in the middle of this dimension.

Based on the foregoing information, Rubin and Coplan (1998, p. 148) presented and validated a Play Observation Scale that includes most of the categories of playing considered thus far. These scholars also reviewed individual developmental differences across infancy, toddlerhood, and preschool, including an important differentiation of solitary playing that could be divided into (1) *solitary-passive,* (2) *solitary-active,* and (3) *reticent,* the last occurring when the child refuses invitations to play by and with other children (pp. 152-154). In addition, Rubin and Coplan traced the origins of individual differences in social play to (1) genetic factors, (2) temperament and physiology, (3) parenting beliefs and practices, and (4) parent-child attachment relationships (pp. 154-158).

Rubin and Coplan (1998) also presented an orthogonal model of high or low Sociability (S) interacting with high or low Emotional Regulation (ER, p. 157) that produces four possible quadrants. When S and ER are high, social competence ensues. When ER is high and S is low, solitary or nonsocial constructive play and exploration ensue. When S is high and ER is low, aggression and hostility (externalizing problems) ensue. When both S and ER are low, reticence, anxiety, and social wariness (internalizing problems) ensue. This is an important model that will be reconsidered and perhaps partially validated in Chapters 6 and 19 of this volume, among other chapters. In addition, Rubin and Coplan (1998) cautioned against assuming Western cultural and usually negative interpretations of nonsocial play as "bad." In China, for instance, "children are encouraged to be dependent, cautious, self-restrained, and behaviorally inhibited" (p. 163).

Given the earlier distinction between toys and games and their composition making up the process of playing and playfulness, according to a simple equation: toys + games = play, we need to expand this distinction into what each of those two components of play means.

THE MEANINGS OF TOYS

There are complete lists of toys available almost anywhere (Sutton-Smith, 1971, 1986; see Resources). The classifications of playing just discussed oversees any possible classification that could be given to toys, from solitary to social, aggressive to nonaggressive, cooperative to competitive, dangerous to safe, and so forth. Additional classifications of toys are found in Chapters 6 and 19 of this volume.

Because toys are ever present in our lives, we need to understand what they mean to us, because they mean different things to different people. More specifically:

1. Toys may mean the existence of a bond between the recipient of a toy and whoever gives a toy to the recipient, creating therefore a communal bond between the two parties, usually parents or relatives.

2. Infants start playing with toys with a minimum of adult supervision except for making toys available to the infant, meaning that this is the beginning of solitariness.

3. Often, when a child or even an adult feels bad or is sick, a toy is given as a concrete form of consolation, as shown by the members of the pottery club who pitied me and gave me some of their products for the final exhibition.

4. Computers and electronic and video machines are the product of present-day technology and to that extent, they represent that technology.

5. Toys can be also conceived as tools, as a way to manipulate a reality that needs fixing, as when I used my bicycle, which I had received for fun with my buddies, to get bread from farmers during World War II.

6. Toys can become stimuli for all kinds of play, including imagination, dramatic play, and competition.

7. Toys always represent a surprise, and to that extent they can be conceived as novelties, new objects that open up new experiences and possibilities.

8. In addition to representing a communal bond between the giver and the recipient of a toy, toys also represent agency, to the extent that they mean action and activity, as discussed in Chapter 19.

9. Toys can be idealized as part of one's armamentarium of memories and past, pleasurable experiences (Sutton-Smith, 1986).

10. Toys are also linked to our identity. Notice how my granddaughter played with dolls and girlish games online, whereas my grandson played with war-like Bionicles. How much did my success in sports in high school become part of my identity as an adolescent and then as an adult?

THE MEANINGS OF GAMES

Apparently play is so difficult to define because the behavior denoted by the term is so ambiguous to the point that additional meanings need to be invoked in trying to define it. What is meant by "meaning" within the context of play? By "meaning" here is meant how playing is interpreted, not only by the players themselves but also by the general public, its observers. Giving meaning to an object, game, or toy involves using other words or different phrases to explain and interpret an action, person, or object. Meaning, therefore, goes above and beyond the literal characteristic that denotes either action, person, or object. Hence, additional meanings are given in this section for the purpose of highlighting characteristics not otherwise considered by the literal definitions or explanations already discussed. Meaning here means an interpretation of what play represents. For instance, rough-and-tumble play among children could be interpreted as fighting (Pellegrini, 1995a). However, for children it may be just a game and nothing else.

To clarify further what play means, one of the major authorities in the study of play, Brian Sutton-Smith (1997) and others resorted to metaphors that illustrate how play might be considered meaningfully:

1. *Play as progress,* considering how we play today as being an advancement from how our forefathers and foremothers used to play. This metaphor might explain why some play authorities lament how play has deteriorated from the openness of the outdoors to the restrictiveness of indoors and computers, questioning whether this is indeed progress or regression.

2. *Play as fate* when, in playing, we leave the outcome in the hands of others, as in gambling.

3. *Play as power* as seen in competitive sports, especially those sports requiring harsh bodily contact and superiority.

4. *Power as identity* when we define ourselves according to the games, toys, or sports we prefer: "I am a Monopoly player," "I am a spelunker."

5. *Play as imagination* when we role-play cowboys and Indians or make-believe stories of kings and queens as well as all the games available on the Internet (Ariel, 2002).

6. *Play as self,* especially when we play by ourselves and become specialized in a particular game, toy, or sport, as in chess. Indeed, in some individuals their game is part of their self-identity, as in "I am a runner," "I am a Monopoly player" (Jackson, 1998).

7. *Play as frivolity* as a waste of time and energy when that time and energy could be spent in some useful or gainful activity. Some people, in fact, see playing as a frivolous activity not worthy of pursuit.

8. *Play as feasts and celebrations* (Isambert, 1969). When we are celebrating a birthday, Christmas, holiday, anniversary, or any special event in our lives, are we playing or what? We are playing as long as we are involved in it. We become observers when we watch and do not participate. When we whoop and holler at the top of our lungs during a football game, are we playing? We are indeed actively involved, because, after all, we could choose not to whoop or holler as some spectators do. Consequently, we would have to include this involvement as playing as well (Sutton-Smith, 2003).

9. *Play as a pathway to personal freedom and community:* "Play is a basic form of activity . . . and can operate in the formation of one's personal world and in the development of love and community" (Sadler, 1969, p. 57).

10. *Play as catharsis* (Ginsberg, 1993): the outward expression of inner feelings, mostly hurt feelings, as seen often in play therapy (Chapter 15 this volume).

11. *Play as danger:* When some individuals run ahead of charging bulls in Pamplona, Spain, they are courting injury and even death. Why are they doing it? In an annual ball game in Florence, Italy, that includes a mixture of soccer, football, wrestling, and even boxing between teams representing different city neighborhoods, there is an ambulance present at a corner of the field of play, with physicians and nurses at the middle line, because inevitably someone is hurt and, in some instances, killed, and not necessarily a player.

12. *Play as challenge:* Eifermann (1971) offered the possibility that play presents a challenge, either in practice or in preparation for a possible future challenge, in either structured or unstructured playing, in competitive games between teams, in competition within teams, and in cooperative games as well.

13. *Play as humor:* Humor is observed in most records of children's play, ranging from smiles to boisterous laughter (Bergen, 2002). This aspect of play is present in most of the playing of older adults, such as the Pigs or the poker clubs described at the outset of this chapter.

PLAY AND PLAYFULNESS

How is play different from playfulness? The former is an activity. The latter is an attitude. Laura Sweeney (2008), for instance, has reviewed the playful attitude of many artists, painters, and poets in her blog, indicating how these great artists considered playfulness an important aspect of their serious work. One, for instance, can be playful at work and consider work a game. Many business tycoons, for instance, may look at their million-dollar dealings as games, approached as being fun to do, where one takes the chance of winning or losing. By the same token, one could play a competitive game in all seriousness. Note how parents become seriously involved in whether their children win or lose at competitive games in which their children supposedly are playing for fun, even though the game is highly contentious. Their children's attitude may be playful, but the parents may become so involved in the game to the point of forgetting their perspective and losing sight of its meaning by becoming abusively obstreperous and demanding during their children's games. Nonetheless, the even presence of just the attitude of playfulness may predict better coping skills than the absence of this attitude, even though girls may score higher on coping skills than boys showing the same degree of playfulness (Sauders, Saver, & Goodale, 1999).

There have been quite a few attempts to define playfulness as well as a dimension along extremes of playfulness and nonplayfulness, with rating scales in general (Lieberman, 1977, pp. 153–161) and one for children (Holmes & Geiger, 2002, pp. 142–143). Playfulness is especially evident in rough-and-tumble playing in boys (Pellegrini, 2002).

WHAT IS NOT PLAY?

In spite of the many ways of describing and classifying play, a clear line is difficult to draw between play and not-play. For instance, is passive entertainment, such as attending concerts, movies, or operas, play even though there may not be active, spontaneous, and voluntary involvement in the process? Yet, watching TV is not play, but interactive TV or Nintendo games are indeed play. Some people may consider shopping without buying as play, and it may be. It depends on the attitude—doing it for "the hell of it." I learned during my courtship days that the meaning of shopping was really different for my wife-to-be than my own meaning of shopping. For her, shopping seemed a serious, excruciating business of comparing, analyzing, considering critically any possible purchase, without even thinking about buying. For me, shopping meant buying something I needed, without any seemingly painful analytic process attached to it. However, when I inquired about the seriousness of such pursuit, she informed me that shopping was a game, a process of exploration, a way of finding out what the cost of any item was with the goal of finding the best possible price for the best possible product. This process satisfied curiosity and an aesthetic need to pursue a definite goal that was superior to any other activity. The process was more fun than the outcome. Whether the item was eventually purchased was secondary to the process of pursuing it—as in a courtship. Once married, when we were looking for a car, in addition to its cost, I would be concerned about its mileage per gallon. She was concerned about its color.

Where can we draw a line between playing and not-playing? For instance, camping may involve playful activities, but is it play in itself? Some people may answer affirmatively to that question. When we are on vacation, actively sightseeing or even passively sunbathing on a beach, would or should that activity be considered play? If we take a cruise, is that play, or is it play only if we play games on board the ship, such as shuffleboard? For many people their hobbies are their games. A hobby that produces a useful product may be play if the product is either kept or given away as a gift. However, if the product is sold, whether for profit or for no profit, that activity is no longer play.

Is reading play? Doubtful but possible, depending on what kind of reading. If I read humorous books before I go to sleep, am I playing or am I not playing? Can work be playful but not play? What is the difference? One way to draw the line is money and time. When money and time are spent in the pursuit of a toy, from an inexpensive one, such as what children receive at fast-food restaurants to a million-dollar yacht, it must be play. However, when money and time change direction, when one is paid for an activity that takes time, that is no longer play. It becomes a job. In high school and college, youths may play a sport for physical education credit, personal interest, and pleasure, but they have to pay tuition to receive that credit. However, when after graduation such a student receives an offer to play on a professional team, it is not longer play. It's a job, even if the player enjoys doing it. The same can be said of college players who receive athletic scholarships.

As noted previously, there is a possibility that play may become an addiction, as seen in many youngsters who play Internet games, or even adults who have become so addicted to the Internet as to forget about family obligations or even paying attention to the needs of intimate others.

Is watching spectator sports or TV programs play? Not if it does not engage physical involvement and is not spontaneous. Many spectators do become involved in the play they are looking at, and this involvement could qualify them as "sports fans." But is watching something play? I guess it depends on what we are watching. Watching birds could be an interesting hobby when it is done "seriously." However, occasional and nonserious bird watching is not play.

Is singing in a choir play? There are more than 28 million Americans who sing in choruses, with adults in more than 15 percent of U.S. households taking part in one or more 250,000 choruses (http://chorusamerica.org/ files). Again, it may depend on what this activity means to the singer, just as in old age (Chapter 16 this volume) volunteering is quite common, but is it play?

As one can see, the line between play and not-play is a difficult one to draw. This is why Sutton-Smith (1997) considered its definition "ambiguous" and drew the line according to how we interpret and give meaning to an activity as play or not-play. Even then, such interpretations may add confusion to the process of defining play. Consequently, we have no choice but to pursue the study of play according to what other professionals call play and accept the position that the line between play and not-play is a difficult one to draw.

IS PLAY NECESSARY?

This question has been asked from times immemorial, and whatever answer one may give to that question, it will never be sufficient or satisfactory. As noted above, many think that play is a superfluous activity and a waste of time. For some of us, play is necessary as much as we need work. I cannot conceive of living without playing. Hence, we need to consider why people do play. If they play, it means that they find it necessary on some level. Otherwise, they would not play. There is little doubt that play is beneficial and has few negative side effects (Sylva, 1984).

HOW DO WE LEARN TO PLAY?

First of all, we learn to play by observing older children and even adults, imitating in some ways what they are doing while playing. The discovery of mirror neurons in both humans and primates goes a long way to explain how we learn by observation and imitation (Iacoboni, Woods, Brass, Bekkering, Mazziotta, & Rizzolatti, 1999). Another way we learn to play is simply through sheer creativity coming from inside us; that is, a child must improvise something to do, whether to kick any object close by, even a ball if available, or build a castle out of something, such as blocks. In many instances, learning how to play involves taking chances in trying to play, even if they involve trial and error.

One important theoretical aspect of play deals with the explanation of play behavior through conditioning. That is, we repeat whatever behavior is reinforced from external rewards, and we decrease behavior that is punished or ignored. However, where is the reinforcement in playing when there is no one there to praise or reward what the children are doing? If there is any reinforcement, it comes from the activity itself and from the internal feelings of satisfaction and pleasure that derive from the activity itself. No external reinforcement is necessary to explain why we play and how we learn to play. Playing is seen as a self-reinforcing activity. However, the ability to speak and to describe what is going on may facilitate observation and imitation of cooperative play being modeled (Jahr & Eldevik, 2002).

This dialogue will be pursued further throughout the chapters of this book, and especially in Chapters 6 and 19 of this volume.

THE STUDY OF PLAY

Since times immemorial, play has been observed impressionistically, rarely with any records to report what was seen. It was only during the nineteenth century that play began to be recorded and reported scientifically using written notes and memories. From occasional and accidental observations about play, the introduction of audio and video recording has produced a gigantic step forward in the professional and scientific study of play. The sandbox and dolls are two of the most frequently used ways to observe play in a way that can be documented (for a complete review of assessment in play, see Gitlin-Weiner, Sandgrund, & Schaefer, 2000, Appendix A). Repeated behavior samples spanning one to more minutes have been another way to measure play activity in addition to ethnographic, anthropological (Schwartzman, 1978, 1985, 1995), and controlled studies. Therefore, throughout this volume these methods of observation, measurement, and active manipulation of factors used to study play will be included, with an evaluation of how reliable and valid these methods may be.

THE FUNCTIONS OF PLAY

Whatever may be said about the functions of play involves a great deal of overlap between concepts because one function is difficult to really separate from any other function (Slowikowski & Kohn, 1998). For the word "function" in the title of this section, one could easily substitute "reasons" for playing. Often, these reasons are very personal and have nothing to do with what may seem irrational or strange, as in the example of shopping as a pursuit game rather than serious acquisition of goods given in the personal narrative at the beginning of the "What Is Not Play?"

section. The following are some of the more common functions of play or reasons for playing.

To add flavor and spice to life: A great deal of our life may consist of repetitious routines that may eventually become boring. What can we do to add spice to our lives? How often can we view the same shows on TV? How often do we have to follow the same routines and responsibilities at home and at work? Clearly, we need to break the cycle of repetitious routines by shifting gears, so to speak, to leave behind what we have been doing. To immerse ourselves in something that is pleasurable and nonroutine is necessary just as much as work is. If our lives are so routine-dominated that we do not have time to play, then there must be something wrong with how we choose to live. We would be taking life too seriously and would allow work or anything else to control and dominate us. Therefore, ultimately the responsibility to play remains on our shoulders. If we do not take that responsibility, no one will take it for us.

To increase pleasure in life: Another way to say what has been said above lies in how we take life and whether we allow the whole weight of life to become a burden that we cannot discharge. Here, one could start to distinguish between legitimate and illegitimate pleasure. Betting on games is gambling. However, when that betting overwhelms anything else, it is evident that we need something else to substitute that is just as pleasurable with no side effects. Playing cards is pleasurable as long there are limits on the betting. However, when one wants to play cards all the time, and loses money at it, it is no longer a pleasure. It becomes an addiction. Perhaps a more appropriate term for "pleasure" would be "enjoyment." If survival is a necessary chore in life, play is an additional enjoyment that helps to make survival worth the struggle.

To decrease inevitable stresses by relaxation: If time is a limited commodity that is constant for all of us, rich, poor, or in between, then in one way or another, either at home or at work or in both, we all are subjected to the inevitable stresses of daily living. Denying the existence of these stresses means that one is either living a charmed existence or denying the existence of those stresses. What can be better than leaving those stresses behind and doing something that is completely different? I know of a couple who, although retired, have continued to work in somewhat stressful professional occupations. Nonetheless, every three weeks, they take a long weekend and leave town for casinos in the adjoining state where, because of their regularity as patrons, board and room are free, and they can gamble all they want. They are extremely happy with this arrangement. Likewise, another couple takes a cruise every three or four months to different parts of the globe.

What about those who cannot afford to leave town or go on a cruise? Where there is a will, there will be a way to play. What does is cost to invite friends for a game of Scrabble? What about inviting a child's friend to play in your home with your child? Children can amuse themselves with rather inexpensive toys. Costs are not as relevant as the desire to play and do something different from the usual.

To cement and enjoy relationships with selected others: After some thirty or forty years of playing together, it is inevitable that some of the players in a card game may have become best friends. Playing together for so many years allowed us to share nuances of our lives that we would have not shared with anybody else. Indeed, I would not be surprised to look back to past friend relationships that lasted and find that they were based on sharing our hurts as well as our pleasures. A few years ago, we were asked to travel from Atlanta to Chicago for a one-day trip to visit Frank Lloyd Wright's home in Wisconsin with childhood friends of my wife. It was worth driving two days to go and two days to come back to be with those friends for one day. They have passed away now, but the memories and experiences of our pleasurable trip still linger.

How do we select "others"? An answer to this important question will be given in Chapter 19 of this volume.

To educate and learn: Learning and playing are inevitably entwined, especially if the pleasure of playing increases skills that will be necessary later on in life, not only academic but also social skills (Davidson, 1996). Even more importantly than education and skills, play may increase creativity in ways that would be difficult if not impossible to achieve otherwise (Yawkey, 1986).

CONCLUSION

Play and playing are as necessary for life as are air, food, shelter, and work. Whether play may produce short- or long-term results is a secondary issue that will be pursued throughout the course of this book. Is play good for you, or is this just a figment of this or other writers' imagination? It will be worthwhile to attempt to answer this question in the remainder of this book.

2

PLAY ACROSS HISTORY AND INTO CYBERSPACE

This chapter does not aspire to be a detailed record of how play has existed as long as the known existence of human life. For reasons of space, the history of play cannot be the focus of this book. The interested reader will find ample information on this matter in Caplan and Caplan (1973), Cohen (1987), Saracho and Spodek (1998a), and Markman (2004) as secondary sources of information on which the present discussion relies unabashedly.

ANTIQUITY

We must not forget that the Greeks have some of the first recorded history of games—as shown in special venues set up for games such as the Olympic Games (Caplan & Caplan, 1973, p. 256; Mergen, 1995). By the same token, the Romans' passion for contests is shown in the Colosseum, where deadly "games" were held, pitting gladiators against each other or men against ferocious animals, with the Emperor's thumb up or down signifying life or death. Across the Atlantic at Monte Albano, overlooking the southern Mexican city of Oaxaca, Mayans played ball inside a large rectangular pit in the ground, and the team that lost the game also lost their lives. The spirit of the times, for both the Roman and the Mayan venues on different continents, might have been approximately the same: human lives seemed to be expendable as entertainment (an issue discussed at the time, in Rome, by Marcus Tullius Cicero and Marcus Fabius Quintilian).

THE MIDDLE AGES

For the medieval period in Europe, comparatively little scholarly study of play can be found, but during this period the nobility disported themselves at the hunt and at the tournament, where knights tested their abilities and courage against each other in a contest intended to be less lethal than the battlefield. The horseless common people played such games as golf and various kinds of football, both mentioned in documents by the fifteenth century.

THE EUROPEAN RENAISSANCE

A recommended history of playing after the Middle Ages can be found in the account of Caplan and Caplan (1973, 255–292). The rest of this chapter is dedicated to modern pioneers of play (292–303), as well as to more recent toy designers and the commercial toy business (see Appendix A).

THE EIGHTEENTH CENTURY

During the eighteenth century, there was an advent of creative geniuses who emphasized the importance of education, especially with handicapped children. One cannot forget Jean-Jacques Rousseau, the French philosopher who emphasized the importance of play education for life. Subsequent reformers included Jacob Rodrigue Péreire and—especially—the Swiss Johann Heinrich Pestalozzi, who was the first to establish schools to train children to use their sensory-motor skills in self-directed activities and frequent contacts with nature. Pestalozzi was also the first educator to question the practice of requiring memorization without an understanding of what has been memorized.

In England, Scotland, and the United States, Robert Owen established the first infant schools and preached unceasingly about the importance of education.

THE NINETEENTH CENTURY

In the early nineteenth century in Germany, Friedrich Wilhelm August Froebel, a student of Pestalozzi, was the first to create a large variety of toys that would impart to the child notions of colors, shapes, sizes, and numbers. Simple manipulation of materials, games, stories, songs, group activities, and pleasant surroundings would increase the child's attention and application and, therefore, learning. Froebel also opened the first kindergarten, where women teachers were employed.

Also during this century, a French physician, Edward Sequin, was the first to institute controlled observations in the study of children and, inevitably, of their playing behavior—especially in developmentally disabled children. In the United States, William James's notions about education influenced educators such as Elizabeth Palmer Peabody, Milton Bradley, and Susan Elizabeth Blow, who attempted to add a play modality to their programs.

THE TWENTIETH CENTURY

In the twentieth-century United States, the most influential philosopher of education was John Dewey, who stressed the simple notion of learning by doing rather than memorizing. He influenced other educators, such as William Heard Kilpatrick, Margaret McMillan, and Caroline Pratt. Pratt was considered a great progressive preschool educator and educational toymaker, introducing play materials into the school curriculum. Harriet M. Johnson was a pioneer in the nursery school movement at the beginning of this century.

These leaders in the United States found a kindred spirit in Maria Montessori, an Italian who was globally influential in founding schools using her methods of letting the child learn at the child's own pace, rather than at the pace of a school curriculum.

Johan Huizinga can be credited with emphasizing the importance of play for its own sake, rather than for educational purposes. His ideas will be revisited in the next chapter of this volume, dedicated more specifically to theories about play, rather than just the education of children.

There is no need to attempt to list all the games that were played in the last century here. In addition to the resources reviewed in Appendix A, Sutton-Smith and Rosenberg (1961, pp. 20-31) list 180 games played during the first sixty years of the twentieth century. These researchers also classified games according to whether they are preferred by boys, by girls, or both and by type as follows (Sutton-Smith & Rosenberg, 1961, pp. 32-47):

- Imitative or make-believe activities
- Singing games
- Dialogue games
- Leader games
- Chasing

- Central-person guessing and acting
- Undifferentiated team guessing and acting
- Games featuring a central person of low power
- Individual skill games
- Skilled pastimes
- Undifferentiated team games
- Indoor or backyard physical skill
- Board or card games
- Major sports
- Cooperative guessing and acting games
- Couple and kissing games

It might be interesting to quote Sutton-Smith and Rosenberg's major conclusion about changes in gender differences of games for boys and girls:

> [That] the responses of girls have become increasingly like those of the boys as the sixty years have passed is not unexpected, in the light of the well-known changes in women's roles in American culture during this period of time. (48)

During the last part of the twentieth century, the advent of electronic portable and nonportable toys and games predicted their increasing influence in the next century, above and beyond gender differences.

THE TWENTY-FIRST CENTURY

The new century has seen electronic toys and Internet games become so prevalent that children who can afford them will be outdoors only during school recess—and at no other time, either at school or in their neighborhoods. Scholars in different countries, using different ways to evaluate these practices, have come largely to the same conclusions: that these practices can be dangerous (Ciofi & Graziano, 2003; Goldstein, Buckingham, & Brougere, 2004; Roberts & Foehr, 2004). Here is where the corrective influence of the family must be considered, possibly counteracting these practices with outdoor activities such as camping and vacations to mountains or seashores. Schools also may have a corrective influence, by helping students become interested in sports that require active outdoor participation, such as track and field or football.

As a child psychotherapist, I would be concerned about the possibility that children sharing their innermost feelings with each other in blogs or chat rooms may reinforce each other in failing to recognize the serious-ness of personal and relational issues. Eventually, those same children, when they grow up needing psychotherapy, may try to obtain it in the same way they have done since their childhood—online from their peers rather than talking face to face with professionals. One does not need to be an expert to make this inevitable prediction (Derrig-Palumbo & Zeine, 2005).

Issues of play and the media will be covered in greater detail in Chapter 17.

CONCLUSION

This brief overview of the historical foundations of play does not even begin to scratch the surface of the topic. Sources cited at the beginning of this chapter, supplemented with more recent references, could easily be expanded into a complete book by itself, a goal that goes above and beyond the aim of this book.

3

WHAT THE EXPERTS SAY ABOUT PLAY

All work and no play makes Jack and Jill very dull persons

(Paraphrase of an old saying)

The previous chapter discussed some early apologists of play, those who supported the value of play within the field of education but did not have a theory or model of play. Consequently, as a psychologist, I wondered whether my discipline would consider the importance of play as previous apologists, including William James and John Dewey, have done. If play is so important, why don't psychological personality, communication, and relationship science theories include it? A superficial perusal of the contents of major treatises in those areas failed to find any references to play, with the sole exception of Erikson's theory (Ewen, 1988). Even more relevant, an important treatise on adult development (Demick & Andreoletti, 2003) did not make any reference to play. Yet play, in its various forms, occupies a great part of our lives from infancy to senility (Orthner, Barnett-Morris, & Mancini, 1994; Wade, 1985). This conclusion, therefore, could mean that there is a disconnect between current major personality, communication, and relationship science and play theorists. Yet major play theorists have had a great deal to say about personality, communication, and relationships (Caplan & Caplan, 1973; Cohen, 1987; Cotter, 2004; Gilmore, 1982; Levy, 1978; Markman, 2004; Saracho & Spodek, 1998a, b).

In other words, major theories of personality, socialization, communication, and relationships have essentially ignored the crucial importance of play, making those theories incomplete and, therefore, inadequate. Play could be considered the Cinderella of most theories about human behavior. Why should play be included in personality and intimate relationships theories? How can we have a theory of socialization and relational competence throughout the life cycle that does not include playing? Answers to this question will be given in Chapters 6 and 19 of this volume.

The term "theory," however, is so overused in the relevant literature as to lose its meaning. I have argued that most psychological theories confuse theories with paradigms or with models. A *paradigm* is an overarching viewpoint that cannot be validated but that covers many theories. For instance, an emergent interactionism paradigm covers symbolic interactionism in sociology, relationship science, and relational competence theory, among many others (L'Abate, in press b). However, there are two types of theory: informal linear and formal pyramidal hierarchical. For instance, most theories of human behavior covered so far are informal linear, one topic after another topic within a major heading. A formal theory, on the other hand, has a hierarchical layered pyramidal nature, as in biology and other sciences (Harkness, 2007), composed of assumptions and derivations from the assumptions that lead to verifiable models. A formal theory differs from an informal one to the extent that the former contains models, while the latter does not.

Hence, a formal hierarchical theory is similar to the organizational chart of any industrial, religious, political, or military organization. A hierarchical theory of this kind, with assumptions and derivations from assumptions about play competence, will be presented in Chapter 19 of this volume.

In the meantime, in this chapter I shall condense some of the most influential "theories" (also described as "models") of play behavior, using secondary rather than primary sources for the sake of convenience and compact presentation. Readers interested in further information on theories of play may consult the sources listed in the References.

MAJOR PAST PLAY THEORISTS

Early conceptualizations of play treated it as (1) *relaxation* or *restoration* of energy exhausted during work, (2) *surplus energy* for whatever strength is left after work, (3) *recapitulation* of previous developmental stages already experienced by the human race, or (4) *practice* or *exercise* for future work roles in adulthood (Saracho & Spodek, 1998a, pp. 5–6).

Subsequent dynamic theories that have dominated the play landscape include (1) *psychoanalysis* (S. Freud), which viewed play as the representation of unconscious or unexpressed conflicts; (2) *constructivism* (J. Piaget), which viewed play as the outcome of two sequential processes necessary to learn: assimilation and accommodation; and (3) *social learning,* which views playing as the outcome of imitation (Saracho & Spodek, 1998a, pp. 5-9). Hopefully, relational competence theory (RCT) will represent a more encompassing view of play than presented in previous theories.

The following pioneers, evolving from and on the basis of previous apologists of play, began to offer explanations and theoretical models of play to the point that they are still relevant at the present time.

Friedrich Wilhelm August Froebel

This pioneer believed so much in the importance of play that he not only made it part of an educational curriculum but also created a variety of play materials that could be used by children to manipulate actively and enjoy. In addition, Froebel fostered the importance of physical skills and training, or what we would call "physical education." He also employed women as being more relevant to working with children. These breakthroughs at both conceptual and practical levels influenced educators throughout Europe and United States, in ways that were eventually expanded and applied, among others, Maria Montessori in Italy and the rest of the world and Caroline Pratt in the United States.

Johan Huizinga

There is no question that Huizinga may have been the most influential scholar in the study of play in the past century, just as Sutton-Smith may be the most influential play scholar in this century. As Henricks (2002, p. 24) argued, Huizinga, even after publication of his ground-breaking book *Homo ludens: A study of the play element in culture* (1938/1955), "stood on the shoulders of giants ... (and) ... modern scholars stand (on his) shoulders ... What (Karl) Marx is to the study of work[,] so Huizinga is to the study of play." *Homo ludens,* the playing man, is one member of a triumvirate along with *homo sapiens* ("man the knower") and *homo faber* ("man the maker"). By emphasizing the equal importance of play with knowledge and with production, Huizinga established play as one important aspect of life. He championed the importance of imagination and created the first list of characteristics that define play as being different from other human activities, that is, that play is (1) voluntary, (2) not ordinary or real, (3) secluded or limited in space and time, (4) has order and creates order, (5) surrounds itself with secrecy to the point that play-ers set themselves up as different from others by the clothes or uniform they wear, the equipment they use, and even the language that is specific to the play and not used anywhere else. In this regard, Huizinga empha-sized the importance of culture in determining the nature and the limits of play. Play has a social and cultural function in the development of civ-ilization.

MAJOR PLAY THEORISTS IN THE TWENTIETH CENTURY

To cover this section I shall rely on Levy's (1978) work because no other work that I know can rival it in covering present-day theories of play in a clear, critical, and straightforward manner. Consequently, Levy's excellent contribution will be condensed here. He follows a multidiscipli-nary paradigm, categorizing theories in the study of play as follows:

1. Classical theories of play include (a) the surplus energy theory of play, already noted, which views play as being motivated by an overabundance of energy and by innate motivation to be active; (b) evolutionary theories, emphasizing instincts and survival of the fittest; (c) the recapitulation the-ory, which holds that through play we replicate behavioral traits handed down to us since prehistory, such as climbing, swinging, throwing, catching, running, and yelling; (d) the recreation theory of play, which sees play as being motivated by a deficit in energy that needs to be restored; and (e) relaxation from other tiresome activities, be they physical or intellectual.

2. Psychoanalytic theories of play include (a) Sigmund Freud's emphasis on unconscious motivation and stages of psychosexual development (oral, anal, phallic, genital), the oedipal conflict, and structure of personality composed of the id, ego, and superego; (b) Eric Erikson's theory of development in eight stages: trust versus mistrust, autonomy versus shame and doubt, initiative ver-sus guilt, industry versus inferiority, identity versus confusion, intimacy versus isolation, generativity versus stagnation, and integrity versus despair.

   From its very beginnings, child psychoanalysis has relied on observations of children at play in both natural and therapeutic settings as a source of information about the mental life of children. Play is known to be an effective means for the child to come to understand and cope with unhappiness and conflict. These and other meanings of play have ramifi-cations throughout adolescence and even adulthood, so that play is a cru-cial subject of study for clinicians (Solnit, Cohen, & Neubauer, 1993).

3. Developmental theories of play include, first and foremost, Piaget's develop-mental theory, which emphasizes accommodation, adaptation, assimilation, and the following ontogenetic stages of cognitive development: (a) sensorimotor

(0-2 years), (b) preoperational (2-7 years), (c) operational (7-12 years), and (d) formally operational (from 12 years to old age). Within each of these stages Piaget placed different kinds of play as relevant to that stage. A major viewpoint of Piaget that remains controversial to this day is that play arises or emerges from inside the child without external opportunities and stimulations. For instance, he never mentioned the presence and influence of the mother in his observations of play in children and attributed to children types of thinking peculiar to autism or schizophrenia. For relevant but critical reviews of Piaget's theorizing about play, see Sutton-Smith (1982) and Smolucha and Smolucha (1998), who conclude that

> the empirical basis for Piaget's theory—the idea that play originates from the child's own solitary activities rather than interactions with caregivers—was greatly overstated by researchers during the 1960s and 1970s. A careful reading of the research literature reveals that researchers appear to have ignored instances of caregiver-child interactions and restricted their observations to what the child could accomplish alone or with children of the same attainment level; thus little evidence of early collaborative play was discovered (p. 41).

On the other hand, Kavanaugh and Engel (1998) credited Piaget for his pioneering work about pretend play in children, which has become one of the major research areas in the study of play. As discussed in greater detail in Chapter 8, pretend play indicates a simulation and acting as if the child were making up or enacting a role, and activity, or even a drama. There are various types of pretend play: (1) solitary, (2) social, (3) with adults, and (4) with peers. These scholars also expanded pretend play to narratives, through which children as well as adults express and share their thoughts and feelings with others, as in storytelling. Roskos and Neuman (1998) extended pretend and storytelling to language use and literacy by including narrative theories.

4. Ecological theories of play emphasize (a) interactions among settings, such as home, school, and playground with qualities of toys used, (b) personality dispositions, such as achievement, power, dominance, and affiliation, (c) individual states, such as anxiety, tiredness, boredom, and relaxation. Ecological theories also emphasize arousal properties in the environment, including properties of the stimulus situation that motivate an individual to play, such as risk, information, novelty, variation, predictability, and meaningfulness, as noted, for instance, in Pellegrini's (1995b) and in Sutton-Smith's (1971) work.

5. Socialization theories emphasize the role of the environment in stimulating and reinforcing play behavior, such as (a) social learning based on observation, imitation, conditioning, and reinforcement or (b) conflict- or competition-acculturation (competition would be preferable to conflict here) of skills, such as building a house; strategies, such as Monopoly; and chances available to play, as in horse racing, dice, or roulette.

Not included in Levy's somewhat outdated summary of recent play theories are the following past and present pioneers, who are worthy of mention if only in a condensed form.

Lev Semenovich Vygotsky

This Russian theorist is still influential even though his most important ideas go back to the mid-1930s. He belongs to the school of play apologists who advocated not just an overall view of play materials but also specific functions for specific toys. A toy is not just a toy; it has more than one meaning for a child, especially a symbolic meaning of dependability, object constancy, and even safety, as noted in Chapter 1 of this volume. Vygotsky developed a hypothesis concerning the origin of play in preschool children. He identified conditions that determine the appearance of this type of play in ontogeny, the biological origin and development of an individual organism from fertilization of the egg cell until death. He demonstrated that play between the early and the preschool period does not arise spontaneously but is the result of educational influences. He established the relevance of play to interpersonal relations, observing that the basic content of play is visible in adult relationships. He pointed out children's techniques of transferring meaning from one object to another and stressed that contradiction and generalization are important in introducing the child to the realm of human relationships. He identified the further development and disintegration of the basic unit of play. He identified real relationships among children in play that constitute the practice of higher forms of group relations; thus he increased our understanding of the role of play in the mental development of children (El'konin, 1976).

Furthermore, active play fosters cognitive and language skills, that is, an "inner speech" that might not be otherwise available to the child (Holmes & Geiger, 2002; Smolucha & Smolucha, 1998; Welteroth, 2002). Vygotsky saw play, such as dramatic/symbolic play, as basic to cognitive development, to the point that a whole educational curriculum should be planned around it (Cotter, 2004). It might be relevant to include the rules of dialogue, which apply to play as well, as can be seen by substituting "play" for "dialogue" in the following rules:

- Dialogue occurs in an environment of trust.
- Dialogue involves taking turns.
- Every one is invited to dialogue.
- Understand what is acceptable.
- Be mindful of others.
- Respect the ideas of others.
- Let others have their ways sometime (Cotter, 2004, p. 335).

As Smolucha and Smolucha (1998) concluded their review:

> The importance of Vygotsky's theory lies in its view of creativity as a higher mental function capable of maturing beyond the skill levels evident in childhood, thus Vygotsky removed creativity from the sphere of simple regressive behavior (p. 51).

As Pellegrini (1998) paraphrased Vygotsky's thinking:

> A child may make a broom a horse because of her desire to own and ride a horse. Correspondingly, as children are realizing the unrealizable in play, they are also confronted with the desire to impose societal rules on their play (p. 225). . . . Thus in play we have a wonderful mixture of children being motivated and this motivation is directed toward highly sophisticated goals. For this reason, Vygotsky believed, children tend to exhibit higher levels of competence in play than in more traditional assessment contexts. (p. 226).

This area of research has suffered from methodological problems partly because of a lack of procedural detail in the original Soviet writings. These difficulties, however, may have been overcome, to the extent that carefully conducted research into private speech provides one of the best ways into an understanding of the central issues of verbal mediation and internalization (Livod & Fernyhough, 1999).

Both Piaget and Vygotsky emphasized the importance of symbolic play, which enables the child to incorporate literacy content with a positive influence on early literacy development. This importance has been supported by research by Wolfgang and Sanders (1982; Wolfgang, Stannard, & Jones, 2003) and Pellegrini (1995a, 1998, 2002).

Jerome Bruner

This American psychologist was greatly influenced by the ideas of Vygotsky about the importance of dramatic play in fostering imagination and creativity through the use of symbolic interpretations of meaning, in reaction to the rigid behavioristic thinking of the post–World War II era (Wagner, 2004).

Brian Sutton-Smith

In addition to his 1997 major contribution to the *Ambiguity of Play*, more recently, Sutton-Smith (2002) added deep play (gambling and dogfights in the southern United States), contact sports, celebrations, and monitored-play forms (as discussed in Chapter 6), found in adventures and explorations and mind play performances. This play scholar, theorist, and researcher, to whom this book is dedicated, is responsible for what was included in Chapter 1 in terms of the various meanings (i.e., metaphors) of play (Sutton-Smith, 1997), and he is cited often throughout the course of this work as well as by most scholars and researchers in the study of play (Pellegrini, 1995a, b). He is also responsible for including sports, holiday celebrations, and holiday rituals within the realm of play. His major contribution lies in emphasizing the scientific study of play, and distinguishing play as related to secondary emotions, associated mostly with activity in the frontal lobes of the neocortex, rather than to primary (flight or flight) emotions, which are associated with activity in the limbic system of the brain, following the theory of Demasio (1994). Sutton-Smith (2002, p. 5) describes the latter type of emotions as follows:

> These emotions still occur for ourselves when we are suddenly startled or threatened and our heart beats faster, or when we tremble, perspire, are enraged, are suffering a painful loss, or, alternatively, when we are suddenly overwhelmed by feelings of surprise, triumph, joy, or love. These primary emotions propel us into action when emergencies arrive.

Here is how Sutton-Smith describes secondary emotions:

> These developments in the frontal lobes of the neocortex require more contemplative decision making in thoughts and actions and were associated with attempts to secure survival through careful delays and reconsiderations. The difference between the two emotional systems seems to be something like the difference between passion and perspicacity, or between intense emotional extremities and more controllable emotional fictions, aesthetics, and imaginings.

From this distinction, it follows that play theories can be divided into those that emphasize irrationality and disorder as related to primary emotions, such as those involving the possibility of serious damage and perhaps death (as in deep games or mountain climbing), versus theories that emphasize rationality and normality based on control of play as related to secondary emotions, where the possibility of a dangerous outcome is minor if not minimal or nonexistent. Following this important distinction, Sutton-Smith was able to relate different kinds of play theorists according to which emotions they relied on, a suggestion worth following up (see Chapter 19).

Sutton-Smith's theory, therefore, rests on the assumptions (2002, p. 14) that (1) there is an evolutionary discontinuity between "reptilian" (primary emotions) and "mammalian" (primary and secondary emotions) behavior, (2) all types of play can be similarly treated, (3) play can be interpreted mainly in terms of secondary emotions, (4) the mammalian brain has the capacity to make simulative maps of its own activity, (5) play simulation rests on the evolutionary emotional duality between primary and secondary emotions, resulting in the revitalization of the players, and (6) recapitulation theory is relevant to all types of play. Recapitulation theory held that stages of embryonic development of the individual organism mirror the morphological stages of evolutionary development characteristic of the species, often stated as "ontogeny recapitulates phylogeny." Unfortunately for Sutton-Smith, and perhaps unbeknownst to him, this theory was abandoned in the twentieth century when embryology showed no consistent correspondence between ontogeny and phylogeny.

Dorothy L. Singer and Jerome L. Singer

This chapter cannot be closed without mentioning the groundbreaking research by a couple of fellow psychologists that is a distinct contribution to the study of play in childhood. For them and for others influenced by them (Ariel, 2002), dramatic and imaginative role-play is the "precursor" of subjective thought, daydreaming, and adult pretending games. They demonstrated how helping parents and teachers themselves learn imaginative play was a much more effective and even efficient way to help children become more imaginative and perhaps more effective players (Singer, 1995; Singer, Singer, & Schweder, 2004). See also Appendix A for their contribution.

Judy S. DeLoache

This researcher and her collaborators have developed ingenious tasks to achieve an understanding of symbolic play in children, such as photographs, scale models, dolls, and small bricks (Uttal et al., 1998). Perhaps a summary of this research represents in part their contribution to play:

> Given the ubiquity of symbols in the lives of young children and the importance of symbols in human culture and communication, one might suppose that a basic understanding of the nature of symbols would come quite early and relatively easily—that children could really "see through" at least some symbols to what they represent. Our research indicates that this is not the case: one can never take for granted that a young child will appreciate the representational nature and role of any given symbol (p. 60).
>
> Rather than viewing play as universally positive, we see it as a two-edged sword. Play certainly is vital to cognitive development. However, just because children have played with an object, does not mean that they have learned from the experience (p. 76).

This is a rather unusual conclusion in a field where theory has been accepted as gospel and ideas have been assumed to be reality.

David A. Rosenbaum and Anthony D. Pellegrini on Play as Physical Activity

David Rosenbaum's contribution (2005) had nothing to do with play, and he did not mention it. However, he had a great deal to say about the widespread neglect of motor behaviors and movements as the "Cinderella of psychology." If we can conceive of play as consisting, at least in part, of actions and movements, whether externally motor or internally intellectual, as noted in the beginning of this chapter, this neglect applies as well and specifically to play. Consequently, play scholars and researchers should be grateful to Rosenbaum for pointing to this deficiency in the science of psychology and, as I have pointed out, especially in personality theory. Since play and movement go together as nonverbal behaviors, the study of play would be directly related to the study of motor control and movements, as discussed further in Chapters 6 and 19 of this volume.

The importance of play as a physical activity was emphasized by Pellegrini and Smith (1998a), who considered it within a context of playfulness "combined with a dimension of physical vigor." These scholars distinguished among three "kinds of physical activity play with consecutive age peaks: (1) rhythmic [stereotypes], peaking in infancy, which may improve control of specific motor patterns"; (2) "exercise play," peaking during preschool years, which may incidentally also improve physical strength and endurance; and (3) "rough-and-tumble play, peaking in middle childhood," which possesses a distinctive social component in terms of a dimension of dominance-submission. Whether rough-and-tumble play may help future fighting skills is still an equivocal possibility. Gender differences, with a greater preponderance of males over females, characterize the latter two kinds of activity play. A criticism of such distinction lies in the difficulty to define "pure" play separate and distinct from other activities (McCune, 1998), while Byers (1998) questions whether the age distribution of play provides clues about the biological nature of play as a physical activity, and whether the latter represents an example of performance-dependent development during sensitive periods, as suggested by Pellegrini and Smith.

This view has brought about some interesting reactions and amplifications in the literature. Bjorklund and Brown (1998), for instance, proposed instead that

> humans may have evolved a special sensitivity to certain types of social information during rough-and-tumble play that facilitates social cognition. The cognitive benefits of physical play [may provide] a break from demanding intellectual tasks, [possibly related] to gender differences in spatial cognition.

McCune (1998) suggests that

play has been difficult to define because it occurs as an aspect of many activities rather than being limited to a specific kind of activity; for instance, rarely it occurs in isolation. [The] immediate and ultimate functions of play can be discerned in the simplest physical activity play.

Peter Rosenbaum (1998) comments that function might be

considered in terms of beneficial immediate and deferred consequences in physical, cognitive, and social domains. Studies of the development of children with disorders of motor function may afford opportunities, [so far] unexploited, to understand the importance of motor function to overall child development.

CONCLUSION

Unfortunately, there is not nearly enough space and time to give credit and recognition to the many unmentioned brave and ingenious pioneers who have contributed to our enjoyment, and the enjoyment of our children and grandchildren, of play and to making play an important part of our lives. The rest of this book is written in the hope of making amends for the brevity and superficiality of this and the previous chapter.

4

WHAT CULTURES HAVE TO DO WITH PLAY

Despite the heart-warming rhetoric we dish out in our teacher-training classes, children do not have unlimited imagination; their make-believe and, by extension, other play forms are constrained by the roles, scripts, and props of the culture they live in.

(Lancy, 2002, p. 56)

American children make up 4% of the world's population, but they consume more than 40% of the world's toys. In 2006, volunteers picked up 68,700 lbs of toys and 33,469 lbs of diapers during worldwide beach cleanups.

(*Mother Jones*, May-June 2008, p. 25)

Play has become an integral part of the early childhood curriculum in the developing countries of the world and it is gradually being integrated into educational efforts in societies that have historically embraced a rigid academic curriculum for young children . . . . Not should we treat cultural norms and practices as static. As individual societies move toward implementing society-wide early childhood education programs, we must be aware of the social and technological changes that affect parent-child and peer relationships.

(Roopnarine, Lasker, Sacks, & Stores, 1998, pp. 195, 210).

Culture has everything to do with play, as Huizinga was the first theorist to point out (Henricks, 2002), in spite of criticisms about his notions

(Nagel, 1998). Toys and games represent the culture they come from (Haight & Black, 2001; Kehily & Swann, 2003; Lieberman, 1977; Renson, 1998; Roopnarine et al., 1998; Schwartzman, 1978, 1985, 1995; Sutton-Smith, 1986). However, once this categorical answer is given, we need to make sure there is sufficient evidence to support it. There are some cultures that discourage play because children are still thought of as workers necessary to the survival and welfare of family members, as was the case in Western societies for centuries and still is the case in some African and Asian countries; on the other hand, there have also been cultures that value play, especially in children (Caplan & Caplan, 1973, pp. 232–254).

Play is a universal, natural, and pleasurable experience, and in children as well as in some adults, it is an integral part of their lives. Play's very nature is social, and by being social it is inextricably linked to culture. Although play is universal, the way play looks and works differs across and within cultures. Despite the diversity of play in different cultures, various aspects of play appear universal because play is integrally related to other major characteristics of all cultures, such as religion, levels of subsistence, social complexity, and child-rearing customs (Schaefer, McCormick, & Ohnogi, 2005).

The nature of children's play across cultures can be reduced to four major types: (1) play as imitation of and/or preparation for adult life, (2) play as a game or sports activity for physical skill, (3) play as a projective or an expressive activity, and (4) play as a pastime. In particular, some forms of children's play in all cultures can be characterized by imitation of the activities of the adult world. Furthermore, types and extents of play are universally related to particular types of child-rearing practices. Even in cultures that put children to work with chores and economically based activities at an early age, the children play during free time or entwine play with the course of work/chores. It is important, therefore, to obtain information about ethnicity and other cultural characteristics of a neighborhood and families, as well as the cultural meaning and significance of children's play. The most valuable information can come from observing and talking with individuals representing different cultural groups, and from participating in their family events, celebrations, and rituals (Drewes, 2005).

A sociocultural approach about play has much to offer toward an understanding of development during toddlerhood. Social processes that contribute to socioemotional development in the second and third years of life need to be integrated within the cultural experience and context. These processes, in addition to play, involve attention and emotion regulation (Perez & Gauvain, 2007). Another factor that seems forgotten in these approaches is memory, to the extent that the more pleasurable the experience of play is, the greater the chances that the child's positive memories may offset unpleasant ones.

Hence, this chapter is concerned with the influence of cultures on play. Of course, even within a given culture there may be a wide range of play practices. Play practice is by necessity dependent on socioeconomic status (SES), since this factor in and of itself may include different cultures: the culture of the rich and the culture of the poor, as well as the culture of those in between (Doyle, Ceschin, Tessier, & Doehring, 1991; Hunnicutt, 1985; McLoyd, 1985). For instance, although middle-class preschoolers may engage in higher levels of play and talk more than lower-class peers, the quality of language used by the two groups may not differ.

With age, play roles may become more socially coordinated, the duration of play episodes may increase, and language certainly becomes more complex. However, social class groups may not differ on these measures. Consequently, if a developmental lag is not found, then other explanations of social class differences and classroom strategies may be necessary. Middle-class children may also more likely to show elaboration in fantasy play episodes than working-class counterparts, who might be more likely to show replication in their use of toys without as many words (Fein & Stork, 1981). This possibility may raise questions on whether there is a developmental lag in the fantasy play of children from lower SES (Smith & Dodsworth, 1978).

Another factor may be how gender is treated in a culture. What does it mean from the viewpoint of playing when, in certain countries, women are forced to use clothing that hides the human body completely and are segregated from men from an early age? How will these practices imposed on women in the name of some religious beliefs affect the playing of boys and girls, if there is any play in cultures of this kind? Although gender will be covered toward the end of Chapter 5 in terms of age-appropriate differences, SES will be covered throughout this work in the sense that both factors, gender and SES, could be conceived as different cultures throughout the life cycle (von Zuben, Crist, & Mayberry, 1991).

Play is most commonly conceived of as an intrinsically motivated universal behavior in children, not only present but also qualitatively similar in all cultures. This conception of play has limited play theory because of the tendency to see the play of children of highly educated Euro-Americans as representative of all children's play. An alternative conception of play is as a culturally structured activity that varies widely across cultures as well as within them, as a result of differences in child-rearing beliefs, values, and practices.

Play varies across cultures not only in its content, in the types of social interactions experienced during play, and in the resources that are made available for play, including material objects, space, and time, but also in the relation that play has to other everyday activities. Ultimately, to the extent that both the quality and quantity of play varies across cultures, one must question the role of play in promoting universal developmental outcomes. The meaning that players ascribe to play is an essential aspect of this somewhat different position, as discussed in Chapter 1 of this volume (Gaskins, Haight, & Lancy, 2006).

Chronological age (CA) will be covered in Chapters 7 through 13. Another important factor in play—the presence, type, and degree of physical and mental disabilities, which may distort, distract, and delay playing—will be also covered in each chapter when appropriate, relevant, and available in the literature (Bishop, 2004; Cicchetti, 1985; Wade & Hoover, 1985). This population includes the following subgroups: (1) preterm infants, (2) infants exposed prenatally to drugs, (3) children with visual impairments, (4) children with delayed language, (5) children with hearing difficulties, (6) children with cognitive delays, including how they play with objects and symbolic play, (7) children with attention-deficit/hyperactivity disorder, (8) children with autism, and (9) victims of abuse (Hughes, 1998).

In a comparison of South African and Israeli preschool children of lower- and middle-class economic background, SES seemed to be the overwhelming factor in determining the observed levels of imaginative play. Perhaps, deficits in imaginative play among lower-class children might be created not by the lack of experiences or stimulation per se but rather by the failure of lower-class parents to help their children with the integration of the plethora of stimuli that confront them in everyday life. Most of the specific home background factors thought to be particularly important for the development of imaginative play in children are culture-bound (Ariel, 2002; Udwin & Shmukler, 1981).

Toddlers and kindergarten children tend to produce and share important elements of their peer cultures that contribute to the reproduction of basic features of the American class structure and socialization (Corsaro, 1993). Here is where the peer culture does play an important role, not as a unitary whole but as a differentiated social system comprising various groups and different types of players. Within the context of peer culture, toys play an important role as entry vehicles and social markers. Play periods are indeed the social arenas whereby the dynamics of the peer culture are enacted (Elgas, Klein, Kantor, & Fernie, 1988).

A qualitative and quantitative reanalysis of data on children's play from the Six Culture Study collected in the 1950s used a running-record procedure that offers a picture of the worlds of childhood at a time when communities were more isolated and less influenced by commercial and technological advances that have produced changes in those very cultures. Children in all communities studied seemed to have an appetite for self-expression, peer collaboration, exploration, rehearsal, imagination, and problem solving. Their outlets were socially mediated and took many forms of play and work, with not necessarily clear boundary lines dividing them in communities where children were more helpful at work.

Both play and work seemed to enable children to build their repertoire of skills and schemes and to exercise and extend their knowledge and control over their environments. Cultural norms and opportunities determined the degree to which play was "stimulated by the physical and social environments." Key factors include whether adults considered play a good use of children's time or just an annoyance, whether adults preferred to preserve tradition or instead to instigate innovation, and "whether the environment provided easy access to models and materials for creative and constructive play." Nevertheless, play of several kinds was observed in each community and dependent on the environment only for reinforcement, not for instigation (Edwards, 2000).

As indicated above, one important aspect of the culture is the relationship between work and play. While the ratio between play and work changes over chronological age, from mostly play to mostly work, this ratio is also influenced by cultural values and practices. For instance:

> Perhaps nowhere else in the world is the work/play connection more evident than in some African societies. While earlier accounts portrayed African children as aimless and passive, often imitating their parents, more recent descriptions have considered the expressiveness and contributions of play to personality and the socioecological context within which play occurs. (Roopnarine et al., 1998, p. 202)

For instance, in some African countries, children who accompanied their parents to work in the fields often copied those adult roles in their pretend play. Within a culture, one must distinguish between traditional and newly acquired games, and between formal and informal settings. For instance, the introduction of television may produce some changes in what might have been traditional forms of play, while children may engage in fantasy and pretend play while in the fields where their parents work, rather than in school or in regular playgrounds (Roopnarine et al., 1998, pp. 205–206):

> In some cultures, the availability of play spaces is at a premium. As the rain forests disappear in Africa and South America, the habitats of the Aka, Efe,

and other hunting-gathering societies are endangered and families and children are becoming increasingly displaced." (Roopnarine et al., 1998, p. 208)

Exploration about the common features of the peekaboo game across seventeen cultures, for instance, through observations and interviews included gestures and vocalizations of U.S. and European mothers and their infants, and may lead to an understanding of why this game is so similar across diverse cultures and why, for both mothers and infants, this game is a source of universal delight (Fernald & O'Neill, 1993).

Things get complicated when various languages are present in a multicultural context when children play sociodramatically. Countering a deficit perspective, which focuses on what children from nondominant cultures do not know, the notion of syncretism, the integration of play elements from two or three cultures, may be useful in illuminating children's expertise and intentionality as they blend knowledge from multiple worlds to reinvent cultural practices and create new spaces for learning though play (Long, Volk, & Gregory, 2007).

THE EFFECT OF CULTURE ON PLAY

The major effect that culture exerts on playing, from the viewpoint of U.S. culture, is to stress the differences that inevitably exist between those in that culture and others, in terms of what is considered acceptable and appropriate (Kearns, Edwards, & Carlucci, 2004). Here is what I have been able to gather about the nature of play in various cultures.

Africa

This continent has experienced and is still experiencing tumultuous political, regional, and ethnic changes that have resulted in genocides, oppressions, poverty, and disease (especially HIV/AIDS) producing continuously unstable environments. Within this context observations and conclusions reached about play within the last decade may no longer be valid.

Botswana: Age- and gender-specific results from object, pretend, and rough-and-tumble play shed light about the relationship between local ecology and time allocated to play in an agrarian society such as that of Botswana. Play time allocation for girls tends to decrease much faster than for boys because of the community's need of the girls' homemaking skills. Eventually boys are trained to hunt, while girls are trained to take responsibility for homemaking chores (Bock, 2005). Therefore, this culture reminds us of what was happening in Europe hundreds of years ago and is still going on in many developing countries, where survival takes precedence over entertainment.

Nigeria: Research performed in this country, focused on the play of children from the Igbo ethnic group, produced a list of artificial and natural materials that differentiated these children from their American counterparts. American children tended to play with artificial materials, while Igbo children relied to a greater extent on naturally available materials (Nwokah & Ikekeonwu, 1998, p. 65). Igbo children may play hand-clap and step dance, hide-and-seek, land nuts, hop-scotch, duck fight, seed throw, role-play of leopard and sheep, the imaginary corpse of a European, and fire on the mountain. American children, on the other hand may tend to play bicycle racing, checkers, hide-and-seek, alligator, tag, king of the mountain, blind man's bluff, red rover, and car racing.

The list of penalties for breaking possessions and rules might be quite extensive among the Igbo children, ranging from mild to harsh, while there were only four penalties exacted from the American children: playing "dead" for a set time, running around the circle again, missing a turn, or being put out of the game (Nwokah & Ikekeonwu, 1998, p. 68).

Among the Bachama tribe of Nigeria, the antics of clan joking partners at funeral ceremonies for the elders serve to ease the transition of the soul to the status of ancestor, an example that broadens the domain of play and culture (Stevens, 1991).

West Africa: A series of studies about young children's play in one West Africa context (Senegal) focused on the relationship between work and play as well as on the emergence of gender differences in children's play. "Play-work" and work provide examples from two- to six-year-old children where work and play are entwined. This overlap is also relevant to the gendered divisions of labor in adolescence and adulthood (Bloch & Adler, 1994).

Children of the Kpelle people of Liberia and Guinea, West Africa, who grow up neither spending thousands of hours in quiet study nor receiving a heavy dose of parental tutelage, provide a more universal understanding of child development. Acknowledging the centrality of play in children's lives, Kpelle parents expect their children to play "on the mother ground": in open spaces adjacent to the areas where adults are likely to be working. Here, children observe the work that adults perform as they engage in voluntary activities or routines that serve a clear enculturating function. Games, folklore, and other routines influence the child's early development. Such enduring routines for raising children may be universal and not limited to rural societies, even though they take a variety of forms depending on the society (Lancy, 1996).

Asia

Comparisons between Asian and Euro-American parents of preschool-aged children, obtained through interviews, questionnaires, and diaries of their children's daily activities, focused on the parents' beliefs about the purpose and nature of play.

> [Euro-American parents believed] that play is an important vehicle for early development, while Asian parents saw little developmental value in it. On the other hand, Asian parents believed more strongly than Euro[-American parents] in the importance of an early start in the academic training of their children. These contrasting beliefs were instantiated in parental practices at home regarding the use of time and the provision of toys. (Parmar, Harkness, & Super, 2004)

Let's see how these conclusions apply to specific Asian countries.

Australia: Logo computing competence in preschoolers seems to differ according to gender, with specific characteristics of girls' and boys' play that might account for their differential effect on Logo competence (Elliott, 1993).

Boys with developmental coordination disorder may be lower in self-appraisal of leisure-needs satisfaction and overall life satisfaction than boys without that disorder, suggesting that perceived freedom in leisure ("comprising competence, depth of involvement, and perceived control over leisure outcomes") may be significant mechanisms "influencing leisure-time participation and life satisfaction," at least in boys (Poulsen, Ziviani, & Cuskelly, 2007).

In another study,

> Based on ideas from subjective uncertainty reduction theory, the extent to which individuals hold similar sports team preferences to their family and friends was examined in Australian high school students aged 15.5 ± 1 years. The extent to which perceived sports importance and personal need for structure might be influential in the development of team identification was assessed. Results indicated that preferences for sports teams were significantly related to the preferences of family and friends. Students who perceived the sport to be important to them identified with the team more than those who perceived the sport to be less important. Students high on personal need for structure apparently scored higher in cognitive/affective team identification than those low in this need. Students with different needs for structure did not differ in their scores on other dimensions of team identification.
>
> These results support the notion that cognitive/emotional attachment to sports teams are influenced by perceptions of the importance of the sport and by needs for subjective structure. It is possible that other psychological motives, such as desire for self-esteem, may facilitate the development of evaluative dimensions of team identification. (Dimmock & Grove, 2006)

This study tends to support Model[12] about Priorities in developmental relational play competence, summarized in Chapter 19 of this volume.

The majority of older people tend to lead relatively sedentary lives. Despite being older and in poorer health, retirement village residents report greater frequency of participation in leisure-time physical activities, such as walking, dancing, and lawn bowls, than older Australian living in the community (Miller & Buys, 2007).

China: Social and cognitive complexity in the play of Chinese and American children was evaluated with ninety Chinese and fifty American kindergarten students who participated in 15 plays with two degrees of dimensional difficulty. Their play behavior was videotaped and rated according to (1) social (onlooking, solitary, associative, and cooperative) development, (2) cognitive (practice, symbolization, game regulation) development, and (3) age. Levels of social and cognitive development predictably advanced with age, with a positive correlation between higher level of cognitive play behavior and higher level of social skill development. Differences between Chinese and Americans in the forms and contents of play and in social and cognitive levels were reported in terms of cultural background influences (Yang, Zou, & Bergen, 1995).

When the effects of ethnicity, age, and gender were examined on competitive versus cooperative interactions of forty Chinese and forty U.S. pairs in a game-playing situation in preschool/childcare centers, samples were divided into younger (2 years 9 months to 4 years 11 months) and older (4 years 3 months to 5 years 11 months) age groups. Participants in each group were assigned to boy, girl, or mixed pairs to play a marble-pull game. Of the pairs, 86 percent achieved equal/near-equal scores, suggesting an awareness of equality and fairness. There was a tendency for female pairs to attain equal/ near equal scores. Chinese participants, as a whole, were more competitive than their American counterparts (Sparkes, 1991).

Role-play behavior in middle school seems to vary through situation control, meaning that the validity of a conclusion was the highest when the situational format was ideographic (individualized) in its interactional context, less demanding, and unstructured. Gender, age, and previous level of assertiveness seem to affect role-play behavior (Ziangdong & Zheng, 1998). Reading more than mahjongg playing seems to be beneficial to the elderly (Ho, Chan, & Kong, 2005).

Guam: Adolescent girls "with greater body mass [may be] more likely to engage in physical fights (aggression) and to participate in team sports (competitiveness). Ethnic differences [suggest] the possibility that individuals with lower body mass may be less likely to participate in physically aggressive acts" and sport teams (Pinhey, 2002). It would be relevant to find which theoretical framework would account for these findings, except perhaps models in play competence theory (see Chapter 19 in this volume).

India: India, especially western India, provides an important basis for comparison between an old, complex civilization and the present. Defining features of life in India "provide some common concepts and Hindu ideals that are expressed in Indian society" and that provide the contextual factors that influence adult–child and child–child play around the following issues: (1) cultural, social, and cognitive messages conveyed during adult–child play, (2) child–child play in formal and informal settings, (3) play training studies as a mechanism to provide cognitive and social enrichment for children, (4) the role of objects and materials in the play of Indian children, and (5) culturally relevant practices in early childhood education (Roopnarine, 1994).

In developing countries, play in children has been stunted by hunger, malnutrition, and disease, with many children required to work from a very early age. In India, therefore, class, tribe, and SES are factors that need to be taken into consideration. Only children from well-to-do families have the chance to be exposed to toys and games (Singh, 2004).

Japan: "There are serious problems with young parents who did not have enough opportunities for play during their childhood. Japan is still a Confucian country—its influence has lessened a bit recently." Japan is still a rigidly hierarchical and male-oriented society, and the competition to be accepted into restricted numbers of students in the most prestigious universities has left very little time for child or even adult play. If play is present, it is in the service of producing educational gains rather than play for the intrinsic pleasure of play itself. This kind of rigid orientation can be related to an epidemic of children refusing to go to school. In few words, the Japanese culture is not the most conducive to free and spontaneous play (Okuda, 2004, p. 67).

In spite of such a bleak view of play in Japan, there is actually a greater deal of play orientation in Japanese preschools than there is even in the United States. Consequently, it would be relevant to compare Japanese with American preschools according to how much playfulness is present in either setting. When playfulness is evaluated by teachers, American children are perceived as being more playful than their Japanese counterparts. The latter showed much less heterogeneity than the former, suggesting that Japanese teachers, valuing conformity and equality in children more than we do here, may not value or even allow individual differences in playfulness as much as their American counterparts do (Taylor, Rogers, & Kaiser, 1999).

A comparison of thirty-eight U.S. and forty Japanese toddlers (aged 13 months) and their mothers on "dimensions of language and play" on the basis of home interviews and videotaped interactions, resulted in the finding that in both cultures and both domains,

> individual variation in toddlers was associated with individual variation in mothers. In general, the frequency and variance of language and play activities were similar in the two groups. American toddlers were more advanced in both productive and receptive vocabularies than their Japanese counterparts, and this cultural difference was matched by the tendency for American mothers to label and describe properties, objects, and events in the environment, more frequently. In contrast, Japanese toddlers were more advanced in symbolic play, and their advanced play was matched by more advanced play in Japanese mothers, particularly for "other-directed" acts of pretense. (Tamis-LeMonda et al., 1992)

Currently common Japanese belief structures and views about the nature of the child as well as theories of education in their relation to play are discussed from a historical viewpoint of traditional theories of play. Changes and problems associated with increased urbanization and technological growth in Japan after World War II have influenced how children play and the role of play in early childhood education (Takeuchi, 1994). Perhaps it may be better to provide "natural" play activities that encourage children to think logico-mathematically than to conceptualize specific standards for 3- to 6-year–olds' mathematical education (Kamii & Kato, 2005).

Nepal: It is unclear to what degree mothers structure, or scaffold, children's early play differently in different cultures. Culture-specific and ecological factors may affect a mother's inclination and motivation to play with her child, her scaffolding behaviors, her involvement in play, and the type and kind of play she engages in. In this study, preliminary descriptions of how play is defined, perceived, and valued were explored in a sample of fifteen rural Nepali mothers. This study meant to describe the kind of play interactions these mothers have with their children, whose ages ranged from 12 to 36 months. A qualitative method of research was used to address the research questions. Data were collected through participant observations, videotapes of mother–child play in the course of everyday activity in the home, and interviews and discussions with the mothers based on the videotaped activities between them and their children. From these data, it appears that play is an integral aspect of the mother–child interaction in daily care routines and is seen as a valuable means of keeping the child engaged, managing the child's behavior, and encouraging the child's cooperation. The mothers of this study had a positive attitude toward play and were aware of the developmental impact it had on their children. Perhaps early childhood educators and practitioners might be able to utilize these results to inform their work and develop relevant curricula (Rajouria, 2002).

New Guinea: Pretend play of Huli children tends to imitate and reproduce the adult culture as well as the production of unique peer cultures. This description raises questions about the line between description and interpretation of play, depending on whether observers are anthropologists or psychologists (Corsaro, 1998). This issue of where and how to draw the line between description and explanation will be raised again in Chapter 19 of this volume.

New Zealand: Participation of preschool boys might be significantly greater than that of girls in the areas with blocks and wheeled toys and less than that of girls in the family area. Teachers may tend to spend more time in girl-preferred areas. In spite of these differences, the breakdown of play stereotypes might be occurring, even though some areas of difference still remain (Smith, 1983).

Philippines: Philippine students (aged 12 to 22 years) seem to report less physical activity than U.S. students, as reported in the Youth Risk Behavior Scale. Those students who scored high on shyness apparently participate in vigorous physical activity less often than those who scored within average or low ranges on the same scale. Students scoring high on shyness also seem less likely to play on sports teams (Page & Zarco, 2001).

Polynesia: Young Marquesan children between 2 and 5 years of age learn to balance autonomy in group participation by transiting from toddlerhood in the family into their first nonfamily peer group while engaging in play. Play is the "work" of childhood, which enables children to "develop autonomous selves and acquire sophisticated social skills." Apparently, these children learn to manage themselves efficiently without adult help or supervision. They teach each other interaction rules and the values of their group and learn to exercise autonomy within the structures and obligations of this stable group (Martini, 1994).

South Korea: Extensive research comparing children's play in South Korea with that in the United States brought about the following conclusion (Tudge, Lee, & Putman, 1998, pp. 87–88):

> It is clear that there are some striking cross-cultural similarities in terms of both the amount and types of play in which these young children were involved. Play, as one might expect from a group of two- to four-year-olds living in most societies, occupied a great proportion of their time. Along

with the cross-societal similarities, however, age within-society differences as a function both of social class and gender. . . . it is important to take into account within-society differences . . . These children's play, and the ways in which their partners play with them, both reflect cultural differences and serve to recreate them . . . focusing on social class and gender revealed striking differences within each society, some of which (particularly associated with class) were mirrored in each society.

Acculturation of the parenting and play attitudes of 108 Korean mothers who had immigrated to the United States and their young children's social play, compared to 52 European American mothers, was evaluated with the Parents as Teachers Inventory and a play questionnaire. Additionally, observers recorded children's social and play behavior during free play activities in their preschool, and teachers rated their social behavior. Korean American (KA) mothers were also administered a measure of acculturation. Those KA mothers who had assimilated an acculturation style were more accepting and encouraging of children's creativity and play, reporting more parent–child play at home than mothers with an integrated, marginal, or separated acculturation style. Children of assimilated and integrated mothers engaged in more frequent pretend play and were rated by their teachers as being more difficult to deal with. These differences suggest how distinct cultures of family life and childhood may manifest themselves as Korean immigrant families individually adapt to life in the United States (Farver & Lee-Shin, 2000).

Taiwan: Pretend play in Taiwanese kindergarten, besides what can be expected of social participation, tends to be influenced by materials, ideas, or reactions of other playmates; personal motivation; and previous experiences with play. Social custom and convention served as symbolic foundations to understand pretend play in these children, where ownership of play objects was one source of conflict between boys and girls (Lin & Reifel, 1999).

However, the highly competitive, exam-oriented educational system causes parents to value academic and educational performance to the point that play takes a back seat place in such priorities where success in school is equated with success in life (Chang, 2004). This harsh conclusion is supported by the need to advocate the children's right to play in similar cultures in Taiwan and mainland China kindergartens. To reach this goal, the following steps have been recommended:

1. Help parents understand that young children's play is different from the play of older children.
2. Help parents distinguish between play for educational purposes and play just for fun, without any opportunistic value attached to it.

3. Help parents realize that developmentally appropriate play may help rather than hinder educational achievement.

4. Help parents realize that certain kinds of play can bring about certain kinds of learning and even achievement within the context of the child's overall well-being.

5. Help parents integrate intellectually and practically a Montessori perspective on free activity versus regulated and restricting educational practices. (Lin, Johnson, & Johnson, 2004, p. 108)

Play behaviors of Chinese children in Taiwan cover four major issues: (1) the Chinese perspective on play, (2) Chinese children's play behavior within a developmental framework, (3) current play behaviors in Chinese children and play differences across cultures, and (4) adults' perceptions of children's play. An observational study of play categories and play deficits with sixty-two kindergarten children from middle-class families as well as a questionnaire study of Taiwanese mothers' attitudes toward play tended to support the validity of these four issues (Pan, 1994).

In structured interviews with sixteen Taiwanese mothers of children with Down syndrome, these mothers stressed cognitive, emotional, and physical outcomes more than mothers of normally developing children did. They valued also a range of maternal roles in supporting these outcomes, such as facilitator, caregiver, director, and entertainer. However, the relative emphases placed by these mothers on benefits and roles within these roles differed from those of mothers of normally developing children. In responding to their children's disabilities, mothers placed equal value on the emotional and physical benefits associated primarily with the children's motor development and health, including also greater emphasis on facilitator and caregiver roles in helping their children achieve those benefits. Differences between these mothers according to two groups, pessimistic and optimistic, tended to produce different outcomes on their children's socialization (Chen, 2001).

Central America

Mexico: Ecological observations of play aggression among forty-eight Zapotec-speaking children aged 3 to 8 years showed that rates of play aggression were not significantly different between boys and girls. However, mixed-gender matches during aggressive play occurred less often than same-gender matches. Play partners were closer in age than chance would predict, with initiators tending to be slightly older than recipients, except when boys initiated aggression toward girls. Injuries during play aggression occurred infrequently, and children were more likely to stay together following play than following serious aggression. These observations tend to support the hypothesis that play aggression serves an evolutionary function of allowing children to practice adult fighting and/or hunting skills under relatively safe conditions (Fry, 1990).

Videotapes of sixty children (aged 18 to 36 months) pretend-playing with their mothers in the United States and Mexico illustrate mutual involvement in social play as well as maternal play behaviors. In this study, "Contextual features were observed, recorded, and analyzed using an activity setting model." Mothers were also interviewed about the value of children's play. Although children's pretend play and mother–child mutual involvement increased with age in both samples, U.S. mother–child pairs accounted for the greater proportion of interactive social play and pretend play episodes. There were also cultural differences in behaviors that mothers used to structure play and in mothers' value of children's play (Farver & Howes, 1993).

"Self-consciousness, lack of self-discipline, interest, company, enjoyment, and knowledge" might be the most predominant factors constraining leisure-time physical activities in both Mexican and European Americans in South Texas (Dergance, Calmbach, Dhada, Miles, Hazuda, & Moulton, 2003).

Europe

Austria: From 1983 to 1987 a longitudinal empirical study was conducted to assess the long-term effects of the Viennese Play Curriculum, which integrates play into the existing elementary school curriculum. Four different domains were studied: emotional attitudes toward learning, social behavior, achievement orientation, and creativity. These qualities seemed to have been produced to a greater extent in experimental than in control schools (Hartmann & Rollett, 1994).

Estonia: Significant gender differences in play could appear in the social domain of dominance in 4- and 5-year olds as well as in the prevailing types of rules within each domain (dominant versus nondominant). One study revealed that

> Boys referred to moral rules more often than girls did. In the category of moral rules, boys were significantly more likely to bring up justice and rights issues than girls were. In the category of conventional rules, girls may focus on miscellaneous and general conventions and boys on the destruction of property. Moral rules were applied more frequently in conflict situations. Regardless, of gender, [however,] rules of justice were the most likely moral rules to engender conflicts. (Tulviste & Koor, 2005)

Former Yugoslavia: An important article has been published about the results of war stress on children who were continuously subjected to deadly and daily bombardments and crossfire bullets during the wars in the Balkan region. Of course, a child's reactions depend on age, cognitive and emotional capacity, and availability of caring adults and attachment figures. Regressive and repetitive play is evident rather than usual or creative play, an important comparison that will be used in Chapter 19 of this volume. Resilience factors to stress are individual (age, basic personality strength, previous similar experiences, adaptability, temperament, self-respect, positive self-concept, inner locus of control, extroversion, activity, and sociability). Also related to resilience in children are the characteristics of the traumatic event (type, suddenness/unexpectedness, and exposure length). The child's personal and subjective evaluation of the traumatic event, of course, is also important, including the child's own and parental reactions to the event and parental responsiveness to the child's needs, including the presence of an intact family and its financial situation (Lisul, 2004).

Germany: As in Latin America and New Orleans, carnival during the pre-Lenten season is a widespread form of play throughout Germany. Nonetheless, there are distinct differences between southwestern and eastern regions of Germany due mainly to religious practices and to political constraints during the 40 years of Communist oppression, respectively (McMahon, 1999).

Play and behavior categories in eight preschoolers (mean age 40 months) in Italy with eight preschoolers (mean age 48 months) in Germany from an average of fifty 5-minute videotaped observation sessions in Germany and thirty-eight such sessions in Italy were analyzed. Results revealed differences in "looking around," "body contact," "talking to somebody," "automanipulation," and "number of children playing together." German children also showed more distal behavior (e.g., smiling, talking). In both cultures children preferred same-gender children for social play and same-gender children for parallel play, with a decline of interactions with the teacher and "looking around" over the year. Gender differences were also found in both samples for "object conflict" (Hold-Cavell, Attili, & Schleidt, 1986).

Boys' play may be more strongly gender-typed than girls' play. Play with same-gender figures might more likely occur in the presence of an opposite-gender peer. A double play set might increase the similarity of boys' and girls' play, at least in kindergarten. Compared with boys and girls who played alone, children who played in pairs might show tendencies toward masculine-role behavioral characteristics. Overall, girls seem to be less influenced by the presence of another child. Consequently, gender-typing varies significantly with the specific conditions of the play situation (Trautner, 1995). It would be important to see whether this gender-typing is present in other cultures, such as the North American one.

Among the elderly, a German study found that

> age, vision, intellectual functioning, out-of-home everyday functioning, and emotional well-being are largely independent of regional

and societal macro contexts. The study further finds that vision seems to mediate

> the effect of age on out-of-home activities of daily living and leisure activities while intellectual functioning may mediate the effect of vision on out-of-home activities. Effects on emotional well-being might be mediated by out-of-home leisure activities.

Hence, if these observations are valid, vision turns out to be a crucial variable on how leisure time can be used inside and outside the home (Heyl, Wahl, & Mollenkopf, 2005). This factor may cut across gender, SES, ethnic, and cultural differences.

Greece: Play has been claimed to relate with divergent thinking ability. Therefore, it might be important to see whether "fluency and flexibility in movement patterns" correlates with play (Trevlas et al., 2003). Production of such qualities may indicate divergent and critical thinking, as they may be "related to a variety of psychological elements (physical spontaneity, social spontaneity, and cognitive spontaneity, manifest joy, sense of humor)" that altogether could contribute to playfulness as "an internal personality characteristic," at least in Greek children. There may be "a significant correlation between total playfulness and motor fluency and flexibility," suggesting that "playfulness and motor creativity [may be] interconnected" (Trevlas et al., 2003). These results may need to be compared with those of Morrison, Bundy, & Fisher (1991), reported in Chapter 8 of this volume.

Italy: See the discussion of Germany for a comparative study of play in both cultures (Hold-Cavell, Attili, & Schleidt, 1986); see the discussion of the United Kingdom for a comparative study of war play in that culture and Italy (Constable, Genta, Zucchini, Smith, & Harker (1992). An anthropological review of children's play in a small town in central Italy included an examination of the social and caregiving routines of twenty infants, in conjunction with an ethnographic study of family life and child development. During five follow-ups from 1980–1981 to 1991, information was gathered about parental beliefs regarding child behavior and temperament, the role of schooling in its relationship to play, and strategies of care in the early childhood period. Educators in a second Italian community considered children's play as a major component of early childhood curriculum (New, 1994).

Gender appropriateness in five playground activities (play-fighting, play-chasing, real fighting, soccer, and skipping) in elementary-school-age children in England and Italy may be a function of some degree of gender stereotyping, except for playchasing. However, there may be a trend in both countries for the degree of gender stereotyping to lessen with age. It may occur at an earlier age in England than in Italy for traditionally male activities and may be more obvious for girls than boys. There may be a culture difference in the perception of skipping (Carvalho, Smith, Hunter, & Costabile, 1990).

Netherlands: Gender differences found repeatedly in the United States that show boys having greater attachment to performance versus relationship and avoidance goals in girls were not replicated with a sample of Dutch children, perhaps because of differences in the value systems of the two countries (Van Rossum, 1998). The physical redevelopment of a playground, according to such aspects as complexity, manipulability, and feasibility for different activities, may be more enjoyable for children than for adults (Van Andel, 1985).

Portugal: Extensive industrialization, crowding, and their stress-related outcomes have produced a remarkable increase in bullying, a school problem that needed to be evaluated through interviews with approximately 2,300 students. The results show that about 25 percent of these students had been subjected to bullying attacks. The majority of these attacks consisted of asking for money, calling names, threats of bodily harm, taking personal possessions by force, and actual physical violence. In addition to playgrounds, bullying occurred in practically all places not supervised by adults. Bullying and underachievement were found to be related. An intervention program patterned after those already implemented in the United Kingdom and Norway is proposed, but it will need the support of the whole educational system of Portugal (Pereira, 2004).

Russia: Play orientation, at least in Russia, may be more stable among proletarian and peasant than among children of the "intelligentsia" with a minimum of gender differences (Zeiliger & Levina, 1995).

Sweden: Viking Kubb is a Scandinavian game that dates to the tenth century and is available to all players from elementary school children to senior citizens, one on one and up to twelve players. It can be played almost anywhere, depending on the age and skill level of participants. It consists of one king and, for each side, five knights (kubbs) and six wooden sticks to knock adversary pieces over, which is part of the game. Illustrations of how the game is played, how pieces are placed, another Viking chessboard, and a burnball field are available in Juhlin (2004).

A comparison of twenty entire Swedish and American families according to the tempo of interactions on the Lausanne Triadic Play paradigm when infants were approximately 3 months old, yielded some interesting results. Coding systems developed separately for each country "described a distinct difference in the tempo of play between American and Swedish families. Overall, although there were many similarities between countries, American families were found to have a faster pace in triadic play than Swedish families." This difference can be attributed to the faster pace of the American over the Swedish culture (Hedenbro, Shapiro, & Gottman, 2006).

Retrospective reports from students between 20 and 62 years of age about their play memories from childhood to adulthood showed that ages 7 to 12 years had a special significance in the play memory of places in the physical environment (Sandberg, 2003).

An ethnographic study of preschool and preadolescent children's "production and participation in play and games in an Italian preschool and an afterschool program in a Swedish elementary school" showed some interesting results:

> Most traditional theoretical and empirical work on children's play and games has focused on the contributions of these activities for children's development of social and communicative skills. Other research has extended this developmental focus by examining play and games as valued activities in children's production, organization, and maintenance of their peer cultures. This [study] extends this work by examining play and games as part of a process of interpretive reproduction of children's lives. Children in the production of play and games simultaneously use (as well as refine and develop) a wide range of communicative skills, collectively participate in and extend their peer cultures, and appropriate features of, and develop an orientation to, the wider adult culture. (Evaldsson & Corsaro, 1998)

United Kingdom and Italy: Parents of children between 2 and 6 years of age in both countries acknowledged that boys would be significantly more likely to engage in war play—either social or solitary, most commonly weapon play, but also play with combat figures and acting out a combat role. Parental attitudes, television, and peers (including older siblings) appeared as common sources of influence. Parents expressed a range of views about how to respond to war play, varying from discouraging it (more common if the children did not engage in war play), to allowing it with limits, to allowing it unconditionally. There was more of a consensus that war toys should not be allowed in school and that playground supervisors and teachers should try to turn war play toward more constructive ends. These results tend to confirm a general dimension of restrictiveness–permissiveness with regard to war play activities, linked to attitudes about rough-and-tumble and pretend play in the Italian sample but not in the English sample (Constable et al., 1992).

At least in England, children might use the means available to them to construct gender in their playgrounds, and this construction might also be involved in reproduction of hegemonic cultural identities and relations of power. However, playgrounds and teachers have a great deal to do with how children will be open to SES, age, gender, and ethnic differences (Epstein, Kehily, Macan Ghaill, & Redman, 2001).

From undergraduates' observations of playgrounds in various primary schools, the following classification of playing resulted: jokes, traditional rhymes and games, football, media influences, and narrative fantasy games. Recent media influences have been absorbed into the culture and language of the playground. The most relevant of all the observations were gender differences. Girls often might tend to play games that involved verbal interaction in small, cohesive groups, whereas boys may tend to spend more time in rough-and-tumble games requiring physical activity (Grugeon, 2004).

Complexity of games tends to increase with age in both U.S. and English first-grade playgrounds. However, American children may play games more frequently, especially simple games, relative to English children. Facility of games may tend to forecast adjustment to school and social skills, but only in U.S. children (Pellegrini, Blatchford, Kato, & Baines, 2004).

Nothing specific about play in preschool settings in Northern Ireland has been learned, except about the importance and value of creating an audiovisual methodology that will yield valid and reliable conclusions (McCooney, 2004). Investigators who are contemplating the use of audiovisual recordings may profit by reading this article.

Middle East

Dubai: Stoecklin and White (2004) studied the play behavior of children from a heterogeneous multicultural culture in a Discovery Center in the town of Dubai. Here is what they concluded after years of study and follow-up:

1. Mothers are attending the center in greater numbers and learning to spend more time playing with their children.

2. Especially, Arab and Western fathers have become more involved with their children.

3. Parents have learned to give children the freedom to play with what and how they want, rather than controlling their play behavior.

4. Schools in the area are visiting this center in increasing numbers, leaning to use its available resources.

5. "Children from all ethnic backgrounds have been playing and having fun together."An important development for Arab parents and children has been exposure to the written medium in a culture where the major communication medium is oral.

6. Both parents and children have learned to value their own cultural values without devaluing the cultural heritage of other cultures.

7. Nannies from many other countries who work for local families have learned to use the center as a gathering place for comfort and support.

8. Local schools requested information on how to integrate play in their own educational curriculum (Stoecklin & White, 2004, p. 224).

Iran and Turkey: A play box containing thirty wooden pieces was developed and tested with forty-seven Iranian and fifty-three Turkish preschoolers. Consistency in play was found through repeated administrations. Differences in the use of space were noted between the two groups as well as SES differences in the Iranian sample. A surprising finding was absence of SES differences among the Turkish sample, possibly attributable to the nature and influence of their preschool program (Bower, Ilgaz-Carden, & Noori, 1982). Action in and of itself in toddlers and preschoolers helps to enhance narrative development with clear episodic structures as they move from one stage to another (Ilgaz & Aksu-Koc, 2005).

Israel: In an important contribution to the study of imaginative play, Ariel (2002) embedded it within the cultural parameters, family structure, standards of living, family values, and child-rearing values and practices (pp. 112–113) of Jewish, kibbutz and town, urban Arab, and Bedouin children. He distinguished among levels of make-believe play according to content, creativity, stylistic formats, nature of play groups, nature of leadership of play groups, and nature of play-relevant social control (p. 114). He concluded these comparisons thus:

> I tend toward constructivistic approaches, according to which make-believe play is an original, creative, cultural artifact, as opposed to functionalistic views according to which make-believe play is a way of practicing adult roles. The main dimension along which the make-believe play of children of different societies is compared is *modernity versus traditionality*. (p. 115)

Lebanon: Boys as a group seem more aggressive than girls and may exhibit more imitative aggression after viewing both a violent film and real-life violence. Girls may not be more violent after viewing film aggression but might be more affected by real-life violence. These results suggest that one effect of war on children is to increase their acts of antisocial aggression (Day & Ghandour, 1984).

North and Central America

Greenland: Story-knifing is a form of play where each storyteller illustrates a tale by drawing symbols in the mud with a flat knife. Observations of this form of play of a small group of young girls in one Yup'ik Eskimo village examine the process of story-knifing in the lives of these young girls, the utensils they use, the places they select for this game, and the types of stories they tell. Interviews with Yup'ik women regarding their childhood story-knifing experiences illustrate how this game is closely related to the whole cultural context, providing a forum for girls to learn about kinship patterns, gender roles, and community names and values. It is also a way in which children learn and practice cognitive skills necessary to survive in the communities in which they live (deMarrais, Nelson, & Baker, 1994).

Puerto Rico: Empirical research on Puerto Rican children's play and contemporary views of play by a group of mainland (migrant and non-migrant) parents gives reliable information about attitudes toward play activities of their primary-school-aged children and how play relates to issues that pertain to early childhood education. Within-group differences in perceptions of play highlight the existence of two differing contexts for playing in the home and in the school. Both contexts provide different opportunities for acculturations and assimilation in the United States (Soto & Negron, 1994).

United States: Play in this country represents the mosaic of various ethnic groups that differ in historical and cultural roots. For instance, Miami, Florida, is a microcosm of such ethnic differences among African Americans, Haitians, and Cubans. Comparisons of Haitian and African American mother–infant dyads' interactions during feeding and play were used as an example that illustrated cultural persistence despite attempts to acculturate these groups. A slow pattern of acculturation was observed by comparing second-generation Cuban mother–infant dyads with similar-SES native African American mother–infant dyads (Field, 1993).

"The emergence and use of concepts of race in preadolescents' collaborative peer cultures and interactions" was studied using an interactionist approach, where the observer was actually involved with the youth he was studying:

> [Kids] established and negotiated race category membership and then evaluated each other's actions accordingly, and informed how they used clique

dynamics in structuring peer relations in two racially varied recreational settings. Children in the predominantly white setting and the multiracial setting appropriated, used, and negotiated race somewhat similarly, particularly regarding the invisibility and nascent emergence of whiteness as a racial category and the assumption of a shared culture and connection among kids of color. They differed, though, in how they complicated and resisted race-based clique dynamics. Because of the presence of kids of color, the greater range of relational options available to youths in the multiracial setting introduced a wider range of power dynamics into clique structures and more instability and fluidity into conceptions of race, thus disrupting easy definitions of in-group and out-group membership and affecting the social negotiation of identity in the children's peer cultures. (Moore, 2002)

South America

Argentina: Comparisons of thirty-nine Argentine and forty-three U.S. children aged 20 months and their mothers "on exploratory, symbolic, and social play and interaction" produced "patterns of cultural similarity and difference." For instance, in both samples, "boys engaged in more exploratory play than girls," who in turn "engaged in more symbolic play than boys." In addition,

> Mothers of boys engaged in more exploratory play than mothers of girls, and mothers of girls engaged in more symbolic play than mothers of boys. Moreover, in both cultures, individual variation in children's exploratory and symbolic play was specifically associated with individual variation in mothers' exploratory and symbolic play, respectively. Between cultures, U.S. children and mothers engaged in more exploratory play, whereas Argentine children and their mothers engaged in more symbolic play. Moreover, Argentine mothers exceeded U.S. mothers in social play and verbal praise of their children. (Bornstein, Haynes, Pascual, Painter, & Galperin, 1999)

Overall, the study found that "Argentine and U.S. dyads utilized different modes of exploration, representation, and interaction—emphasizing other-directed acts of pretense versus functional and combinatorial exploration," with differences in allocentric (external) versus idiocentric (internal) emphases (Bornstein, Haynes, Pascual, Painter, & Galperin, 1999).

Brazil: Brazil is a superficially exuberant multicultural country composed of many ethnic minorities, such as native peoples, Africans, and immigrants from Portugal and many European countries. "Spontaneity and creativity have been the strongest elements of the Brazilian culture and they have permeated all of our play and cultural activities." (Flores-Martins, 2004, p. 64)

There are frequent religious celebrations and gastronomic festivals, where dancing, body painting, and loud percussion music are ever present. The favorable climate enables ample opportunities for children's playgrounds, including miles of open beaches. Unfortunately, these assets have become a mixed blessing. Open and free spaces have become increasingly subjected to violence and vandalism, rendering play dangerous except in protected school playgrounds or adult- and police-supervised public parks. The Brazilian Association for the Child's Right to Play has used the proclamation issued in 1977 by the International Play Association (2004) to involve political, public, and private organizations in supporting the importance of children having safe and sound environments in which to play (Brincandando). This movement has been also active in training play workers to qualify as formal supervisors and facilitators of children's play, not without difficulties (Flores-Martins, 2004).

Natives in the northern part of Brazil who still have hunting and gathering societies allow the opportunity to observe human nature as may have appeared centuries ago anywhere else in the world. These cultures have made it possible to classify play games according to a typology that in some ways amplifies and supplements those presented in Chapter 1 of this volume (Gosso, Otta, Morais, De Lima, Ribeiro, & Bussad, 2005).

1. Exercise with wide movements, such as running, jumping, sliding, and climbing

2. Exercise with movements based on objects, such as stilts or flicking objects into the air

3. Object play of fine movements to manipulate and move objects such as bows and arrows

4. Construction games in which materials are combined to create a new product, such as modeling sand or making baskets

5. Social contingency games as a response to invitations from others, such as peekaboo or tickling

6. Rough-and-tumble play involving vigorous and close physical contact, such as wrestling or pursuit-and-escape based on sheer playfulness

7. Fantasy play, giving real or imaginary objects' qualities to otherwise inert objects, such as using a stick as a canoe, simulating domestic scenes, or imitating roles of other people, including the shaman

8. Games with explicit rules such as reciprocally throwing a ball at a distance or using dice with turn taking

Colombia: A four-year long study of street children in Bogotá from 5 to 17 years of age suggested how play may provide a framework for understanding these children and the nature of play, by acquiring immediate survival skills and preparing for adulthood. These children are perceived negatively by society because they live out of adult control. However, the creativity and adult modeling that are viewed as destructive and limiting in their play is considered desirable in the play of adult-supervised children. Many of these street children did seem to exhibit characteristics of psychological health and resourcefulness (Tyler, Holliday, Tyler, & Echeverry, 1987).

DISCUSSION

Hopefully, these summaries about play in different cultures will help us value how lucky children in the United States are in being allowed to have time and support to enjoy playing as fun, because, as they will learn as they grow up, there will be serious constraints on their play time. These constraints will test motivation to play at various stages of the life cycle. However, the cultural dilemma of traditional games (Renson, 1998) is found in the many transitions that are occurring in those cultures, such as deforestation in Brazil. For instance, the Internet and TV have increased the globalization of culture and, with this process, perhaps the homogenization of play. The Olympic Games shown on TV, for instance, have also increased the awareness and influence of certain sports across cultures. If children in developing countries are given inexpensive computers to study and learn, inevitably they will be able to connect with other children across countries and cultures, increasing the process of homogenization in play. This transition can be seen by going back to isolated cultures not yet influenced by mass markets and media. For instance, a count of how 140 children (aged 3 to 10 years) in six different communities scored on measures of creative-constructive, fantasy, role, and rule-controlled games showed significant differences among children from different countries, with children from Kenya and India scoring lowest overall, those from the Philippines and Mexico scoring intermediate, and those from Japan and the United States scoring highest (Edwards, 2000). Consequently, cultural norms and opportunities—or whether adults encouraged work or play—determine whether children have the "freedom for exploration and motivation to practice adult roles through play" if the environment provides "easy access to models and materials for creative and constructive play" (Edwards, 2000). This conclusion will be discussed further in Chapter 6 and tested in Appendix B.

CONCLUSION

There is no question, therefore, that culture has almost everything to do with play, as shown by so many differences among cultures. Nonetheless, there are similarities in the necessity and function of play. Whether play continues beyond childhood, for instance, is an important issue. How much play is affected by age, gender, and SES is an issue that will be covered throughout this volume. However, the connection between culture and play in children is mediated by parents, a topic covered in the next chapter.

5

WHAT PARENTS AND ADULTS HAVE TO DO WITH PLAY AND GENDER

Parents and other adults have everything, or almost everything, to do with play in children (assuming, of course, that the adults are able to be truly caring and competent adults in the full meaning of the term). The developmental level of parents, as we shall see, has a great deal to do with how they are effective in transmitting their culture to their children through play. As we have already learned from the previous chapter of this volume, children's play depends on the culture transmitted to them, and parents and other adults in children's lives are the intermediaries and transmitters of that culture. What parents have acquired and know about play will be transferred to the child almost automatically, including views about play in general, as well as preferences and biases in particular. They can be the facilitators and encouragers as well as the inhibitors of play (Lieberman, 1977, pp. 99–100).

Parents and other adults help to provide children with a structure to encourage play, and that structure has the function of a construction scaffold, providing support until the child's ability to self-support in the activity is built up. For example, as I described in Chapter 1, my mother made connections to make sure I became involved in playing Monopoly with other children. Mothers seem more involved in their preschoolers' play than fathers (Vandermaas-Peeler et al., 2002). Whether parents' involvement in their children' play changes as a function of gender and age of the child is still open to question. For instance, fathers may become more involved with their sons than with their daughters when the children reach high school and perhaps take an interest in team sports.

Both psychobiological and cultural perspectives on parent–child play include a variety of disciplines including anthropology, developmental psychology, education, ethnology, and medicine. Parent–child play provides an interesting problem for evolutionary analysis, because the style and amount of parent–child play varies enormously among species, among cultures, and within cultures. Parent–child play is found in very few species besides humans, precluding easy or specious generalizations about parent–child play (Power, 1993).

There are certain consistent relationships between home environment factors and cognitive development during the first five years of life (Gottfried, 1985, p. 184). Positive factors include the following:

1. Availability and variety of stimulus materials (i.e., toys), availability being primarily relevant to the first nine months of life, whereas variety may become more critical as the child gets older (Bradley, 1985)

2. Responsivity of the proximal environment, including physical, emotional, economic, and intellectual resources

3. Regularity of scheduling, which depends on age and ability level of caretakers

Negative factors include the following:

1. Ambient background noise, such as caretakers arguing or fighting, which may be particularly relevant to male and at-risk infants, adding unneeded stress on infants

2. Overcrowding, which may restrict type and frequency of positive nurturance and support

3. Physical restraints on exploration, preventing the child from moving around the immediate physical environment (Wachs, 1985)

4. Domestic violence

As an illustration of the effects of domestic violence, thirty preschool girls attending Head Start programs without any history of domestic violence were evaluated from their parents' demographic information and completion of the Caregiver-Teacher Behavioral Report Form. The children participated in 25-minute videotaped free-play sessions. The girls who might have been exposed to intercaregiver violence demonstrated more externalizing problems and aggressive play themes than girls without indications of parental violence (Berger, 2001). Girls, however, may tend to represent their parents "more positively, regardless of family circumstances. Boys, especially those who [do] not visit regularly with their fathers," may have "negative representations of their mothers." Apparently,

"severity of violence [does] not predict negative parental representations" (Stover et al., 2006).

Aggressive and socially unskilled playground behaviors may find their
origins in early family relationships (Pettit & Harrist, 1993). Indeed,

> there is a growing number of preschoolers presenting at clinics with high
> levels of aggression.These children are at risk for developing conduct disor-
> ders, especially when the symptoms are severe.Treatment for older children
> with aggressive symptoms has often relied on teaching their parents behav-
> ior management techniques but has ignored affective and relationship
> issues. (Landy & Menna, 2001)

These issues include

> the mother's difficulty in tolerating and modulating the child's negative
> affect, reluctance to enter the play metaphor, and failure to gradually move
> aggressive play to more prosocial themes. (Landy & Menna, 2001)

The rest of this chapter will be devoted to a more specific review of
how parents, together or separately, relate to their children's play and to
the development of gender differences in play.

INFLUENCE OF PARENTS AND OTHER ADULTS ON CHILDREN'S PLAY

Children's Play with the Entire Family

When children play with another sibling, mother, or father, apparently
siblings engage in more prosocial and agonistic interactions when alone
with each other than with the other parent, while there may not be any
differences between sibling interactions with mother and with father.
Apparently, paternal negative behavior may be associated with sibling
agonistic behavior when children are left alone. However, mother–child
and sibling interactions may not be significantly associated. Nonetheless,
reciprocity in positive and negative behaviors directed by children to
parents and vice versa might be evident, perhaps demonstrating syn-
chrony in the pattern of exchange. These possibilities underscore the
necessity of studying both parents to understand more fully the dynamics of play involving both parents (Dubrow & Howe, 1999).

Parents as Playmates

Parents and caretakers are the primary models of play and playfulness
available to the child (Beckwith, 1985) to the point that co-parenting
from infancy, as assessed by family play, tends to predict marital stability
(Schoppe-Sullinvan, Mangeldorf, Frosch, & McHale, 2004). However, to

assume that all parents are equipped and motivated to behave and become playmates to their children is incorrect (Duarte, 2004; Singer, 1995). That assumption applies to teachers as well. Both parties need to be helped in learning how to play with their children. Whatever they might have learned about play as children is no longer sufficient or appropriate because of dramatic changes that have occurred in the last generation. For instance, many children have learned how to play with computers. These are skills that were unknown to many parents (and especially grandparents!). One way to appraise such a knowledge is through informal questioning, which should help parents and teachers become aware of their knowledge and skills (Duarte, 2004, p. 228), including a theory-derived structured interview about play (Appendix C).

With infants, mothers may play more conventional limb movement games and more distal, visual, attention-maintaining games, while fathers may play more proximal, arousing, idiosyncratic limb movement games. Interactive games with parents, even during the first 6 months of infancy, seem to provide differential experiences for the infant. These games may have developmental significance in selectively facilitating the acquisition of social and cognitive skills (Yogman, 1981).

Fathers seem to control and direct their children more often than do mothers, while mothers are more quiet than fathers during play with their children. Children apparently control, direct, and actively follow their fathers more than their mothers, engaging in more lead-taking with their fathers than with their mothers. Boys seem to display more physical warmth to mothers than do girls, while boys may tend to praise their fathers more than do girls (Bright & Stockdale, 1984).

Children's behavioral orientations on the playground and peer status may be linked to maternal and parental disciplinary strategies. The development of peer competence may be related to global parenting styles as well. Apparently, children acquire social knowledge and behavior from parental inductive and power-assertive disciplinary strategies (Hart, De Wolf, & Burts, 1993). Differential patterns of maternal and paternal behavior may be associated with the social competence of boys and girls. Paternal physical play and engagement and maternal verbal behavior may be positively related to children's peer relations, especially in boys. Paternal directiveness may be negatively related to popularity for boys and girls, while maternal directiveness could be linked positively with popularity for girls. Opportunities for learning to regulate affect could possibly contribute to those relationships, illustrating linkages between family and peer social systems (MacDonald & Parke, 1984).

Conclusions about parent–child physical play and salience of father–infant rough play may be limited to some cultures rather than being a universal pattern. For instance, Indian parents are not vigorous play partners with infants. In India, mothers may be more likely to engage in object-mediated play with their children than are fathers (Roopnarine, Ahmeduzzaman, Hossain, & Riegraf, 1992). The influence of culture and SES may affect the physical activity of low-income preschoolers, who spent 58 percent of free-play time in sedentary activities and seemed vigorously active only for 11 percent of the time. Family risk for cardiovascular disease, parent physical activity, and father body mass index may account for significant amounts of variance in the child's play activity. Therefore, it is possible that the effects of parental role modeling on child physical activity levels may extend to free-play settings beyond the confines of the immediate home environment (Sallis, Patterson, McKenzie, & Nader, 1988).

Keren and colleagues found that co-parenting style "marked by cooperation and autonomy [could predict] symbolic play during a triadic family session." Child intelligence could also predict the level of "symbolic play beyond the parent's style during triadic but not dyadic interactions." These results may indicate the importance of "increasing symbolic play in young children" through early interventions (Keren, Feldman, Namdari-Weinbaum, Spitzer, & Tyano, 2005).

Mother–child attachment could be related to play engagement and (in boys) peer popularity. Father–child attachment could be related to play quality and friendly–cooperative behavior. Fathers of more securely attached children may issue more directives, and their children may make more suggestions and positive responses. Attachment and play seem to correlate with peer behavior, yet both factors appear to be relatively independent of each other (Kerns & Barth, 1995).

More competent parents, defined by self-report questionnaires to determine degrees of self-efficacy, optimistic trust, and an active, competent coping style, seem to treat their children as being more capable and resourceful, showing generally warm and positive feelings, and being more helpful with problem-solving. Consequently, these and other results summarized above confirm that parental competence relates to parental behavior and to their styles of interaction, which are part of the socialization context of their children (Mondell & Tyler, 1981).

The Mother's Influence on the Child's Play

The mother's mood, competence, and attitude are crucial influences on the child's play. Will her positive mood and attitude become assets to the child's eventual affective, cognitive, and social development, or will the negative aspects of a sad mood, incompetence, and negative attitude hinder the child's play and, eventually, overall development? How the mother will interact with the child may determine the positive or negative outcome of that child's development and ability to play. Levenstein (1985) identified at least ten items in the mother's interactive behavior that need consideration because they are linked significantly to the child's responsible, cognitive, and task orientation and emotional stability:

1. Giving label information on what kind of toy is present
2. Giving information about the color of the toy
3. Verbalizing actions but commenting on what is going on between the child, the toy, and her presence and actions
4. Giving number and shape information
5. Questioning child, soliciting information
6. Praising the child's involvement in playing with the toy
7. Stimulating divergent usages of the toy
8. Smiling and making positive gestures toward the child
9. Replying to child's implicit or explicit questions
10. Not reacting to the child

In addition to these ten items, Caldwell (1985) describes four additional positive, possibly crucially influential actions that parents in general can take:

1. Teaching common, popular games as well as games that are not as popular and that are off the beaten path, to help the child become familiar with different possibilities that might enhance creativity
2. Recognizing that not all toys are only for play and fun and that some toys and games need manipulation and, in some cases, problem-solving abilities
3. Anticipating that some toys and games eventually will play out and be outdated and eventually discarded from the child's interest
4. Encouraging children to learn to play with other children as well as with other adults, even above and beyond their caretakers

Caldwell and Bradley (Gottfried, 1985, p. 182) developed a forty-five-item questionnaire that measured six dimensions of home environment directly related to the proximal context of play:

1. Emotional and verbal responsivity of mother
2. Avoidance of restriction and punishment
3. Organization of the physical and temporal environment
4. Provision of appropriate play materials
5. Maternal involvement with the child
6. Opportunities for variety in daily stimulation

These scales administered to mothers in four different studies (Gottfried, 1985, p. 184) were highly correlated to a standard measure of intelligence

(Stanford-Binet) two years after administration. On the basis of these results, Gottfried concluded that:

> First, the most potent and pervasive early home environment variables that correlated with cognitive development during infancy and the preschool years are Play Materials and Maternal (parental) involvement. Second, with advancement in age, the relationship between Play Materials, Maternal Involvement, and cognitive development become increasingly strong. (p. 185)

For example, mothers' and children's imaginative play might be positively and significantly correlated, but only within each session of play with preschool boys and girls, not across sessions of play. Furthermore, contrary to predictions from the extant literature, children's divergent thinking ability and spontaneous fantasy play at nursery school might not be significantly related to either mothers' or children's imaginative behavior (Johnson, 1978).

Infants' play might become more "sophisticated" when they are playing with their mothers than when playing with a peer or alone. For 2-year-olds, peers may exercise an inhibitory effect on both elicitation and expansion of conventional and symbolic play. However, both processes may be reserved for more competent members of a culture (Turkheimer, Bakeman, & Adamson, 1989).

Mothers' pretend behaviors may not change a great deal as infants age, but there may be some scenario differences, where consistency of "particular maternal pretend behaviors [might be] associated with children engaging in pretend behaviors and smiling" (Lillard et al., 2007). In the rest of this chapter, we shall see whether these conclusions are valid and reliable.

On the negative side of mothers' influences, neglecting mothers seem less developmentally appropriate than non-neglecting mothers in play interactions with their children and showed greater difficulty interacting with them. These results, if valid and reliable, suggest that early childhood interventions should include sensitizing potentially neglectful mothers to their children's development (Fagan & Dore, 1993).

Mothers' understanding of emotions within themselves and in their children is crucial to their everyday interactions with their children, including play (Haight & Sachs, 1995). In this regard, there might be significant relationships "between parenting styles and children's negative affect in the prediction of play" behaviors (Lagace-Segui & d'Entremont, 2006). Emotion-coaching parenting, for instance, might be "negatively related to rough-and-tumble play for children low in negative affect but not for children high in negative affect" (Lagace-Segui & d'Entremont, 2006). Maternal stress, even on a prenatal basis, seems to produce less functional and more stereotyped toy play, with less diversity in their children, compared to children with low-prenatal-stress mothers (Laplante, Zelazo, Brunet, & King, 2007). Disrupted or unresolved maternal attachment may be responsible for producing disorganized attachment in infants, as shown by their behavior problems and play interactions (Madigan, Moran, Schuengel, Pederson, & Otten, 2007).

One study found that

> some forms of maternal play [could] be interpreted positively, leading to healthy development or [could] have negative effects leading to emotional and cognitive vulnerability in children and adolescents. (Reissland, Shepherd, & Herrera, 2005)

For instance, maternal mood states may be related to mothers' play interactions with their children, more specifically maternal well-being and their touching "as well as gaze-direction and emotional expressions by their infants." Nondepressed mothers may tend to nestle a toy up to their babies significantly more than "mothers reporting a depressed mood":

> Infants of mothers with depressed moods looked significantly less frequently at their mothers and showed significantly more negative expressions than infants of non-depressed mothers. These differences in maternal play interactions [may] indicate that mothers with depressed mood play with their babies in such a way as to elicit negative emotional reactions as well as gaze avoidance from their baby. (Reissland, Shepherd, & Herrera, 2005)

Contrasting cultural perspectives, of course, may be a relevant factor in considering mother–child play interactions. The anthropological rather than psychological perspective, for instance, notes that in some cultures there is often an absence of mother–child play, and it seeks to provide possible explanations for such an absence. The psychological perspective sometimes limits itself to the upper strata of modern society, whereas anthropology focuses on all levels of a culture. These contrasting perspectives suggest that a "culture-specific child-rearing strategy may be quite incongruent with native belief and practice" (Lancy, 2007).

Mothers' Scaffolding of a Child's Play

Even indirectly, scaffolding, defined earlier in this chapter, is an important aspect of how mothers arrange situations to ensure play situations for their children. For instance, my mother arranged with one of her women friends to have me go to her house to play Monopoly with that woman's son and his friends. I would have not learned Monopoly otherwise. She also arranged for an older son of another friend to take me under his wings and introduce me to Greco-Roman wrestling, in part to offset the vacuum produced by my father's absence during World War II. That vacuum was also offset by our pastor, Tullio Vinay, who "forced" me to act in various church-related plays. These skills were useful years later in Greenville, North Carolina, in playing the Greek landlord in *My Sister Eileen* and the Italian smuggler in Agatha Christie's *Three Blind Mice*.

Scaffolding was also studied in fourteen South African Bantu mothers' object play with their infants aged 26 to 50 months. The task consisted of how mothers adjusted their teaching strategies as infants played with a standard play object over a six-month period. As a result of these strategies changing over time, "infants became more competent at performing the required actions with the object over time." These findings are comparable to those of mother–child play in Western cultures (Richter, Grieve, & Austin, 1988).

Fathers' Influence and Involvement in Their Child's Play

Mothers' play with their children, as just discussed, has been studied much more frequently than fathers' influence and involvement in the same area. Fathers' sensitivity and challenging in play interactions with their children can be predicted from their care-giving quality, at least between 1 and 4 years of age. Sensitivity, challenging, and care-giving skills may all be closely linked to fathers' own internal working models of attachment. When qualities of attachment are evaluated in both parents, they may be related to their children's attachment security at age 6.

> Fathers' play sensitivity and infant-mother quality of attachment may predict children's internal working model of attachment at age 10, but not vice versa. Dimensions of adolescents' attachment representations could be predicted by fathers' play sensitivity alone. Consequently, fathers' play sensitivity may be a better predictor of the child's long-term attachment than the early infant–father security of attachment. (Grossman et al., 2002)

Admirable is the attempt to create supervised play areas in prison visiting rooms to provide a framework where children could play in a safe and structured fashion with materials appropriate to their developmental needs. In this way, both parents, but especially fathers, could function in a relatively "normal" manner, perhaps promoting the mental health of the whole family (Hughes, 1982).

Other Adults' Influence on Children's Play

Adults other than parents, including teachers and child-care workers, can also influence a child's play. Guided by an adult, play can contribute to emerging literacy by motivating a child to learn the skills that are prerequisites for success in kindergarten and during the elementary school years (Singer, Singer, & Schweder, 2004). When the adult–child dyad is observed while focusing on physical construction with Lego blocks, this interaction is "interspersed with conversations and other activities, introduced by adults and also by the children" (Ireson & Blay, 1999). Even minimal praise can have immediate positive outcomes (Goetz, 1981), even though long-term effects still need to be established. Children tend to use "a variety of devices to influence the direction and focus of the activity"; these possibilities indicate how "children not only play an active role in their own learning [but] they are also active partners in constructing the activity itself" (Ireson & Blay, 1999).

A simple training procedure consisting of adult-delivered prompts and social reinforcement may increase imitation by children with mental retardation (MR) of the free-play behavior of their classmates without MR. Maintenance of peer-imitation effects may increase reciprocal social interaction between children with and children without MR, in either training or nontraining conditions (Peck, Apolloni, Cooke, & Raver, 1978). Differential advantages of play-tutored children may be few and perhaps limited to sociodramatic play experience (Smith & Syddall, 1978).

Planned participation by toddler boys in sociodramatic play opportunities and play-tutoring may increase their intellectual level somewhat by building language competence (Levy, Schaefer, & Phelps, 1986). That play and learning are inseparable from and intertwined with joy, creativity, creations of meaning, and children's possibilities to control and form goals shows how important is the role of adults, and especially teachers, in providing a context where the child is free to explore and to learn (Johansson & Samuelson, 2006). High levels of adult direction may increase the amount of time children spend with toys and may have a stronger effect on social interaction than on manipulation of objects. Boys may be more exploratory than girls, who instead may engage in more social interaction (Vlietstra, 1978), a possible gender difference to be discussed at greater length toward the end of this chapter.

Links between imaginative play and communication underline the importance of play as a tool for developing oral language in preschoolers. Imaginative play supposedly expedites growth, development, and continued expansion of communication abilities. Using imaginative play as a tool for oral language growth requires a certain amount of the child's internal control, free of reality constraints, that increases internal motivation to become involved in and to perform make-believe activities. In this process, the caretaker plays a major role in the provision of cues to the child. Cues determine the degree of control, reality, and motivation. Some of the more important cues are based on the arrangement of the environment, use of space, and selection of play materials. In the early preschool years, the caregiver can build on the child's immediate need to act out sensory impressions in dramatic play. The caregiver could provide a model of the playful person by the use of playful gestures. Such behaviors may startle youngsters out of vagueness into purposeful activity, stretch their cognitive capacities, and broaden their verbal skills. The caretaker can also provide a model of playfulness by using verbal expressions regarding characters or themes in the play scenario, providing also pretend cues for sociodramatic play (Yawkey & Hrncir, 1983).

GENDER DIFFERENCES ACROSS THE LIFE CYCLE

The literature is pretty clear: boys are different from girls, but how? Here is what Zahn-Waxler, Shirtcliff, and Marceau (2008) concluded:

> Boys' play themes emphasize action, attention to objects and construction, and personal achievement and power. Girls' play is less hierarchical and more reciprocal, nurturing and affiliative in nature. It often involves relationship and family themes. . . . It is no coincidence that so much of the play during childhood appears preparatory for differential sex roles and activities, i.e., exploration, dominance, and competition for boys versus caregiving, cooperation, and affiliation for girls. These robust sex differences in play are present throughout childhood. (pp. 280, 290)

Gender differences across the life cycle may be due to influences from the children themselves as they bring into the playground whatever they have learned from their parents or caretakers, just as much as bringing home what they might have learned from the playground. In the years between preschool and puberty, the free play of children occurs largely in gender-segregated groups. Some differences in the socialization setting provided by all-boy and all-girl playgroups may be due to a variety of reasons; for instance, approaching playmates of the same gender may be less anxiety- or insecurity-provoking than avoiding playmates of the opposite gender. Gender-differentiated play styles and modes may also be due to peer influence. Three classes of possible explanatory processes may be occurring in such segregation: biological factors, socialization pressures from adults, and gender cognitions. "Masculinity" and "femininity" as dimensions of individual differences may not be linked to preference for same-gender playmates, but these two aspects of gender-typing may require different explanations, as discussed in the rest of this section (Maccoby, 1989).

Gender segregation may occur for reasons other than a simple socialization explanation; rather, differences in interactional style may cause children to prefer playmates of the same gender, leading to segregated play. Boys, for instance, have often been found to display rough-and-tumble and verbally dominant behaviors during social interactions, whereas girls are more likely to engage in more socially skilled activities. According to the play style compatibility hypothesis, girls may find boys' play to be aversive and thus segregate according to gender during play. Cognitive factors, such as awareness of gender categories, could also play a role in such differences. Comparing rough-and-tumble versus friendly play, younger girls may prefer rough-and-tumble in girls but friendly play in boys. Older children may display same-gender bias, with friendly play perhaps being more liked than rough-and-tumble and dominant play, suggesting socialization effects in this age group (Tietz, 1998).

In addition, the three factors mentioned above may be used subsequently to explain gender-related differences in the following areas:

(1) gender self-concepts, stereotypes, and attitudes; (2) gender-typed play; (3) sports; (4) social interaction and social norms; (5) academic motivation and achievement; and (6) household labor. (Leaper & Friedman, 2007)

The socialization of gender-related variations in these areas both reflects and perpetuates gender divisions and inequalities in the larger society (Leaper & Friedman, 2007). Activity level and task performance may produce different patterns of responses for boys and girls (Fagot, 1984).

When gender segregation and cross-gender play are viewed from a comparative perspective, some level of gender segregation seems to be a universal feature of children's play. Taking an interpretive view, on the other hand, children in some peer cultures emphasize gender differences and ritualize cross-gender interactions, while in other cultures children seldom enforce gender boundaries. Gender identity varies in salience and practice among Italian children, lower-class African American children, and upper-middle-class white American children. Thus, studying gender segregation as something that is constructed and negotiated in children's peer cultures, rather than [as] a universal phenomenon that is strictly based on biological or cognitive factors, may provide a clearer picture of these differences. (Aydt, 2003)

Parental Influences on Gender Differences and Gender-Typing

Gender differences in play behavior may be related to parental interactive style. For instance, in preschoolers, boys' play contains more aggressive themes, while girls' play contains more nurturing themes. Mothers may display more caring themes during play with both sons and daughters, while fathers may display more repair and construction themes.

Mothers and fathers' facilitative-creative interaction style may predict the level of the child's symbolic play. One study found that

> Boys may be more likely to play physically than girls, whereas the latter could be more likely to engage in pretense play than boys. Both boys and girls may tend to engage in pretense play in the presence of mothers than in the presence of fathers. Moreover, parents of girls could be more likely to become involved in pretense play than parents of boys. Parents of girls could be more likely to comply with their children's play directives than were fathers. These trends suggest that parents may contribute to children's gender specific styles of play, influencing their play interests by modeling particular play behaviors and/or providing differential patterns of reinforcement for boys and girls. (Lindsay, Mize, & Pettit, 1997)

These gender-specific trends were replicated during pretend play sessions; parents and daughters, particularly mothers and daughters, engaged in more pretend play than did parents and sons. Fathers and sons tend to engage in more physical play than did fathers and daughters. These trends suggest that context may play an important role in gender-differentiated patterns of parent–child play behavior. As for children's peer play behavior, the study found that

> consistent with previous evidence, girls may be more likely than boys to engage peers in pretend play, whereas boys might be more likely than girls to play physically with peers. Children whose parents engage in more pretense play could engage in more pretend play with a peer, whereas children whose parents engage in more physical play might engage in more physical play with a peer. These trends suggest that parents may contribute to children's gender-typed play behaviors with peers. (Lindsey, 2001)

Gender Differences in Infants

There is a question on whether to believe adults' reports of gender-stereotyped behavior in their interactions with infants (Zucker & Corter, 1980). There is no sufficient research to settle such a question at this time.

Gender Differences in Preschoolers

Many children may have already learned to avoid opposite-gender activities by the time they enter nursery school, while gender-role learning during the preschool period appears to involve increasing attention to same-gender activities (Connor & Serbin, 1977). When toys are separated according to their gendered characteristics, feminine toy preference may be positively related to interactions with girls, whereas masculine toy choice might be positively associated with interactions with boys. For older girls, feminine toy choice might be positively related to interactions with girls. However, large girls may tend to play with masculine toys (Eisenberg-Berg, Boothby, & Matson, 1979). In the search for "gender-neutral" toys, a farm set comprising a tractor, trailer, farm animals, fences, and a wrench might be suitable for children's imaginative play including "junk" toys (Stagnitti, Rodger, & Clarke, 1997). Whether these toys have potential for research and clinical work remains to be seen.

Gender differences are a function of culture and how parents or caretakers promote and promulgate that function to the child since infancy. As indicated in the previous chapter, SES and age are important factors to consider in addition to gender (Doyle, Ceschin, Tessier, & Doehring, 1991). Apparently, preschoolers may tend to select playmates not only according to gender but also according to race (Fishbein & Imai, 1993) and peer group (Fetter, 1997).

Race may be a factor in multiethnic cultures but not in homogeneous ones. Since these areas have been already covered or will be covered in the rest of this volume, this section will be devoted to gender differences as produced by biological and cultural influences. However, it should be noted that many gender differences that have existed in the past may tend to diminish as women want and receive greater equality with men (Carvalho, Smith, Hunter, & Costabile, 1990). This equality has been seen in the growth of women's teams in basketball, soccer, softball, and many other sports. Another factor in the equalization of gender differences has been the availability of Internet games (see Appendix A).

Preschoolers tend to rate toys according to their gender appropriateness and expected cultural directions, but with lower agreement than adults: younger children may assign fewer toys exclusively to the opposite gender than older children. Girls may tend to play longer with gender-neutral and equally long with feminine and masculine toys. Boys may tend to play longer with masculine and equally long with feminine and neutral toys. With increasing age, both genders may tend to play longer with feminine toys, with no age differences for masculine and neutral toys. Children may be highly concordant in their verbal gender-typing and play. For instance, younger children may play with a smaller proportion of self-defined gender-inappropriate toys, but there may not be any age differences in the proportion of playtime spent with these toys. Even though parents may expect their children to play with culturally defined gender-appropriate toys, generally their expectations may turn out to be inaccurate (Schau, Kahn, Diepold, & Cherry, 1980).

Toy preferences, at least in early childhood, may follow rigidly stereotyped gender differences even when children are told about certain toys being appropriate for both genders (Trasher, Nurss, & Brogan, 1980).

More specifically, girls may engage in more constructive play while boys may be more interested in functional play, with solitary play representing a less mature form of play (Johnson, Ershler, & Bell, 1980). If play with a particular toy changes how children interact and thus their social pretend play, then toys might indirectly influence the development of social competence. Same-gender pairs might engage in more social pretend play than mixed-gender pairs. Furthermore, same-gender pairs who play with "gender-appropriate toys" might engage in more social pretend play than same-gender pairs who play with "gender-inappropriate" toys (Grinder, 1995). However, age might be a factor to include in these possibilities.

Level of gender constancy might be related to playmate choice in social interaction. Girls who may have acquired an understanding that gender might be temporally but not situationally stable seem to engage in more same-gender social interactions than girls who understood gender as being invariant across situations. Preschoolers at all levels of gender constancy might become more gender-typed in their toy and activity preferences when they play alone and when they play in parallel or interact with same-gender peers but not when they play in parallel in mixed-gender groups. Boys but not girls might become more gender-typed in activity preferences in mixed-gender social interactions. At least for girls, gender concepts may include an organizing role in gender-role development by motivating children to seek social contexts in which to acquire and practice gender-appropriate behaviors (Smetana & Letourmeau, 1984).

There may be a moderate negative relation between opposite-gender peer interaction and preference for same-gender toy play. Gender of playmate prior to contact with a toy could be unrelated to the gender-typing of subsequent toy use. Especially for boys, there may be a match between peer interaction during play and the gender-typing of ongoing toy play. Apparently, there is more pressure for boys than for girls to avoid gender-inappropriate play activities (Eisenberg, Tryon, & Cameron, 1984). The issue here is to discover where this pressure comes from among biology, culture, parents, teachers, and peers. The answer may lay in the possibility that play with "boys' toys" may contribute to the development of spatial abilities, while "girls' toys" may contribute to the development of verbal abilities with the consequent possibility that girls may develop a relative deficit in visual-spatial performance while boys develop a relative deficit in verbal performance (Serbin & Conner, 1979). This hypothesis needs further empirical verification.

Of course, educational programs in classrooms may influence play development, and such programs may affect boys and girls differentially

(Johnson & Ershler, 1981). For instance, children's life work of constructing and maintaining gendered social orders in their lived everyday worlds
may be due, in some part, to girls' turning the boys' masculine practices
of ritualizing threats into a performance. By so doing, apparently, some
girls might be aware of the masculine discourse, but they do not actually
own it in the ways that boys do. In this way, gender may not be established as a social identity but as a dynamic practice that is ongoing, built
by relational encounters and shaped by the collective performances of its
participants (Danby, 1998).

Play constructions using blocks by girls might be characterized by
more "enclosure-ness" than those built by boys, who in turn might construct with greater "tower-ness" than girls. Boys might also use a greater
variety of toy constructions than girls (Goodfader, 1982). These possible
differences might support the research by Erik Erikson (1972) as well as
psychoanalytic and social learning theories discussed in Chapter 3 of this
volume. However, one could also attribute these differences in terms of
dominance versus social inclusiveness, if at all.

Story enactments of violence in post-divorce children may predict

> negative social behavior in child care for both boys and girls. Other, nonvi-
> olent story enactments might be strongly associated with gender, suggesting
> that gender socialization may play a significant role in children's play repre-
> sentations of violence and caring. (Page & Bretherton, 2003)

In addition to these seemingly external factors—parents' and teacher's
influences, ethnicity, age, and gender—there may also be individual differences due to temperamental characteristics such as arousability (how
quickly or how slowly a child may react to external stimuli) as discussed
in Chapters 7 and 19 of this volume. High arousability and same-gender
peer play may interact to predict behavior problems. For boys high in
arousability, play with same-gender peers may increase the chance of
problem behaviors. In contrast, "arousable girls who played with other
girls [might be] relatively unlikely to show problem behaviors" (Fabes,
Shepard, Guthrie, & Martin, 1997). The variability of gender-typed behaviors
within individuals or within genders might be more present in girls than
in boys (Green, Bigler, & Catherwood, 2004).

Young children "in kindergarten, first grade, and second grade [may
perceive] classroom activities in terms of what [could be] considered to
be work and what they considered to be play" (Wing, 1995). Distinguishing factors between work and play include

> the obligatory nature of activities, the cognitive and physical effort required,
> involvement and evaluation of the teacher, and the fun that children experi-
> enced while engaged in a given activity. (Wing, 1995)

Some activities may be viewed as falling "in between" pure work and pure play, suggesting the possibility of a work–play curriculum that would incorporate the children's characterizations (Wing, 1995).

Gender Differences in Elementary School

A pronounced aspect of elementary school is the division of children's play groups by gender (Moore, 1986; Pellegrini & Davis, 1993). This preference for same-gender peers, or gender segregation, begins during the late-toddler and early preschool periods and increases with age. Its prominence across cultures suggests that it is an important aspect of the child's social development, yet no one seems to understand fully why this phenomenon occurs, as noted at the beginning of this section. At least in elementary school, when gender is held constant, girls seem to prefer a nonwrestling peer while boys may prefer a wrestling peer, at least in pictures of this sport. In fact, gender may be a stronger predictor of children's peer preferences than play styles (Percer, 2002).

Predictably, according to still acceptable gender stereotypes, at least in second grade, boys seem to engage in

> more aggressive rough-and-tumble play as well as more functional, solitary-dramatic, and exploratory play, tending to become more involved in group play, whereas girls seem to produce more parallel and constructive play as well as more peer conversations. By the fourth grade, these differences may become maximized, so that boys may produce more games with rules while girls may exhibit more parallel-constructive activity. (Moller, Hymel, & Rubin, 1992)

In spite of these conclusions, perhaps derived from fairly SES-homogeneous schools, children in racially heterogeneous schools may construct and experience gender according to groups and activities in working-class communities rather than other influences. Fourth- and fifth-graders, mostly white with a sizable minority of Latino, Chicano, or African American children, tend to segregate and isolate themselves according to ethnicity. As a consequence of such ethnic differences, the organization and meaning of gender in play is influenced by age, ethnicity, race, gender, and social class. These factors, however, may shift as a function of the social context. Consequently, gender identity may not develop just as a function of socialization and difference, but as a social process involving groups of children. The group one joins may influence one's identity more than what parents or teachers may have represented (Thorpe, 1993).

Girls' dominance in jumping rope seems to change over time. In mixed groups, where boys might be learning how to jump, girls frequently might set the agenda on how the game is to be played. However, as boys gain greater proficiency in the game, they seem to become equal partners in calling plays and making decisions. Rather than evidence of differences in directive forms related to gender, this phenomenon seems to be a case in which the ability to use actions that tell others what to do in very direct fashion in cross-gender interactions is changing over time as children become more relatively skilled in the activity (Goodwin, 2001).

Finally, as one study found,

> Racial positioning and gender of African American girls [may hold] different meanings according to the context, that is, whether the setting is rural vs. urban, inner city versus suburbs, large versus small city, etc. The impact of race and gender as intersecting forces on girls' peer interactions [must be] considered. (Scott, 2002)

Gender Differences in Middle School

The observations about ethnic differences in elementary schools in the United States seem to be validated by mixed-race schools in the United Kingdom (Boulton & Smith, 1992). At both 8 and 11 years of age, most common categories of behavior engaged in seem to consist of "sociable activities and rule games":

> Older children seem to spend significantly more time in rule games and significantly less time alone than younger children. Girls seem to spend significantly more time in sociable activities and significantly less time alone than boys. (Boulton, 1992)

Middle school children's feelings at being excluded by other groups are now becoming prominent and relevant to the inevitable process of group inclusion and exclusion. Older boys may be "largely responsible for the lack of mixed-age and mixed-gender play on the playground" (Boulton, 1992). It remains to be seen whether these conclusions could replicate themselves in the United States.

Gender Differences in High School

Not a great deal of research could be found on gender differences in play at this stage, even though team sports such as baseball and basketball are still played according to gender. The sole exception to this conclusion lies in a study that found ethnically diverse high school girls participating in a basketball team, scoring above the mean on masculine gender-role identity. They were classified as androgynous or masculine in regard to gender-role identity, scoring above the median on six of eight domains of self-concept. Sport participation factors of ability and persistence might be related to certain domains of self-concept, but not to gender-role identity. Overall sports participation might be viewed positively and worthy of continuation (Britsch, 2000).

Gender Differences in College

On retrospective reports about their favorite games, toys, and hobbies and favorite exercise and sports in elementary, high school, and college, undergraduates often indicate that

> similarities and differences have varied as a function of what kind of play. For both genders, games may tend to be home-based and individual or dyadic play, while sports may tend to be viewed as group, public-based play. Whereas team sports play might have been most frequent in childhood for both genders and decreased in frequency from childhood to adulthood, the decrease in team, as compared to individual and dyadic, sports might be more dramatic for girls than for boys. (Vaughter, Sadh, & Vozzola, 1994)

Masculine and androgynous childhood activities may play a role in the development of skills necessary for achievement in mathematics and physical sciences, which are salient in male-dominated professions such as engineering and science (Cooper & Robinson, 1989).

> Playing with "masculine" (rather than "feminine") toys and games, playing in predominantly male or mixed-gender groups, and being considered a tomboy may help distinguish between women who later become college athletes and those who did not. Therefore, childhood play activities might be considered, along with other agents of socialization (i.e., family, peers, coaches), as important factors in predicting future sports participation. (Giuliano, Popp, & Knight, 2000)

Tomboyism may be statistically quite common, but there is little indication that it is abnormal (Hyde, Rosenberg, & Behrman, 1977).

Playing violent games might result in more aggression than playing a nonviolent game, with men being more affected by the game than women, with the possibility that there may be potential differences in aggressive style between men and women (Bartholow & Anderson, 2002).

Gender Differences in Adulthood

In a study of forty-four adults shown an edited videotape of "playful and aggressive fighting involving middle school pupils,"

> each participant was asked to say whether he or she thought each episode was playful or aggressive and then to give the reasons for that judgment. The

20 males and 22 of the 24 females showed significant agreement with the standard view of these episodes. Adult men were more likely to view aggressive episodes mistakenly as playful than to view playful episodes mistakenly as aggressive, with the opposite being the case for the women. The most frequently reported criteria for deciding were the nature of the physical actions, inferences about action/intent, facial expressions, and whether the children remained together or separate[] after the interaction. (Boulton, 1993)

CONCLUSION

Parents, and especially mothers during infancy and preschool years, are very crucial in making toys and games available to their children and making sure that their choice and usage of toys is age- and gender-appropriate within the constraints of a culture and of SES. Within this age context, gender differences may be produced by the interaction of culture, parental influences, and SES.

6

Chronological Age Is Not the Same as Development in Play

Play is not only a behavioral phenomenon, it is also a developmental one with its own distinctive sequences.

(Herron & Sutton-Smith, 1971, p. 267)

How young you are does not mean you are old enough to play, just as how old you are does not mean you are young enough to play.

The purpose of this chapter is to introduce a model of play development that demonstrates definite developmental stages and substages in sequences of behavior from exploration, aggression, and construction. However, before introducing this model, we need to define the terms necessary to distinguish among chronological age (CA), development, and socialization, because these three terms are important parts of play.

DEFINITION OF TERMS

We need to distinguish between CA and development. CA is characterized by five major stages: (1) childhood, from birth to 12 years, with substages of infancy (from 2 to 23 months), preschool (from 2 to 5 years), school (from 6 to 12 years); (2) adolescence (from 13 to 17 years); (3) early adulthood, from 18 to 30 years; (4) mature adulthood, from 31 to 60 years; and (5) old age or seniority, from 61 years to death. CA is a definite factor that needs to be acknowledged from the outset (Lindley, 1997).

Development, on the other hand, is a much more difficult term to define, because we must specify the aspect of behavior whose development we are interested in. Development can be emotional, physical, intellectual, and social, to mention just a few dimensions. In each, development applies to play: how, how well, how much, and with whom one plays. Consequently, how old a person is chronologically does not mean that development in play follows the same sequence. A young person may play an adult game such as chess. Because adults play tennis or golf, that does not mean that children cannot play either game. CA, whether in play or in anything else, is counted in days, months, and years. It is a physiologically, physically inevitable process with a definite beginning and a definite end, although the timing of the end is unknown. We all go through it regardless of gender, SES, and education. We may retard some of its effects and prolong this process according to how we take care of ourselves through physical, emotional, and relational care. However, whether we like it or not, this process comes to an end, and there is no way to stop it.

Play development and socialization, on the other hand, are also two different processes that are independent of CA. Development is understood to be an internal physical process, how an individual receives information, food, liquids, nurturance, and how he or she uses whatever has been supplied through years of gradual growth, determined in some ways, as discussed in Chapters 4 and 5 in this volume, by the culture in which the individual grows. The process of assimilation and accommodation in development is universal, as Piaget indicated years ago (1972). How rapidly or how slowly development occurs results from native qualities as well as environmental ones, such as culture. It may vary according to what kind of nutrition, clothing, and shelter are available; think of the difference in growth in height between second-generation and first-generation Italian and Greek immigrants in the United States. However, what and how the external world is received—that is, how tangible goods such as nutrition and intangible ones such as nurturance and education are processed by an individual—relates to a process of socialization according to progressive and sequential stages of what we play and how we play, how we learn to play, and how we stop playing, regardless of age. CA is predictable and specific, whereas development as the result of the continuous interplay between CA and environment is not.

Development, then, is the outcome of how the individual receives and processes internally whatever is given from the external environment. Given the same external input, development differs as a result of factors internal to the individual. For instance, there are distinct physical differences in gender, and given the same information received from the environment, individuals of the two genders may process that information differently. Children and adults with physical disabilities are not going to be able to learn some games, although they may be able to master some others, perhaps better than physically healthy players, as in, for instance, wheelchair competitions of leg-handicapped players.

Socialization, on the other hand, is what is available outside of the individual according to the individual's culture and caretakers. As we have seen in Chapter 4 of this volume, each culture has different types of toys and games, rules, expectations, and restraints or freedoms about play that differ from one culture to another. Within each culture there is a myriad of parental practices that affect playing.

For instance, Tiger Woods, one of the greatest golf players of all time, learned to play at a very early age under the tutelage of his father, who was very fond of this game and knowledgeable in it. Likewise, Venus and Serena Williams did not become tennis champions by themselves; their father nurtured and coached them from a very early age. Maria Sharapova has been (and still is) receiving support from her father since an early age when he brought her to the Florida Tennis Academy from Russia to become a champion. These women did not become champions by chance. They started to play tennis at an early age, often practicing under the initiative of their fathers, who were also fond of and knowledgeable about that game. Millions of other children did not have the involvement and investment of their parents to transform them from mere players to giant money-making machines. In general, both golf and tennis are "adult" sports. One of my uncles started playing as a teenager with his brothers and sisters in my maternal grandfather's tennis court, and he played it until he was 75 years old.

Starting to play a game can occur at different stages of CA. I did not start playing tennis until I was over 30 years old, and consequently I enjoyed playing it, but I never became good at it. However, I had to quit playing it in my sixties because of an arthritic neck and spine. I never started to exercise on a foam mattress until I was in my seventies. One can start and quit playing any time one wants to; for example, I quit doing tai-chi after four years because I found it boring. However, I could not quit getting old.

What type of toy or game one can choose is largely determined by the culture and by parents who transmit that culture according to what the child can or cannot play within their larger immediate context, gender, SES, and age (Wade, 1985). My mother, some of her sisters, and some of her brothers learned to play tennis in the only tennis court that was available at that time in their town—the one built by their father. Had there not been a tennis court, they would never have learned to play tennis.

Because of this variability in starting, continuing, and stopping, it is impossible to divide and subdivide play development or socialization, especially when we do not have an idea of what process and what path both development and socialization follow. We have a clear and predictable trajectory about various stages of the life cycle according to gross chronological criteria such as infancy, preschool, elementary school, high school, college, maturity, middle age, and old age (Elkind, 2007). Even though the specific years defining each stage may vary from one source to another, there is consensus about the existence of those stages.

However, what about play development and socialization? We have already reviewed most theories of play development in Chapter 3. Nonetheless, is there a way to divide and subdivide stages of development and socialization in a more objective and empirically grounded way than what has been theorized to date? Perhaps there is. To begin with, the relationship among CA, development, and socialization are described in Figure 6.1, showing how all three processes are related to different aspects of play.

Development applies to emotions, intelligence, physique, social skills, humor, and awareness of self and others (Higgins, 2005) as a function of gender, age, and other intrinsic characteristics biologically and as a function of socialization culturally, including SES, education, and other social factors. I have proposed (L'Abate, 2005; see Chapter 19, this volume) that the infant is born into a world of space, as assessed by who and how the child is approached or avoided, by a caring, smiling, and soothing caretaker or by a rough, nasty, dour one, with all the possibilities in between these extremes. At this age, the child may tend to discharge any emotional or physical discomfort immediately, on the one hand, or may tend to keep the discomfort in, delaying expressing it through crying or whining, on the other. After the first two years of life the child enters a world of time, where past, present, and future with time become differentiated into hours, days, weeks, and years. Here is where the child learns to control by balancing appropriately approach/avoidance and discharge/delay functions. Within this visible development, there is also a development that is internal and that needs to be elicited to be studied. One important aspect of development and socialization that deserves mentioning is awareness: how a child becomes aware of self, others, and the environment according to predictable stages, such as *instrumental* (what one does), *monitored* (continuously watching self), and *expectant* of a better future (Higgins, 2005).

The first stage of awareness is physical and postnatal, when memory is strictly limited to the perception of the immediate concrete self and

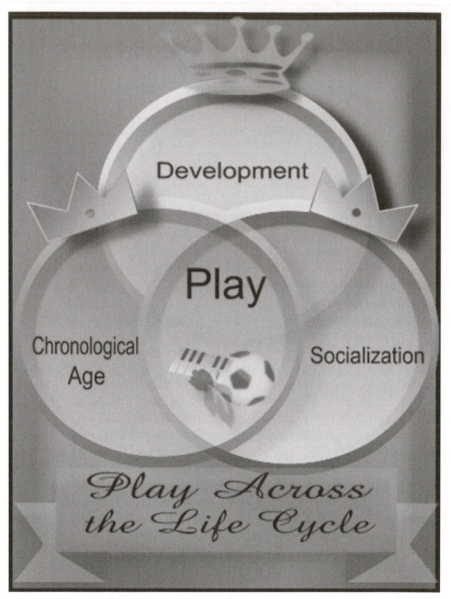

Figure 6.1 Effect on play of the interrelationships among chronological age, development, and socialization.

others. The second stage is social, between 6 and 12 months, when the memory of people around allows recognition of them, and the beginnings of language, communication, and social sharing occur within the constancy of reliable routines and the presence of the same objects and, of course, toys. The third stage, between 18 and 23 months, is cognitive, where there is memory of events, routines, and categories of people and objects with the emerging perspective of self ("I") and others ("You"), and an awareness of body self and of an objective self. The fourth stage occurs between 2 and 4 years of age and is reflective, with a memory of specific events shared with others and an awareness of the experiences of self and the experiences of others, what has been referred to as the theory of mind, with an increasing understanding of social and physical causality. The fifth stage, between 3 and 6 years, is narrative, when memory becomes autobiographical, including stories of self and others with an understanding of what is real and what is imaginary, as represented by pretending and making up stories. The sixth stage, between 6 and 10 years of age, is cultural, where there is an increasing understanding of external representations, different roles and responsibilities, and different settings and institutions (Nelson, 2005, p. 127). What is lacking in this *normative* classification of levels of awareness are physical, gender, intellectual, and cultural constraints, which may modify, retard, and lengthen the duration of each stage.

Consequently, we will need to consider other developmental stages specifically focused on play socialization. How these stages correspond to those proposed above is a crucial issue for future research.

DEVELOPMENTAL STAGES IN PLAY SOCIALIZATION

As reviewed in Chapter 3, various theorists have developed or suggested different stages of development, from Piaget's sensorimotor, symbolic, and rule games to Erikson's autocosmic, microcosmic, and macrocosmic levels of play. However, these suggested developments relate to the early life of the child and not to the whole process of play development across the life cycle. Hence, we need a framework for play development that is encompassing and applicable at various sequences of socialization in play.

Pellegrini (1998, p. 228, p. 228) summarized six stages in the first 54 months of development that include age in months and salient issue: (1) 0–3 months, physiological regulation; (2) 3–6 months, tension management; (3) 6–12 months, establishing attachment relationship; (4) 12–18 months, exploration and mastery; (5) 18–30 months, autonomy; (6) impulse management, sex role identification, and peer relationships. What is important here is to expand such a summary of stages to the rest of the life cycle. A feeble attempt to complete this summary of stages in development will be made in this chapter and in the rest of this volume.

Ariel (2002, pp. 83–85) proposed another model of how make-believe play develops as a function of the child's general development in four areas characterized by complexity, abstraction, depth, and objectivity. He distinguished among seven main stages: (1) sense perception and attention, (2) memory, (3) creativity and problem solving, (4) insight/self-awareness, (5) organization and planning, (6) knowledge and understanding, and (7) socialization.

It would be useful but difficult to attempt an integration of both Pellegrini's and Ariel's models by developing a supermodel that would include both chronological and developmental stages. Nonetheless, such integration will be attempted in Chapter 19 of this volume, when the information contained in many chapters will be processed.

THE IMPORTANCE OF STRUCTURE IN PLAY

Structure achieves meaning at different levels of play, ranging from the nature of the toy object (simple to complex, colorful to colorless), the surrounding setting (outdoors or indoors, large or small, enclosed or open), and the rules or lack of rules related to toy usage and playing among players, and the degree of structure ranges from lack of structure at one extreme to extremely detailed structure at the other. Why is structure important? Because structure determines the process of play. It could be said that there is no such a thing as lack of structure, because by just giving a toy to a child a structure is created. Adding another toy or another play increases the structure and determines the process that will occur consequently (Getz & Berndt, 1982; Hogg, Rogers, & Sebba, 1988).

Structure in play could also be defined by the amount of adult-directed activity. For instance, in urban Head Start classes high in structure (defined in this manner), preschoolers may engage in less prosocial behavior to peers, less imaginative play, but less aggression than preschoolers in low-structure classes, but there may be slightly more friendly peer interactions. However, preschoolers in high-structure classes might be more attentive in circle time and tend to clean up more after free play, even though they might not show more independent task persistence. Consequently, these possibilities suggest that high levels of adult direction may produce greater conformity when adults are present but do not facilitate independent task-oriented behavior (Huston-Stein, Friedrich-Cofer, & Susman, 1977).

Structure may also refer to the degree of realism or fantasy in toys, where more unstructured toys may increase pretend play even though preschoolers may tend to play longer with high-structure, that is, more realistic, toys. Unstructured toys could be associated with high playing time only when they are presented before high- or moderate-structure toys. Apparently, children show a greater variety rather than amount of pretend play behavior with unstructured toys (McGhee, Ethridge, & Benz, 1984).

Structure could also refer to the nature of the toys themselves. For instance, five sets of nine pieces to fit into 5-inch form-boards could be used as puzzles (indicating the presence of convergent activity) or as play blocks (divergent activity). Differences in the use of toys according to this dichotomy may influence the way children will think (divergently or convergently) and, consequently, behavior, not only in play but also in real-life situations (Pepler & Ross, 1981).

GAMES AND TOYS THROUGHOUT THE LIFE CYCLE: A DEVELOPMENTAL MODEL

The objective of this section is to evaluate the plethora of therapeutic games and toys available commercially according to an empirically based model. Unfortunately, this model is based only on boys' playing rather than girls'. Therefore, it is offered here with a proviso not to generalize it to girls' play behavior, a topic that I intend to expand in its own right through the course of this book.

There are so many supposedly educational, recreational, and therapeutic games and toys that it would be practically impossible for many teachers, school counselors, child therapists, and even pediatricians to be informed of the availability of all these games. For example, a single, representative brochure of creative therapy games contains some 152 games and toys for different genders, ages, intellectual level, and nature of the child's disturbance. In addition to chain toy and game stores such as Toys "R" Us, there are at least six or seven other publishers who also produce brochures with as many other games and toys. However, I know of no brochures concerning toys and games throughout the life cycle (Appendix A).

For instance, on the basis of observations made from 1965 to 1975 at a monitored play-therapy room built at Georgia State University, I was able to develop the model of play development presented here. I am also reproducing the original research because it appeared in a practically unknown publication (L'Abate, 1979; Appendix B). In processing thousands of data points, as shown in Figure 6.2, I was able to discriminate an initial exploratory stage, followed by a second, aggressive stage, followed

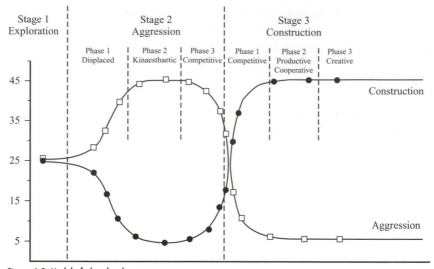

Figure 6.2 Model of play development.

by a constructive stage, and a final goodbye stage. As you can see, each stage could be subdivided into substages or phases that include most of the dimensions that will be elaborated in the chapters to follow in this volume.

This model is fundamental to various models of a hierarchical theory of play presented in Chapter 19 of this volume. What is the relevance of this model for play and playful activities throughout the life cycle? Let me try to answer this question in detail. This figure shows that in the beginning stage of exploration both aggression and construction are of equal importance; exploration at the beginning may include both aggression and construction. However, after the initial stage, the second stage of aggression takes over and increases until the third stage of construction takes over. Within each stage there are distinct phases distinguished by different kinds of toys and different kinds of games. The third stage of nonaggressive positive playing includes a first competitive substage without construction, while in the second and third substages something is built, constructed, or produced, as explained further below.

THE DEVELOPMENTAL PLAY MODEL EXPLAINED

This section would provide a developmental classification of toys and games available commercially, according to the model presented in Figure 6.2. This model will make it easier for readers to see how play can be described according to a predictable developmental process separate from CA. Furthermore, the classification of toys and games derived from this model would allow selection of the most appropriate game and toy that could given to an individual according to what stage of development that individual might be in. It would be impossible for most play professionals to review and become knowledgeable on all the games and toys in existence. The same process of classification is necessary for a systematic presentation and ordering of most games and toys (Barnett & Kane, 1985a, b; Herron & Sutton-Smith, 1971; Kleiber & Richards, 1985). Information about publishing houses that sell toys and games mostly at pre–high school and older stages is available in Appendix A.

Play development as a progressive process with a predictable path has been proposed by quite a few play scholars, as discussed in Chapter 3 of this volume. For instance, as already noted, Elkind (2007) suggested four major chronological stages of play development: (1) infancy and early childhood, (2) elementary school years (ages 6 to 12), (3) adolescence, and (4) adulthood. This model is inadequate because it does not take into account that individuals mature at different rates and that they develop their play interests with minimum regard to CA. It does not take into account developmental stages independent from CA. That suggestion, therefore, needs to be refined according to substages within each stage given by Elkind and, especially, expanded according to various stages of adulthood to seniority.

Each of the stages and substages in the development of play will be expanded in the rest of this chapter.

Importance of Exploration in Playing Development

Exploration, the active manipulation of playing, is usually reserved to infancy (Sutton-Smith, 1986, p. 13), but it is clearly present in early childhood (Pellegrini & Gustafson, 2005; Schneider, 1983). There are some scholars who differentiate exploration as not really being "play" because play in and of itself seems conceptually distinct and has different developmental trajectories and possibly different functions (Pellegrini & Gustafson, 2005). However, be that as it may, I believe that exploration is a necessary introduction to play as a process that goes on across the life cycle. In high school I explored mountain climbing and skiing in the Italian Alps, but I could not do either in the flat plains of Kansas (where I had naïvely supposed I would be able to look out the window of my college dormitory in Hillsboro and see the Rockies to the west but saw only fields of wheat and foraging cows). Exploration is present even when adults who can afford them look for a sports car or even a yacht. No one is going to buy an expensive toy without comparing models, costs, colors, and convenience, that is: exploration (Hutt, 1971, 1982; Pellegrini & Gustafson, 2005; Sutton-Smith, 1986, p. 130).

Emotionally, exploration includes curiosity, interest, and joy (Fahndrich & Schneider, 1987). There is a faint possibility that in preschoolers exploration is related to divergent thinking (Goodwin, Sawyers, & Bailey, 1988), even though there may be a complex reciprocal causality in which the development of divergent problem-solving skills may facilitate the development of play skills and vice versa (Wyver & Spence, 1999). However, more reliable evidence will be needed to support this possibility.

In addition to investigation, exploration is also characterized by active manipulation of objects. Investigation usually occurs at the beginning and is followed by manipulation, where children seem to engage in a greater variety of activities and change activities more often than do college students (Vlietstra, 1978). From manual manipulation, the child often may progress to symbolic pretend play, suggesting the importance of interactions among a child's cognitive abilities, interactions with others, parental knowledge about play, and the child's culture (Tamis-LeMonda & Bornstein, 1996). Exploratory and manipulatory characteristics of play could contribute to a general problem-solving ability that can be specifically applied to successful solutions of tasks (Barnett, 1985).

The level of complexity of a toy or game, of course, is relevant to how much time is spent and at what age a toy or game is easy or difficult to solve (Vandenberg, 1981), depending also on the level of intelligence (Switzky, Ludwig, & Haywood, 1979). Consequently, it would be difficult if not impossible for a child learning to play without an initial observation, investigation, and subsequent active manipulation of an object, before understanding the toylike qualities and gamelike possibilities that that object may possess.

Additionally, choices that children make in choosing toys, games, and even playmates appear to be in some way related to their enduring styles, whether their locus of control is external (field-dependent) or internal (field-independent) (Saracho, 1989). This aspect will receive more attention in Chapter 19 of this volume.

Importance of Aggression in Play Development

Interestingly, most treatises about play, including those on play therapy, where aggression is more relevant, make only passing mentions of aggression in play. For instance, Gitlin-Weiner, Sandgrund, and Schaefer (2000) mention aggression in children's relationships on only one page, even though aggression is a very important topic at various personal, interpersonal, cultural, and societal levels. Nonetheless, a cursory review about aggression in secondary references found only a few references. Schwartzman (1978) suggested that childhood aggression becomes or is channeled into competition in youth sports and games. Herron and Sutton-Smith (1971) referred to aggression as well as construction and competition, all topics that are included in the model shown in Figure 6.2 and expanded here. Elkind (2007) devoted two pages to aggression, as if it did not exist in playing, let alone in real life. Bertilson (1991) and Erikson (1982), however, provided two excellent although by now unfortunately outdated introductions to aggression, the first from the viewpoint of personality, the second from psychoanalytic theory. Goldstein (1995) reviewed the literature on aggression and play in gender differences: boys are relatively more aggressive than girls, especially in reference to war play (p. 132). Goldstein also differentiated between television violence and video games with violent themes (p. 136). Stories with aggressive content may tend to reinforce aggressive responses (Larder, 1962).

Schaefer (1993) cited quite a few references to acting-out and catharsis but not on aggression per se. In his (1999) volume Schaefer had only one reference to "acting out," even though one chapter by this writer (L'Abate, 1999) contained many examples and even workbooks about anger, hostility, and aggression in children and youth. By the same token, Shirk and Russell (1996) had quite a few references about aggression in terms of two case examples (pp. 263–266; pp. 282–284) and from the viewpoint of cognitive misattributions (p. 80) and schema (p. 226), nonverbal decoding biases (p. 80), problem-solving deficits (p. 266), and speech (pp. 104–105). The latest *Encyclopedia of Children, Adolescents, and the Media* (Jensen-Arnett, 2007, Appendix A) has quite a few entries about aggression but none on construction and constructive toys, which, on the other hand, received frequent references in Caplan and Caplan (1973) and other sources (Lancy, 2002, p. 57), not to mention Sutton-Smith (Herron & Sutton-Smith, 1971, 1982; Sutton-Smith, 1986).

This point is made because both aggression, in its many expressions, and construction, in its many indirect expressions, competition, and cooperation, enter prominently in the model shown in Figure 6.2. These expressions are present in everyday life and in almost all kinds of playing (Lieberman, 1977, pp. 79–80; Patterson, 2004, p. 30). It is evident, for instance, in play-fighting and rough-and-tumble play (Fry, 2005, pp. 54–85).

There are quite a few primary references to play behavior, especially in preschoolers, where it is important to differentiate between aggressors and victims. Aggressive incidents usually occur in 10–14 percent of the cases. The predominance of male participation in aggressive behavior, particularly physical aggression, is clearly visible (Gunnarson, 1997).

Therefore, gender differences in aggression, as shown in how my two grandchildren differed from each other according to stereotypical gender differences as described in Chapter 1, are important. As Hay observes in a 2007 study,

Nearly a century of observational studies and more recent longitudinal surveys reveal that, in infancy, girls and boys use force at similar rates. Over the next few years boys become significantly more aggressive. Alternative hypotheses accounting for this widening gender gap include (1) normative patterns of male escalation and female desistance, (2) boys' preference for active play that promotes aggression versus girls' tendency to hide aggression, (3) girls' use of alternative, perhaps indirect, forms of aggression, (4) boys' increased risk for the cognitive and emotional problems linked to aggression, (5) boys' sensitivity to situational triggers that promote aggression, and (6) boys' vulnerability to adverse rearing environments. Evidence bearing on each hypothesis is mixed; in general, the overall difference between genders appears to be produced by a minority of boys who deploy aggression at high rates.

Three general principles govern the emergence of gender differences in aggression: (1) female precocity, (2) male vulnerability, and (3) the salience of sex as a social category that shapes children's lives. (Hay, 2007)

Another possibility about gender differences may lie in differential modeling from parental figures. At least in extremes, mothers tend to model the importance of others more than themselves, training girls toward selflessness, letting others win at one's expense, while fathers tend to model importance of self over the importance of others, training boys toward selfishness and winning at the expense of others, including aggression (L'Abate, 2005). This possibility will be explained further in Chapter 19 of this volume.

Aggression may vary as a function of age and peer group status in preschoolers. For instance, aggression can be proactive/overt, instrumental/bullying, and relational. Boys may tend to show "more proactive/overt and instrumental/bullying aggression than girls," while girls may tend to show more relational aggression than boys. The latter seem to be more aggressive "according to their peer group status." That is,

Children classified as "nuclear" in their peer group may show higher frequencies of relational aggression than children who were classified otherwise. Children classified as "isolated" suffered more than others from relational aggression. (Hatakeyama & Yamazaki, 2002)

Hatakeyama and Yamazaki's study is important because it contains a distinction among types of aggression, a distinction that adds to different kinds of aggressive behaviors shown in Figure 6.2 and discussed in Appendix B.

Organized games on a playground, such as rope jumping and foot racing, coupled with an infrequently used time-out procedure for aggressive play, may significantly reduce the frequency of inappropriate aggressive incidents. This possibility suggests that in dealing with large groups of children, antecedent playground manipulations may be more practical than providing consequences for aggressive behavior exhibited by already identified children (Murphy, Hutchinson, & Bailey, 1983).

It is important to differentiate children who are hyperactive and perhaps aggressive from children who are truly aggressive and may appear hyperactive, as well as children who are both hyperactive and aggressive. Significant differentiation (up to 86 percent) can be achieved from behaviors exhibited in two different play settings (free and restricted) and in the restricted academic period. One study notes that "Children with externalizing disorders can be distinguished in light of their observed clinical behavior in the restricted academic setting," which makes it possible to discriminate aggression from hyperactivity validly (Roberts, 1990).

Antecedent conditions for distinguishing aggressive behaviors from hyperactivity include situations where (1) children are seeking entry in a play activity and are denied it or (2) another child interrupts an ongoing activity. In hyperactive children, aggression can be almost 14 times greater for seeking/interrupted activity than for ongoing social play. Furthermore, percentages of negative responses from peers to aggression on the playground can reach almost three times previously documented rates for children without hyperactivity (Stormont, Zentall, Beyda, Javorsky, & Belfiore, 2000). Dominance and aggression are clearly related, to the point that the competition between highly dominant preschoolers may be directed toward similarly dominant peers (Straver & Straver, 1978). Aggressive kindergarten children may not differ from nonaggressive children in symbolic play (Young, 1995), an important possibility that needs to be researched further.

Cooperative and aggressive behaviors can be modified almost at will by how teachers tend to make nonevaluative comments about either behavior, leading to another important distinction between verbal and nonverbal aggression (Slaby & Crowley, 1977). Cooperative behavior can be rewarded, thus decreasing the frequency of aggressive behavior (Stafford & Stafford, 1995).

Boys, however, do not have a monopoly on aggression. Girls in a relationally aggressive way may spend more time engaged in social conversation with one specific peer and less time in cooperative play than girls in a nonaggressive group (Isobe, Kirk, Filho, & Maeda, 2004).

From these primary and secondary sources one can conclude that (1) aggression is an important stage of development for some but not for all children, because (2) not all children are aggressive, (3) aggression may be more prominent in disturbed or troubled children, and (3) boys tend to be more aggressive than girls. Consequently, it might be important to study aggression under controlled experimental conditions that allow reliable measurement of aggression rather than study aggression under uncontrolled conditions that cannot be measured reliably.

Importance of Cooperation and Competition in Play Development

Cooperative and competitive playing could be the defining extremes of a dimension in which some play could be described as noncompetitive and noncooperative somewhere in the neutral middle, depending also on the setting. For instance, cooperative play may appear to increase significantly outdoors more than indoors, but noncooperative play may also tend to increase significantly indoors (Orlick, 1981).

Cooperation and cooperation in play, of course, are present at every age and stage of development but may develop rapidly at certain ages and plateau at others. For instance, group play might not be the culmination of a linear developmental process. Cooperation may vary along a continuum of its own, with large variations between groups within each age group (Garnier & Latour, 1994). Cross-culturally (Lancy, 2002, p. 57) competition and cooperation are the hallmarks of playing in early childhood (Beal, 1998, pp. 215–218; Pellegrini & Gustafson, 2005, pp. 114–115) as well as in adolescents in the United States (Erikson, 1971, 1982, p. 128). Of course, competition and cooperation endure across the life cycle, even though they are, strangely, not considered in representative developmental treatises (Demick & Andreoletti, 2003) or personality theories (Maddi, 1989). This noteworthy absence makes one wonder about the validity of certain developmental or personality theories if they do not contain these topics, let alone play, as discussed in Chapter 19 of this volume.

Cooperation and competition go hand in hand between multiplayer groups. Members of one group with a minimum of two players need to cooperate to play with members of another team similarly constituted in number of players. Both behaviors may have been produced through natural selection, including the ability to compromise among members of the same team (Boulton & Smith, 1992). It is doubtful whether an evolutionary approach can explain cooperation, competition, and the middle point of compromise along a continuum. All three behaviors can be explained by necessity and by the nature of the game. Archery or biking may be solitary games, but they become competitive when players are in a competitive tournament or when players are grouped together to represent a nation or a neighborhood. The toy itself generates the nature of the play and whether the play demands a cooperative or competitive framework. Of course, cooperation may tend to engender more positive behaviors, while competition may engender more negative behaviors (Einlinson et al., 2000).

Cooperation could be directed toward constructive, playful, or destructive (warlike) purposes. Winning or losing in the Roman Colosseum or playing ball for the Mayans in Monte Albán was a life-or-death struggle: the participant survived if he obliterated his adversary, with no choices for compromise. Modern representations of these sports are still visible on TV, where players in warrior-like clothing shoot at an adversary who is thrown in a water pool for losing in a symbolic reenactment of traditional games from the past.

The bottom line on this section lies in the possibility that if a teacher emphasizes, teaches, and rewards cooperation, she or he will receive back cooperative behavior from children. If the teacher emphasizes, teaches, and rewards competition, the chances are high that he or she will receive back competitive behavior in play (Lejeune, 1995). Of course, such a simplistic conclusion needs to be qualified and specified further. Nonetheless, the possibility still remains that both behaviors exist in life and both are needed to live as effective players and citizens. The issue will need specification of what kind of cooperation and what kind of competition need to be emphasized.

One step toward answering that question lies in gender differences in social dominance and cooperative play among preschoolers. Same-gender and opposite-gender dyads identified as being high or low in play dominance patterns suggested that children with a dominant personality could lead children with low-dominance personality during play. When girls were paired with boys, girls seemed to lead more when the play was of a feminine rather than masculine nature. Girls might also show higher amounts of cooperative play than boys, while boys might show higher parallel play than girls. During an activity of a feminine nature, there may be higher levels of cooperative play than in a masculine activity, with more parallel play during masculine compared to a feminine activity. Same- and mixed-gender pairings seem to display more cooperative than parallel play, a rather inconsistent pattern from past research. In line with cultural stereotypes, girls may exhibit more feminine themes in play than boys, who, on the other hand, may exhibit more masculine themes than girls, including the superhero theme (Neppi, 1997).

This conclusion was supported by the nature of protagonists in children's narratives from dramatic play. Girls seem to favor protagonists with qualities such as lovingness, graciousness, and attractiveness, while boys seem to favor protagonists with physical power (Kyratzis, 1999).

Importance of Construction in Play Development

Constructive play occurs when children use play materials to produce something that lies at the intersection between functional and dramatic play (Christie & Johnsen, 1987).

Advanced constructional play at an early age may lead to mathematical achievement (Stannard, Wolfgang, Jones, & Phelps, 2001; Wolfgang, Stannard, & Jones, 2003). Constructive play may increase perspective-taking, the child's ability to see someone else's viewpoint (Burns & Brainerd, 1979) as well as higher mathematical achievement (Stannard et al., 2001; Wolfgang et al., 2003).

An important issue that is relevant to the model and its results (Appendix B) deals with the degree of structure present while the child plays, such as materials only (Play-Doh and blocks), materials plus unstructured props, and materials plus model/instructions. There may be an increase in constructive play when a child is able to impose a structure on the play situation, with a parallel decrease of constructive play when limits are set by a teacher. If this pattern is reliable and valid, it suggests that high levels of teacher structuring may not provide children opportunities for problem-solving and, in some cases, for creativity (Tegano, Lookabaugh, May, & Burdette, 1991).

Complexity of preschoolers' block constructions, as a way to assess an understanding of children's development, seems to increase with CA, while another study points out that the time that a child might be "involved with block construction activity could have a positive effect on block construction complexity. Gender [apparently does not seem to] influence block construction complexity" (Frances, Milton, & Phelps, 2001). Of course, color may play a prominent role in play behavior, especially with blocks or similar toys (Gramza & Witt, 1969).

Constructive and constructive/symbolic play could offer the transformational basis for much of children's earliest forms of written language, where writing and language development seem to be intrinsically interwoven (Neves & Reifel, 2002).

The Importance of Creativity in Play Development

Whether creativity can be thought or learned is a possibility that needs to be explored further, assuming that creativity in play can be evaluated reliably. Verbal elaboration, for instance, could be used to facilitate creative play through preparation of a play space, encouraging talk during play, and listening evaluatively to what the child is saying during play. Consequently, rather than being an artifact of incidental learning, creative play could be planned and structured actively within a preschool curriculum (Harrington, 1987).

More specifically, creativity is represented by what a child does with whatever materials are available to build something new that integrates parts that may have not been thought to be related with each other. The best example of creativity I have seen was when some children reached this final stage of constructing a fort with logs in the constructive play-room and then went into the adjacent aggressive playroom and brought back both Indians and soldiers into the fort compound. Some of the children who reached this level where not problematic. They were included in the study to see whether "normal" children would follow the same progressive sequence of play stages followed by "disturbed" children. They did (Appendix B).

CLASSIFICATIONS OF GAMES AND TOYS

The literature on classifications of toys and games seems to lack any systematic proposal. For instance, Sutton-Smith (1971, 1986) proposed quite a few classifications of games and plays. Elkind (2007) classified games and toys according to two criteria: (1) developmentally, such as Teletubbies, Baby Einstein, CDs and videos for preschoolers, Leapfrog Products, and computer games for infants, toddlers, preschoolers, and school-age children, including Piglet's Big Game, Spy Fox, and Professor Fizzwizzle, among others; and (2) structurally, according to their physical characteristics, such as (a) sensational, according to touch and texture, (b) microchips, (c) character building through heroes or heroines, (d) skills for boys and skills for girls (according to stereotypes of the two genders), and (e) to foster education.

On the other hand, from the model shown in Figure 6.2, I have developed a classification of toys (Table 6.1) that represents various stages of development in play and possibly play-therapy. These stages of development were not available in the literature 35 years ago when I conducted this study. However, Pellegrini and Gustafson (2005, p. 121) did present object use categories and tool use subcategories that come close to the model presented here. An even more complex, hierarchical framework for the classification of toys and games is presented in Chapter 19 of this volume (Figure 19.1).

Essentially, this classification of toys may be necessary for the construction of a virtual reality play (therapy) room, also elaborated in Chapter 15 of this volume. It would be important to see whether this model is valid throughout the various life-cycle stages reviewed in this volume. For instance, the first stage of exploration features in Herron and Sutton-Smith (1971), although it is not contained in most references cited above.

Table 6.1
Games and Toys Used at Various Stages of Play Development

A. First Stage: Exploration

Players are free to become acquainted and to visit various toys and games available to them within environmental limits provided by culture, family, and the immediate educational SES (Sutton-Smith, 1986, p. 143). This stage is present throughout a lifetime, because we all explore and manipulate new toys, be they computers, phones, camcorders, cars, or yachts.

B. Second Stage: Aggression

This stage may differ in the intensity and severity of aggression, but its existence cannot be denied. It may be more extreme in disturbed and troubled individuals, but in one way or another the potential for aggression (flight or fight) is present in all of us. In the first two substages, choice of toys and games and actions may stem from primary emotions, while in the second and third substages they may stem from secondary emotions requiring a certain degree of rationality, as described by Sutton-Smith (2002) and as discussed further in Chapter 19 of this volume.

Consequently, it is important to distinguish among at least three kinds of aggressive play according to the toys used:

1. *Displaced aggression*: guns of any type, especially machine guns directed toward imaginary threatening human beings. In adulthood this level is present in hunting and, unfortunately, in wars. Guns that shoot water or paintballs also enjoy great popularity with children of all ages. As shown by the results of the original study (L'Abate, 1979, Appendix B), there is a significant but negative correlation between intelligence and frequency of shooting, that is, the brighter the individual, the fewer the shots fired. It does not take a great deal of intelligence to pull the trigger of a gun. It takes a much higher level of intelligence not to pull it.

2. *Kinesthetic aggression*: any toy that involves hitting, such as a hammer, or throwing or shooting at inanimate targets, such as in archery, water pistols, or the like. This phase is present in adulthood in sports such as target shooting, archery competitions, and ball throwing, such as basketball or football. The level of intelligence here is somewhat higher because a higher level of skill may be necessary. Note that up to this point children have been playing by themselves, seldom acknowledging the presence of the therapist.

3. *Competitive aggression*: toys that involve aggressive competition between two people or two teams, as in physical sports involving various degrees of body contact, such as hockey and football, baseball, or basketball; board games involving airplanes, cannons, missiles, nations, armies, or soldiers involved in warfare. In these games one side wins at the expense of the other. During this stage, children started to communicate with the therapist to engage him or her in competition. From this stage on, children became more available to speaking and working with the therapist.

Table 6.1
(continued)

C. Third Stage: Nonaggressive Constructive Playing

In this stage, constructions apply to the second and third substages because the first substage, Competition, does not involve construction per se. However, this is the most important substage, because it includes the most frequently used games.

1. *Competition without Aggression*: This stage includes any *competitive* game or sport that does not involve much if any body contact among players, such as bingo, cards, bowling, tennis, swimming, or peaceful board games, such as Monopoly, involving competition, where there is a winner and there is a loser. This type of play is present and most frequent at various stages of the life cycle. It is characterized by two major qualities in addition to being competitive, as determined by one player winning and the other player losing: (1) *reactivity*, to the point that the game is in response or answer to moves initiated by self or by other, and (2) *repetitive* in the sense that the process is essentially structured and governed by rules and regulations, including time limits and penalties for not following or obeying rules. Nothing concrete, however, is built, constructed, or created in these games. The notion of reactivity-repetition will be expanded in Chapter 19 of this volume.

2. *Cooperative Construction*: This substage covers any game, toy, or task involving concrete building or constructing something, such as castle, forts, houses built of Lego, logs, plastic bricks, plaster of Paris, or the like, following instructions or making up constructions according to given models or instructions.

3. *Creative Construction*: In this substage, games or tasks allow players to integrate, find out, or put together any of the previous toys or games, even aggressive ones, into a new, originally creative fashion with an unexpected but integrated combination of various toys, games, or materials, with either an original use of materials or an unusual combination of various materials that go above and beyond given or set instructions. It can be self-initiated or it can occur with other players.

D. Fourth and Final Stage: Letting Go

At this final stage the player reviews all the toys or games that have been played, as a form of saying goodbye and going on to better or different things. Some toys are kept throughout a lifetime as mementos of early, pleasurable times. Nonetheless, as time goes by we all must say goodbye to old toys and games.

As noted, competition and creativity are topics cited quite frequently in most secondary references, but not as much as aggression. Consequently, from the model shown earlier (Figure 6.1), it is possible to suggest a list of toys relevant to the various stages of development (Table 6.1).

Hence, this model could serve as a basis for classification of toys and games according to criteria found in the model across the life cycle. Instead of a chaotic hodgepodge of toys without any theoretical or empirical rationale, this model classifies toys according to the appropriate age, gender, stage, and substage of development independent of CA, but still dependent on the intellectual level and personality characteristics of the player, such as internalization, externalization, and severe psychopathology (Barnett & Kane, 1985b). Functional players might gravitate toward games with a minimum of hostile aggression and a maximum of cooperation. Internalizing players may direct aggression toward self and not toward others. Externalizing players might enjoy attacking others and defending themselves from attacks. Dysfunctional players may gravitate toward aggressive toys and games, moving inconsistently and contradictorily from one type of toy to another, even though the developmental sequence suggested here is still followed.

How does this model apply to play and play therapy throughout the life cycle? This question will be answered in the following chapters and especially in Chapter 19.

As noted, the major shortcoming of this model is its masculine-dominated nature. Another model, more appropriate to girls and women, may be necessary and will be attempted throughout the course of writing this book, if at all possible. At least in the early years, the most frequently occurring activities may include cutting and pasting, painting and crayoning, sand and water, and books. Play activities may engage nonsocial functions that may be less complex and mature than those used in social constructive fashion, where girls may engage in more art work and less block and vehicle play than boys, thus indicating a lack of change in toy preferences across sexes over a period of more than 40 years (Rubin, 1977). Whether these gender differences hold up at the present time is an issue already discussed in Chapter 4 and throughout the following chapters.

CONCLUSION

The results of the model presented in this chapter can be described by three basic styles of playing: (1) Aggressive style, contained and described by the second stage and its three phases included in Figure 6.2 and Table 6.1; (2) Competitive, Reactive/Repetitive style in Stage 3, implicit in competitively repetitious games, where one party wins at the expense of the other player, players, team, or teams with only accidental or without intended body contact, and (3) Constructive. Constructive style can be differentiated into Conductive, when one player self-initiates playing or takes the lead and directs the play or construction if there are other players involved, and Cooperative, present when all players involved play together for a common goal of building something found in instructions. A Creative style exists when the player by him- or herself or players in unison build something that integrates a completely novel and never-thought-of creation, without following instructions or existing patterns. These three basic styles will be expanded by evidence gathered in the following chapters and forming one of sixteen models in a hierarchical theory of play competence, presented in Chapter 19.

Part II

CHRONOLOGICAL STAGES OF PLAY

Chronological stages in life as well as in play are arbitrary and relative. Nonetheless, this is the way development is evaluated by age and by gender. Any other alternative, reviewed in Chapter 2 of this volume, would have been even more controversial and perhaps, inadequate.

7

INFANCY

What is of most interest to human infants throughout the first year are the sights, sounds, touch, and movement of people. Over this period, the infant's consciousness grows rapidly from fleeting levels of awareness interspersed with long period of sleep to sustained periods of engagement with the physical and social world.

(Nelson, 2005, pp. 126–127)

Infants' play is influenced by physiological prenatal and natal actors that determine their temperament as well as their emotions (Kagan, 2007). How and how rapidly infants react to internal and external events is called reactivity (Charles & Carstensen, 2007; Rothbart & Sheese, 2007). Indeed, reactivity may be one of the most enduring aspects of temperament. When infants are divided into high- and low-reactivity categories, a host of physiological and characteriological differences show up. For instance, "few high reactive infants become consistently spontaneous, sociable, high risk-takers, and few low-reactives become hypervigilant, shy, and risk-averse adolescents" (Kagan, 2007, p. 187). For readers desirous to learn more about reactivity, I recommend Kagan's book and the two secondary sources cited above.

What I have written about reactivity in Chapter 19 of this volume as well as in previous writings (L'Abate, 2005; L'Abate & Cusinato, 2007) must be coupled with another feature: repetitiveness. We tend to repeat ourselves when we are in a reactive mode. We can readily see this pattern in many political debates where candidates react repeatedly to each other's accusations and blaming. If adults do it, infants tend to do it more, but they let go as they become more mature and proactive rather than reactive. Many of us, however—even politicians, it seems—cannot let go of this childish, destructive pattern as we supposedly grow up.

Another instance in which physiology may interact with the immediate environment can be found in the continuous interactions between infants and their mothers where, for instance, there may be differences in measures of spatial relations between anemic and non-anemic infants. After all, infants are first born in a world of space, where distance from caretakers is a crucial dimension, and eventually grow up in a world of time, where control is a crucial dimension (see Chapter 19). In 71% of anemic infants, the duration of child-initiated body contact with their mothers might be high compared with a level of contact in only 26% of non-anemic babies. Mothers of anemic infants seemed to spend less time at a distance from them, were less likely to break close contact, and were more likely to reestablish close contact if the baby moved away. This increase in body contact could be interpreted as a reflection of fearfulness, hesitancy, or inactivity. Iron deficiency, therefore, among many other chemical factors, could have a strong effect on the infant and how the mother responds to her or him (Lozoff, Klein, Nelson, McClish, et al., 1998).

At this stage, the most important aspect lies on whom and what the infant is taught to approach and to avoid in a world of space and distance. The infant is rewarded by food, touch, the 3HC (hugging, holding, huddling, and cuddling; L'Abate, 2001), smiling and laughing, and is discouraged from approaching possibly dangerous and painful situations—people as well as objects, toys, and even pets. If people, objects, toys, and pets are not rewarding, the infant will learn to avoid them. Unfortunately, in their helpless position, infants are not able to avoid people, objects, toys, or pets that may be forced on them unwittingly, producing an approach–avoidance conflict that may last a lifetime (Blue, 1986; Kidd & Kidd, 1987; L'Abate, 2007; Triebenbacher, 1998). If people, objects, toys, or pets are rewarding, the infant will continue to want to stay and even play with them (see Chapter 19, this volume). This level of proximity has been fully explained and expanded by a very influential attachment model that, however, has failed thus far to consider play as a part of our development and socialization (Mikulincer & Shaver, 2007).

The temporal stability and convergent validity of infant temperament may vary as a function of age even within months in infancy. Stability can be noted for temperamental dimensions of activity, rhythmicity, intensity, mood, and persistence, including smiling and vocalizing in a later stage of infancy. Convergent validity can be noted for attentive behaviors and comparable gaze aversion and nondistractibility, distress in eyebrow behavior, and negative mood. Babies with easier temperaments tend to vocalize more and cry less frequently during their play interactions than hard-temperament babies (Field et al., 1987). As infants become more interested in their nonsocial surroundings, triadic play, where a toy is added to infants' play with their caregivers, becomes an increasingly frequent play context. Yet, little is known about the emergence of triadic play within the first year of life. Identifying the play contexts in which infants participate is integral to understanding the processes by which infants develop into increasingly competent social beings (Colburne, 2001).

The mutual influence of mother and infant on the context of early play interactions, whereby the content of play is modified with the infant's development, is crucial to play development. Infants tend to become more autonomous in toy play with age, while mothers may provide fewer demonstrations of the toys and may tend to use fewer physical interventions with older infants. Additionally, the play context may strongly influence infants' communicative development. Infants' nonverbal communicative behavior, indeed, may tend to differ during triadic play. Seven-month-olds may gaze more toward their mothers' faces and may display higher levels of smiling than the 4-month-olds when social and functional toys were used. During this period the highest levels of social play may tend to occur. Consequently, at 7 months, it appears that infants may be more responsive to triadic play with certain toys and may engage with their mothers to a greater degree, as measured by infant gazing and smiling. Different triadic play contexts within which mothers and infants engage as well as the communicative contexts promoted by the use of different toys could underscore the diverse learning opportunities available to infants during triadic play (Colburne, 2001).

Triangulation in infancy is the infant's capacity to handle more than one interaction and share affection with both parents. This capacity may vary "when recruited in functional versus problematic" child–parent alliances. Possibly,

an infant under stress when interacting with one parent will protest at that parent and also at the other. Such [may be] the case when, for example, the father acts intrusively while playing with [the] baby. [. . .] The regulation of this dyadic intrusion-avoidance pattern at family level depends on the family alliance. When coparenting is supportive, the mother [may validate] the infant's bid for help without interfering with the father. Thus, the problematic pattern [could be] contained in the dyad, and the infant's triangular capacities remain in the service of developmental goals. But when coparenting is hostile-competitive, the mother [may ignore] the infant's bid or [could engage] with [the infant] in a way that interferes with [the] play with [the] father. In this case, the infant's triangular capacities [could be] used to relieve tensions between the parents. (Fivaz-Depeusinge & Favez, 2006)

This situation may perhaps make the infant assume the role of Rescuer, while the parents simultaneously assume and switch roles of Rescuer, Victim, and Persecutor. This triangulation, therefore, might not exist in peaceful parents–infant relationships, but it could become the basis for the pathogenic Drama Triangle explained in Chapter 19 of this volume.

Home environment might relate more systematically to highest levels of exploration displayed in free play (called performance) than does executive capacity, the ability to make decisions. Infants evaluated as securely attached to their parents might be more free to attend to the immediate environment beyond the attachment figure in play, and thus might display a smaller gap between the most sophisticated play levels exhibited in free and elicited play. Therefore, there might be a certain degree of stability of individual differences between infancy and subsequent developmental periods (Belsky, Garduque, & Hencir, 1984).

During infancy, "narrative vocalizations, spontaneous play, and elicited appropriate play" might be considered as the primary measures to evaluate symbolic play style (Dixon & Shore, 1991). Symbolic play and use of toys might be significantly and positively related. However, language and symbolic play abilities have been claimed to be unrelated in infancy (Russell & Russnaik, 1981), a conclusion that needs to be questioned and verified.

As a study from the year 2000 points out, "Various theoretical accounts propose that an important developmental relation exists between joint attention, play, and imitation abilities. However, very little empirical evidence supports these claims" about these abilities and a theory of mind (Chapman et al. 2000). Theory of mind includes the ability to imagine or make deductions about the mental states of another individual. What does the other individual know? What actions is that individual likely to take? Theory of mind is an essential component of attributing beliefs, intentions, and desires to others, specifically in order to predict their behavior. It begins to appear around 4 years of age in human beings (American Psychological Association, 2007, *Dictionary of Psychology*).

A small sample [of thirteen infants], for whom measures of play, joint attention, and imitation had been collected at 20 months of age, was followed-up longitudinally at 44 months, and a battery of theory of mind measures was conducted. [See also Lillard, 1998.] Language and IQ were measured at both timepoints. Imitation ability at 20 months was longitudinally associated with expressive, but not receptive, language ability at 44 months. In contrast, only the joint attention behaviours of gaze switches between an adult and an active toy and looking to an adult during ambiguous goal detection task at 20 months were longitudinally associated with theory of mind ability at 44 months. [... Joint] attention, play, imitation, and language with theory of mind might form part of a shared social-communicative representational system in infancy that becomes increasingly specialised and differentiated as development progresses. (Chapman et al., 2000)

Long-term memory was evaluated at 10 months of age by teaching twenty infants to

operate a toy in their homes and testing after 4 months, along with twenty age-matched controls who had not been instructed to operate the same toy. Experienced infants appeared to be more willing to remain in the play situation, relearning faster than controls, and one operated the toy spontaneously. Eighteen months later, two subgroups of five children each and age-matched controls were observed in a laboratory playroom. Only children with experiences at both 10 and 14 months operated the toy without being shown. Children with a single 14-month experience made equivalent numbers of toy contacts and successful responses.

This experiment is important also in demonstrating the beginning of an automatic if not unconscious level in awareness underlying some of our behavior during adulthood (Myers, Perris, & Speaker, 1994).

DEVIANCY IN INFANCY

In a follow-up of preterm and full-term infants after 5 years, the former preterm participants seemed to show slight delays in cognitive functioning. Measures of development and language at 13.5 and 22 months and relational play at 22 months seem to be more predictive of cognitive outcome. Children with behavior problems at 5 years may differ from those without problems in terms of their play and language skills. Measures of development, particularly language development, and of play appeared to be predictive of later cognitive and behavioral functioning (McDonald, Sigman, & Ungerer, 1989).

In infancy it may be already possible to detect early signs of autism. Even though there may not be biological tests or a single reliable measure with which to confirm a diagnosis of autism, the relative invisibility of this disorder in infancy implies that its diagnosis does not occur until well after language has failed to develop—usually between 3 and 4 years of age. Nonetheless, there is often the possibility that some parents may become aware of differences much earlier than that age period, to the extent that 50% of parents of autistic children report that they suspected the existence of a problem before their child was one year of age. What do these parents notice in the first 12 months that evaluation tools and practitioners cannot? Home videos taken during infancy involving various activities, and especially the use of toys and games as well as playful interactions between child and parent, may provide an answer to this question (St. Clair, Danon-Boileau, & Trevarthen, 2007).

CONCLUSION

Even though the literature about play in infancy may seem limited (as obtained by cross-indexing "infancy" with "play" in Internet search engines), in spite of the enormous amount of data about infancy, whatever has been summarized in this chapter indicates how is it is practically impossible to separate play from the immediate influences from the distal and proximal physical and human environment during this period. What happens at this stage of development has substantial implications for what will happen for the rest of a child's life.

8

NURSERY, PRESCHOOL, AND KINDERGARTEN

A certain degree of reflection on states of self and other can be achieved through the imagination, either in thought or in play.... Children's play may come to invoke aspects of this landscape [of consciousness] as children begin to collaborate on imaginative play scenarios, but play also begins as the simple playing out of everyday events.... Between age 3 to 5 years, children come to contribute more to the construction of accounts of past experience and to participate in the making of narratives about their own lives.... Most notable is the newly emerging sense of self that is situated in time.

(Nelson, 2005, pp. 130, 134)

The second and third years of life are a time of momentous growth and change. Leaving infancy behind, toddlers become increasingly independent as they begin to speak, walk, and participate actively in their widening social world. This pivotal period involves social and emotional transitions and pathways by which children develop socioemotional competence with emerging specific abilities, as shown in increasing individual differences in specific play activities. No single behavior can be used as a yardstick of socioemotional competence. There is a continuing interplay among codeveloping systems that moves the toddler forward (Brownell & Kopp, 2007). Through narrative and group dramatic play, the toddler begins to develop a sense of self, an identity. Collaborative self-construction may be seen in linguistic forms preschoolers use while constructing narratives with their protagonists. Girls' protagonists, for instance, may value qualities of lovingness, graciousness, and attractiveness, while the protagonists that boys construct seem to value power. Girls may rely on narratives for self-construction more than boys do (Kyratzis, 1999). Both factors, which could be called *communal* for characteristics valued stereotypically by women and *agentic* for characteristics valued stereotypically by men, will be reconsidered in a relational theory of play competence in Chapter 19 of this volume.

PLAY IN PRESCHOOL AND THE THEORY OF MIND

During this period of life children start developing ideas about what other children or even adults may think, feel, and act, including what roles they may play, the so-called theory of mind, already considered in the previous chapter. In playing tag, for instance, it may be much easier for children at ages 5 to 6 years to change roles among chasing, catching, or running away than for 4-year-olds. Six-year-old chasers may tend to chase more than two escapers at the same time more frequently than 4-year-olds do. Age, therefore, is an important factor in how children become conscious of relations with others, even in a seemingly simple game such as tag (Tanaka, 2005). A vast majority of all toy materials can be used in an isolated context at one time or another, suggesting the importance of selecting toys that clearly set the occasion for positive social interaction (Hendrickson, Strain, Tremblay, & Shores, 1981).

Possession of toys may indicate a failure to appreciate the feelings of other children with regard to ownership and use of particular toys. Possession episodes may be positively associated with competitive behaviors and negatively related to positive social responses both situationally and dispositionally. Disputes following possession claims frequently may result in the termination or disruption of the social interaction. Children who frequently engage in possession disputes might also engage in more aggressive actions and fewer affiliative ones than their less possession-oriented classmates (Ramsey, 1987).

INITIATION OF PLAY INTERACTIONS

There may be obvious

age differences in initiation styles during ages 3 and 4 [with] various implicit strategies besides direct and explicit ones to initiate interactions with peers. Three-year-olds [may imitate] others' behavior to engage peers more often than did 4-year-olds. Between ages 3 and 4, children [may] use implicit strategies and [may] participate in peer play more often. (Matsui, 2000)

However, "in the latter half period of 4 years," they may tend "more to invite peers to join in their activities and to attract peers' attention" (Matsui, 2000). The number of explicit entry attempts may tend to increase "as children became more familiar with the rules of entry into preschool play" (Matsui, 2000).

Additionally, four-year-olds may tend to use few play-implicit strategies appropriate for such play, even though they may also employ many explicit play entries. In constructive play, for instance, players may enter and leave the play scene by carrying and constructing materials. Pretend play may be going on simultaneously. Participants seem to engage others' attention, or attempt explicit entry. In sand play, when occurring in an outdoor space, 3-year-olds may tend to use many implicit strategies of calling to peers, presenting their own activities, and providing the necessary equipment for playing. In motoric play, 3- and 4-year-olds may tend to mix with each other through engaging in similar body movements. Rule play could follow fixed sequences: 4- and 5-year-olds often may attempt explicit entry (Matsui et al., 2001).

Younger children may tend to initiate interactions at lower rates than the norm, reciprocating interaction invitations at a higher probability level, perhaps "demonstrating the power of peer social [interactions] to produce reciprocal responding." Girls and low-interactor boys typically may tend to receive more initiations than they make to peers (Greenwood, Walker, Todd, & Hops, 1981). Older and younger children may tend to interact primarily with their own age groups rather than with cross-age peers; such interactions may involve low levels of play (Roopnarine, 1981).

The quality of initiation may be important. For instance, friendly initiations could be associated with more frequent "agree" responses, demanding initiation with more frequent coercive responses, and whiny initiations with more "ignore" responses. The frequency with which an initiation mode is employed could be associated with its efficacy in eliciting agree responses. In addition to reciprocal patterns, complementarity in the demanding initiation mode may be present. Therefore, both reciprocal and complementary social interactions of preschool children could be considered as the first step toward a functional analysis of play initiations at this age (Leiter, 1977).

MOTOR ACTIVITY IN PLAY

Children with motor impairments may be able to compensate for their limitations by developing areas of strength that would allow them to play normally (Morrison, Bundy, & Fisher, 1991). This possibility was studied in greater detail by Trevlas et al., (2003) with Greek children (Chapter 4 this volume). Recorder data show that boys may be more active then girls, correlating with teachers' rating of the same motor behavior (Halverson & Waldrop, 1973). Attending a playground may have a significantly more beneficial outcome on children than not attending; the effect of the variety of activities in which children were encouraged to engage may have been augmented by the warmth, interest, and participation of playground leaders (Turner, 1974).

Pretend imagery may improve learning to dance in preschoolers, in comparison to traditional teaching, by improving visual fixation on the instructor, increasing children's engagement and enjoyment while learning to dance, decreasing the need for promoting and time to recall, and decreasing the amount of time needed to learn the skill of dancing. If these results are reliable, then pretend imagery could be used within a variety of teaching contexts (Sacha & Russ, 2006).

SOLITARY AND SOCIAL PLAY

As is the case with most psychological behaviors, social play is a complex entity that carries with it a variety of psychological meanings. Nonsocial play is even more complex and multidimensional. The content of children's play activities should be considered within a given social context. Variables in the social context within which play activities are considered include (1) the developmental course of social participation from infancy and toddlerhood to preschool period; (2) the social significance of sociodramatic play; (3) the social significance of social interaction; (4) origins of individual differences in social play, such as genetic factors, temperament and physiology; (5) parenting beliefs and behaviors together with parent–child attachment relationships; and (6) developmental models and outcomes of social and nonsocial play (Rubin & Coplan, 1998). Preschool experience and attendance may tend to relate to play behavior and to improved measures of social interaction, except for aggressive behavior, which actually may increase with preschool experience (Shea, 1981).

Developmentally, 2-year-olds might go through successive stages of predominantly solitary, then parallel, then group play, but many others do not. Some 3- and 4-year-olds may alternate periods of predominantly group play and periods of predominantly solitary play, suggesting the importance of maturity in both solitary and parallel play (Smith, 1978). Children exhibiting high levels of peer play interactions might demonstrate more competent emotional regulation; that is, control, initiation, self-determination, and receptive vocabulary skills. Positive results of assessments of engagement in play early in the school year might be associated with lower levels of aggressive, shy, and withdrawn adjustment problems at the end of the year. Children who might tend to interact successfully with peers early in the year seem to evidence greater cognitive, social, and movement/coordination outcomes. Disruptive and disconnected peer play behaviors might be associated with negative emotional and behavioral outcomes (Fantuzzo, Sekino, & Cohen, 2004).

Multiple forms of solitary play can be assessed reliably with a Preschool Play Behavior Scale that can be administered to teachers and parents (Rubin & Coplan, 1998). Certain toys may promote cooperative or isolated or solitary play (Rodney, 1997). Solitude may provide benefits not otherwise accrued by social play, because the "capacity to play alone is an important developmental step" (Katz & Bucholz, 1999). However, "the benefits of solitude in early childhood [may not have] been fully researched" (Katz & Bucholz, 1999).

"Current research on solitary play most often views solitary in contrast to social play and focuses on how low rates of social [interactions] may negatively affect preschoolers." Children who play on their own without interacting with peers "may be at risk for social, [cognitive,] and social-cognitive problems" (Lloyd & Howe, 2003). However, this position has been questioned by recent literature that reveals that some forms of nonsocial activity may be constructive and adaptive. A more positive way to view solitary play may

> help teachers discriminate between healthy, productive solo activity and problematic social withdrawal. Children who play alone more than is typical fall into four groups: (1) shy, (2) nonshy soloists, (3) isolated, and (4) depressed. Only the [last] two groups present clear concerns during the preschool years. Solo play should be viewed as a capacity in its own right, not in contrast to social play. (Katz & Bucholz, 1999)

Nonsocial-functional sensorimotor and dramatic activities may correlate negatively with measures of competence, whereas parallel-constructive activities generally may correlate positively with them, supporting the position that not all solitary play may be beneficial (Rubin, 1982). There is a difference between solitary play and social withdrawal. The latter may be found in internalizing disorders, such as depression, anxiety, and loneliness. Different types of social withdrawal may have different relationships with behavior problems: (1) watcher children who may engage in onlooker behavior and low levels of solitary-constructive play; (2) actor/explorers who engaged in solitary-dramatic and solitary-exploratory play, and (3) off-task/immature children who exhibited unoccupied behavior and solitary-functional play. It is likely that the third group of children may be at higher risk for future disorders than the first two groups (Wasserstein, 1997).

Social toys consist of blocks, balls, vehicles, and puppets. Isolate toys consist of books, paper and crayons, Play-Doh, and puzzles. Mixed toys consist of both social and isolate toys. Under conditions in which social toys are available, children generally may tend to engage in more interactions and less toy play as compared to other conditions. Groups of children with and without disabilities may tend to interact more than groups in which children with disabilities played separately from those without (Beckman & Kohl, 1984).

FREE VERSUS STRUCTURED PLAY

What are the component skills of spontaneous cooperative play in preschool? Early techniques of spontaneous cooperation tend to be action-oriented, and self-reference statements seem to contribute to a thematic dialogue. Advanced techniques may consist of informing possible play partners in the use of toys with suggestions on how to interact. Five-year-olds may be better able than 4-year-olds to respond to the demand characteristics of a structured rather than a free setting. However, in addition to age, there may also be gender differences that need to be considered together with types of play materials.

Preschoolers tend to engage in significantly more "solitary-functional and parallel-functional play" and in less "parallel-constructive, parallel-dramatic, and group dramatic play" than kindergarteners (Rubin, Watson, & Jambor, 1978). The latter, in turn, may display "less unoccupied, onlooker, solitary, [and] functional" activity and more group and dramatic play than preschoolers (Rubin, Watson, & Jambor, 1978).

IMAGINATIVE PLAY AS A FORERUNNER OF PRETEND PLAY

Early childhood play could foreshadow the form and complexity of ongoing adult consciousness. Imaginative play, especially, could become the forerunner of pretend play but also a precursor of narrative consciousness (Pellegrini, 1984). The beginnings of make-believe play from about two years of age may start with transitional objects, play with soft toys, or imaginary playmates. The roles of pretending and story-telling play contribute not only to sheer enjoyment but also to an array of cognitive, social, and emotional skills. Here is where adults can play roles of nurturers and enhancers of such play. Through these roles, there is the development of certain aspects of adult consciousness, such as wakeful perception, identification, labeling, and encoding, guided imagery, mental trial actions, and playfulness. These features of childhood play may be seen to foreshadow another array of functions in ongoing conscious thought, especially its narrative components and its role as a "theater" for prioritizing, decision making, contextualizing, and creativity (Singer & Singer, 2006).

Imaginative play (the introduction by a child of settings, times, and character changes not immediately present in the immediate environment), is probably one of the major forms of play in preschool and early childhood-age children. Although such make-believe games are less likely to be expressed aloud after ages 7–8, there is reason to believe the interest in such play continues into adolescence and becomes a part of the adolescent's daydreaming. There is a growing body of evidence suggesting that pretending games not only are enjoyable for children but also play a part in their acquisition of varied vocabulary imagery skill development, ability to tolerate waiting periods, and empathy and social-role mastery. Consequently, both parents and teachers should be encouraged and sometimes helped to enhance imaginative play in their children (Singer, 1977).

Symbolic maturity (the ability to think and speak according to abstract rather than concrete words) is a function of age; the older the child, the greater the level of symbolic maturity in play. Mental age may tend to correlate positively with symbolic play performance. Children living with their families were found to have a greater ability to symbolize, that is, to play symbolically, than children living without their families in an orphanage (Besevegis, Coulacoglou, Mitsotakis, Arabatzi, & Tsitsikas, 1988). However, unless the children in the two groups were matched on such factors as age and gender, these results must be considered tentative and in need of replication.

One of the factors that may be related to imagery and symbolic play may be phonological awareness (the ability to utter speech sounds that are appropriate to one's age). A positive relationship may exits between the amount of symbolic play in preschool and literacy. In first grade, children with high phonological awareness may continue to do better on literacy measures than children with low phonological awareness. The performance of the latter group on literacy measures at kindergarten seems to be a reliable indicator of whether they will have reading difficulty in first grade (Bergen & Mauer, 2000). Firstborns may also exhibit higher levels of symbolic play than later-born preschoolers (Kowalski, Wyer, Masselos, & De Lacey, 2004). There may be improvement in imaginative play following associated learning (Szabo & Shapiro, 1983).

"Ideational fluency and fantasy predisposition [may be] related to naturally occurring imaginative play" behavior (Moran, Sawyers, Fu, & Milgram, 1984). Both 4- and 5-year-olds may understand the demands of telling a story, but only 5-year-olds may have a usable mental model of a story (Benson, 1993).

When sociodramatic play is focused on specific themes or topics, it may lead to a higher quality of make-believe play, in which children enact more roles outside the home, utilize more aspects of their roles, demonstrate higher levels of symbolic prop use, and play longer (Bagley & Klass, 1998).

Imaginative play training with seriously traumatized preschoolers tends to produce significant post-training increments in levels of imaginative play, positive emotionality, prosocial behaviors, and measures of divergent thinking and storytelling skills, also decreasing levels of overt aggression. Age, nonverbal intelligence, and fantasy predisposition may also influence the children's responsiveness to the training program, with younger, high-fantasy, and high-IQ children being most susceptible to the influence of training exercises (Udwin, 1983).

Leader/follower play styles allow a classification of children as Lords, Bishops, Serfs, and Vassals. Lords and Bishops are those who exhibit more frequent leadership behaviors, while Serfs show mostly follower behaviors. Vassals' behaviors might fall in between. Pairing leaders with followers might reduce aggressive behaviors in the classroom, as much as verbal reinforcement might also reduce such behavior (Segal, Peck, Vega-Lahr, & Field, 1987).

Results of preschool assessments of imaginative predisposition seem to be related to subsequent third–grade assessment results. Early assessments might be predictive and strongly related to third-grade expression of imagination, creativity, and other related cognitive and emotional features such as reading, language comprehension, independence and maturity (Shmukler, 1983).

IMAGINARY COMPANIONS

Evoked or imaginary companions may also pertain to the phenomenon of children's invisible companions. Preschool girls observed in dyadic play interactions in nursery schools apparently attribute to them primarily the functional roles of playmate and interlocutor and secondarily the role of companion in everyday activities. During dyadic play girls with imaginary companions seemed to use significantly more of their speech to communicate than girls without imaginary companions. They also seemed to engage significantly more often in pretend play and in negotiations about it. During their play with dolls, girls with imaginary companions seemed to use the dolls significantly more often as active agents and attributed to the imaginary companions psychological and relational characteristics while acknowledging at the same time that they do not really exist. Supposedly, imaginary companions emerge naturally because of the inherently dialogical structure of mental processes and the intersubjective nature of human development (Papastathopoulos & Kugiumutzakis, 2007). Unfortunately, no additional references about this fascinating topic could be found to either support or question the conclusions from this source. For instance, imaginary companions could be understood of as one type of pretend play. However, what kinds of children make them up and why do other children not use or need them? Unless individual differences about this phenomenon can be studied further, it may continue to remain an interesting but still poorly understood and rarely studied play behavior.

PRETEND PLAY

Pretend play is the earmark of this age period and has received more research attention than any other kind of play during this age period (Bretherton, 1985; Cohen, 1987; Dunn, 1985; Kavanaugh, 2006; McLoyd, 1985; Shine & Acosta, 2000; Smith, 2005). Make-believe play tends to express the young child's emerging capacity to engage in counterfactual or would-be-thinking. Three processes have been proposed in the literature that may

> enable preschoolers to create joint make-believe play worlds with others: [enabling the child] to (1) manage multiple roles as playwrights and actors, (2) invent novel plots, and (3) deliberately blur the boundary between reality and pretense. (Bretherton, 1989)

Of these three social and cognitive processes, emotional mastery is the only one that could not be equally exercised in nonpretend contexts. Well-adjusted, secure children may be "most able to benefit from the opportunity for emotional mastery offered by sociodramatic play, whereas less well-adjusted, insecure children [might] not" (Bretherton, 1989). There are different types of pretend play, such as pretense in and of itself, solitary pretend, social pretend, and narrative (Kavanaugh & Engel, 1998).

Pretend play is a ubiquitous activity of early childhood. Although of long-standing interest to researchers, it has proved somewhat elusive to research as compared to, say, language. Since the seminal work of Parten (1932) and Piaget (1972), two waves of research have made good progress, the first in the late 1970s, and the second beginning in the 1990s and continuing today. Among the many outstanding issues related to pretending in toddlerhood, one set of issues concerns understanding pretending both as a mental state and as an activity in its own rights: how pretend events are cognitively represented (Lillard et al., 2007).

Pretend play in which the child assumes completely different roles to act or enacts different sequences is a pronounced and important stage in play development. The great many individual differences in the outset and nature of this play may depend partially on the child's relationship to the caretaker and to siblings. There are a great many developmental trajectories through which children acquire and express their understanding of social situations through nonverbal rather than verbal means. These early pretend experiences could have important implications for the child's socioemotive and cognitive understanding of other people's actions and feelings (Dunn, 1985; Youngblade & Dunn, 1995).

When pretend play of family life is directed toward the aggravation end of a politeness continuum, using doll house play, children portray family life more realistically, that is, as

> rich in aggravations. A specific type of escalation, called threat-tell sequences, showed how the children moved successfully from a metapragmatic level to a pragmatic level and at times ultimately to a level of embodied action. Focusing in depth on children's embodied role play directives in face-to-face interaction, [. . .] politeness models need to be expanded in order to account for aggravated moves and paradoxical communication. (Aronsson & Thorell, 1999)

Young children might develop ease and skill in pretending from early, enjoyable experiences engaging in pretend play with adults. There is a difference between the kind of play talk that labels and describes objects and activities and the talk of pretend play, which is based on symbolic transformations of the real world and communication of novel information. Children's exposure to and participation in pretend play talk in the preschool years might be related to their emergent literacy skills when they reach kindergarten (Katz, 2001).

The benefits of social pretend play in children could be interpreted from two points of view: evolutionary and educational. From the first viewpoint, pretend play is universal across cultures, and like any other activity it incurs time and energy cost. If that is the case, then there should be benefits. Although this viewpoint is not prescriptive about what the benefits might be, they should be universally applicable. Furthermore, given that the costs of pretend play are relatively low, benefits might also be low or modest in nature.

A contention, based almost entirely on studies in Western societies, could be made that educationally, pretend play is associated with advanced language, use of mental-state terms, and practice of theory-of-mind-type understandings, perhaps especially with more fantasy figures. However, correlational and experimental evidence does not support any strong model of the causative influence of pretend play on other cognitive or social skills, including theory of mind. Outcomes are patchy. It seems reasonable to argue that pretend play might have originated as a spinoff of our greater intelligence and language skills, and that only as we evolved culturally into settled farming communities and then urban industrialized societies might we have found pretend play to be one useful way to facilitate skill acquisition—subsistence skills in farming communities and, eventually, more creative and cognitive skills in modern urban societies. Indeed, a play ethos in modern societies might be functional in raising levels of scaffolding for pretend play and, therefore, actual levels of pretend play in children, well above what might be normally expected evolutionarily. Whether this heightened scaffolding actually has all the benefits intended and expected is still to be fully demonstrated. At least, children enjoy these activities and we are usually willing partners in this culturally inspired endeavor (Smith, 2005).

A complete understanding of social development during play requires an analysis not only of the child's development but also of operationalizing factors for each child and the development of individual children. Group improvisations of play could result in the development of a classroom's social culture. Two levels of analysis that are often neglected by developmental psychologists are the oral culture and the peer group. Pretend play might help children to form personalities and develop their social skills. Indeed, pretend play is essential for the normal development of a wide range of social, cognitive, and language skills (Sawyer, 2001).

A "significant increase in cognitive behavior" could occur in child-directed pretend play than in teacher-directed pretend play. During child-directed play there may occur a "significant positive correlation between children's cognitive and affective behavior" and "teachers' behavioral stimuli and cognitive behavior, as opposed to teacher-directed play, where the teacher's stimuli correlated with children's affective behavior." These results suggest that to learn, at least in the early years, there needs to be a "balanced development of the cognitive and affective domains" as two synergistic processes in child-directed play (Gmitrova & Gmitrov, 2004).

PLAY, LITERACY, AND LANGUAGE DEVELOPMENT

Debates about early childhood curricula tend to pit teacher-centered and skill-oriented approaches against child-centered or play-oriented approaches, as was the case centuries ago (see Chapter 3). Even though the value of teacher-directed and skill-oriented literacy activities for young children is recognized, the discussion may become too one-sided and unbalanced. Years of developmental research have demonstrated that young children have different interests, cognitive styles, and ways of grasping the world from adults, with important implications for their modes of learning. Thus, we should not be quick to fill up preschool classrooms exclusively with adult-centered, skill-based activities that may be foreign to a child's perspective. We need to balance these didactic skill-based activities with more child-centered activities within the preschool curriculum (Nicolopoulou, McDowell, & Brockmeyer, 2006).

Furthermore, the polarization between teacher-directed and child-centered approaches often poses a false dichotomy. Increasing evidence suggests that early childhood education is most effective when it successfully combines both kinds of educational activities. Even teacher-directed and skill-oriented activities themselves can become more engaging and more meaningful for children when they are linked to child-centered and play-oriented activities. Thus, a genuine integration between didactic and child-centered approaches is advocated to allow them to complement and support each other. Activities that systematically integrate symbolic play with narrative, such as journal writing, can be especially valuable, effective, and rewarding (Nicolopoulou, McDowell, & Brockmeyer, 2006).

The language of social pretending, for instance, may differ from that of other social activities at various levels of language organization. Some of these differences in the language of social pretending seem to appear at different ages during the preschool years (Garvey & Kramer, 1989). Improvisational conversations of play may suggest how social development could follow a path of increasing interactional complexity (Sawyer, 1997). Narrative and pretend play are two expressions of symbolic thought that have important implications for an understanding of the nonliteral, fictive world that emerges during childhood (Kavanaugh & Engel, 1998).

There is a definite link between play and language development, making play an effective intervention for stimulating language development. Play can stimulate innovation in language, introduce and clarify new words and concepts, motivate language use and practice, develop metalinguistic awareness, and encourage verbal thinking (Levy, 1984).

The cognitive view of play in literacy development focuses on mental processes that appear to link play with literacy-related activities. The ecological stance examines opportunities to engage in literacy-related activities in specific environments. The social-cultural perspective stresses the importance of the interface between literacy and play cultures at home, community, and the school, including also work (Roskos & Christie, 2000).

PLAY IN EXCEPTIONAL CHILDREN

It is important to have available valid and reliable instruments to evaluate play in functional as well as dysfunctional preschoolers (Harrison & Kielhofner, 1986; Howard, 1986). Social pretend play is one way to study exceptional children, including those prenatally exposed to controlled substances, who tend to obtain lower scores on intelligence tests and on expressive language skills than comparable children not exposed to controlled substances. Structure, as noted in Chapter 6 of this volume, may be important in assisting the substance-exposed child to focus on a task or skill. Otherwise, these children do not differ from other children in the proportion of time spent in pretend play, solitary play, and nonplay (Barbieri-Weldge, 1997).

Children with Disabilities

Language delays or the discrepancy between chronological age and language level may tend to produce less mature patterns of play than those observed in language-competent children (Sherrod, Stewert, & Cavallaro, 1984). In children with disabilities, cooperative play may be "significantly more likely when social [rather than isolate] toys [are] available," while collaborative play may occur only rarely with isolate toys. Social toys may tend to support "a more equal balance between parallel and cooperative play" (Ivory & McCullum, 1999).

There is

a high level of similarity between the types of activities that children with and without disabilities [may select] during play. Typically developing children [seem to spend] less time interacting with their peers with disabilities than expected, while children with disabilities may interact less with their typically developing peers than [might be] expected. An understanding of disability [may predict a] stated preference to play with hypothetical peers with disabilities. (Hestenes & Carroll, 2000)

The children's age and teacher presence may predict actual interactions among peers with disabilities, but "an understanding of disability or stated playmate preference" does not appear to do so (Hestenes & Carroll, 2000). An issue here lies in the definition of expectations and understanding of play between children with and without disabilities. Without quantifiable measures of expectations and understanding, it would be very difficult to believe in the validity and reliability of these results.

A 2004 study found that "The influence of [a] partner's developmental age on social play was different depending on the developmental age of the focal child" (Skinner, Buysse, & Bailey, 2004). If this is a reliable conclusion, it could suggest that some advantages may accrue to preschoolers with disabilities from mixed-age play groupings depending on the child's developmental age and the age of available social partners (Skinner, Buysse, & Bailey, 2004). Teachers should consider pairing a child with delayed play skills with another child with higher play skills (Tanta, Deitz, White, & Billingsley, 2005).

There may be an inverse relationship between complex play and social interaction in preschoolers with pervasive developmental disorder. These children's play within a social interaction may tend to be less complex than their play outside of the interaction. Therefore, social interventions should be implemented within the context of play activities that can be mastered by the child rather than those activities that the child is experiencing difficulty of learning (Pierce-Jordan & Lifter, 2005).

The level, complexity, and initiation of play behavior may differ among handicapped segregated preschoolers and kindergarteners, who may perform worse than mainstreamed children with and without handicaps (Federlein, Lessen-Firestone, & Elliott, 1982). Severely handicapped children showed "more prosocial, child-directed, and less teacher-oriented, teacher-initiated behavior" compared to their normal peers in integrated and non-integrated play situations (Field, Roseman, de Stefano, & Koewler, 1982). Although normal children continued to relate more frequently to their own classmates, the handicapped children appeared to watch and make as many social overtures to their normal peers as to their classmates. The direction of these effects suggests that

> normal preschoolers continue to play as if undisturbed by the addition of less developed children, whereas the handicapped children [appear to] make the greater effort to assimilate themselves into the ongoing stream of activity. (Field, Roseman, de Stefano, & Koewler, 1982)

Children with Mental Retardation

The relationships among group, setting, and variation in the play-developmental age imply the need for a multi-contextual understanding of children's play and the use of play for a more contextual understanding of retardation (Malone, 2006).

Emotionally or Socially Maladjusted Children

Socially maladjusted preschoolers may engage in more nonsocial activities and be more involved in more teacher-oriented interactions. Nonmaladjusted children may engage in more unoccupied and onlooker behaviors and greater involvement in group play. However, in considering these possible differences, one must also consider the ways in which specific teacher behaviors, such as teacher directiveness, may be related to the social status and social skill level of socially maladjusted children (Factor & Frankie, 1980).

Separation anxiety-proneness and peer affiliation may be factors influencing the quality and quantity of play. Low-anxiety preschoolers may tend to play more, show more mature play, and watch peers less when alone than highly anxious children, who may fail to show any play increase but may tend to watch peers longer when alone. A measure of separation anxiety may predict preschool differences more sensitively than a measure of general anxiety (McIntyre, Lounsbury, Hamilton, & Mantooth, 1980).

Free play of 4.5- to 6.5-year-old "normal" children, scored for quality and time, was observed to yield significant correlations with intellectual level that remained the same even when talk was deleted from play protocols. However, free play scores for 67- to 111-month-old severely disturbed boys significantly differentiated two subgroups differing in degree of pathology, with an apparent significant improvement from pre- to post-treatment periods, indicating that pretreatment scores were significantly correlated with improvement assessments at a 2-year follow-up (Clune, Paolella, & Foley, 1979). The "normal" control group did not, however, match the age range of the group of disturbed children.

Sensory impairment, measured by space and material management and participation, does not seem to affect the play of preschoolers with this impairment in comparison to children who do not suffer by this impairment. It looks as if these children may be able to compensate for their deficits by playing in an age-appropriate manner. Nonetheless, in spite of their efforts, the quality of and ability to modulate their movements in play, impressionistically observed, appeared to be poorer than those of normal children (Bundy, 1989). Symbolic play may be a helpful adjunct to assess intellectual level and play behavior in developmentally disabled preschoolers (Power, House, & Radcliffe, 1989).

Abused, Neglected, and Maltreated Children

Because play is an important developmental process influencing and influenced by socialization, physical abuse may adversely affect the developmental play age of children. Deficits in developmental play age and play imitation might be present in abused children compared to nonabused counterparts (Howard, 1986). Physically abused and neglected children may become more antisocial, disruptive, and aggressive on one hand, and more passive on the other, than children abused in other ways. Sexually abused children may tend to be relatively quiet. Peer interactions in the two groups of clinically referred children may be less positive than those of the control group (Fagot, Hagan, Youngblade, & Potter, 1989).

Exposure to imaginative play in children institutionalized for deleterious family backgrounds seems to benefit them by imaginative play training; they show improvements in positive emotionality, prosocial behaviors, and measures of divergent thinking and storytelling skills and also decreasing levels of overt aggression. Age, nonverbal intelligence, and fantasy predisposition might influence the children's responsiveness to imaginative play training, with younger, high-fantasy and high-IQ children apparently being more susceptible to the influences of training exercises (Udwin, 1983).

Maltreated children may engage in less overall play and greater functional or sensorimotor play than nonmaltreated children. They may also engage in more transitional behavior and aggression, seemingly be less competent with peers, and be perceived by teachers as more emotionally disturbed (Alessandri, 1991).

Maltreated children seem to show "significantly poorer skill in initiating interactions with peers and maintaining self-control, as well as a greater number of problem behaviors. Significant correlations of moderate strength [may exist] between social participation in play and social skills," whereas social skill might be related positively to interactive play and negatively to solitary play (Darwish et al., 2001).

CONCLUSION

There is no doubt, therefore, on the basis of all that has been written about play during this period, that the preschool period may be the most critical for overall emotional, intellectual, and interpersonal development across the life cycle. One critical issue that derives from this information refers to the presence or absence of pretend play in development. If pretend play does present, is it solitary or social? For instance, social pretend play being present in my grandson's early childhood consisted of hundreds of hours on pretend play with his Bionicles and staging fights between the good ones (his) and the bad ones (mine). I am pleasurably aware of this behavior being present in my granddaughter's behavior since I was the recipient of literally hundreds of imaginary pizzas, drinks, desserts, and entrées during this period of her life. Consequently, future research would need to tease out factors of pretend versus nonpretend play existence. If pretend play is not visible, then what would its absence indicate? Would it be replaced with fantasy and rumination? If pretend play does exist, what are the differences and outcomes between solitary versus social pretend play?

9

ELEMENTARY SCHOOL

Play as perceived by adults during the elementary school period has changed drastically from what it was perceived to be during the first half of the last century. At that time, play was supposed to have a purpose. These perceptions developed as a response to urbanization and industrialization. This development can be observed in the increased impersonality and organization of play, which might be associated with an increased frequency of stories about city life and city work. By the 1940s, play activities for children met with approval; however, there still lingered a growing need to justify play, and the appropriate balance between work and play remained unclear even at mid-century (King, 1991). Play may now be viewed by adults as a necessity equal to any other educational activity. However, more information about this possibility needs to be gathered, especially at the elementary school level.

THE NATURE OF THE GAME

Two types of play—the transformation of toys from one function to another (for instance, making a car into a robot) and representational cars and figures—may produce different interactions among same-age, same-gender dyads. Children playing with Transformers may engage in more parallel play and manipulative activity, while children playing with representational toys may display more social and more symbolic play (Bagley & Chaille, 1996).These results suggest that the nature of the toy and game needs to be taken into consideration before any other factor is added.

THE PLAYGROUND IN ELEMENTARY SCHOOL

As pretend play seemed relevant to study play in the preschool period (Chapter 8 this volume), so is the playground during this period, as shown by how much has been written on both topics, especially on attitudes between the sexes, boys' irrevocable devotion to fighting and football, the art of storytelling, friendships and enmities, the excited interest in sex, and above all, the hilarity that pervades the playground (Opie, 1993).The elementary school playground offers children a cultural event of great endurance as well as regular patterning by age, gender, and form of play. In some ways, one could argue that the playground has "festival" characteristics and that its preservation against current attempts to abolish or limit it deserves support on the basis of children's rights within the limits of their capacities (Sutton-Smith, 1990).

Recess on the playground has important educational and developmental consequences. Timing and duration of recess relate to playground activity, and possibly to classroom behavior, in ways that interact with age, gender, and temperament (Pellegrini & Smith, 1993). Boys and girls tend to self-select themselves into different environments to engage in preferred forms of play. Only boys' behavior tends to appear strongly related to adaptation and maladaptation. On the playground the boys' propensity for active, outdoor play could be useful to gauge children's social-cognitive status (Pellegrini, 1990; Serbin et al., 1993). Boys in particular seem to be more socially interactive following a long delay compared to a short delay to be allowed on the playground. Inattention seems to be higher indoors rather than outdoors (Pellegrini, Huberty, & Jones, 1995). Somehow, boys seem to be the most favorite target for research on play in playgrounds, where activity and flexibility of temperament may correlate significantly with the vigor level in rough-and-tumble play (Pellegrini, 1993).

By the same token, among girls, not only does playing hopscotch involve rotating through various positions, but girls animatedly dispute, resist, and probe the boundaries of rules as referees and players seem to build the game event. Positions may be highlighted not merely through words but also through intensified intonation contours of utterances and through embodied performances, within the built social world of the game grid and a framework for the interpretation of moves (Goodwin, 1995).

In a school in which the student population is drawn from a variety of ethnic backgrounds, the level of skill and interest that different boys display toward soccer games is likely to be, in part, culturally located. For teachers and administrators working in such settings, these cultural differences raise important questions as to which activities should be promoted among which groups of students, paying attention also to inevitable gender differences (Young, 1985).

When a playground is redesigned, it seems that the new physical setting may generate more conflicts and stress than does the human quality of the setting, which seems to engender more harmonious relationships among children (Moore, 1986). Clendaniel (2008) contends that in the past two decades, playgrounds have gotten safer, more streamlined, and progressively worse—too structured, standard, and unimaginative. Now innovators are taking playgrounds more seriously than ever. Historically, in the 1980s a rash of lawsuits were brought by parents whose children had been injured in playgrounds across the nation. As a result, attempts were made to minimize the possibility of injury by using new, safer equipment that would meet the playgrounds' requirement to include complexity, challenge, some risk, flexibility, and adaptability, including an emphasis on allowing for "free play"—allowing children to play in an unstructured setting in which they can create their own scenarios, learn to cooperate with other children on their own, and confront to a certain extent some risks. Designers of playgrounds are now including toys that allow a variety of play applications, such as plastic blocks, water, and sand, all relatively safe materials to play with.

Clendaniel (2008) gives three examples of model playgrounds, such as a nontraditional one in Berkeley, California, where children play with scrap materials such as old tires and available "junk" rather than ready-made toys created on the basis of what commercial producers "think" children will like. In New York city, Imagination Park is filled with hundreds of blue foam blocks of various shapes and sizes that children can use to build whatever they like. Another exemplary playground, cited by Clendaniel, also in New York City, is Teardrop Park, where prebuilt structures are eliminated in favor of natural elements so that the natural landscape itself is the playground, where children are encouraged to explore and try out whatever is available outdoors. Whether these innovations will spark replications elsewhere remains to be seen. The concept is interesting and challenging. However, if the risks to children are too high, innovation, fortunately or unfortunately, may have to give way to safety.

PLAY IN EXCEPTIONAL CHILDREN

There is comparable variability in socioeconomic status (SES) for learning-disabled and nonhandicapped pupils, suggesting that SES, regardless of the presence or absence of disability, may be a factor to consider in studying play (Ochoa & Palmer, 1991). Children at risk for emotional problems differ from controls on measures of make-believe with objects, make-believe with action/situations, and verbal communication (Poidevant & Spruill, 1993). Children with moderate, mild, or borderline retardation seem to interact more with adults than with nonretarded peers. Otherwise, they do not differ from their controls on the playground (Roberts, Pratt, & Leach, 1991).

Aggressive children receiving cognitive-behavioral and attention/play interventions seem to improve significantly more than children exposed to cognitive and behavioral training without attention/play and show increased prosocial behavior. At a 6-month follow-up, only children exposed to attention/play showed maintenance of improved behaviors. For teachers desirous to learn to control aggression and disruption in the classroom, Embry's (2002) Good Behavior Game (see Chapter 18 this volume) is recommended as the most documented classroom intervention with long-term results. Aerobic exercise for low-functioning students may be an alternative approach to improve children's self-concept, academic grade average, and classroom conduct (Crist, 1995), among other approaches, such as sociodramatic play (Singer & Lythcott, 2002).

Increasing text anxiety might be generally associated with increasing preferences for play with complex jigsaw puzzles. However, intellectual level and need for achievement may confound this conclusion, suggesting different styles of coping depending on intellectual level, anxiety level, and need for achievement (Gilmore, Best, & Eakins, 1980). Children with profound mental retardation interacting with nonhandicapped peers seem to benefit by such a structured program, as evidenced by improvements in both partners (Cole, 1986). Long-term results, however, need to be demonstrated before one type of intervention can be recommended over another. The nature of the game to be played (simple to complex, easy to difficult, solitary to social, etc.), of course, needs to be considered before anything else is planned.

CONCLUSION

In comparing the decreasing amount of information with increasing age, it is clear that from elementary school on to older ages of the life cycle, the play field is open to research.

10

MIDDLE SCHOOL AND PUBERTY

One cannot understand play unless one embeds it within this stage of chronologic age, when children start to deal with menarche in girls and with boys' nascent interests in the opposite gender. Middle school students seem to benefit by a comfortable, contained classroom environment that allows students to interact socially while exploring a wide array of authentic, literacy-enriched activities (Romeo & Young, 1999). Before being adopted, this romantic if not idyllic view of middle school will need a reality check.

Free-time activities at home (listed in one study as "hobbies, sports, toys and games, outdoor play, reading, television viewing, and hanging out") in middle school and high school seem related to the children's emotional and social adjustment, in the sense that the more focused and varied these activities were, the greater the chance of achieving adjustment at this stage (McHale, Crouter, & Tucker, 2001).

At this stage of development, supportive behavior in play becomes crucial in understanding its nature and function to forecast possible consequences for future outcomes. Once nonsupportive play behavior is contained within group-oriented contingencies, supportive behavior may increase (Vidoni & Ward, 2006). At this stage, dramatic play becomes an integral creative process that ranges from suggesting topics and ideas, to the complete development of situations, based on real life or fantastic events. Some themes used by participants for their dramatic play may contain issues concerned with confrontations between adults and children and between peers (gangs, groups, or cliques) (Sierra Restrepo, 1999).

RECESS AND PLAYGROUND PLAY

Recess provides students the opportunity to play and to socialize (i.e., "hang out") in ways that would be impossible to obtain in structured physical education classes. School systems considering substituting physical education for recess should learn what actually occurs during recess and consult with students before reaching a decision (Jarrett & Duckett-Hedgebeth, 2003).

Most bouts of rough-and-tumble play and aggressive fighting are usually dyadic. However, significantly more bouts of rough-and-tumble play may involve three or more participants, with more individual action patterns than aggressive behavior. Aggressive fighting, on the other hand, seems to be more varied in form. Wrestling and chasing may occur more frequently in rough-and-tumble play than in aggressive chasing. Positive and neutral facial expressions may be more characteristic of rough-and-tumble play, while negative facial expressions may be more characteristic of aggressive fighting. Rough-and-tumble initiations may be more likely to receive a similar response and less likely to receive a response than aggressive initiations might (Boulton, 1991).

Partners in rough-and-tumble play seem to like each other more than chance would predict and may tend to be closely matched in strength. Neither initiators of rough-and-tumble episodes nor recipients might be consistently perceived to be the strongest partner. Participants seem to like their partners in a wide range of non-rough-and-tumble activities significantly more than chance would predict. Thus, children could simply choose to spend time with peers whom they like, rather than rough-and-tumble representing a special case. This conclusion appears supported by the fact that children may tend to keep the same partners in a range of playground activities as they seem to do for rough-and-tumble play (Boulton, 1991).

PLAY IN EXCEPTIONAL CHILDREN

When 12- to 13-year-old nonhandicapped volunteer students serve as playground tutors for students with moderate retardation (IQs 44–59) at a regular middle school, they apparently can teach age-appropriate recreation skills to retarded peers. These nonhandicapped students seemed able to improve playground behavior and to facilitate positive interactions between themselves and handicapped children even after a follow-up (Donder & Nietupski, 1981). Children from both regular and special education classrooms seem to show similar perception on both leadership and game playing. However, retarded children may differ significantly in regard to friendship by being more egocentric than their regular classroom peers (Kingsley, Viggiano, & Tout, 1981).

CONCLUSION

There do not seem to exist sufficient studies to draw definite conclusions about play at this age period.

11

HIGH SCHOOL AND ADOLESCENCE

At this age the word "play" is no longer operative. If that term is cross-indexed with "high school," no references will result. Only when "high school" is cross-indexed with "sport" or "team sports" quite a few relevant references will ensue (Kleiber & Richards, 1985). Some of these references will be found in Chapter 4 of this volume (in reference to high school sports in different countries), and some will be found in Chapter 5 (in reference to gender differences).

The major topic perhaps relevant to this age and setting is leadership in its various aspects. For instance, one might suppose that adolescents who perceive their mothers and fathers to exhibit transformational leadership behaviors would themselves display these behaviors. Transformational leadership consists of the ability and skill to produce improvements in followers—more specifically, transformational leadership comprises "idealized influence, inspirational motivation, intellectual stimulation, and individualized consideration" (Zacharatos, Barling, & Kelloway, 2000). If this hypothesis is correct, one would expect that

adolescents who [use] transformational leadership behaviors in a team context (as rated by themselves, their peers, and their coach) would be rated as more effective, satisfying, and effort-evoking leaders by their peers and coaches. (Zacharatos, Barling, & Kelloway, 2000)

This prediction turned out to be supported by evidence. The major conceptual issues regard the "development and effects of transformational leadership in adolescents" (Zacharatos, Barling, & Kelloway, 2000).

Even more specifically,

> baseball and soccer coaches [whose athletes reported] higher levels of task
> and social cohesion [might also be] rated highest in positive feedback and
> training instruction. Successful soccer teams tend to [show] more task cohe-
> sion, [while] unsuccessful baseball teams seem to be less task-cohesive.
> (Murray, 2006)

In both cases, there seems to be a "significant relationship between
team cohesion and leadership behavior," highlighting the importance of
"interdependence in team sports" that can "significantly affect the need
for team cohesion" to contribute to a team success (Murray, 2006).

Interdependence could have moderating effects between leader
behaviors, satisfaction, and performance. "Winning coaches of high-
interdependence sports teams" (e.g., basketball) were described as showing significantly greater leader-initiating structure and less leader
consideration than losing high-interdependence coaches" (Fry, Kerr, &
Lee, 1986).

SPORTS IN EXCEPTIONAL ADOLESCENTS

With minimal instruction but with the use of miniature golf training,
students with severe mental retardation and cerebral palsy seem to
acquire a sequence of skills that enable them to actively participate in the
game (Banks & Aveno, 1986). Whether these gains are long-term or
whether these gains spread to other skills remains to be seen.

CONCLUSION

These meager reports indicate the need for continuing research at this
age and setting. Very likely, this research cannot occur unless a theory
about play competence is introduced, as in Chapter 19 of this volume.

12

COLLEGE AND EARLY ADULTHOOD

A great deal of the literature on play in college and early childhood consists of retrospective accounts of childhood playing, including favorite experiences such as dramatic play with friends or siblings, most often occurring outdoors rather than indoors and seldom including parents or other adults (Henniger, 1994; Strudler & Schaefer, 1997). Solitary play seems to provide the same functions as group play or play with a family pet (Henniger, 1994).

Behavioral, normative, and control beliefs with respect to spending more time on the "beach, jogging or running, mountain climbing, boating, and biking" seem to show

> a partition into beliefs about affective reactions and about costs and benefits. Participation in leisure activities [might be] influenced by these affective and instrumental beliefs [as much as] normative beliefs about the expectations of important others and by control beliefs about required resources and other factors that impede or facilitate leisure participation. (Aizen & Driver, 1991)

Imaginary worlds, as assessed by childhood worldplay, seem to be more prevalent in the memories of high-achieving and creative individuals, social scientists, and artists (Root-Bernstein & Root-Bernstein, 2006). There may be a clear relationship among childhood fantasy behavior, creativity, and an internal epistemic style—how one prefers to acquire knowledge of the world (Hill, 1998) including a regular college course designed to introduce undergraduates to learning more about children's play (Gross, 2003).

Perceptions of aggressive behaviors in preschoolers by male and female college students, preschool teachers, and fifty preservice early childhood teachers may vary depending on personal factors such as gender, whether observers had been engaged in war toy play, and whether they worked in preschool settings. Therefore, observer characteristics may be an important determinant of what should be considered as aggressive behavior in preschoolers (Connor, 1989).

Childhood sexual games, where "a strong relationship [may exist] between abuse and cross-gender play," may be relevant to the "level of physical involvement in the game" (Lamb & Coakley, 1993). This involvement might correlate with the perception of normalcy, producing "a typology of six kinds of sexual play experiences." These results indicate the need to differentiate "childhood sexual abuse from play and gender socialization influences relating to the role rehearsal of coercive or manipulative relationships" (Lamb & Coakley, 1993). On the other hand, the impact of childhood sexual play may be shown in widespread adult cognitive representations of sexuality. While some of these experiences may have been negative, particularly those involving coercion and being caught by an adult who responded negatively, retrospectively the majority of these experiences might be evaluated positively, with female sexual play experiences being rated less favorably by judges than those of males (Reynolds, 1997).

CONCLUSION

The meagerness of information about play at this stage of development indicates the need to research it with more emphasis than done in the past.

13

ADULTHOOD, MIDDLE AGE, AND OLD AGE

Combined with a wise diet, exercise is absolutely vital to gaining and maintaining good health, and it's never too late to begin.

(Anonymous)

We do not cease playing because we grow old; we grow old because we cease playing.

(George Bernard Shaw, 1856–1950)

Fun is like insurance. The older you get the more it costs.

(Kin Hubbard)

The functions of play change as a result of age. While in younger years play was mainly for fun and for the moment, without any thought about consequences in later years, as we mature, play reaches a completely different configuration. Play is no longer fun that we can play or not play at will, even though pleasant memories of ages between 7 and 12 may linger on (Sandberg, 2001). In adulthood, play is necessary because it becomes synonymous with vital "exercise" to maintain health and to prolong life (Bennett, 1985; Blanche, 2002; Chick & Barnett, 1995; McGuire, 1985 a, b; Wade, 1985). As in high school and college, play is now seen in sports activities and exercise. Exercise "is intrinsically motivated [as] part of [an individual's] leisure repertoire. Activities capable of producing perceptions of internal [and] external competence comprise each individual's leisure repertoire" (Mobily, Lemke, Ostiguy, & Woodard, 1993). Exercise and leisure activity participation may be more predictive of better perceived health and greater life satisfaction (Griffin & McKenna, 1998; Menec & Chipperfield, 1997). Indeed, gambling in old age may prolong life (Desai, Maciejewski, Dause, Calderone, & Potenza, 2004). A higher level of education, religious well-being, and perceived health may distinguish regular physical activity participants (i.e., exercise), from nonparticipants in regular physical activities (Guinn & Vincent, 2002).

A leisure repertoire, defined as the particular library of largely intrinsically motivated activities that participants practice on a regular basis, might be determined by two criteria: perceived competence and psychological comfort. Perceived competence (in contrast to objective or actual competence, as reviewed in Chapter 19 of this volume) relates to the individual's judgment of performance compared to the performance of other members of the same age cohort and gender. Psychological comfort refers to an individual's perception of performance judged in relation to personal, internal standards. The leisure repertoire of the elderly is of particular concern because of the abundance of free time accompanying retirement and the age-related deficits limiting one's ability to use free time meaningfully (Mobily, Lemke, & Gisin, 1991). Five factors determine whether a person takes leisure indoors or outdoors: age, gender, domestic circumstances (such as family dynamics); physical status; and mental status (Bond, Clark, Smith, & Harris, 1995; Mancini & Sandifer, 1995).

> Older adults who participate in 20 to 30 minutes of moderate-intensity exercise on most days of the week tend to have better physical function than older persons who are active throughout the day or who are inactive. Any type of activity is better than no activity for protection against functional limitations, but exercise confers greater benefit for physical activity. (Brach, Simonsick, Kritchevsky, Yaffe, & Newman, 2004)

By adulthood, playing transforms itself into exercise. What up to now might have been fun, "just for the hell of it," is no longer fun. Play is no longer voluntary. Now play becomes obligatory if one wants to enjoy and to survive (Birren & Shaie, 1985). Subjective reasons for participation in leisure activities include the need for companionship, novelty, escape, solitude, and expressiveness, where reciprocity and control seem the major dimensions (Purcell & Keller, 1989). However, there are at least three objective reasons for exercising in and beyond adulthood: (1) cardiovascular health, (2) physical flexibility, and (3) intellectual flexibility. Even the term "leisure," frequently used to include play at this stage of maturity, is really no longer conceived as something that needs to be filled in at will. "Leisure" at this stage means forced exercise if one wants to live well and long. At this stage, one tends to prefer a variety of players of different ages. However, as we age we are more likely to select players of our own age (McGuire, 1985 a, b), as described in my groups of poker players in Chapter 1 of this volume.

Growing old means a decrease in family and other responsibilities, thus fewer worries and more time for relaxation, such as hobbies and leisure-time activities. Perhaps there is an increase in wisdom and understanding as a result of experiences accumulated over the years. However, with old age comes greater selectivity in how to use time and resources (Carstensen, 1992). Other advantages may include more time to enjoy families and friends, greater freedom to choose lifestyle, and financial benefits accrued by a lifetime of work (Luszki & Luszki, 1985).

Such an idyllic view of growing old, however, is corrected by disadvantages such as increasing physical frailness, memory loss, and loss of loved ones. Perhaps a more realistic view of growing old lies in a balance of work and play, even when work is not longer paid but becomes a hobby (Marino-Schorn, 1986). Time spent in work and leisure seems to correlate more highly with high levels of life satisfaction than does time spent in daily living tasks and rest. Life satisfaction may increase by emphasizing interests, values, personal causation, and responsibility balanced with work and leisure (Smith, Kielhofner, & Watts, 1986).

Old age brings the choice of either expanding or restricting one's horizons, usually depending on socioeconomic status (SES) (Howe, 1987) and rural versus urban residence (McCormick & McGuire, 1996). Expanders tend to alter their leisure patterns by adding new activities throughout the life span, whereas contractors seem to have learned most of their outdoor recreation activities before 21 years of age (McGuire, Dottavio, & O'Leary, 1987).

If they had to live their lives over again, retired male participants would have sought more education, and women would have spent more time developing their intellectual faculties (DeGenova, 1992). Old age means dealing with inevitable losses of loved ones after many years of companionship. For bereaved men, mourning the loss of their wives, mixed group and social leisure activities seem to moderate the effect of stress on physical health (Fitzpatrick, Spiro, Kressin, Greene, & Bossé, 2001).

The concept of cognitive reserve suggests that innate intelligence or aspects of life experience such as educational or occupational attainments may supply a reserve in the form of a set of skills or repertoires that allow some people to cope with progressive age deficits better than others.

Lifestyle characteristics, such as

> engagement in leisure activities of an intellectual and social nature, seem
> associated with slower cognitive decline in healthy elderly and may reduce
> the risk of incident dementia

by tolerating more appropriately the incipient loss of memory (Scarmeas &
Stern, 2003).

A great deal is already known about the protective effects of leisure
time involving physical activity against decline in perceived health
(Hirschfelder & Reilly, 2007). However, although energy expenditure of
weekly leisure time physical activity may "not prove to be a protective
factor against the risk of decline in perceived health, global level, intensity, and type" of weekly exercise do seem to provide some benefits
"among middle-aged and older [individuals] with good perceived health"
(Malmberg, Miilunpalo, Pasanen, Vuori, & Oia, 2005). "A broad spectrum of
activities" containing more than one mental, physical, and social component seems to be more beneficial than engagement in only one type of
activity (Karp et al., 2006). In addition, cognitive activity participation
may be associated with lower risk of development of mild memory
impairment even after excluding individuals at the early stages of dementia
(Verghese et al., 2006).

"Studies comparing physical activity in caregivers and non-caregivers
should assess activities performed during routine [caregiving] tasks"
(Fredman, Bertrand, Martire, Hochberg, & Harris, 2006). With the "graying
of America" and the ever-increasing numbers of retired and aging individuals, it is crucial that a variety of options be available to choose from:

> A large body of research indicates that being physically active is beneficial
> for the prevention, management, and treatment of the chronic conditions
> and illnesses most prevalent in older adults and that increased physical
> activity increases the quality and years of healthy life. (Hirschfelder & Reilly,
> 2007, p. 121)

Volunteering is an activity mostly preferred in old age. However, what
about play? Clearly, sedentary play such as bingo won't cut it. Active,
nonsedentary play should be encouraged and rewarded in addition or as
an alternative to "volunteerism as a behavioral intervention" (Hirschfelder &
Reilly, 2007, p. 127). What about conceiving of volunteerism as a form of
old-age playing? Volunteerism is self-initiated, it is pleasurable, it is different from other activities, and it is rewarding for its own sake. Aren't these
the very qualities of play? Here is where the attitude of playfulness
(Chapter 1 this volume) could become relevant. If this were the case,
then one could conclude that in old age, volunteering could be

considered as a form of play. If volunteering is a prescribable activity as a health promotion strategy in old age (Hirschfelder & Reilly, 2007, p. 129), what about prescribing *active* play as well? This should be an activity just as important as volunteering, and certainly more important than bingo.

LEISURE, PLAY, AND RETIREMENT

In France and Germany around the turn of the last century there was a close connection made between old age and retirement to the extent to which society accepts work-free retirement. In labor circles of both countries, labor-free retirement seems to have originated in the early phase of the welfare state. Labor movements in both countries had significant influence in attempting to provide for old age. The German labor movement believed that old-age pensions were primarily a compensation for the reduction in income on reaching an advanced age. In contrast, French society supported the idea of welfare security for the old. Along with criticisms of state social systems, the purpose of providing for the old is at the center of comparing contrary forms that obliged to work in old age or receive a well-earned retirement (Schniederwind, 1997).

"With the exception of time constraints, [most] outdoor recreation constraints [seem more] important to elderly, [women] or minority respondents with lower SES" (Shores, Scott, & Floyd, 2007). An interesting classification of outdoor recreation activities (Jackson, 1987) divides them into (1) *appreciative,* such as cross-country skiing, hiking, and canoeing, (2) *consumptive,* such as fishing and hunting, and (3) *mechanized,* such as motorboating, snowmobiling, and trail biking. Participants in appreciative activities seem to hold stronger proenvironmental attitudes than participants in consumptive or mechanized activities, suggesting that "outdoor recreation participation [may be] more strongly related to attitudes [toward] specific aspects of the environment necessary [to pursue] such activities than to attitudes [toward] more distant environmental issues" (Jackson, 1986). Type, intensity, frequency, and duration of physical activity are measures that could and perhaps should be applied to play as well.

SPECIFIC SPORTS IN MATURITY AND OLD AGE

Involvement in different recreational activities, such as golf, downhill skiing, and windsurfing, seems stable over time related to activity and length of participation (Havitz & Howard, 1995), implying a specialization necessary to master one sport at a time with little if any diversification of sports with age.

Basketball: Apparently, superior basketball women players are different from superior women players in bowling, field hockey, and golf on a variety of personality dimensions such as socialization, well-being, good impression, communality, flexibility, and femininity. Apparently, the superior basketball players seem more inhibited, more shy and awkward in social behavior, and more immature intellectually and socially than the superior players in other sports (Johnson, 1972). Given the unusual nature of these results, they will need to be replicated with more recent data using a procedure controlling for or disaggregating social class variables, and also including superior men players in the same sports to avoid jumping to invalid conclusions.

Bingo:

Stigmas about [the] "little old ladies" in bingo halls highlight a leisure phenomenon that has received very little research. Although bingo is a sedentary leisure choice, the game seems harshly judged by society [although] players themselves [report] compelling reasons to play that relate to enjoyment of their leisure time and the enhancement of their well-being. (Cousins & Witcher, 2004)

This appears to be more important to the players than the gambling aspect of the game. Most bingo players are identified as being female, relatively elderly, living in rental accommodations, and receiving federal income supplements (O'Brian-Cousins & Witcher, 2007).

Bowling: Mental skills training is just as important as the physical skills necessary to play this sport (Mesagno, 2006).

Camping: This is usually a form of family leisure in which many families attend family camps, with immediate and long-term benefits for everyone (Agate and Covey, 2007).

Gambling: In addition to bingo, already discussed, this activity includes a vast range of possible types of gambling, including scratch and lottery tickets, casino games, dog and horse races, football pools, golf matches, local poker and other card games, bookies, dice games, video poker in a bar, dog or cock fights, off-track betting, and sweepstakes (Lange, 2001).

"With the [question] of gambling in its many forms across the American landscape, the question arises as to how senior citizens have been [affected]." Though casino gambling may not yet be "a major threat to the elderly, more extensive research needs to be [performed] to assess [its] individual and social costs and benefits" as a social activity (Stitt, Giacopassi, & Nichols, 2003).

> Younger age, greater social support, and alcohol use in the past year [seem to] remain strongly and independently associated with gambling. Longitudinally, age, [gender,] social support, alcohol use, and gambling are predictive of future gambling activity, that [may] offer a forum [for] social support to older adults who are often isolated as they age. (Bilt, Dodge, Panday, Shaffer, & Ganguli, 2004)

Elderly gamblers seem to be the least likely to obtain information about the casino they use for gambling and the least likely to use the Internet for this information. They seem to prefer to visit casinos on weekdays and may indicate an interest in buying weekday package trips that include stops at various casinos. There does not seem to be any difference in overall spending and gambling behavior between elderly and younger counterparts, at least in Midwestern USA (Moufakkir, 2006). About

> one-half of those aged 65 years and older [apparently] participated in casino gaming in 1998 (approximately 16 million). This number is expected to increase with the increasing number of casinos and the growing number of the elderly. However, research on the elderly who participate in this type of recreation is less visible in the academic literature [which has traditionally focused on gaming as an] addiction or on the economic and social impacts of casino gaming development on local economies. (Singh, Moufakkir, & Holecek, 2007)

University students who define themselves as gamblers seem to participate in twice as many forms of gambling as those who classified themselves as nongamblers.

Golf: This sport has received more publications for its inclusion at old age, including training (Saunders, 2005), ethnic differences (Dawkins, 2003; Scarboro & Husain, 2006), its historical background (Varner & Knottnerus, 2002), flow frequency and importance of pre-performance psychological state on the quality of the sport experience (Catley & Duda, 1997), motivations and constraints, novelty (Petrick, Backman, Bixler, & Norman, 2001), and even a state hospital golf course and its possible benefits to staff and patients (Bigelow & Roberts, 1968).

Hiking and Hunting: Elderly hunters are able to negotiate their environments as well as younger hunters, despite declining spatial and cognitive skills (Hill, 1992).

However, as a 1998 study that is also relevant to old hunters found, "Regardless of whether the lost person" in the wilderness is "hiking, cross-country skiing, or mountain biking, quantitative [i.e., distance-related] differences" among these individuals are consistent with a "common-sense geographical distinction between front and back country wilderness," in contrast to qualitative factors for "lost persons who walk away from interpersonal conflict or are despondent" (Heth & Cornell, 1998). However, there seem to be different social values and interpersonal conflict among hikers and mountain hikers (Catothers, Vaske, & Donnelly, 2001).

CONCLUSION

No other references could be found on cards, dancing, jogging, kayaking, Nintendo, Pilates, shuffleboard, tai chi, tennis, walking, weights, yoga, or television gambling in old age, even though a more thorough search may produce more information on these topics if desired. Refer to Table 19.1 for a tentative classification of playing.

Part III

THE USEFULNESS OF PLAY

This part of the book is devoted to applications of play in its multifaceted possibilities. Elsewhere (Harwood & L'Abate, 2009), I made the point that play is the cheapest and best form of self-help. From this viewpoint, if physical, economic, and financial survival is our first priority and enjoyment is a close second, then play is just as important to our survival as anything else. This is why a playful attitude is just as crucial even in school and work. It helps reduce school and work as drudgery. This is why children must be given as many opportunities to play as much and as often as possible, and I do not mean watching television mindlessly. Interactive participation, sensory-motor involvement, and challenging play pursuits with and without peers need to be rewarded.

Unfortunately, in some highly competitive cultures, such as Japan, the emphasis on studying and preparing for entrance examinations is so fierce that children and adolescents have to forgo play completely. We hope that it will not be necessary for such competitiveness to spill over into the United States, because an appropriate balance of play and work is as necessary as breathing air and eating.

14

PHYSICAL, EMOTIONAL, INTELLECTUAL, AND RELATIONAL BENEFITS

Hypothesized benefits of play range from the individual's cognitive, social, physical, and/or emotional development to the general preparation for adult skilled action, the perpetuation of the species, or the aesthetic appreciation of the world and its cultures. (Barnett, 1990)

More specifically, play plays an important role in convergent and divergent thinking, problem-solving ability, language development, emotional development, and social adjustment through communication and integration (Barnett, 1990).

These benefits, a generation later, are no longer regarded as hypothetical. As pointed out in the book *Play = Learning*,

Why is it that the best and brightest of our children are arriving at college too burned-out to profit from the smorgasbord of intellectual delights that they are offered? Why is it that some preschools and kindergartens have a majority of children struggling to master cognitive tasks that are inappropriate for their age? Why is playtime often considered to be time unproductively spent? Answers to these questions [seem to] stem from a single source: in the rush to create a generation of Einsteins, [U.S.] culture [may have] forgotten about the importance of play for children's development. (Singer, Golinkoff, & Hirsh-Pasek, 2006)

How many ways does play facilitate development across emotional, cognitive, behavioral, and relational domains? "Over forty years of developmental research indicates that play has enormous benefits to offer," not only to children but even to adults across the life cycle (Singer, Golinkoff, & Hirsh-Pasek, 2006). Obesity and hypertension, among many other disorders that have reached epidemic proportions, are not going to be reduced by words alone, and medication will only foster passive dependence without personal engagement and responsibility. Play provides children as well as adults with the opportunity to maximize attention span, not to mention: "learn to get along with peers, cultivate creativity, work through emotions, and gain the academic skills that are the foundation for later learning (Singer, Golinkoff, & Hirsh-Pasek, 2006). In short, play has powerful effects in the intellectual, social, and emotional spheres.

In Russia, Aleksandr Zaporozhets (1905–1981) (Trifonova, 2006), a theorist unavailable to Western scholars and researchers of play (and who was not included in Chapter 3 of this volume because of being ignored by the extant literature), added to the literature by emphasizing play activities as one aspect of education. He advocated a tendency common to present-day preschoolers' development by matching visual with motor activities to accelerate learning and problem-solving. The meanings and benefits of play for this process can be seen in illustrative videogames, combining pictures with actions. Children play for the experience of control, for curiosity, for intrinsic motivation of fun, and to learn. The various types of play, including sensorimotor, dramatic symbolic, and games with rules, are all intertwined with developmental stages, as argued in Chapter 6 of this volume. Play activity stimulates the brain, lubricates action, and previews later life. Among the more important gains is a facilitation of symbolic manipulation.

Play may well be underutilized as a learning strategy and may be nearly completely ignored by many educational reformers, despite the hundreds of empirical citations documenting its power in cognitive and language development, the growth of imagination and creativity, and the development of social competence (Hellendoorn, van der Kooii, & Sutton-Smith, 1994; Mann, 1996).

One advantage of play not mentioned above lies in its functioning like a vaccine in terms of its ease of administration, long term results, cost-effectiveness in the long run, and lack of side effects. Each of these benefits has been discussed at length by Embry (2002) and L'Abate (2007).

THE ROLE OF PLAY IN LANGUAGE DEVELOPMENT

As one study asks: Does play contribute to language development, and is play "a useful intervention technique for increasing the language competence of young children?" The study found that, indeed, "There is a definite link between language and play," suggesting that play is an effective intervention to stimulate language development by introducing and "clarifying new words and concepts, motivating language use and practice, developing metalinguistic awareness, and encouraging verbal thinking" (Levy, 1984).

CONCLUSION

It is questionable whether this chapter should have been written, because it includes redundant information interspersed throughout this volume. To say that play is beneficial is by now an understatement. We need to specify how and what it does to be beneficial, especially when it can be applied to improve troubled or handicapped behavior, as discussed in the next two chapters of this volume.

15

IN THEIR BEST INTEREST: PLAY THERAPY FOR CHILDREN

Lauren S. Wynne[1] and Luciano L'Abate

> Play allows us to develop alternatives to violence and despair; it helps us learn perseverance and gain optimism.
>
> Stuart Brown, M.D., Psychiatrist

This chapter is not meant to be a review of the existing literature and research on play therapy. As indicated in the Preface, the number of specific play therapy references matches if not overpasses the number of play behavior references in general. Consequently, the contents of this chapter will be selective and limited to those references that seem relevant to the aims of this book: play therapy across the life cycle. This chapter will be limited to play therapy with children, while Chapter 16 in this volume will be devoted to play as a rehabilitation method for participants of all ages.

The reader should note from the outset that, just as there is a disconnect between play and personality theorists, as indicated in Chapters 3 and 19 of this volume, there is also a disconnect between play scholars and play therapists. To that extent theorists in both fields do not cite each other. Play therapists as a whole, and we are sure there are exceptions, do not pay attention to theory, research, and findings about play from scholars and researchers in this field. Most play theorists are not

[1]Lauren Stern Wynne, Ph.D., LPC, RPT-S, Assistant Professor, Georgia State University, Department of Counseling & Psychological Services, P.O. Box 3980, Atlanta, GA 30302–3980

usually considered in the play therapy literature. All the reader need do to verify whether this conclusion is valid is to check selected play treatises found throughout this volume and play therapy treatises (Kaduson & Schaefer, 2000; O'Connor, 2000; Russ, 2004; Schaefer, 1993; Shirk & Russell, 1996). Surely there are reasons for this disconnect. However, one reason lies in not having available a theory that integrates and links play with its applications in therapy and rehabilitation, as discussed in greater detail in Chapter 19 of this volume.

WHY PLAY THERAPY?

When adults interact with a therapist, they are developmentally able (in most cases) to voice their feelings and share their concerns with their therapist. Children, on the other hand, must rely on play because it is the mode of communication that (in most cases) is their natural way of expressing themselves in a holistic manner. In this way, children can share their feelings and thoughts through the behavioral expression of play without being limited by a need on the therapist's part for words. Even children who do not speak much or at all can make meaningful therapeutic progress in a playroom that allows for multiple means of self-expression. With this in mind, a play therapist is able to work with children who either cannot talk or choose not to talk, which becomes especially relevant when working with children who may be struggling with speech/language difficulties (Danger & Landreth, 2005), selective mutism (Post, 2001), or the consequences of trauma (Crenshaw & Hardy, 2007; Van der Kolk, 2003).

According to Landreth (2001), the symbolic meaning of play is paramount to the therapeutic process and enables the child to communicate: (a) what he or she has experienced; (b) his or her reaction to and feelings about what was experienced; (c) his or her wishes, wants, or needs in general and in relation to the experience; and (d) his or her self-perceptions. For example, the first author can recall working with an 8-year-old boy in a school-based play therapy setting who was referred for encopresis (bowel incontinence) during the school day and disruptive classroom behavior. He was not a quiet child in most settings. However, in the playroom he typically chose not to speak in words. He did play in several thematic ways across the fifteen or so sessions. He would usually play out a fight scene with the same five miniatures in the sandtray. Four of the five miniatures were picked on by the largest miniature, which he would ferociously crash into them over and over and then bury each one of them in the sand as he laughed.

The second theme in his play centered on using art materials (e.g., Popsicle sticks, tape, glue, pipe cleaners, and cardboard) to construct walls and barriers that he would use to protect the four miniatures that were being harassed in each session. The third theme in his play occurred each time I indicated he had five minutes left to play. He would immediately disengage from the fight scenes or barrier building to draw a picture of a face that either had a frown or a straight-line mouth. The only complete sentence he would share during each session occurred just before our time ended. He would show his picture to me and say, "That's my (step)-dad," and walk out of the playroom. He never talked about being abused by his stepfather directly, but he played about it with great depth and regularity. Even though he was capable of talking, he was able to exert power over his experience by playing in a way that felt comfortable and safe to him. This is an example of the cathartic, or abreactive, aspect of play, which allows children to tell their story and process their feelings out in the open.

Play also helps children make sense of their world and develop skills for living and coping as well. When a child plays out a classroom scene where he or she is the teacher and the therapist is the student, the child is probably trying to make sense of the learning environment. If "the teacher" writes some numbers on the board, points to them, and asks "the student" to say what they add up to, he or she is trying to make sense of that interaction from another person's point of view. In that way, the child is trying to master a particular school-based interpersonal interaction. This type of play happens time and again in therapeutic and non-therapeutic settings when children play out kitchen scenes, take care of baby dolls, and "play" school when they are away from it. When children use the metaphorical language of play, they are communicating important information about their worlds (Kottman, 2003) and how they are trying to cope with and master the events of their daily living.

WHAT ARE THE THERAPEUTIC POWERS OF PLAY?

Dr. Brown's statement at the outset of this chapter serves as a guide for the first writer of this chapter as a play therapist. We believe he is speaking to the inherent play processes that propel human development and encourage the best in people. Russ (2004) describes fundamental play processes that are cognitive, affective, and interpersonal in nature. Her conceptualization is rooted in the fields of play and child development and stands out as a way to link what is known about play with how it can be used in developmentally-appropriate and therapeutic ways with children in need. Within each of the play processes are opportunities for problem solving and conflict resolution. The following examples are intended to define the natural therapeutic value of play further.

The cognitive processes incorporate the child's ability to use play to organize information, think divergently, transform objects into symbolic representations, and engage in the "as if" fantasy of role-plays. The first author is reminded of a play therapy group for children who were abandoned by a parent and who used cognitive processes with such skill in their therapeutic experience. One day, they decided to do some role-plays, and each member was cast in the role of mother, father, child, or, believe it or not, refrigerator repairman. One member also used a director's marker to start and stop the action. As a group, they determined multiple ways to act out the conflicts that occurred in their families. Each time, the group focused on the perspective of a different person in the scene (e.g. through the eyes of mom, through the eyes of dad, through the eyes of a child, through the eyes of siblings, through the eyes of an unrelated third party who was merely trying to fix the refrigerator). As they played through different versions of the conflict, they were more able to talk about what they thought about each scene historically and in the moment.

The affective processes of play encompass how play allows children to express their pleasant and unpleasant feeling states in ways they can control and that feel relatively safe. The first author can recall working with a five-year-old boy whose house was hit by a tornado when he was at home with his babysitter. His mom was at work at the time. He was able to utilize the affective processes of play when he would repetitively ask each puppet in the playroom, "Are you my mother? Are YOU my mother?" When the puppets said no, he expressed great frustration in not being able to find his mother no matter how hard he looked. When the bat puppet finally responded that she was his mother (after nearly twenty puppets), he would use the play handcuffs to connect the bat to him and dance around the room saying, "I'm not going to let you get away this time." For this young client, being in a tornado was tough, but being separated from his mother during a tornado was his greatest frustration. He was able to express these negative emotions through play.

From an interpersonal process perspective, Russ (2004) describes play as an activity where children can express empathy, develop an awareness of self and others in relational situations, and find ways to communicate with others. Earlier, a scenario was alluded to in which a child tries to make sense of the teacher–student relationship in the classroom. Whether children play the role of another student in the classroom or the teacher, they are trying to understand what it is like to be another person in that situation, which is like taking a walk in someone else's shoes, as in the theory of mind considered in Chapter 8. This is the core of empathy. On the other hand, children can cast themselves either as therapists or as an object such as a doll or puppet in the child's real-life role. Often this process enables children to communicate what it is like for them emotionally, cognitively, or behaviorally in a manner that feels safe and natural.

The Association for Play Therapy directly addresses the importance of interpersonal processes in the play therapy relationship in its definition of play therapy. One young client once wrote a letter that brought that definition to life. She wanted to find a way to express her deep satisfaction with the time she spent with the first author in the playroom. In her letter she stated, "I want to yell out triumphantly . . . [that she loved me]." She went on to clarify what was so meaningful when she expressed the joy she felt in playing (being able to play) and feeling loved (she and her play were accepted at face value without condition). She had a very strong emotional reaction to the opportunity to simply be herself in the presence of someone who respected her for who she was in that here-and-now moment. She did not elaborate on any specific things that were said or noted any specific techniques used. For her, time together was therapeutically powerful! Ultimately, being able to find a way to express strong feelings appropriately was a giant gain for her and was actually why she was referred to play therapy in the first place.

Whether the play process is cognitive, affective, interpersonal, or problem-solving in nature, interventions based on the processes can encourage therapeutic change and/or strengthen the naturally occurring play processes in children. Please consult Russ (2004) for more information about the role of play processes in play therapy. At this point, a brief allusion to the history of play as a therapeutic modality seems relevant.

HISTORICAL ROOTS OF PLAY THERAPY

According to Carmichael (2006), the earliest inklings of play therapy can be traced back to the mid-eighteenth century, when professionals examined child development as it related to children with special needs. During the nineteenth century, education professionals created state schools for children with disabilities, where they attempted to "train" them to become functional enough to return to their families. Closer to the twentieth century, social workers, psychologists, and psychiatrists started the child guidance movement with the goal of exploring factors that contributed to behavior disorders in juvenile offenders. Around the same time, child advocates were attempting to make child abuse a societal matter instead of a family matter by publicizing the plight of abused children. Their work led to the Society for the Prevention of Cruelty to Children, and laws were created to protect children from abuse and neglect.

The early twentieth century also saw contributions to the play therapy movement from several members of the psychoanalytic community, including Sigmund Freud, Anna Freud, Melanie Klein, and Margaret Lowenfeld, who can be described as mental health practitioners who attempted to create a means of working with children out of the much more adult-oriented practice of psychoanalysis (Carmichael, 2006). These contributors recognized that play had symbolic meaning, that it provided an effective mode for establishing rapport with child clients, and that early intervention was a means of potentially preventing difficulties in adulthood.

Release therapy (Levy, 1938), active play therapy (Solomon, 1955), and structured play therapy (Moustakas, 1959) were more directive in nature and were written about in the early to mid-twentieth century. These approaches relied on therapists encouraging children to re-enact traumatic incidents and to play them out using symbolic substitutions in safe and realistic ways until their frustration, anxiety, or guilt were replaced by appropriate problem-solving.

At the other end of the continuum of therapeutic activity-passivity, Carl Rogers's nondirective therapy served as the basis for the child-centered play therapy movement, which has been further developed, most notably by Axline (1947) and Landreth (2001) during the second half of the twentieth century. This approach places the responsibility for the direction of the therapeutic process in the hands of the child. This faith in the child's ability to make choices, determine his or her play, and control the pace of the therapeutic process emanates from a position of great respect for the child. This respect, along with a genuine desire to accept the child where he or she is, is apparent to the child through the undivided attention of the therapist on him or her and a conveyance of wanting to understand the child via reflections of content and feeling and minimal limit-setting.

It is important to note that play therapy's roots reach far back into the past and are multidisciplinary in nature. Additional contributions related to appropriate settings for the practice of play therapy with individuals versus group formats, the use of parents and teachers as therapeutic agents, and specific play therapy techniques also play a role in the evolution of play therapy. There is no simple way to replicate, condense, or copy the historical, theoretical, and therapeutic background as found in O'Connor (2000). The reader interested in this topic should consult that source above any other for a thorough review of the history of play therapy.

WHAT IS PLAY THERAPY TODAY?

Just as medical interventions are shaped over time, play therapy has evolved into a specialized way of working with children who are experiencing psychological, situational, and behavioral difficulties. Dr. Garry Landreth, founder of the Center for Play Therapy at the University of North Texas, believes that "children must be approached and understood from a developmental perspective." (Landreth 2001, p. 9). Because children are not adults, mental health practitioners must utilize therapeutic approaches that are developmentally appropriate to children's unique levels of cognitive, language, and interpersonal growth, to name a few of the dimensions involved. In very general terms, play therapy consists of a mental health professional in a room full of toys playing or observing the play of a child and commenting on what the child does or says. More specifically, the Association for Play Therapy (APT) states that play therapy is defined as

> the systematic use of a theoretical model to establish an interpersonal process wherein trained play therapists use the therapeutic powers of play to help clients prevent or resolve psychosocial difficulties and achieve optimal growth and development. (Association for Play Therapy [APT], 1977)

The question here arises: "Which theoretical model?" An answer to this question will be attempted in Chapter 19 of this volume.

THEORETICAL MODELS OF PLAY THERAPY

APT's definition of play therapy answers the "what is play therapy?" question, but it remains ambiguous in terms of "how" play therapy is implemented. Play therapists use theoretical models to guide their assessment of children, plan courses of treatment, and make decisions about the direct interventions (e.g., nondirective play, structured group play therapy, sandtray therapy, art therapy, bibliotherapy) and indirect interventions (e.g., parent consultation, filial therapy, Kinder Training) they use on behalf of their child clients inside and outside of the session. The "how" depends in large part on the theoretical orientation from which the play therapist works, and these different approaches can manifest differently in the playroom.

Carmichael (2006) states that a play therapist's choice of theoretical orientation is based on his or her beliefs about what contributes to personality development, the play therapist's role in the helping process, what contributes to and reinforces presenting concerns, what the course of treatment should look like, whether intervention should be directive or nondirective, and other questions. Wynne and White (in press) believe that using a theory to guide therapeutic practice is similar to a motorist using a Global Positioning System (GPS) receiver, which provides information about where a motorist is, the path that got him or her to that point, and instructions for how to get to the next destination. Different play therapists can use different theories to make sense of a child's history, conceptualize where the child is at the present moment, and make decisions about how to proceed. For a thorough review of the major theoretical orientations used by play therapists, please consult Schaefer (2003). It is also possible to examine entire volumes dedicated to the theory and practice of specific systems such as Ecosystemic Play Therapy (O'Connor, 2000), Adlerian Play Therapy (Kottman, 2003), Child-Centered Play Therapy (Landreth, 2001), Developmental Playtherapy (Jennings, 1999), and Theraplay (Jernberg & Booth, 1999).

WHAT IS A REGISTERED PLAY THERAPIST?

The official APT definition highlights that registered play therapists are licensed mental health practitioners with at least a master's degree who have received specialized training, which includes a minimum of 150 hours of specialized play therapy education and hundreds of hours of supervised general clinical and play therapy specific practice. Practitioners of play therapy who are most prepared for this type of work with children have completed coursework and/or approved training in child development, personality theories, principles of psychotherapy, child and adolescent psychopathology, legal and ethical issues in the counseling field, play therapy history, play therapy theories, play therapy techniques and methods, and play therapy applications (APT, 2008). Note, however, that no mention is made of knowledge or information about the field of play divorced from play therapy, supporting our initial point of a disconnect between play as a field of study in its own right and the field of play therapy, also in its own right.

The educational and experiential requirements for play therapists are necessarily rigorous and account for the professionalism of the field and its effectiveness, which will be addressed later in the chapter. It is important to note that some clinicians say they "do" play therapy, but they have not trained or prepared in the manner described earlier. For more information on the specific requirements of play therapists, please refer to the section of the APT's website (http://www.a4pt.org) that outlines how to become a Registered Play Therapist.

WHO NEEDS PLAY THERAPY AND WHERE IS IT OFFERED?

James (1997) begins her text by describing the five categories of children who are likely to come to play therapy. She includes children who have (1) experienced attachment issues with their primary caretakers, (2) been inconsistently conditioned, (3) were born with or developed biological differences, (4) experienced trauma, and (5) experienced social or cultural changes or shock. Play therapy is an appropriate intervention for children who have experienced bond breaks with significant people in their lives; live in situations that are characterized by the confusion of conflict, addiction, and ever-changing rules; are born with or develop physical illnesses or disabilities that interfere with their emotional, social or psychological well-being; have experienced directly or indirectly the trauma of violence, abuse, natural disaster, or accidents; or have been unpleasantly impacted by the myriad of changes and transitions that naturally occur as part of growing up in society (e.g., moving to a new home, changing schools, divorcing parents, or death of a loved one).

Play therapy is utilized in different environments based on the diversity of issues that bring children to counseling. Play therapists work in private practice settings, community agencies, schools, and hospitals, and they respond to the unique concerns of each child client. The type of setting will have an impact on the nature of the concerns that bring a child to counseling, and play therapists will often develop specialized knowledge and skills for using play therapy with specific populations of children. For example, the first author has also worked with children in a private practice setting that focuses on helping clients of all ages ameliorate symptoms of anxiety and stress. In this setting, she might find herself combining exposure therapy, play therapy, and filial therapy to effectively help a six-year-old boy with a severe dog phobia. In a next session, a nine-year-old girl might work through her post-traumatic stress symptoms from being burned in a cooking accident by pretending that the sand in the sandtray is lava or hot tar and deciding which of the miniatures gets burned and which ones do not.

As one can imagine, hospital-based play therapists focus on helping children with the psychological issues that arise from their medical situations. School-based play therapists will often work with children who are struggling with difficulties related to the child's educational environment, such as learning disabilities, peer struggles, and teacher–student conflicts. However, children are usually struggling with more than what got them through the door. At times when consulting with play therapists who work in child advocacy centers devoted to helping children work through the trauma of sexual or physical abuse, the first author is reminded that they often work on their grief over the loss of loved ones, health issues, divorcing parents, and academic struggles *in addition to* the impact of being sexually or physically abused. All people, including children, are unique and multifaceted.

THE PLAYROOM, TOYS, AND MATERIALS

Regardless of the play therapist's work setting, he or she needs to have a space in which children have freedom of movement and the appropriate toys and materials to express themselves effectively through play. Ideally, play therapy will take place in a room that is large enough (12 × 15 feet) and has access to a sink and a bathroom (Landreth, 2002). For many practicing play therapists who have only small or limited types of spaces, play corners or traveling play therapy kits become viable options. It is helpful to have shelves to hold many of the toys from which the children can choose, and they should be at a level within easy reach. At minimum, the toys should be displayed in a manner that is safe, organized, and predictable, so a child can easily find the same toy when he or she comes back for additional sessions. Play therapists with smaller or ever-changing therapeutic spaces may opt to use a large cabinet or rolling suitcase to be opened up whenever and wherever a play therapy session takes place. However, play therapists on the move need to be careful to secure locations that will protect the privacy and confidentiality of their child clients.

Toys in the playroom should (a) facilitate a broad range of expression, (b) allow for verbal and nonverbal expression, (c) be fun in the eyes of the child or children, (d) be able to be used in projective or metaphoric ways, (e) appeal to children at many developmental levels, (f) provide opportunities for mastery and success, (g) allow for individual and interactive play, (h) be multiculturally appropriate, and (i) be safe, clean, and in working order (Gil & Drewes, 2005; Kottman, 2003; Landreth, 2001, Norton & Norton, 1997). The appropriate selection of toys for a therapeutic playroom encourages children to establish a relationship with the therapist, express a range of feelings, play out scenes from their experiences and relationships, learn self-control through limit-testing, and develop self-awareness and self-confidence (Kottman, 2003; Landreth, 2001).

According to Kottman (2003), toys should represent different categories, including "family/nurturing toys, scary toys, aggressive toys, expressive toys, and pretend/fantasy toys." Landreth (2001) provides (Table 15.1) an expanded list of toys that serves as a guide for what is typically found in a therapeutic playroom.

Multiculturally appropriate play therapists will incorporate items that are reflective of the cultures of their clients and are responsive to the clients' needs for safety, respect, and self-expression. Gil & Drewes (2005) offer several suggestions for how to prepare play spaces that reflect cultural diversity in therapeutic ways.

THE ROLE OF SIGNIFICANT ADULTS IN THE PLAY THERAPY PROCESS

Parents are the most important adults in their child's life. Parental involvement is crucial to accurate assessments and successful outcomes in play therapy. It makes sense for parents to be actively included in the therapeutic process of play therapy from the outset. They provide critical information about the child's developmental history, past and present functioning, and strengths and weaknesses. Parent consultation with a play therapist creates opportunities for parents to develop new ways to help their child be successful at home, at school, and at the playground.

The most structured approach to parent involvement in the play therapy process is the incorporation of filial therapy training, which was first described by Bernard Guerney (1964). When filial therapy is used as a model to help strengthen parent–child relationships and help families overcome struggles related to their child's social, emotional, and behavior problems, parents are trained to become the primary therapeutic agents, who learn how to conduct child-centered play sessions with their children at home. Training formats can vary from teaching many parents in a group setting to helping individual parents learn how to incorporate the principles and practices of child-centered play into weekly at-home sessions (L. F. Guerney, 1976, 2003; Bratton, Landreth, Kellam, & Blackard, 2006; VanFleet, 2005). Training can range from weeks to years, depending on the model and can be preventative or remedial in nature. The terms "filial therapy," "filial play therapy," "filial family therapy," and "child–parent relationship therapy" are variations on the same theme.

As a result of favorable filial therapy outcomes and an awareness that teachers are highly significant to school-age children, Kinder Training was developed as a consultation model to help school counselors strengthen teacher–student relationships, improve school behavior, and enhance academic achievement (White, Draper, & Flynt, 2003; White, Flynt, & Jones, 1999; White, Draper, Flynt, & Jones, 2000). While similar to filial therapy in its skills training, Kinder Training also incorporates a component that teaches educators how to conceptualize from an Adlerian standpoint what is happening with students who struggle in the classroom. Draper, White, O'Shaughnessy, Flynt, & Jones (2001) and Post, McCallister, Sheely, Hess, & Flowers (2004) implemented Kinder Training in school environments and published encouraging results, as evidenced by teachers who felt more skillful, prepared, and empathic and children whose problem behaviors decreased, adaptive behaviors increased, and early literacy skills improved after the intervention. Children do seem to benefit when the significant adults in their lives learn the effective strategies associated with filial therapy and Kinder Training.

PLAY THERAPY IN GROUP SETTINGS: THE MORE THE MERRIER?

Group play therapy incorporates the strengths of play therapy with the advantages of group work (Sweeney & Homeyer, 1999). Because the therapeutic process in play therapy is so grounded in relationships, group play therapy provides more opportunities for interpersonal learning than individual play therapy does. Sweeney (1997) believes play therapy in group settings promotes opportunities for children to

- Play in spontaneous ways
- Work through feelings on intrapsychic and interpersonal levels
- Benefit from vicarious learning, catharsis, and increased courage to try new ways of solving problems
- Engage in self-exploration and growth based on feedback from other group members
- Benefit from the limit-setting and reality testing that "anchor" children to reality
- Process concerns in the here-and-now in lieu of fantasy-based or repetitive play
- Try new ways of relating to others, practice new coping skills, and receive help from the play therapist or other members
- Feel less anxious or on the spot than they might in individual play therapy and take cues for how to behave in the group from other children

He also believes group play therapy enables the play therapist to make guesses about how the children function outside of group based on how they function within the group.

Group play therapy can be effectively utilized with children (Shen, 2002), preadolescents (Packman & Bratton, 2003), and adolescents (Draper, Ritter, & Willingham, 2003). However, play therapists will often use different techniques and materials based on the unique developmental level of the group members. Sweeney and Homeyer (1999) provide a thorough introduction to group play therapy, how it can be used with different theoretical orientations and presenting concerns, and techniques that are well-suited to play therapy in group settings.

ASSOCIATED MODALITIES AND TECHNIQUES USED BY PLAY THERAPISTS

Play therapy is one of the expressive therapies and, as such, benefits from its relationship to and collaboration with other expressive therapies. It is common for play therapists to incorporate art assessments and interventions into their work with child clients (Carmichael, 2006). Art can be informative and therapeutic, and it works well with children and adolescents in play therapy settings. Art therapy is a profession with a long history in its own right. For more information about art therapy, the American Art Therapy Association can be found online at http://www.art therapy.org/.

Sandtray therapy is also an appealing therapeutic modality for children and adolescents. It can be used individually or in groups in nondirective and directive ways. Homeyer and Sweeney (2005) provide a useful manual for play therapists interested in creating spaces for and conducting sandtray therapy as part of the play therapy process with children. Interested readers may choose to consult The Sandtray Network (http://www.sandtray.org/) or The Sandplay Therapists of America (http://www.sandplay.org/) for more information.

Entire texts have been devoted to the description of therapeutic uses of childhood games (Cheung, 2006; Schaefer & Reid, 2001). Game playing is a type of play in which many children happily engage; however, game play is inherently more structured and goal-oriented than spontaneous, free play if children are directed to interact in this manner. Games used in play therapy can be developed by the child or the therapist or purchased from a clinician who creates and markets games for therapeutic use. Therapeutic games can help children learn social skills, cope with a divorce, grieve in a developmentally appropriate way, or develop skills for living and learning.

Play therapists also integrate techniques that utilize symbolic play, movement, therapeutic storytelling, role play, music, fantasy play, doll and puppet play, and writing. For more information about the diversity of techniques that can be incorporated into the play therapy process, please consult Schaefer and Cangelosi (2002) and Kaduson and Schaefer (1997).

EFFECTIVENESS OF PLAY THERAPY

There have been some questions about the efficacy and effectiveness of play therapy (Russ, 2004), especially when it consists of single case studies (De Giacomo, 1999). The second author contended years ago (L'Abate, 1968a, b; Schaefer, McCormick, & Ohnogi, 2005) that play therapy needed more empirical evidence not only about its outcome but also about its process. Even though it is assumed that play therapy is beneficial to children, we do not know under which conditions and with what kind of children it works and whether play therapy is a preferred method of treatment rather than family therapy. Charles E. Schaefer, who has dedicated his entire career to play therapy, has not yet answered questions raised about who benefits and does not benefit by play therapy. Two recent treatises about play therapy (Kaduson & Schaefer, 2000; O'Connor, 2000) failed even to mention research as a possibility to learn more about the process and outcome of play therapy. Phillips's review (1985) of empirical research on the process and outcome of play therapy raised serious questions about the empirical foundations of this method of treatment. Early reviews (Millar, 1968) raised serious questions about its effectiveness.

The best that has been accomplished thus far to check on correlates of play behavior consisted of relying on videotaping play behavior (Noble, 1973; Tauber, 1979). As in the case with videotapes of psychotherapy sessions, coding and classifying videotapes is a time-consuming endeavor. Hence, not many participants can be used, and not many researchers can become involved in this type of research unless a grant is received from external sources. As a result of this state of affairs, playrooms in general, as far as these authors know, contain a less than systematic array of toys, selected on the basis of clinical mythology rather than solid observational and reliable evidence. Innovations in play therapy usually consist of group and short-term formats (Landreth, 2001). A possible corrective to the inadequate representation of research in play therapy may be found in Russ's (2004) recent contribution to place play therapy on a firmer empirical base. Reddy, Files-Hall, & Schaefer (2005) also serve as a helpful reference of empirically based play interventions for children that are preventative and remedial in nature, with the hope of using the "first generation" of play intervention research to support and encourage the "second generation" of interventions and outcomes (Gitlin-Weiner,

Sandgrund, & Schaefer, 2000; O'Connor, 2000; Schaefer, 1993, 1999; Shirk & Russell, 1996).

Recently, Ray, Bratton, Rhine, & Jones (2001) conducted a meta-analysis of the existing literature to evaluate all of the empirical research done in the field of play therapy, including 94 outcome studies in which play therapy was conducted by qualified play therapists or paraprofessionals, usually parents or teachers. Results revealed a large positive effect on treatment outcomes across modality, gender, clinical versus non-clinical populations, setting, and theoretical schools of thought. This meta-analysis produced very high mean effect sizes for the 94 total studies $d = .80$; $d = .73$ for 70 studies with no parental involvement; $d = 1.06$ for 28 Filial Therapy studies, involving parents, teachers, and mentors; and $d = 1.15$ for Filial Therapy studies with parents only and no child involvement. Overall, the findings support play therapy as

> an effective intervention for a broad range of children's problems—across both behavioral and humanistic schools of thought, in various settings, across modalities, across age and gender. (Ray, Bratten, et al., 2001)

(Interested readers might want to consult the World of Play Therapy Literature database, which is maintained by the Center for Play Therapy at the University of North Texas. Access to this database can be purchased at http://cpt.unt.edu/shopping/bibliography.aspx.)

It is important to highlight that play therapy effects were found to be greatest when a parent was fully involved in the child's treatment. These results indicate that parental involvement is crucial to the outcome of play therapy. However, there are still conditions where children would need play therapy individually and when it can be used effectively without parental involvement, including institutions such as orphanages, hospitals (Jones & Landreth, 2002), and clinics or when caretakers are either not present or are temporarily unavailable, including play therapy with child victims of abuse and neglect (Mullen, 2002; White, Draper, & Jones, 2001), children who have experienced trauma (Hutchison, 2005), or children who are discouraged (Draper et al., 2001).

PRETEND PLAY IN THERAPY

Four clinical examples of preschool children (three from the inner city) played hide-and-seek games with their therapist. These cases suggest that before such a self–other action game can be played, the child has to establish an attachment to the therapist and to feel safe. Feeling safe means knowing that the self that wants to be out in the world will be accepted and that the therapist will be an affirming partner in the child's actions. Feeling safe also means that the therapist's arms will be open to welcome the child back into the closeness of the holding environment. The fact that the children often hid in an enclosure suggests that the hide-and-seek game could enact a symbolic birth experience that is celebrated by the mother-therapist (Bergman, 1993). This example is the kind of accounting that has given a bad name to psychoanalytically oriented play therapies.

Doll Play Therapy: A number of recent projective doll play interventions may be used to investigate "young children's moral development, attachment [patterns] beyond infancy, and for predicting [behavior] problems" (Woolgar, 1999). These interventions have been implemented with high-risk and clinical populations to evaluate what specific factors influence the quality of projective play responses that may reveal what and how the child is experiencing in the time. "Doll play, and story stem techniques in particular, have become established as powerful tools for eliciting preschoolers' representations about their families or their socio-moral understanding" (Woolgar, 1999).

Sandtray Play Therapy: Sandtray play therapy is a versatile, practical, and relatively inexpensive approach to deal with a variety of problems at various stages of the life cycle. This is a major reason for including this approach in this chapter. It has already found its place in fiction (Kittle, 2005, pp. 123–132). It consists of a tray about $30 \times 20 \times 3$ inches in size filled with sand and in some cases with water; the tray is colored blue on the inside so that water can represent the sea. Individuals, couples, groups, or families can participate by selecting from a vast collection of miniatures representing people, animals, vegetation, buildings, vehicles, fences and signs, natural items, fantasy figures, cartoon characters, religious, spiritual/mystical personalities, military figures, landscaping, household items, foods, fences, and whatever is available in a miniature size that may be appealing to a wide range of participants and of problematic issues and clinical diagnoses. This collection can be visible either on open-shelves or in boxes, arranged systematically by categories that participants can easily observe, choose, place, and arrange on the tray according to either structured or unstructured, nondirective instructions from a therapist.

After an arrangement is completed, participants are asked to explain who the objects chosen are—that is, what meaning they are given, including name, age, and the relationships among themselves and with the immediate environment. Arrangements can vary according to various dimensions, for instance, people vs. objects, closed vs. open spaces, flexible vs. rigid arrangements, organized vs. disorganized, aggressive vs. pacific, empty vs. full.

Supposedly, these arrangements express something about participants and the nature of central and crucial issues in their lives, combining non-verbal and verbal modalities. This approach seems to provide an effective medium of communication, especially in expressing unexpressed, perhaps unconscious issues in participants' lives (Homeyer & Sweeney, 2005; Sweeney & Homeyer, 1999; Turner, 2005).

The reason for being cautious in describing this approach lies in trying to find empirical evidence to validate claims made for its therapeutic effectiveness. Nonetheless, on the face of it, there is no denying the versatility, practicality, and relatively inexpensive nature of this approach. Perhaps, one day, some researcher will come along to support or refute claims made about the clinical usefulness of this interesting approach. A session summary and a peer-feedback form, as well as an annotated bibliography, are available from Dr. Linda E. Homeyer (LHomeyer@txstate.edu). These forms might well compose the beginning of an interesting research program.

PROPOSAL FOR A VIRTUAL PLAY THERAPY PLAYROOM

The purpose of this proposal is to suggest a virtual playroom that follows a process model of play therapy based on results from monitored play therapy research (L'Abate, 1979; Chapter 6 and Appendix B, this volume). One objective of this proposal is to build an online play therapy room. There are so many supposedly therapeutic games and toys available commercially that it would be practically impossible for many teachers, school counselors, child therapists, and even pediatricians to be informed on the availability of these games. For example, in a single, representative brochure of creative therapy games (Western Psychological Services, 2004; see Appendix A of this volume), there were over 150 games and toys to be used for different genders, ages, intellectual levels, and natures of the child's disturbance. As far as the second author knows, there are seven or more other publishers who also produce brochures with as many other games and toys. However, there are no brochures concerning toys and games throughout the life cycle online (Appendix A, this volume).

In spite of a great deal of research on the process and outcome of play therapy, we still do not know what sequential process, if any, is followed by children while they are engaged in play therapy. A review of recent contributions to play therapy (Chethik, 2000; Kaduson & Schaefer, 2000; Landreth, 2001; O'Connor, 2000; Russ, 2004), failed to find references to

Table 15.1
Landreth's recommended list of toys and materials for the playroom

Doll furniture	Egg cartons
Bendable doll family	Sponge, towel
Gumby (bendable nondescript figure)	Soap, brush, comb
Dolls	Crayons, pencils, paper
Doll bed, clothes, etc.	Transparent tape, paste
Pacifier	Toy watch
Nursing bottle (plastic)	Broom, dust pan
Purse and jewelry	Building blocks (different
Chalkboard, chalk	shapes/sizes)
Colored chalk, eraser	Paints, easel, newsprint, brushes
Refrigerator	Play-Doh or clay
Stove	Lone Ranger–type mask
Dishes (plastic)	Pipe cleaners
Pans, silverware	Tongue depressors, Popsicle sticks
Plastic food	Pitcher, dishpan
School bus (Fisher Price type)	Truck, car, airplane, tractor, boat
Pounding bench/hammer	Dart gun
Xylophone	Toy noise-making gun
Cymbals	Balls (large and small)
Drum	Telephone (two)
Toy soldiers and army equipment	Blunt scissors
Firefighter's hat, other hats	Construction paper
Sandbox, large spoon, funnel, pail	Medical kit, Band-Aids
Zoo animals, farm animals	Play money, cash register
Rubber snake, alligator	Rags, old towels
Bobo (bop bag)	Hand puppets (doctor, nurse, police,
Rubber knife	mother, father, sister, brother, baby,
Handcuffs	alligator, wolf)
Rope	Tinkertoys
Empty fruit and vegetable cans	Tissues

stages of development in play therapy. Even a reference about its development (Cohen, 1987) failed to give any suggestion about whether there are any stages in play in general and in play therapy in particular. An outdated primer with contributions by the great theorists about play in the past century failed to provide a model of stages of play development (Piers, 1972). As far as the second author knows, the only reference about stages of development in play was that of Piaget (1951).

As mentioned earlier, the best check on correlates of play behavior was accomplished by videotaping play behavior (Noble, 1973; Tauber, 1979) and analyzing the recordings, an expensive method. A possible corrective to the inadequate representation of research in play therapy may be found in Russ's (2004) recent contribution to place play therapy on a firmer empirical base. Even in this source, however, no mention was made about how children progress through stages of play therapy, making one wonder whether it is at all useful to look for developmental stages in play-therapy, as considered in Chapter 6 of this volume.

The foregoing considerations and results prompted a revisit to the process of monitored play therapy based on a playroom built more than 40 years ago (L'Abate, 1964, 1968a, b, 1971, 1973). Perhaps the same playroom can be replicated virtually in ways that were very impossible to imagine that many years ago. This proposal would include toys and games that are available commercially, according to the theoretical model included in Chapter 6 of this volume, making it easier for professionals dealing with children to find the appropriate game and toy that would be useful in their practice (L'Abate, 2004). It would be impossible for most mental health professionals to review and become knowledgeable in all these games and toys. Mental health professionals dealing with children may be able to find this information online; the second author finds that the same process of classification is necessary for a systematic presentation of most games and toys.

For instance, in a review of therapeutic applications of computers with children, Aymard (1999, p. 310) concluded:

> Opportunities for research and publishing are legion in this burgeoning field. Psychotherapy outcome studies, reviews of children's software, and articles describing new ways of adapting digital technology to special populations are needed. Controlled empirical studies should contrast traditional play therapy techniques with computer play therapy. Although many of the articles in the clinical literature extol the merits of computers in child therapy, the evidence cited to support that assertion is often anecdotal in nature.

The experience and results obtained then (L'Abate, 1979; see Appendix B in this volume) are still relevant today in view of new electronic technologies and computer-based interventions for children (Aymard, 1999; Kijima, Shirakawa, Hirose, & Nihei, 1994). Perhaps, the same playroom can be replicated virtually in ways that were impossible to imagine not so many years ago, from what has been outlined in Figure 6.2 in this volume.

CONCLUSIONS AND RECOMMENDATIONS

Play therapy provides children with an opportunity to express their thoughts, feelings, and behaviors in a safe, developmentally appropriate way in the presence of a caring and specially trained therapist in a setting that allows them to use their natural language, play. Research supports its efficacy with a number of presenting concerns (Ray & Bratton, 2000; Reddy, Files-Hall, & Schaefer, 2005) across a variety of therapeutic settings, modalities and theoretical orientations (Ray, Bratton, Rhine, & Jones, 2001). These findings underscore the significance of play therapy as a therapeutic intervention for children. Current and future collaboration between play theorists and play therapists can only make this intervention more effective as these professionals work together to work for what is in the best interest of children.

16

PLAY AS REHABILITATION

We need to distinguish among the following purposes of play:

- Rehabilitation (a process of returning participants to a previous or higher level of competence)
- Recreation (that is a process of entertainment consisting of playful, leisurely distractions, social support, relaxation, and companionship)
- Therapy (as defined and described in Chapter 15)
- Education (the process of imparting knowledge and information about a given topic)

If these terms and "play" can be clearly defined, then the following list of issues or questions derives from these definitions (Martin, 1963):

- Does too much work and not enough play cause mental illness?
- Are holidays and vacations sometimes harmful to mental health?
- Does participation in athletic activities contribute to mental health?
- Is being a spectator also recreational?
- Can recreation be misused?
- What agencies provide recreational facilities?
- What is recreational therapy?
- Do hobbies contribute to mental health?
- Is there a basic difference between the play and recreational interests of men and women?

- Does children's play serve any functions other than pleasure?
- What is the fundamental feature of children's play?
- Do children's play activities differ according to the age of the child?
- Are play materials helpful to the child's play?
- What accounts for the marked change in school and playground equipment?
- Is it possible to tell whether a child is emotionally ill by the type of play?
- What is the basis for play therapy for children?
- Is recreation of value in a program for children with mental retardation?
- What kind of play is suitable for the child with a disability?

It is hoped that these questions and issues have been answered satisfactorily in chapters throughout this volume or by references that attempted to answer those original but by now outdated issues and questions. However, we need to be sure that we are clear about the distinction between recreation and rehabilitation. In some cases, these terms have been erroneously equated with therapy. For instance, there are various types of so-called "animal-aided therapy" (Fine, 2006; L'Abate, 2007), such as "dolphin-aided therapy," for which there is questionable evidence for their claimed therapeutic effectiveness (Marino & Lilienfeld, 2007). Animals may be a source of companionship, distraction, relaxation, and social support. However, help from them to change behavior for the better, as one should expect from therapy, may be limited to a few cases rather than to the norm (Allen, 2003).

Consequently, this chapter will deal with rehabilitation conceived as a professional (physical, occupational, psychological) relationship between an expert in any of these disciplines and a participant who needs to be brought back to or be elevated to a previous or even higher level of functioning. Particularly, this will be a special type of rehabilitation where play, playful, or play-like activities are used to help participants with disabilities improve their physical, emotional, cognitive, and relational skills. Within the wide range of psychosocial rehabilitation disciplines, mental health services for patients with multiple disorders of personality indicate the need to integrate this discipline within other discipline-specific services, such as occupational, art, music, and movement therapies, including vocational counseling (Richert & Bergland, 1992).

However, the evaluation of psychosocial interventions such as those included in this chapter poses many challenges to maintain a rigorous experimental protocol to deliver these interventions in a uniform format that allows replication. This replicability is especially important in recreational therapy as well as in any kind of interventions (Kolanowski, Buettner, & Moeller, 2006; L'Abate, 2008; Schaefer, McCormick, & Ohnogi, 2005).

ANIMAL-ASSISTED THERAPY

Even though the effectiveness of animal-assisted therapy has been questioned, the presence of a cat or a dog may serve to lower the level of stress on its owner (L'Abate, 2007). The most dramatic differences between animal-assisted therapy and nonanimal therapy seem to be rates of touch: touching animals during this form of therapy may add significantly to participants' engagement in, and initiation of, social behavior (Bernstein, Friedman, & Malaspina, 2000).

ART THERAPY

Art therapy is gaining recognition as a form of psychosocial treatment for both children and adults with cancer. There are at least three different areas of interest to this approach: (1) theory loosely pertaining to art therapy and cancer care, (2) descriptions of the practice of art therapy within the context of cancer care, and (3) reflections of art therapists who have had cancer. However, there has been very little outcome research about art therapy and cancer care. It is customary in the field of art therapy to write in these three modes, with a limited range of studies evaluating the claims of practitioners in this field. Consequently, one is loath to recommend this form of treatment if no evidence to support its clinical usefulness is available (Waller & Sibbett, 2005). A film devoted to illustrating the process and outcome of art therapy suggests that therapeutic effects can be enhanced when its process is specified in replicable stages. Though the film fails to provide convincing evidence of the relationship between the creation of art and the therapeutic transformation of the self, art can help painful memories to surface to a place where they can be faced and released, providing a means of dealing with personal issues (Rubin, 2004). Unfortunately, even though art and other types of release therapies may be useful, there is not sufficient evidence to satisfy a requirement of evidence to show what happens in a typical art therapy situation.

Although most therapies contained in this and the previous chapter require their practitioners to have specialized training and degrees, art therapy apparently may not need special expertise. In fact, art therapy is not sufficient in and of itself; recovery from illness must be based not only on art but also on act, just as social change can only occur when persons become part of a process of social action (Kaplan, 2007). For instance, patients with cancer and patients facing or recovering from surgery for heart conditions may be particularly vulnerable to depression and anxiety, with fatigue as the most prevalent symptom of those undergoing treatment. One could reasonably ask: What, then, are the art and the act necessary for these patients?

Fortunately, a comprehensive overview of similarities and differences among different "arts therapies, music, art [as in painting], drama, and dance movement therapy" around the world integrates research that tends to support them as ancillary approaches to medical treatments (Karkou & Sanderson, 2005). This conclusion seems supported by the research of Bar-Sela, Atid, Danos, Gabay, & Epelbaum (2007) in Israel.

HORTICULTURAL THERAPY

An innovative model program introducing horticultural therapy in a Veterans Affairs Medical Center included goals such as

sensory stimulation, social interaction and integration, feelings that [partici-pants] are essential members of a group, engagements with others in rela-tionships, opportunities for self-esteem and self-worth, and positive enjoyable experiences. (Abbott, Cochran, & Clair, 1997)

Lofty and laudable as such goals may be, their attainment through hor-ticultural therapy may remain a fantasy if no evidence is introduced to support it.

KAYAKING AS RECREATIONAL OCCUPATIONAL THERAPY

This approach has been applied specifically to patients with spinal cord injury, providing possible gains in meaningful time use and con-struction of an identity after a debilitating irreversible injury (Taylor & McGruder, 1996). One cannot help wondering whether the initial novelty of any different or pleasurable activity in and of itself may be sufficient in producing some lasting results.

LEISURE EDUCATION

Individuals who do receive leisure education seem to experience "higher levels of perceived leisure control [and] competence [and] life satisfaction with reduced levels of boredom," but no improvement in "generalized locus of control" (Searle, Mahon, Iso-Ahola, Sdrolias, & van Dyck, 1995). These outcomes seemed to have been sustained seven months later, supporting the conclusion that leisure education may pro-vide a process of fostering feelings of "competence, control, and a sense of independence in older adults" that may generalize over time to other life domains (Searle, Mahon, Iso-Ahola, Sdrolias, & van Dyck, 1998). This generalization *may* occur, but *does* it?

> Older adults with intellectual [disabilities] represent a growing segment of the elderly population in developed and, to some extent, developing nations worldwide. A considerable body of research has addressed this burgeoning demographic over the past 20 years. Although some variations appear within etiological subgroups, the biological processes of aging and related concerns (e.g., changes in [mental] status) are similar [to] people independent of whether a person [is intellectually disabled. The] unique life experiences of individuals with intellectual disabilities, however, introduce social and environmental factors and practices that affect healthy aging and quality [of life] but are less understood. As such, later-life planning is an accepted, although not always practiced, mechanism used and directed by adults without disabilities to plan for their [future] in later life. Planning for this life stage among older adults with intellectual disabilities, if it is done at all, typically is a parent/family–driven process with a limited scope of focus (e.g., guardianship, financial security). Later-life planning and leisure education, [therefore, need] a conceptual rationale to meld these two processes [through principles] and content elements that could facilitate the use of leisure education as a framework for holistically exploring later-life options and issues. (Mactavish & Mahon, 2005)

The use of a leisure intervention may help homeless women who are disaffiliated become less isolated (Klitzing, 2004). However, more evidence will be necessary to prove the effectiveness of any leisure intervention. Post-traumatic stress disorder may have negatively affected leisure life styles of veterans from the war in Vietnam (Harris-Strapko, 2003).

MOVEMENT THERAPY

This approach may include dancing, expressive movements accompanied by music, along a whole spectrum of participants ranging from completely functional to severely dysfunctional (Dulicai & Schelly Hill, 2007). A critical issue is whether exercise in and of itself constitutes part of movement therapy. Perhaps the difference between the two approaches lies in the inclusion and presence of music and rhythm in movements, whereas usually no music is present in exercise. Nonetheless, when physical activity is paired with competitive games in teams within and between hospital wards, it seems that the antisocial behavior of patients may be gradually lessened when bulletins and awards to various teams are publicly displayed. A table of suggested activities for more specific application to particular patient conditions is available, information that would allow replicability of this approach (Campbell & Davis, 1940). No more up-to-date information is available on whether this innovative, seemingly interesting approach has ever been replicated.

MUSIC THERAPY

Music as an intervention for patients with dementia seems to have the strongest research base. However, neither music, art, nor any other recreational intervention will work for all patients with dementia (Gerdner, 2000).

OCCUPATIONAL THERAPY

An understanding of leisure as an area of occupational performance that can contribute to an individual's personal and social development is important to this profession. The knowledge base of leisure found in other disciplines has much to offer in developing this understanding. Social identity and stereotype theories and symbolic interactionism suggest that leisure stereotypes may exist in women and could have an impact on their identity, except perhaps for golf (Taylor et al., 2003).

RECREATIONAL THERAPY

Therapeutic recreation traces its beginnings to 400 B.C. when Socrates and Plato first considered the relationship between physical and mental health. Centuries later, one of the signers of the United States Declaration of Independence, Benjamin Rush, M.D., advocated for recreation in the Pennsylvania Hospital, a psychiatric facility in Philadelphia. It was in the early 1900s, however, that occupational and recreational therapies began to slowly separate and differentiate themselves. The first federal Recreation Act was passed in 1926, and the United States Works Progress Administration began to distribute Recreation Division funds to recreational leaders at various institutions in 1934. Recreation expanded to serve various disability groups, including persons with developmental disabilities, visual impairments and amputations, as well as geriatric populations. Since the 1960s, therapeutic recreation has continued to grow and develop as a profession (Andrews, Gerhart, & Hosack, 2004). This field has grown to the point that there is a *Therapeutic Recreation*

Journal devoted to this type of intervention. Furthermore, it is now possible to link therapeutic recreation to diagnoses given in the International Classification of Functioning, Disability, and Health (ICF) (Porter &
Burlingame, 2006).

Recreational therapy, therefore, has the same foundations as any traditional therapy program and has shown benefits in every facet of human
recovery from trauma to illness. Depending on which area or areas of the
brain are damaged, brain injury can produce losses in movement, sensa-
tion, communication, intellect, and memory. The physical benefits of
recreational therapy may seem self-evident in practically any recreational
activity in which a person participates and can include reduction of
numerous health problems such as high blood pressure, heart disease,
and immune disorders. Other notable benefits claimed for recreational
therapy include improved physical health indicators such as bone density, heart rate, joint mobility, fine and gross motor coordination, balance,
and strength, along with reductions in secondary disabilities such as
decubitus ulcers and urinary tract infections (Sell & Murrey, 2006). Such
extraordinary claims must be accompanied by evidence before one is to
believe them (Colotta, 2006).

Despite evidence documenting the increasing number of youth with
emotional and behavioral disorders, gaps in health care services exist.
College students could provide therapeutic recreation services for these
youth in a non-treatment-oriented community setting. Of course, the
process of identifying potential partnering agencies and developing collaborative partnerships in alternative locations is still beset by potential
shortcomings, but the opportunities for the potentially successful use of
college students in this form of rehabilitation is virtually untapped
(McGhee, Groff, & Russoniello, 2005).

One special type of rehabilitation, cognitive rehabilitation, has been
attempted (White, 1999), but lacking replication, its feasibility for geriatric
stroke patients needs to be evaluated further. Severely mentally ill male
patients who participate in directed recreational activity, either alone or in
groups and with or without extrinsic rewards, may experience a significant decrease in the frequency of bizarre behaviors and an increase in the
frequency of prosocial behaviors (Corrigan, Liberman, & Wong, 1993).

REMOTIVATION THERAPY

Remotivation therapy was originally designed to be used by psychiatric aides in mental institutions to work with their patients in a manner
beyond daily custodial care. Since that time, remotivation therapy has

been used by people in several professions in a variety of settings. Professionals who make use of remotivation therapy include nurses, activity professionals, recreational therapists, social workers, occupational therapists, psychiatrists, psychologists, and more. Each professional contributes a certain aspect of his or her own profession when conducting remotivation therapy sessions. One thing that each of these professionals has in common is that each looks to rehabilitate an individual in some manner. This rehabilitation may involve some form of physical or psychosocial intervention. No matter what type of intervention the professional uses, the overall goal of the sessions is to rehabilitate the patient so that he or she can live as independently as possible with the highest quality of life possible. Therefore, when these professionals make use of this technique, a rehabilitative component is added to remotivation therapy (Dyer & Stotts, 2005).

CREATIVE THERAPIES

A broad spectrum of creative [therapeutic] approaches, such as art, play, dance, music, and drama, and combinations of those, [may be needed] to work with people who have been [traumatized] by experiences of sexual abuse. Many disciplines, including art therapy, play therapy, psychology, dance movement therapy, music therapy, psychiatry, social work, and psychodrama

are included in the process of rehabilitation (Brooke, 2007). However, none of the disciplines included in this spectrum presents evidence or replicable means whereby each approach can be evaluated. What is lacking in many of the approaches contained in this section and in this chapter is reliance on distance, interacting, and writing as a cost-effective, replicable medium of intervention to be added to any rehabilitative process included in these approaches (L'Abate, 2009).

CONCLUSION

A major issue with all types of rehabilitation briefly reviewed here lies in wondering how much play entered in such diverse approaches. Future rehabilitation efforts should be directed toward assessing how much play entered in the rehabilitation effort above and beyond after all other factors specific to a particular approach.

Part IV

Controversies about Play

Controversies about play exist and will continue to exist as long as play is present and practiced, hopefully for all times. Sometimes, one has to read between the lines to discover disagreements and even conflicts between viewpoints, orientations, and practices about play. Clearly, not all controversies about play are covered in this section. However, an attempt will be made to cover some of the most evident.

17

THE TECHNOLOGY OF PLAY TIME AND OF MEDIA TIME

Advances in the technology of play are controversial because we do not know whether this technology helps or hinders the crucial importance of play and its supposed benefits. Severe concerns have been voiced about the violence orientation of media and their encouragement of passive and inert behavior rather than physical activities and imagination (Ciofi & Graziano, 2003; Roberts & Foehr, 2004). Negative results attributed to excessive use of media and technology for play purposes may include increases in aggression, eating disorders, poor school performance, and decrease in social skills, including intimacy. These advances and their concerns are so pronounced that a separate chapter would be needed to cover the ever-growing literature in this area. Included in this technology are passive viewing of television and interactive play with electronic games. What was once considered play or leisure time is now considered media time (Frost, Shin, & Jacobs, 1998, pp. 275–277).

By the same token, technology could be a life-saver at an older age. For instance, technology may inspire activity in older folks. A pedometer, a mechanical device that counts the number of steps one takes while walking, seems to increase the amount of physical activity one takes. Individuals who were using pedometers and preplanning a given number of steps each day might walk about a mile more a day than they previously did. They might also significantly decrease their body mass index, which indicates whether weight falls within a healthy range, as well as blood pressure. Playing video games on the popular Nintendo Wii, which requires physical movements, may provide some exercise as well. Nonetheless, these games are not a substitute for real activity in a competitive game such as tennis.

> If technology hasn't inspired you to get moving, you might want to try it. It's fun to track how many steps you take from your kitchen to the car. And it's neat to watch a tennis game appear in your living room. (*The Erickson Tribune,* April 2008, p. 8)

Toys have been a frequent subject of contemporary claims concerning social problems. Rooted in our culture's long-standing ambivalence regarding leisure and its concerns about children's vulnerability, concerns about troublesome toys also reflect anxiety about children's increased susceptibility to nonfamilial influences, their growing access to toys, and an expanded toy industry, as well as an active social movement sector. "Typically, these claims argue that toys represent undesirable values and that children who play with the toys acquire those values" (Best, 1998). Parallel arguments can be found in claims regarding other forms of popular and material culture. Interactionists "should be wary of making or accepting these claims," because rather than treating children's play as a topic for empirical study, such claims "locate meaning in objects, rather than [in] actors" (Best, 1998). Video modeling technology, for instance, could be applied to "teach pretend play to children with autism" (MacDonald, Clark, Garrigan, & Vangala, 2005).

COMPUTERS

> The computer game industry has become the fastest-growing field in the entertainment industry. However, only a very small number of computer game products overcome the costs of production and generate earnings. According to traditional marketing wisdom, customers' preferences must be analyzed correctly to create successful products, and in the gaming industry such information must be considered during the design process. (Song & Lee, 2007)

Arguments against the use of computers in the classroom originally included their possibly disruptive impact, encouraging children to undertake solitary rather than group activities, thus inhibiting the development of social skills and cooperation. Their use might result in an "overemphasis on academic [preparation] at the expense of play and creativity." Arguments for the use of computers include more active learning, less mental drudgery, presentation of information via varied sensory and conceptual modalities, and learning that can be tailored to individuals. From these pros and cons, one can conclude that the computer "is a piece of technology that is not likely to ruin children but, if accepted and used imaginatively, [might] become a tool that [will] enrich" children's educational environment (Simon, 1985). A great deal of water has passed over the dam since these pros and cons were considered. However, these advantages and disadvantages need to be evaluated with actual outcomes rather than with simple opinions.

Apparently, research on young children and computer technology has shown positive effects on development. However, little effort has been devoted to issues concerning children's play with computers, including the influence of parents on their children's computer play use. Parents may differ in how they deal with their children according to dimensions of instructing, informing, and/or praising the child's performance (Liang, 1999). As computers become more accessible to early childhood classrooms, relationships between computers and play need clarification. A study performed in 1994 (Henniger, 1994) found that although significant improvements had led to more playful computer activities, the best computer software then available still needed additional refinements to approach the effectiveness of more traditional materials in stimulating creative play experiences. Since the time that position was taken, an incredible mass of toys and games has become available on the Internet and may render past attitudes about computer games obsolete (see Appendix A).

During the first month of introduction in the classroom, computers seem to have little uniform impact on the behavior of preschoolers and their teachers. Uniform effects seem to appear two months later, when less unoccupied behavior, less interactive play, and more parallel play occurred when computers were available in the classroom. This change might be accompanied by a decrease in dramatic play and by an increase in functional parallel play. Solitary or constructive activities may not be modified by computers, while functional activities may tend to increase. While computers may not promote solitary functional or solitary dramatic play, they may also fail to encourage parallel constructive or interactive play (Fein, Campbell, & Schwartz, 1987).

TELEVISION

Early studies of prosocial TV alone did not seem to find corresponding outcomes in preschoolers' behaviors. When TV viewing is paired with related play materials, this approach may tend to produce high levels of positive social interaction with peers and adults, of imaginative play, and of assertiveness and aggression. The inclusion of trained teachers in the process may tend to decrease aggressiveness (Friedrich-Cofer et al., 1979) but not to rule obedience and prosocial behavior (Bankart & Anderson, 1979). Exposure to prosocial programs such as *Mister Rogers' Neighborhood* may yield positive changes in preschoolers, especially for less imaginative children, in imaginative play, affect, concentration, and social interaction (Tower, Singer, Singer, & Biggs, 1979).

At least in India, increased amounts of time watching TV might be associated with decreasing amounts of time spent studying and playing in children between 6 and 12 years of age. Approximately 90 percent of the children interviewed apparently adjust their studying time to TV watching (Arya, Sharma, & Dhaliwal, 2001). Whether these results can be generalized to American children remains to be seen.

VIDEO GAMES

There is burgeoning interest in the study of video games. Existing work is limited by the use of correlational designs and is thus unable to make causal inferences [to] remove self-selection biases from observed results. The recent development of online, socially integrated video games such as massively multiplayer online role-playing games (MMORPGs) has created a new experience for gamers, [producing] worse health [and] sleep quality, with greater interference [with] "real life" socializing and academic work. (Song & Lee, 2007)

This in spite of greater enjoyment, greater interest in playing, and greater acquisition of new friendships (Song & Lee, 2007; Smyth, 2007). The negative influence of physical violence and verbal aggression in video games may have lasting effects over the life cycle (Frost et al., 1998, pp. 275–277).

Pervasive gaming, as this field is now called, has great potential as a learning tool and is a striking development in the areas of video games and education. The literature surrounding this field is vast. For instance, pervasive commercially available game systems such as Nokiagame and electronic arts systems such as Majestic use multiple media platforms, such as cell phones, computers, fax machines, television, and newspapers to deliver games in real time (Gee, 2008; Hayes and Games, 2008; Torres & Macedo, 2000; Thomas, 2006).

Specific types of disease-related simulation-based games, such as *Mosquito* and *Parasite,* may help achieve much-needed prevention of diseases such as malaria or dengue fever (Lennon, 2006) and teach information systems development (Martin, 2000). Of course, one needs to differentiate "simulation" from "game" when simulation is playful and when a game is serious (Meadows, 2001). The concept of "competitive fandom" has been used to describe the learning, play, and engagement of fantasy sports (Halverson & Halverson, 2008).

COMMERCIAL PLAY FRANCHISES

One of the most important developments in the field of play has been the tremendous growth of commercial play and game franchises for children. I will let Frost and coworkers (1998) give an opinion about them:

> Growing concerns for children's safety in playgrounds has resulted in national franchise chains of indoor pay-for-play settings. These franchise play environments are typically limited in play value. They emphasized profit over substance and entertainment over play by featuring junk food, birthday parties, violent video games, and gross motor equipment with little attention to creative play. The developers and sponsors of these mega-chains would be well-served by carefully studying the impact of physical play environments on children and implications of play for child development (p. 280). . . . The key issues in quality physical play environments are play value, safety, adult play leadership, zoning and layout, novelty and complexity, structure and realism, and quality and flexibility of space. Finally, the factors that influence the nature of play, for example, family life, television, books, and community experiences, should be carefully assessed to ensure that children have a constructive range of experiences to bring to their play. (p. 281)

Nonetheless, I was glad to receive an invitation from my 8 year-old granddaughter to take her to a Chuck E. Cheese as an example of this commercial enterprise that is slowly blanketing the United States. Where else can a family go to play, where both children and grownups can allow themselves to have fun? Many games require eye–hand coordination, speed, and controlled movements including strength. These outfits are successful because they fill and fulfill a niche in the American culture that is missing. It would be better to play there than sit in front of a television set.

SERIOUS GAMES FOR TRAINING

"A new wave of serious-minded games" is now in development in a variety of business, commercial, industrial, and even legal enterprises (Musgrove, 2008). Former Supreme Court Justice Sandra Day O'Connor, for instance, is overseeing a game that

> puts players into the shoes of a judge charged with sorting out First Amendment issues raised when a school [tried] to discipline students for wearing T-shirts with provocative messages. (Musgrove, 2008)

Three-fourths of 150 large U.S. companies were found to use games as training tools. Simulation games, for instance, are now used to train police and firefighters to coordinate during crises. Suzanne Seggerman, co-founder and president of Games for Change, argues that topics such as globalization, poverty, and the environment should not be tackled through game-like approaches. An online *ReDistricting Game* can be used to teach how congressional district maps can sway elections. "The corporate world has already taken notice of the educational possibilities of games." One successful such game, *Darfur Is Dying*, had at least one million hits online. As Seggerman concluded: "I do not think games have to be funny. I think games have to be engaging" (Musgrove, 2008).

A defense company uses video game hardware to make controls more intuitive for pilots flying drones in the Middle East (Wardell, 2008). Appelman and Wilson (2006, p. 415) listed and spelled out six characteristics of "all games":

1. Challenge: goals and tasks
2. Rules: instructions that govern how the game works
3. Interaction: the user's relation with aspects of the game
4. Contrivance: modification of realism to benefit game play
5. Obstacles: encountered elements of the game
6. Closure: an end to the game

These authors also list four expected outcomes that should be derived from playing these games (Appelman and Wilson, 2006, p. 416):

1. Increased skill
2. Understanding of the implementation of a process
3. Deeper understanding of relationships and concepts
4. Awareness of cross-training needs

CONCLUSION

There is no doubt that play has an important role in its various aspects, manifestations, and settings, from the funny to the serious. If there is anything to regret about all these aspects and manifestations, it is that there should be more of them.

18

What Teachers and Coaches Think about Play

Perhaps this chapter should have followed Chapter 5 about the influence of parents on children's play and of gender differences. However, while in the early years of a child's life the parents, especially the mother, are actively involved in the hands-on process of actively playing with their children, it is literally impossible for teachers to be involved directly with children on a one-to-one basis because of the many children present and the educational context of playing. Furthermore, in preschool and kindergarten, teachers can be actively involved perhaps because of smaller numbers of children and the requirement of playing being primary to the secondary process of learning. From the first grade on, however, learning takes precedence over play—assuming, of course, that play does not involve learning. Here lies one of the major controversies in the history of play (Caplan & Caplan, 1973; Cohen, 1987; Clements & Fiorentino, 2004). Here lie controversies about how recess and team sports become recognized in academic curricula as important parts of children's play. In high schools, especially in small Southern and Southwestern towns, high school playing becomes a competitive spectator sport for lack of other social amenities.

Moreno (1946) was one of the pioneers to advocate the use of role playing and improvisation in psychodrama. More than 50 years ago, he argued that the curriculum of progressive kindergartens for preschool children was limited to play, dancing, music, and singing. He felt that a criticism of this system was necessary because the problem of a curriculum for play schools needed to consider three elements:

1. The age-old habit of surrounding the child with finished playthings or with play materials for the making of toys encourages in the child the conception of a mechanical universe of which the child is the only uninhibited ruler; the cruelty and lack of sympathy that children often display towards living beings is due to the prolonged occupation with inanimate objects.

2. The curriculum must be partly enlarged by the addition of topics that are offered to the public school and high school student, to be presented and experienced on a correspondingly lower level.

3. Techniques of teaching these topics in accordance with spontaneity principles have to be invented.

Additionally, play may be part of a theory of play based on emotions, considering play as parody of emotional vulnerability (Lytle, 2003), as discussed at greater length in Chapter 19 of this volume. These criticisms were valid years ago and have made an impact in education circles. Whether they are valid at the present time remains to be seen.

The relationships between teachers and play curriculum vary according to two approaches: work skills versus free play. In the work-skill curriculums, children attend scheduled classes and follow prescribed instructional routines, whereas the free-play curriculum is concerned with the "social and emotional development of the child [through an] emphasis on [the] teacher–child and child–classmate" play interactions. The roles of teachers in each of these curricula can be illustrated from scenes from two different classrooms. In defense of the free-play approach, the adult's role in children's play is crucial. The "arrangement, interpretation, and intervention" by adults can facilitate, "encourage, and expand children's involvement in play" (Ariel, 2002). Consequently, it is important that educational curriculums for teachers include training in play activities to enhance teachers' encouragement of quality play. Play intervention training should include

> broadening the teacher role from *facilitator* to *participator*. As the teacher role expands to that of an active member of the play environment, it must [also] expand to that of communicator to the public on the value of the play curriculum. (Green, 1984)

Whether this viewpoint is still valid remains on the shoulders of educators rather than play activists.

Another moot issue deals with the relationship between school readiness, the ability to cope with the demands of teaching, and preschool play. Here, the teacher's role becomes crucial in determining and "ensuring that play is used effectively to promote school readiness" (Bredekamp,

2004). Teachers need to be aware that not all play automatically promotes school readiness, producing possible role conflicts among the roles that teachers need to play, such as promoter of motivation, referee of conflict with children and among children, facilitator of positive play experiences, and counselor for impressionable or special occasions such as children crying or hurting themselves on the playground. In this regard, encouragement of dramatic play seems related to "school readiness skills — self-regulation, higher-order social skills, language, and early literacy skills such as symbolic [representations] and print awareness" (Bredekamp, 2004).

Therefore, in this chapter I shall include what teachers think about playing according to the chronological stages included in previous chapters. Teachers, indeed, are a major source of information about children's playing before elementary school. After kindergarten, teachers may be involved as supervisors of the children's playgrounds during recess. Similarities and differences between Froebel (see Chapter 3 this volume) and Russian Activity Theory play scholars Elkonini and Leontyev in respect to the role of play in child development at preschool age fail to demonstrate which approach is preferable based on published research rather than just theory (Arce, 2006). The optimal classroom for facilitating peer interactions and fantasy play among middle-class preschool children seems to feature a low teacher/child ratio and partitioned special play areas (Field, 1980).

Recess time in schools is the time children can play almost at will. Its importance has many educational implications. To ascertain play opportunities occurring in schools, a survey of "teachers' attitudes toward play and provision of play for children" (Pellegrini, 1995b) in grades 1 to 6, found information about amount of recess time provided, ranging from 0 to 65 minutes with a mean of 19 minutes. The study found that

> Teachers from rural areas [seemed to provide] more play time than teachers from suburban areas, who in turn provided more play time than teachers in urban areas. (Pellegrini, 1995b)

Play time also seems to be influenced by the teachers' attitudes. Teachers who indicate generally positive attitudes toward play may tend to allot more play time in school. Teachers from upper grade levels, who are more likely to perceive greater pressure to provide highly structured academic instructional programs, may tend to de-emphasize the role and value of play, allotting less play time. Therefore, children who are given less recess time may also likely have teachers who report less positive attitudes toward play (Newman, Brody, & Beauchamp, 1996).

BLURRING THE LINES BETWEEN WORK AND PLAY

A new category of classroom learning activities contains elements of play and work. This new category blurs the lines between work and play, promotes sharing control of classroom activities, and encourages spontaneity in learning experiences (Cooney, Gupta, & O'Laughlin, 2000). As with many ideas, fads, and fashions in the field of education, this category seems in need of further conceptual and empirical evidence.

PLAY AS AN OPPORTUNITY FOR LITERACY

The word "opportunity" is used in the active sense for both the availability of play in children's lives and how settings are organized structurally and normatively to press for literacy activity in play. Literacy-play connections exist in two domains: (1) the psychological, which focuses on relationships between pretense and literacy-related discourse that occur in play texts, and (2) the ecological, which explores forces from the environment that press on children's literacy behavior within the play context. As practical implications of these connections, they could be applied to the creation of literacy-enriched play opportunities for young children, particularly in educational settings (Roskos & Neuman, 1998).

INFANTS, TODDLERS, AND PRESCHOOLERS

According to teachers' perceptions about the role that playgrounds may play in the play behavior of first year infants, gathered from questionnaires and interviews, playgrounds may play a major role in language and intellectual development with emotional maturity playing a minor role. Playgrounds may allow children to integrate themselves as well or better than infants raised without a playground (Rogers, Wheeler, & McLaughlin, 1977).

Wolfgang and Sanders (1982) developed a teacher behavior continuum (TBC)

> as an explicit model for teachers to use in effectively directing the play of young children. [This continuum] suggests a progression across a power continuum using the minimum level of control to sustain play.

Play is classified as sensorimotor or representational (including symbolic and construction play). Three teacher behaviors are presented to support this play: "directive statements, modeling, and physical intervention" (Wolfgang and Sanders, 1982). Typical examples of play situations found in preschool and day-care settings demonstrate how the TBC can add to the "teacher's ability to structure and facilitate learning while maintaining an open and dynamic play environment" (Wolfgang and Sanders, 1982). It will be important to check on whether this approach has been applied by teachers or whether it was a one-shot one-time deal lost in the vast literature on teacher training for play activities.

To integrate Piaget's (1962), Vygotsky's (Chapter 3 this volume), and Erikson's (Chapter 3 this volume) theories about oral language acquisition, emergent literacy, and developmental play, a process approach to teaching and learning in preschool years is suggested. This approach involves child-initiated play in a prepared environment with social interaction and mediation as the media to encourage the formation of symbolic mental representations. Once symbolic representations are acquired, the processes of decentralization, decontextualization, and integration can be stressed and the physical, intellectual, emotional, and social growth of the preoperational child might be facilitated (Lauritzen, 1992). This suggestion sounds plausible, but where is the evidence that it has been implemented?

Teachers tended to report difficulties in distinguishing playful from real fighting for about one-third of 20 videos of fighting episodes. They also thought that play fighting was about twice as frequent as real fighting and that nearly one-third of play fighting episodes would turn into real fighting. Teachers tended to agree with children about the nature of episodes. These results indicate that there may be disagreements among teachers, children, and outside observers concerning playful and real fights (Schafer & Smith, 1996).

"The nature, frequency, and patterns of preschoolers' sexual play and behavior" are of concern to teachers as well as parents (Davies, Glaser, & Kossoff, 2000). Teachers reported about

> children's curiosity about genitalia, looking and limited touching were more commonly observed, and drawing or modeling of genitalia and simulating sexual intercourse were also reported. Children inserting anything into another child and oral–genital contact [were] rarely observed

but they were also at the highest level of concern, leading to interventions (Davies, Glaser, & Kossoff, 2000).

ELEMENTARY SCHOOL

There are a variety of playlike strategies that teachers can implement to control and improve disruptive behavior in the classroom; one is humor, the other is the Good Behavior Game (GBG; Embry, 2002). When discipline becomes a problem, humor as play interactions may provide stability and a platform in which teachers may gain more respect from children who do not wish to damage the relationship that has been already established. The language of "humor as play" could have the potential to become a powerful tool for teaching in ways that have not been tapped by traditional teaching methods (Fitzsimmons & McKennzie, 2003).

> A "behavioral vaccine" provides an inoculation against morbidity or mortality, impacting physical, mental, or behavior disorders. (Embry, 2002)

A simple behavioral strategy such as the GBG reinforces inhibition of classroom aggressive, impulsive, and disruptive behavior in a group context and "has substantial previous research to consider its use" in the classroom (Embry, 2002). The GBG is the only classroom practice that has been documented to produce long-term effects, including lowering the "incidence of substance [abuse], antisocial behavior, and other adverse developmental [and] social consequences, [with] very favorable cost-effectiveness ratios" (Embry, 2002). This method should be part of any curriculum to teach teachers how to deal with aggressive and disruptive children at any age.

Another school-based short-term intervention for teaching isolated children how to engage in play with other children involves (1) teaching children how to recognize whether a group is open to newcomers, (2) getting them to compile ideas for entering a group, (3) role playing, and (4) having them practice on the playground. This technique has been used with impulsive third-grade boys, fifth-grade boys with attention deficit disorder and aggressive behaviors, shy fifth-grade girls, and elementary-age language/learning disabled students in a self-contained classroom (Mackle, 1987). If this type of intervention has been replicated elsewhere, then it would be worthy of comparison with the GBG. However, if no replication exists, then the GBG is recommended over any other approach.

MIDDLE SCHOOL

The present author was not able to find relevant references concerning the functions of teachers or coaches at the middle school age level. That conclusion does not mean that references do not exist.

HIGH SCHOOL COACHES

A coach's gender and sport team membership may determine how much self-disclosing behavior will occur. High school girls disclosed the same amount to either male or female coaches but less than what they would disclose to their parents or to friends of either gender. Girls in cross-country teams seem to disclose more than those on gymnastic, volleyball, and basketball teams. Topics of disclosure to female coaches seem to be primarily concerned with self-concept development and role clarification, whereas topics of disclosure to male coaches seemed primarily concerned with school matters and interactions with significant males. Although the amount of disclosure to a female coach might be positively correlated with the athlete's disclosure to strangers, disclosure to a male coach might be positively correlated with her disclosure to friends (Officer & Rosenfeld, 1985). Apparently, desirable qualities provided by coaches seem unrelated to gender, age, or sport membership (Chen & Rikli, 2003).

Many coaches use at least some of the principles of coaching from sports psychology, even though their students may not be aware or know which skill is being used in the coaching process. Furthermore, students might not know that they could be practicing the same skill the coach is using, so that they can apply it to themselves. A written curriculum based on science could supply coaches with written goals and benchmarks so that all coaches could be working toward the same goal of producing a successful outcome, just as in any other academic department functions. The written nature of this curriculum allows its replication and evaluation from coaches who might not have followed explicit guidelines and criteria thus far (Lyons, 2001).

REFEREES

Apparently "college basketball referees [seem to] call a significantly higher number of fouls against a team that is leading a game when the game is televised" regionally, perhaps promoting "dramatic suspense to attract and maintain television viewers" (Thu et al., 2002).

CONCLUSION

This chapter has barely covered a variety of topics that constitute the distal rather than proximal context of play. How is one able to cover so many topics without any organizing framework or even theory? An answer to this question will be attempted in the next chapter of this volume.

Part V

CONCLUSION

19

A HIERARCHICAL THEORY OF PLAY COMPETENCE

It is proposed that the theories of the function of play, especially those emphasizing mastery of the environment, mastery of painful experience, and pleasure in function, should be uniformly extended to include play activity throughout the life of the individual and not limited to childhood or special categories of adults.

(Adatto, 1964, p. 839)

[A] play theory that is only about progress and deals only with some small part of the population (children) could hardly claim to be an encompassing one ... A play theory of any comprehensiveness must grasp this strange companionship of the very young and the very old, the first waiting to begin and the second to finish.

(Sutton-Smith, 1997, p. 48)

With Sutton-Smith (1997), I do not believe that we can or should have a theory of play separate and independent from a theory of behavior and human relationships. The reason why a theory of play does not fully exist as yet or has not yet been found satisfactory is because there might have not been an existing validated theory of relational competence wide enough and deep enough to encompass play. Furthermore, we cannot have a theory, even though past theories have done so, about human behavior and relationships separate from their proximal and distal environment (Lytle, 2003), family, friends, and neighbors. As noted in

Chapter 3 of this volume, most personality theories have not included play in their formulations, with the exception of psychoanalytic explanations such as Erikson; as a whole, play theorists have not been included in communication, personality, or relationship theories to describe and explain play. Why? Perhaps, because most theorists in these three different disciplines apparently do not value play sufficiently to include it as an important aspect of communication, personality, and relationship development and socialization, which I have consistently emphasized (L'Abate, 1994; 2005, pp. 148–150).

Consequently, this concluding chapter will attempt to include, describe and perhaps explain, play within the hierarchical framework of relational competence theory, which has been validated from its inception independently (L'Abate, in press b), indirectly, and directly in its sixteen models (L'Abate, 2005, 2008, in press b; L'Abate, Cusinato, Maino, Colesso, & Scilletta, in press; L'Abate & Cusinato, 2007; L'Abate & De Giacomo, 2003).

DEFINITIONS OF TERMS

The four terms in the phrase "hierarchical theory of relational competence," of which three occur in this chapter's title, need to be defined to make sure of what is meant by each term as it applies to play:

Hierarchical: Hierarchy means a layered structure similar to the table of organization of any political, industrial, military, or commercial enterprise (Table 19.1) with its (1) top level (like the president or chief operating officer), in this case Play itself; (2) two "vice-presidents," Toys and Games; (3) six "managers," Age, Gender, Socioeconomic Status (SES), Culture, Ethnic Origin, and Play Competence (which is elaborated in Table 19.2), which set the constraints and the nature of toys and games; (4) at a lower level, categories as to who, if anyone, dictates and supervises how a toy or game is to be played, ranging from free play with no instructions whatever, through written instructions, suggestions, and guidelines, sometimes coupled with examples of how the game should be played, to definite rules and regulations about the constraints of the game, complete with uniformed officials with standard signals to indicate fouls or errors; (5) categories of indoor and outdoor play; (6) whether the play should be solitary or social, with some games, such as those on the Internet listed in Appendix A, that can be played both by oneself or with one or multiple other players; and (7) finally, illustrative lists of the enormous varieties of toys and games available these days that fit into the bottom of this hierarchy. I have not attempted to include all the possible toys and games available, because it would take more space than could be allotted to it.

Table 19.1
A Hierarchical Framework for Play Behavior

Level 1.		Play		
Level 2.	Toys		Games*	
Level 3.	Age, Gender, SES, Culture, Ethnicity, and Relational Competence (Table 19.2)			
Level 4.	Free/Guided/Controlled/Refereed			
Level 5.	Indoor		Outdoor	
Level 6.	Solitary		Solitary	
Level 7.		Appreciative	Consumptive	Mechanized
	Blocks	Skiing	Fishing	Motor boating
	Build-N-Roll	Canoeing	Hunting	Trail biking
	Internet games (see Appendix A)			
	Nintendo			
	Social		Social	
		Basketball	Baseball	
		Bingo Football	Golf	
		Bowling	Soccer	
		Boxing	Tag	
		Cards (poker, bridge, etc.)	Tennis	
		Ice hockey	Volleyball	

*This list is meant to be illustrative, not exhaustive. For complete lists of toys and games see Sutton-Smith (1971) or Herron and Sutton-Smith (1971).

Once the reader has envisaged such a structure in Table 19.1, perhaps the hierarchical framework in Table 19.2 might make more sense, because now we enter into the theoretical rather than the concrete world of play. However, before we go any further, we need to specify what a theory is and what it does.

Theory: This term applies to any speculative body or structure of inter-related concepts or principles that aims at explaining or predicting a number of interrelated behaviors. In our case, play can be evaluated by observation, measurement, and experimental manipulation. The theory summarized here has been evaluated in many ways over the last decade (L'Abate et al., in press), but it differs from traditional informal and linear theories of communication, personality, and personal relationships to the

Table 19.2
Hierarchical Framework for a Theory of Play Competence

Requirements for a Theory of Playful Competence

Verifiability	Applicability	Redundancy	Fruitfulness

Metatheoretical Assumptions about Relationships

	Width[1]	Depth[2]	Settings[3]
Models	ERAAwC[1]	Levels of Interpretation[2]	
	Emotionality	Description	Home/ Playground
	Rationality	Presentation	School/work
	Activity	Phenotype	Transit
	Awareness	Explanation	Transitory
	Context	Genotype Generational-developmental	

Theoretical Assumptions about Relationships

Models	Ability to Love[4]	Ability to Control Self[5]	Both Abilities[6]	Contents[7]
Dimensions	Distance Approach/ Avoidance	Control Discharge/ Delay	Functionality High/ Middle/ Low	Modalities Being/ Doing/ Having

Models of the Theory

Dimensions	Likeness Continuum[8]	AA/RR/ CCCC[9]	Functionality[10]	Selfhood[11]	Play and Priorities[12]
a.	Symbiosis/ Alienation	Abusive/ Apathetic	Divisive	No-self	Vertical: Self/ intimates
b.	Sameness/ Oppositeness	Reactive/ Repetitive	Subtractive/ Static	Selfless/ Selfish	Horizontal: Settings
c.	Similarity/ Differentness	Conductive/ Creative	Additive/ Multiplicative	Selful	

Applications of the Theory

Models	Distance Regulation[13]	Drama Triangle[14]	Intimacy[15]	Negotiation[16]
Dimensions	Pursuer/ Distancer/ Regulator	Victim/ Persecutor/ Rescuer	Sharing joys, hurts, & fears of being hurt	Structure/ Process (Ill, Skill, Will)

extent that by being hierarchically framed, it contains models that can be verified one by one. To the extent that its models may be valid, so much more valid will be the theory.

Relational: Play is a relational behavior because it occurs between one individual alone and the individual's environment or among individuals through the mediation of objects used as toys. These toys influence players reciprocally and interactively just as players also influence toys by manipulating them according to their desires, fantasies, likes, and wishes. Additionally, players play with other players in a variety of relationships that need to be specified. Play, therefore, in and of itself, is an exquisitely relational activity, unless one were to consider internal unexpressed fantasies and ruminations as play. However, if these fantasies remain inside the player's mind and are not expressed, they could not be observed and studied unless they were captured by an external observer and perhaps elicited by a toy (Midley & Morris, 2006).

Competence: This term means how effective players are in manipulating toys and interacting with each other through toys and games. This competence can be superior, mediocre, or poor (Creasey, Jarvis, & Berk, 1998). If the term means how effective a player is, why not use the term "effectiveness" instead? The reason is that a player could be highly effective at one game and unable to play some other game. Play competence, therefore, is the sum total of effectiveness in a variety of games and may vary from superior to inadequate with objects and with people. Consequently, play competence indicates at what level an individual is effective in playing with other people and with objects, in this case toys and games. Competence arises or emerges from interactions among people with objects. In this case, those objects are toys and games, as outlined in Chapter 6 of this volume.

In trying to define competence I have been helped by Creasey et al. (1998), who conclude their search for acceptable definitions of competence by stating that "socially competent children exhibit a positive demeanor around or toward others, have accurate social information-processing abilities, and display social behaviors that lead them to be well liked by others" (p. 118).

These scholars went on to review theories of social competence and the influence of familiar and extrafamilial systems, narrowing them down to those already reviewed in Chapter 3 of this volume, including the psychoanalytic theory of Freud, the cognitive-developmental theory of Piaget, Vygotsky's sociocultural theory, and ethological theory. On the basis of their review, Creasey et al. concluded that "each of the theoretical positions discussed supports the idea that play and social competence are interrelated. However, each perspective highlights different pathways to this conclusion" (Creasey et al., 1998, p. 123).

If this conclusion is correct, any attempt to improve on previous theorizing would have to include the previous theories that lead to this conclusion. According to these scholars, "Play is a reflection of factors underlying social competence" (Creasey et al., 1998, p. 124), to the point that play competence and social competence seem synonymous terms. Factors contributing to play competence include (1) emotional attachment to caregivers, (2) effective child rearing, and (3) effective peer relations. If not synonymous with social competence, at least play is a facilitator of social competence (Creasey et al., 1998, pp. 123–132).

One important distinction in Table 19.1 relates to the separation between solitary and social games. Solitary playing, such as fishing, for instance, essentially suggests a denial of dependence on others, even though a coach may have been used. This reliance on an expert to help and lead one off the court indicates that there is not such a thing as "independence" in play. Even in solitary play there is still reliance on an object, be it a golf club or a tennis racquet. Therefore, playing, whether solitary or social, always implies a certain degree of interdependence (Fry, Kerr, & Lee, 1986; Murray, 2006), as noted in Chapter 11 of this volume. This interdependence is visible in how cooperative one is with a coach and with other team players, how much critical feedback is used, and how goal-oriented one is. In short, we need a theory of play competence that will include all the factors included in Table 19.1. This distinction shows the relative inadequacy of a simple dichotomy between solitary and social play because one could be playing golf or tennis by oneself but still be part of a team. However, up to the present, no better distinction has been made.

To achieve the goal of including play within a more encompassing theoretical framework, a hierarchical theory of relational competence will be applied to play (Table 19.2), or, to put it another way, a theory of play competence will be embedded within a hierarchical theory of relational competence. However, the theory needs to be explained briefly first, and then it must be shown how play fits inside the theory or how play is an extension or application of the theory.

A HIERARCHICAL THEORY OF RELATIONAL COMPETENCE

This theory is also hierarchical to the extent that is composed of layers (Table 19.2) of (1) meta-theoretical assumptions about past knowledge, with three models about width (Model^1), depth (Model^2), and settings where play occurs (Model[3]); (2) theoretical assumptions about play competence, including the ability to love (Model[4]), the ability to control self in play (Model[5]), levels of functionality-dysfunctionality in play (Model[6]), and the Triangle of Living in play (Model[7]); (3) the theory itself, composed of five normative models about developmental self-differentiation in play Identity (Model[8]), play Styles in intimate relationships (Mode[9]), play Interactions between objects and people (Model[10]), Selfhood (Model[11]), and play Priorities (Model[12]); and (4) applications of the theory to four specific topics: distance regulation in play (Model[13]), the Drama Triangle in play (Model[14]), Intimacy in play (Model[15]), and the structure and process of Negotiation over problem-solving in play (Model[16]).

The theory is relational to the extent that it describes and explains an individual's relationships with toys and games and with other players, referees, and observers, including family members and friends. However, this extension is different from the original theory in that while the overall theory is concerned with both functional and severely dysfunctional relationships, its application treats play as being more positive than negative, more functional than dysfunctional. There may be shades of positive and shades of negative. However, severe psychopathology does not enter in this expansion to play because, as we have seen in previous chapters of this volume, it takes a fairly functional individual to be willing and able to play. As Creasey et al. (1998, pp. 118–119) argued,

> Secure emotional relationships with caregivers were theorized to predict the child's active exploration of social environments, shape expectancies and perceptions of future interactions, encourage appropriate affect during social transgressions, and predict successful integration into the peer group.

In short, it takes a fairly functional individual to be able to play. Yet, play can be used to help dysfunctional individuals become more functional, as reviewed in Chapters 6, 15, and 16 and Appendix B of this volume.

REQUIREMENTS FOR A THEORY OF PLAY COMPETENCE

Any theory of any kind, to be called a theory rather than a paradigm or a model, needs to include models in a formal hierarchical fashion as shown in Table 19.2. Models are the irreducible components of a theory. They are the foundations of any theory, as the line employees of a company or the foot soldiers of an army. They are responsible for representing the theory, and to the extent that the models are valid, so is the theory. However, to obtain a certain amount of credence—to be believed—a formal theory of play must fulfill at least four requirements:

(1) Verifiability, (2) Comprehensiveness or Applicability, (3) Redundancy or Usefulness, and (4) Fruitfulness.

Verifiability: This term means that the models of the theory can be repeatedly checked by different observers to be related to reality and not to wishful thinking, fantasy, or dreams. Consequently, models must be evaluated by experiments and by controlled observations. Rather than simply answering the question, "How many angels are playing on the head of a pin?" the goal is to compare the answer with what the model says we should expect the answer to be. For us to believe in the reality of a model, we need to have different sources of information or viewpoints agree to the existence of that reality. Think about witnesses to a car crash. They may have different views of the crash depending from what direction or position witnesses saw the crash. However, all agree that a crash did happen. Accounts of how and why it occurred (for example, whether it was an accident) may depend of the point of view of each witness—the Rashomon effect.

Therefore, the theory should be *verifiable,* and possibly to a certain degree *validated,* to offer a needed, believable, and solid foundation to describe and explain play behavior (L'Abate et al., in press). More than one source attests to the real existence of that behavior. As we have seen throughout the previous chapters, especially Chapters 1 and 3, there are a great many ideas, meanings, theories, and metaphors about play. There is also a great deal of information about play, which in one way or another has been condensed and considered in the previous pages of this volume. Some information is reliable; that is, we can believe in its being real and valid because multiple researchers have confirmed it. Some evidence can be believed; some cannot or has not been replicated and therefore cannot be said to be valid as yet. That is why most results are qualified ("might," "seems," "could," "may") rather than verified ("are").

Consequently, if a theory is offered to describe and explain play, it would help if we could believe in the fact that the theory underlying play is provisionally valid and validated. It is real to the extent that different sources tell us that we can believe in it. The way models of this theory are framed allows both direct and indirect, formal and informal evaluation of each model for its reliability (we can believe it will happen again) and validity (we can believe it is real, it actually exists). Indeed, the seemingly abstract nature of the theory and its models relevant to play can be reduced to a very simple, concretely structured interview about play behavior (Appendix C) and a Planned Parenting protocol (L'Abate, 2009).

Comprehensiveness and Applicability: A theory should be comprehensive (inclusive) enough to cover and account for as many types of play possible and imaginable. That is, the theory should be able to describe and account for play in different settings—home, playgrounds, gyms, ski slopes, playing fields—and different kinds of toys and games. This is a tall order to fulfill, but if the theory underlying it is comprehensive enough, the hope of achieving such a goal may make it a worthwhile endeavor.

Redundancy: As already introduced on the requirement of verifiability, this requirement means that we should be able to look at play from a variety of viewpoints that, in this case, would be models of the theory. For instance, a child playing Nintendo, four men playing poker, two children playing ball, or a person climbing a mountain can be viewed from a variety of vantage points included in previous chapters of this volume and in the models of the theory. This criterion will become important when we try to describe, let alone explain, games and play. Another way to explain redundancy deals with overlap among different models, or correlations and connections among various models. For instance, play can be described and perhaps explained by many if not most models of the theory in ways that overlap and correlate with each other as part of a hierarchical framework. Examples of how this requirement is present in this theory will be given later in this chapter.

Fruitfulness: This requirement means that the theory has led to a great many experiments and research from a variety of sources. Relational competence theory (RCT) is still in its infancy in this regard.

Theory and Classification

An important function of any theory is to classify behaviors or relationships it claims to describe and explain. Consequently, one goal of this hierarchical play competence theory is to classify toys and games according to a verified and verifiable framework, as already discussed and presented in Chapter 6 (Figure 6.2) where different stages of play development also yielded a classification of toys and games that is also relevant to this theory, admittedly more related in some regards to masculine than to feminine aspects. Table 19.1 shows a classification of play behavior that is independent of relational competence theory to the extent that it is theory-free but connected to the theory through the necessity of encompassing play behavior along a major dimension of competence–incompetence.

Description and Explanation

Another function of a theory is description, that is, by classifying toys and games appropriately, in a manner that is reliable and valid, as done in Chapter 6 of this volume (Table 6.1), it is possible to reach a more adequate and satisfactory description of toys and games. However, how is description different from explanation? One can describe a toy or a game accurately, it can be photographed and audio- or videotaped, but does that description have anything to do with explanation?

Here the hierarchical nature of the theory comes into function with its requirement of redundancy. A toy in and by itself does not need to be explained. It exists and we can describe its color, composition, and texture as well as other special features. We can take pictures of that toy. Its existence is validated by its very presence; we can touch, handle, and manipulate it at will. As noted, toys can be also classified according to what was presented in Table 6.1 of this volume. Play behavior, on the other hand—how one plays with a toy and with other players—is more dynamic and much more difficult and complex first to describe and second to explain. Nonetheless it can be recorded faithfully via videos, as in various studies cited throughout the course of this volume.

Explanation, on the other hand, consists of looking at play from different viewpoints, and here the requirement of redundancy comes into play. It means that by looking at a game from different viewpoints or models of the theory, we are now explaining that game. Explanation therefore, will be considered once all the models of the theory have been presented, and the requirement of redundancy used to "explain" play. Explanation is closely related to interpretation, how one tries to make sense of play using different models available within a theory. For instance, in Chapter 13, I suggested that volunteering in old age could be interpreted as a form of play, admittedly a long shot, but a possible interpretation nevertheless.

Rather than explain the theory in greater detail, which has been done at length in various publications (L'Abate, 2005; L'Abate & Cusinato, 2007; L'Abate & De Giacomo, 2003) and validated repeatedly (L'Abate et al., in press), models of the theory will be explained in their specific applications and extensions to play behavior.

PLAY IN DEVELOPMENTAL RELATIONAL COMPETENCE THEORY

The assumptions and models of this theory will be explained here in their expansion to play and not to any other areas already covered in previous publications. While this theory has been applied to verbal and written media (L'Abate, 2005, 2008; L'Abate & Cusinato, 2007; L'Abate & De Giacomo, 2003), its expansion to play represents its application to the nonverbal medium, as requested by David Rosenbaum (2005) cited in

Chapter 3 of this volume. The models will be distinguished by super-script numbers from Model[1] through Model[16].

Meta-theoretical Assumptions

These assumptions go beyond the theory itself and include whatever knowledge has been accumulated thus far about human relationships, and by extension, play. Therefore, no psychological relational theory can ignore them, let alone play in this case. Furthermore, all models of the theory from Model[4] to Model[16] rely in one way or another to these three models. For instance, models of the theory will have to rely and to link to the five components of Model[1] because these components are necessary to function and to play. They are the foundations that determine the rest of the structure underlying them. Without them there would not be any models, and without models there would not be a theory.

Model[1]:

Play includes five components of functioning necessary according to a validated information-processing circular model:

1. *Emotionality*: This component includes how players indicate how they feel about a toy or a game, how they receive internal and external information that is experienced subjectively as being experienced literally in the gut and in the body (sweating, pulse rate, blood pressure) rather than in the head. This is the bottom line of our existence, how we experience playing, but we will need to add another model (Model[15]) to achieve a fuller understanding to what is meant by this component.

2. *Rationality*: This component represents how players think about playing, processing information received and how they plan to proceed in playing with this information.

3. *Activity*: This component includes movements and words expressed during play or participation in a game (i.e., what children do and say while playing).

4. *Awareness*: This component includes whatever and however players communicate how they are aware of and understand what is going on before, during, and after they play.

5. *Context*: This component includes proximal and distal settings surrounding a particular game or play.

These five components, abbreviated as ERAAwC, need further elaboration, because they constitute the bases for the whole theory:

Emotionality (E): This component represents what is experienced subjectively from internal and external events (Aizen & Driver, 1991). The infant is born with this component, as shown by crying and laughing. Two exemplary philosophical schools that represent this component are existentialism and phenomenology. This affective component, when elicited, includes dimensions of pleasant to unpleasant, intense to weak, and activation or arousal to deactivation or nonarousal (Blanche, 2002; L'Abate, 2008, in press a). When Sutton-Smith (2002) used the term "emotions," as discussed in Chapter 3 of this volume, he failed to discriminate between how we experience pleasant or unpleasant events on the receptive, internally subjective input side—what and how we feel—from the expressive, external output side, as visible emotions in Activity (Lytle, 2003). Pleasant or painful events are experienced first, and passing and processed through Rationality, they are then expressed on the output side as Activity. Emotionality is the internal experience of an event. Activity is the emotional expression of that internal experience that is visible and recordable. Sometimes feelings can be inferred from a child's play. However, it is much better to ask a player directly rather than to infer indirectly (Appendix C).

In reading Sutton-Smith's brilliant distinction between primary and secondary emotions, it seems clear to me that he commits the same error that many emotion scholars have committed for years and that I have criticized repeatedly (L'Abate, 1997, in press b): coupling, matching, and equating internal, subjective experience with external and visible expression without distinction between the two processes (L'Abate, 2005, in press a). Coan and Allen (2007) have finally corrected this erroneous equation by differentiating clearly between eliciting subjective feelings and experience at the receptive, input end and expressing emotions at the output end. We may become emotionally attached to a toy or game, but eventually we may have to discard it because it is no longer workable, useful, or appropriate. By the same token, we may become attached affectionately to old-time friends we used to play with in our childhood, adolescence, college, and adulthood. During play in preschool children, for instance, emotionality or affect was shown by happy expressions that lead to a greater number of cooperative episodes and language (Marcus, 1987).

This component, therefore, distinguishes between experience at the receptive, subjective input side, called here Emotionality in contrast to expressed emotions, which are seen in the component of Activity mediated by Rationality, as discussed below. Consequently, within Emotionality I would locate the "primary feelings" discussed by Sutton-Smith (Chapter 3 this volume), while I would locate his "secondary emotions" in the Activity component, with Rationality intervening between the two. Here, I would expand on DeMasio's (1994) distinction of primary feelings, which are directly related to cerebral functioning, more specifically, the limbic system. Here is where primary feelings need another differentiation, along a dimension of pleasantness to unpleasantness.

More recent evidence allows us perhaps to locate pleasant feelings in the medial orbitofrontal cortex and basal ganglia, while unpleasant feelings might be localized in the parietal and cingulate cortex (Beer & Lombardo, 2007).

Emotion regulation and emotion understanding are directly related to

> children's emotional competence with peers. High levels of pretend play [may be] associated with high emotion understanding. However, different patterns of associations [may exist between] boys and girls. (Lindsey & Colwell, 2003)

"High emotion regulation and emotional competence" may be stronger in girls than in boys, while "physical play may be associated with boys" more than with girls (Lindsey & Colwell, 2003). These possible trends may explain why children's emotional "competence with peers may account for associations between children's play and the quality of peer relationships" (Lindsey & Colwell, 2003).

These conclusions are supported by the possibility that preschoolers with adequate and appropriate emotion self-regulation skills in pretend play situations may show

> better emotion regulation in [daily] life. Regular pretend play with a more experienced play partner [may be] related to higher frequency of adaptive affect [i.e., emotionality], empathy, and emotional [awareness] in [daily] interactions. Continuing a pretend play game when faced with a negatively valenced event [could also be] related to emotion regulation in the wider context

whereas "effective solutions"—that is, activity—for the same event may not be related (Galver & Evans, 2001).

Rationality (R): This component includes thinking, intelligence, planning, and inventiveness or creativity, as well as social intelligence, what is called cognition in most psychological treatises. The major theoretical schools of thought underlying this component are psychoanalysis, rationalism, cognitive science, and theory of mind (Lillard, 1998). Piaget (1972) represented this school well. Rationality may vary from very limited thinking, as in quick-paced games requiring immediate reaction such as boxing, basketball, hockey, or volleyball, to a great deal of planning and thinking, as in such games as chess or bridge. Here is where planning, plotting, and discussing possible strategies to win over an adversary require a realistic appraisal of pros and cons necessary for a victory or for a successful completion of a game. The function of Rationality, therefore, is to plan, plot, problem-solve, and prepare for the future, thinking ahead of the curve.

Activity (A): This is instrumental behavior that can be registered, recorded, photographed, or videotaped, including mastery and creativity in performance and production of play (Blanche, 2002). Behaviorism and empiricism are the two major schools of thought that stress the importance of this component. Activity can be measured according to its frequency, duration, rate, intensity, and direction. This definition includes what have been referred to as "secondary emotions": what is expressed outwardly, verbally or nonverbally, and that can therefore be recorded and evaluated like any other activity. What is not expressed verbally, nonverbally, or in writing remains inside the individual and, if painful and unexpressed, may fester and damage that individual. Because they are controlled, linked to, and modulated by Rationality, secondary emotions might be localized in the frontal lobes. Here is where emotions can be classified as positive or negative according to their personal and interpersonal and contextual impact (L'Abate, in press, b). Play by this definition becomes an Activity that can be observed, measured, and reproducible. Play can be effortful and does not exist without some effort (Eisenberg, Hofer, & Vaughan, 2007).

Awareness (Aw): This behavior is difficult to observe because it occurs internally, unconsciously, semi-consciously, and often consciously, as a personal, internal dialogue, for example, when a player becomes conscious of errors that decrease the possibility of a victory and changes the play accordingly to correct the errors and increase the chances of winning (Stegge & Terwogt 2007). Specifically, the term refers to an awareness of the self "as an independent experiencer and agent . . . as a matter of degree " (Kinsbourne, 2005, p. 153). If the self cannot do it, a coach, if present, or other players, will perform the same feedback, corrective function. However, Aw can be evaluated through intensive interviews (Appendix C; Ariel, 2002; Blanche, 2002). The function of Aw is to correct and possibly change errors made in the past. It may be called reflection, insight, and, perhaps even better, a feedback function to change E, R, A, and C (L'Abate, 2005).

There are two types of Aw, one directed internally toward the self (Kinsbourne, 2005) and the other externally directed toward one's immediate (proximal) and past (distal) Context. Self-awareness is the crucial feedback system that occurs right after A, allowing for change to occur by going back reflexively either to E, R, Aw, and presently to Context. This process demonstrates the circularity of this model. There are really no major schools of thought that emphasize this component except for Eastern philosophies, New Age practices, relaxation, mindfulness, and the like, including the contribution by Terrace and Metcalfe (2005).

While R deals with the present and future, how to regulate plans and strategies of play, Aw deals with the present as related to the past. It involves reflection and consideration of internal processes, such as E, R, and A as well of contextual processes, such as Context—what is going on around a player. In relying on and relating to the past, Aw needs to rely on working, long-term episodic memory. Without memory there is no Aw (Terrace & Metcalfe, 2005). Therefore, one way to differentiate R from Aw lies in the possibility that R may deal with the present by planning for the future, while Aw lies also in the present but may attempt to correct errors by reflecting on the past. Here is where so-called meta-cognition, thinking about thinking, comes into play. Aw may also possess motivational, developmental aspects that have been reviewed in Chapter 6 of this volume (Higgins, 2005). Furthermore, to the extent that Aw relies on the management, use, perception, and understanding of emotions, here is where emotional intelligence (Mayer, Salovey, & Caruso, 2008) could be placed because it occurs in the present and in retrospect of what we do, including play.

Context (C): This is the immediate circumscribed proximal situation in which play is occurring, as perceived subjectively (Aw) by players involved. It could be organized voluntarily and embedded in extra-familial, extra-educational, extra-occupational activities along a dimension from little to a great deal of structure (Cutler & Danigelis, 1993). Contextualism is the major school of thought that has stressed the importance of this component, including the nature of the relationship between players and toys, players and games, and among players and how players perceive subjective physical and social environment, including observers (Lin & Reifel, 1999). There are at least four such contexts: (1) *family* as the context of intimate relationships, (2) *technology* as the context of fate (Pershing, 2006), (3) *education* as the context of growth and progress, and (4) the *marketplace* surrounding toys, as the context of ideology and power (Sutton-Smith, 1986, p. 245). The physical nature of the distal objective environmental context, or setting, is described by Model^3.

Model^2:

Play occurs at various levels of analysis, observation, and interpretation. The most evident level is *descriptive,* consisting of a *presentation* sublevel, that is, social appearance, the external social façade of impression formation—how players present themselves to other players or to observers, at first blush and superficially. This level is present and evident in pretend play, when children assume roles and parts that are completely made up (Ariel, 2002), and in the social presentational façade of adult individuals who want to make a good impression at all costs, even if this level is completely different from how they behave with intimates (close, committed, prolonged, and interdependent), the next private or phenotypical sublevel. Indeed, the ephemeral and improvised nature of pretend play does not allow parents to infer social competence from play scores on a Child-Initiated Pretend Play Assessment (Swindells and Stagnitti, 2006). On the other hand, engaging children in symbolic play while incorporating literacy content into such play can have a positive influence on early literacy development (Isenberg & Jacob, 1983).

The next sublevel, the *phenotype,* is private, addressing how players play and behave when no one is looking; for example, the nice-looking, courteous player at the presentational level may play "dirty" and try to win at all costs, even by breaking the rules of the game. The child who pretends playing Savior or Rescuer or Victim roles may be a Persecutor in the privacy of intimate relationships. This is the actual reality of how players play when, under prolonged interactions, superficial appearances disappear to show how the player and the game really are. That nice, courteous player, at first glance, may be a real nasty one to other players or to loved ones in the privacy of the home. At this level it is possible to deceive, when there is discrepancy between the presentation sublevel of superficial social appearance and the phenotype sublevel of what is going on in the reality as perceived by the player, other players, and observers—between what is real and what is not real.

This is the level where player may show their true colors, so to speak, when the pretend façade gives way to the actual person as shown under the stress of prolonged intimate interactions (Boyd, McLearen, Meyer, & Denney, 2007; Sutton-Smith, 1986, pp. 219–222; Vandenberg, 1998). Preschoolers who display more jointly constructed pretense in their play may be able to better distinguish between appearance and reality (Schwebel, Rosen, & Singer, 1999).

The next level, the *explanatory* level, consists of an internal or *genotype* sublevel about how players feel about themselves as individuals and as players: "I am a good/lousy player," "I am good at T-ball but lousy at soccer," "I am good at any game I play," or "I cannot play at all." This is the sublevel that has produced hypothetical or inferred non-relational or monadic constructs such as "Ego" or "Self-esteem." However, these inferred or hypothetical terms are nonrelational. Instead, relational terms, such as Emotionality, Identity (Model[8]) or Importance (Model[11]) are preferable. This sublevel will be expanded in most models of the theory because it is too important to leave it as it is here.

The historic *generational-developmental* or intergenerational sublevel indicates (i.e., explains) how toys and games are part of the family lore, as tennis was for my mother's family and eventually for me. This is where socialization, culture, and parental practices come into being.

Model[3]:

Play occurs in various settings that can be objectively observed, recorded, and measured in terms of square feet, width, length, or height: indoors/outdoors, or in homes, playgrounds, gardens, parks, schools, gymnasia, swimming pools, hills, and mountains, or even different areas of the same playground (Brenner & Omark, 1979; Clendaniel, 2008; Sandberg, 2003). Within these settings there are objective rules (Table 19.1) that regulate how a game should be played. For instance, there are differences in leisure activities between resort village and community residents (Miller & Buys, 2007). Skills in the playground can be also assessed reliably (Butcher, 1991). In the last generation, at least in the United States, there has been a growth of commercial entertainment centers where children and adults can play various games, possibly accompanied by eating (see Chapter 17 this volume).

Settings can be divided according to what functions they serve, as in the *home, school/work, transit* (such as buses, bicycles, cars, hotels, and planes), and *transitory* (such as playgrounds, playing fields, swimming pools, or gyms).

Oldenburg (1999) calls home the first place, work, the second place, and various types of meeting places, third. He left out, however, the increasing importance of school and of transit, the fourth place, when dealing with play. For instance, playing teams transit from one play venue to another in buses, cars, or planes. Play venues are temporary and transitory as well, while play takes second priority, after school, in childhood and falls to third or fourth in priority, after work, in adulthood. This model also includes the distinction between settings needed for survival *(home, school, and work)* and settings needed for enjoyment *(playgrounds* or *computers)*. The latter are settings relevant to play (Slowikowski & Kohn, 1998). As Frost, Shin, and Jacobs (1998, p. 255) contended, "The materials, equipment, and context for play (indoors and outdoors) influence children's play preferences and behaviors."

Even more specifically, years ago, town children may have preferred movies and bicycles while country children may have preferred hunting, horseback riding, climbing of trees and porches, anty-over, teeter-totter, singing, and whistling. The greater variety of play among country children could be explained by the smaller groups of children who played together and the less inhibition by ridicule, and also to the freedom from the restrictions of a city environment (Lehman, 1926). However, almost a century later, differences between town and country children may have disappeared due to the introduction of television and the ready availability of toys and computers in both settings.

Playgrounds for preschool children could be conceived as an expansion of the teaching environment in terms of their creative potential in providing opportunities for sensorimotor, symbolic, and construction play (Clendaniel, 2008; Hart, DeWolf, & Burts, 1993; Phelps, 1984). In Scandinavia, for instance, it has become popular for kindergartners to spend more time outdoors in the natural environment. Some kindergartens are organized as outdoor schools, where children aged 3 to 6 years spend all or most of the day outdoors. This practice seems to have positive effects on children in terms of increases in creative play, play activities, and play forms, including a decrease in sicknesses compared to children in traditional indoor kindergartens. The most evident outcome of an outdoor setting seems an improvement in motor fitness, suggesting that the natural environment may be a stimulating arena for learning in general, and for motor fitness training in particular (Fiortoft & Ingunn, 2001). These claims seem supported by results obtained earlier by Hart and Sheenan (1986).

Gender differences in the physical environment may be extremely important, as already reviewed in Chapter 5 of this volume:

> There is a growing body of evidence for gender differences in choices of play environments and activities. Boys prefer outdoor environments, and girls prefer indoor environments. Early exposure to particular toys and equipment has pronounced effect on differences in spatial abilities between boys and girls ... Boys' preferences for larger outdoor spaces influence the development of spatial orientation. In addition, there are play differences in the games and use of play space between boys and girls. (Frost et al., 1998, p. 259)

This model will be expanded in Model[12], where players and would-be players need to set priorities about how play fits into their lives and relationships.

Age, of course, even more than development per se, has a great deal to do with the choice of a setting; a school recess playground in childhood is quite different from a tennis or golf court in middle age or a bingo hall in old age (Pellegrini & Perlmutter, 1989). With age, the freedom of the playground and even of the classroom becomes restricted more and more, to the point of disappearing completely in high school, let alone college (Fantuzzo, Sekino, & Cohen, 2004; Wilburn, 1998).

When children report about their physical play in a playground domain, it is possible to identify those children who may lack in movement competence (Watkinson et al., 2001). In old age, elderly people may use urban shopping centers (malls) as places for exercise in inclement weather and for social exchange, where age, gender, educational level, and feelings of loneliness may be significant factors (Graham, Graham, & MacLean, 1991).

Assumptions of the Theory

The following are the assumptions that are basic to the expansion of the theory to more detailed models. Sequentially, even though these assumptions are based on meta-theoretical assumptions, they form the bases for models of the theory and of its applications (Table 19.2). They function as intermediaries between meta-theoretical assumptions and other models of the theory and its applications.

Model[4]:

The major dimension of this model is distance, defined by extremes in approach and extremes in avoidance, with functionality an appropriate balance between the two extremes. Distance takes place in a space that could vary from a tiny closet, a floor, or a small table to the whole universe (Lin & Reifel, 1999, pp. 161–163; Williams & Bargh, 2008). Play in this model involves approaching something and/or somebody we like and avoiding something or somebody we do not like. Distance from something or somebody can vary from close body contact and body movements that move one toward something or somebody (such as in dancing) to movements away from something or somebody (as in tag), or a toy, game, or potential player we do not like.

Teasing, disputing, and playing as aspects of interactions may be related to the use of space. Teasing, for instance, may occur when space is restricted. Disputing may occur as the "result of invaded space," while "playing requires shared space and varying levels of cooperation" (Voss, 1997). As a result of the focus on the relationship between space and interaction, "important power asymmetries [may] appear. Since boys are more likely to initiate invasions, and more likely to determine the rules [and terms] of play, they [apparently may learn to] maintain a greater amount of power and control" (Voss, 1997). Density controls space available, and how much space is available may be related to aggression (Ginsburg, Pollman, Wauson, & Hope, 1977).

Essentially, this model concerns how much space is available, from a closet to a football field, and how the player moves within this space by going toward and going away from something or somebody (Duarte, 2004). Even symbolically, an object is necessary to play, whereas an adversary is neutral. The game lies in the object being approached. Spatial density (how much space is available for a number of players), spatial arrangements and use are important characteristics of physical environments, as specified in Model[3] (Frost et al., 1998).

Consequently, approach could be indirect and neutral (as in darts), direct and neutral (as in football), indirect and symbolic (as in chess), direct and symbolic (as in marbles), indirect and actual (as in ball tag), or direct and actual (as in boxing) (Sutton-Smith (1971, p. 306. At a more abstract level, this dimension subsumes *community* or the ability to *love,* how close or distant we are from people, toys, and games we like or dislike and from each other emotionally (Sutton-Smith, 1986, p. 143). The importance of love in relation to morbidity and mortality has been reviewed by Carter (2007), Fricchione (2007), Ghafoori and Hierholzer (2007), Koenig (2007), and Levin (2007). However, love in and of itself is not sufficient. We may love someone to play with or toy or a game and want to approach either, but it takes more than love to achieve play competence. The more we love to play, however, the longer we may live.

Model[5]:

This model is defined by a temporal dimension of control or self-regulation, that is, play as *agency* and activity rather than play as *community* as in being together without competition and minimum value to performance, production, or problem-solving (Eisenberg et al., 2007; Sutton-Smith, 1986, pp. 191–218). The dimension of self-control is defined by two extremes: at one end there is *discharge,* as in impulsivity and disinhibition, and, on the other end, *delay,* as in inhibition and constraint (Kagan, 2007), as seen also in high or low delay play skills (Tanta, Deitz, White, & Billingsley, 2005) and low or high "arousability" (Fabes, Shapard, Guthrie, & Martin, 1997). How rapidly or how slowly does the player move? How intense is the game? On one end of this dimension, there may be immediate high reactivity in discharge of energy and strength, as in body contact sports such as boxing and hockey with little if any R. On the other end, there may be a strong delay or low reactivity as required by moves in bridge and in chess, with R being present and necessary to win (Freeman & Brown, 2004). Like distance, control is a two-way street; it can be attributed to self, where the locus of control is seen as internal ("I made a mistake and I lost the game"), or control can be attributed outside the self, as in external locus of control ("The referee was unfair and gave points to the adversary team").

Here is where gender differences should be noted, as reviewed in Chapter 5 of this volume. Normatively and stereotypically speaking, boys and men tend to discharge while girls tend to delay. In their extremes, these differences transform themselves, with adult men ending up in jails and penitentiaries and adult women tending to become depressed and relying on medication to relieve this condition (Zahn-Waxler, Shirtcliff, & Marceau, 2008).

Temporal aspects of play also include the amount of time required to enter complex forms of play, length of play segments, and percentage of total play time spent in complex play (De Long et al., 1994). Games that require special control could include Performance Reversal, Rule Complexity, Spatial Obstacles, Territorial Imagery, Ecological Territory, Immunity Symbols, Prop Imagery, Types of Props, and Spatial Deployment of Players (Sutton-Smith, 1986, p. 143). Play requires discharge of time and energy: it takes time and energy to play (Lin & Reifel, 1999, pp. 163–164).

Vygotsky (see Chapter 3 of this volume) assumed that socio-dramatic play in early childhood contributes importantly to the development of self-regulation, allowing us to explore whether the link between the discharge and delay processes differs between impulsive (i.e., high-discharge) and nonimpulsive (low-discharge = delay) preschoolers. Complex socio-dramatic play does seem to predict development of self-regulation, whereas solitary dramatic play may be negatively related with improvement in performance. The relationship between complex socio-dramatic play and self-regulation may be particularly stronger in high-impulsive children but not for low-impulsive ones. Consequently, there is the possibility that Vygotsky' assumption may apply especially to impulsive, discharge-oriented children (Elias & Berk, 2002).

The need for valid and reliable observation methods to assess self-regulation in children has been highlighted by McCabe, Rebello-Britto, Harnandez, and Brooks-Gunn (2004). For instance, children exhibiting high levels of peer-play interactions may demonstrate more competent emotional regulation, initiative, and self-determination and better receptive vocabulary skills. Positive engagement in play early in the school year could be associated with lower levels of aggressive, shy, and withdrawn adjustment problems at the end of the year. Children who successfully tend to interact with peers early in the year may evidence greater cognitive, social, and movement/coordination outcomes. Disruptive and disconnected peer play, on the other hand, may be associated with negative emotional and behavioral outcomes (Fantuzzo et al., 2004).

Model[6]:

Combining how one plays in approaching and avoiding toys and games with others and how one discharges or delays in playing determines the level of effectiveness and competence in play. In addition to evidence to support a two-factor model of distance and self-control, both Model[4] and Model[5] are supported by Ariel's (2002, pp. 34–41) contention that "Proximity and control are key concepts in the analysis of interpersonal relations" (p. 34). In this theory both distance and control are key abilities on which to base a description and possibly an understanding of play. Instead of proximity and control, Purcell and Keller (1989) suggest two dimensions of reciprocity and control, suggesting that the ability to love (i.e., approach) is based on reciprocity, because without this aspect there would not be a relationship, only a one-way street.

These abstract concepts are translated into play by concrete games in which both distance and control are paramount. Examples of proximity dimensions in play are degrees of territorial participation, as well as physical closeness ranging from wrestling on one hand to tennis on the other. Images of control are roles played and activities with set limits on what can or cannot be played (Ariel, 2002). "Structures in space" delineate the child's movements within the "spatial potentials and constraints" determined by the nature of the toy. "Structures in time describe how movements and movement ideas [are] strung together" in sequences as well as in how much time is spent on a particular toy or game (Young, 2003). The duality of our existence, the communal (Model[4]) and the agentic (Model[5]), is further highlighted by gender differences as shown already in preschoolers, with girls seemingly stressing communal values, such as lovingness, graciousness, and attractiveness, versus boys valuing action and physical power (Kyratzis, 1999).

If one balances approach–avoidance and discharge tendencies according to appropriate rules and regulations, the level of play competence and effectiveness may be quite high. However, one could play well in space but be too quick or too slow in control, decreasing the effectiveness of playing. By the same token, there may be a balance in controls and an imbalance and deficits in distance that may reduce play effectiveness. If there are imbalances and deficits in both distance and controls, there will be a reduced level of play competence and effectiveness. The nature and level of playing will also be considered in the next model. An attempt to relate communal and agentic motives to sports participation failed to find any correlation among them (Benton, 1999), very likely because both agentic and communal qualities arise from the interaction of the individual with a specific setting and not from internal "motives."

Model[7]:

The two previous assumptions, Model[4] and Model[5], separately or together (Model[6]), deal with the processes of playing without regard to contents. However, these processes need to be coupled with contents. To account adequately for play, we need a classification of contents—what is exchanged between players and toys and games and among players. These contents are found in the Triangle of Life, composed of the modalities of Being, Doing, and Having. Being includes Love (Model[4]) and Intimacy (Model[15]). Doing includes Information (rules and regulations on how to play) and Services (what needs to be done to accomplish and prepare for a game). Having includes Money necessary to play and to buy goods or Possessions (objects and equipment necessary to play).

Games, therefore, can be classified according to which modality is used for exchanges between players and toys, players and players, and players and observers. More specifically, play means Being (Presence) emotionally and physically present—focused—with somebody and with something for the sake of self, rather than Doing (Performance) or Having (Production) for the sake of self and intimate others. *Well-being* is composed of "health, harmony with spouse [or partner], harmony with children, self-acceptance, positive relations, purpose in life, and personal growth" (Sastre, 1999), all components that require the importance of unconditional love for self and intimates, regardless of IQ, SES, education, or occupation.

Payment to a player for playing means the game is no longer play— it's a job. In fact, playing is so important that some people who can afford to spend billions of dollars for the pleasure of playing. Think about the multimillion-dollar yachts brought strictly for pleasure and nothing else.

Being games require closeness with oneself. They represent solitary play and social play for the pleasure of being by oneself and together with loved ones, more importantly than what is being done. Examples include the walkers in Salamanca, Spain, circulating around a fountain arm in arm like the spokes of a wheel (see the Preface), or the group of women who call themselves Pigs in Chapter 1 of this volume. *Doing* games require *Performance,* as in the physical activity and movements necessary to draw, paint, build, or play competitive games, such as throwing a ball (Byers, 1998; Mobily, Lemke, & Gisin, 1991; Pellegrini & Smith, 1998a). *Having* includes money and possessions, such as the make-believe money in Monopoly or similar board games, or real money exchanged in adult games, as in gambling. Performance also connotes the *quality* of playing (sloppy, careful, cooperative, nasty, aggressive, etc.). *Production* connotes the *quantity* of how many toys and games are available to players. How realistic and structured play materials are do have an effect on how players will react to them (Frost et al., 1998, pp. 270–275).

> Establishing the ground of play entails an active reworking of the playground's material resources and involves a system for the production and exchange of valued goods. Character within [a] game is carried outside the ground of play in which it is produced, allowing for an account of development not as [an] individual construction of cognitive structures, but as the social production of human individuals. (Packer, 1994)

When Performance is combined with Production, it results in Power. Here is where toy companies and manufactures come into being (Aycock, 1998; Kleine, 1995). Here is where play becomes a business and is no longer play, even though toys are the basis for playing (Hohn, 2008; Pershing, 2006). Play by Being Present together with relevant others occurs for the sake of self, as in ritual playing of cards on New Year's Eve. No money is necessary, as in certain games made with one's hands. In Performing or Producing, on the other hand, something occurs for the sake of others. Think about the billions of dollars that are received in the toy industry (Hohn, 2008). Here is where power is paramount (Caplan & Caplan, 1973; Sutton-Smith, 1986, p. 245). It takes time and money to play: that is also the difference between play and work. The direction of money is reversed from one to the other. It takes time and money to play, but eventually it takes work to receive money to play.

Normative Models of the Theory Proper

Model[8]:

This is a very crucial model for describing and explaining play from a developmental viewpoint, as discussed already in Chapter 6 of this volume. Here is where play becomes part of one's identity as developed, sometimes from resembling important intimates, or childhood friends, or movie actors (Baumeister & Sanders, 1989; Jackson, 1998; Sutton-Smith, 1986, p. 205). However, how do we describe identity: "Who am I"? An important part of our developmental identity over the life-cycle is composed also of who we are as players: "I was a soccer, skier, and tennis player and am now a poker player."

Most literature on this subject still uses a dichotomy of similar/dissimilar to describe how we grow up learning to differentiate ourselves from those close to us or the games we play. Developmentally, we develop such an identity not only according to that dichotomy, but also according to a dialectical dimension of resemblance or likeness composed by various degrees of similarity and dissimilarity according to a curvilinear distribution (Cusinato & Colesso, 2008). This dichotomy is still present, especially in gender differences, as reviewed in Chapter 5 of this volume. The child starts with a same–different dichotomy between self and others according to gender. However, at the child grows older, this dichotomy differentiates itself according to a continuum of likeness or resemblance.

This resemblance varies along a continuum ranging from (1) *symbiosis,* as seen in children who assume the same role as their parents had as players, or the relationships that Tiger Woods, Maria Sharapova, or the Williams sisters had with their fathers, or children who follow in the same professional footsteps as their parents in play, as players or as referees; (2) *sameness,* when conformity is required by players, with no deviations or criticisms allowed, as included in Authoritarianism, Conservativism, and Religiousness (Koenig & Bouchard, 2006), which is true of most team sports and many games; (3) *similarity,* when players follow some qualities handed out by tradition or rules but do not conform blindly to external constraints (Wade, 1985) or else some games are similar to other games, such as Australian Rules football or rugby are similar but also somewhat different from American football; (4) *differentness,* when a player plays within the rules but adds an additional personal quality of being free from tradition or external demands, rules, and regulations, as in skateboarding (Beal, 1998), or when members of one team perceive themselves as being together in the pursuit of winning against the members of a different team; (5) *oppositeness,* when the player does not conform and rebels against traditions, rules, and regulations to do the opposite of and against what is required, as discussed by Myers (1998) and by Duncan (1998) and found in second-generation Mexican, Central American, and African American fifth-grade girls by Goodwin, Goodwin, and Yaeger-Dror (2002); (6) *alienation,* when the player is excluded from and plays completely outside of traditions, rules, and regulations, as in mountain climbing, which has its own methods and equipment but is a completely isolated sport. Developmentally, this continuum of likeness viewed initially within the dichotomy of similar–dissimilar may be present from the time children are in a nursery (Tsujino, 1978).

Here is where creativity in play comes into being, as a combination of similarity with differentness, when players combine in a new creation from parts that are similar but that are also different, as considered in Chapter 6 of this volume. With time, developmentally this dichotomy does become a continuum that is relevant to creativity in playing. It means putting together what is similar with what is different, oftentimes bordering on oppositeness, when one goes against the grain of established tradition and invents something new that has not be thought before. Think about the millions of dollars that Monopoly has brought into the United States worldwide as a brilliant, creative game that also possesses educational qualities. The field of play is now full of innovations representing the integration of past toys and games combined with some new and different visual and concrete forms.

This continuum allows us also to view biological, cultural/ethnic, gender, and SES factors as dimensions rather than just as categories, as considered particularly in Chapters 4, 5, 6, and generally in previous chapters of this volume. The developmental aspect of this continuum consists of how we learn certain skills as play in an early or even later age, as when

I learned to play tennis in my thirties, for instance. Dramatic play in high school may become a full-time vocation or part-time avocation, or a specific sport might continue as an avocation throughout our lives, or become a full-time job as long as age and health allow. Dramatic play in adulthood, for instance, is often based on early experiences in high school and even earlier expanded across our lives as a livelihood or as a hobby. I did not play the Greek landlord in *My Sister Eileen* or the Italian smuggler in *Three Blind Mice* out of the blue without prior exposure to being on a stage in front of an audience (Chapter 1). I had had experience as a player in early church pageants and holiday plays.

This Model[8] is directly basic to the two following models.

Model[9]:

Style in play is defined by (1) *preferences,* "the choices a child makes in regard to settings, toys, types of play, roles assumed in play and playmates," (2) *attitudes,* "the mood or affect the child exhibits, the consistency or variability of moods, and humor," (3) *approach,* the manner in which the child's attitude propels the child toward a specific play activity, including direction or whatever motivates a child to "action, focus or involvement in activity, and spontaneity in play," and (4) *social reciprocity,* "the amount of social interaction or 'give and take'" involved in what a child brings to and takes from the play situation (Knox, 1997).

More specifically, the dialectical aspect of the underlying continuum of likeness or resemblance, which is mostly below the level of Awareness (A) in Model[1], pairs Symbiosis and Alienation together to produce an Aggressive-Abusive (AA) play style to the extent that in this style the danger of injury and even death is the greatest, as in boxing, hockey, or mountain climbing. Pairing Sameness with Oppositeness produces a Reactive-Repetitive (RR) play style, found in most competitive sports not requiring harsh physical contact, such as Trivial Pursuit, Olympic-type wrestling, or tennis (Kagan, 2007; Chapter 7 this volume), while pairing Similarity with Differentness produces various styles: *Conductive/Creative/Constructive/Cooperative* (CCCC) as found in fantasy, imagination, make-believe, pretend, or doing something positively.

CCCC is the most functional style. RR is borderline to the extent that creativity is limited, especially in team sports, while AA could be conceived as dysfunctional. A major distinction between CCCC and RR (Traumatic) play was proposed by Lisul (2004, p. 56) from her involvement with children who experienced the war in Belgrade, Yugoslavia. Creative play seems characterized by (1) always being for fun, (2) emotional distance, (3) hedonistic quality, (4) spontaneous, (5) dynamic and full of movement, (6) flexible roles, (7) tranquilizing effect on anxiety and help in problem-solving, and (8) providing togetherness among children in a group. Repetitive play, on the other hand, seems characterized by (1) causing anxiety, (2) no emotional distance, (3) dark hedonistic quality, (4) being compulsive, not spontaneous, (5) being stereotypic and static, (6) inflexible roles and lack of creativity, (7) becoming regressive rather than progressive, and (8) causing distance rather than closeness among children.

The issue raised by this important distinction is whether there is the possibility of reactive play being positive or whether all reactive play is negative. The repetitive-reactive quality of play can be distinguished according to the differentiation made in Chapter 6, Figure 6.2, between aggressive and nonaggressive competition, where Reactivity and Repetitiveness (RR) are characteristics of games requiring aggressive competition, such as football, rather than nonaggressive competition, such as tennis (Land, 2003). An Abusive-Aggressive (AA) style is present in kinesthetic aggression, requiring harsh physical movements, as in hockey or football, while displaced aggression could be found in hunting. Reactivity diminishes with age, explaining why more games in old age are essentially passive, such as bingo (Charles & Carstensen, 2007).

This model is supported by Saracho's (1997, 1998, 1999) conceptualization and review of research about cognitive styles in play. She differentiated between field-dependent (FD), global and undifferentiated, and field-independent (FI), analytic and differentiated, styles in children's play, suggesting different ways to process information. FD players possess the following characteristics (Saracho, 1998, p. 242):

1. They "rely on surrounding [proximal] perceptual field"
2. They "experience their environment in a relatively global fashion by conforming to the effects of the prevailing field or context"
3. They "are dependent on authority"
4. They "search for facial cues in those around them as a source of information"
5. They "are strongly interested in people"
6. They "get [close to players] with whom they are interacting"
7. They "have sensitivity to others, which helps them to acquire social skills"
8. They "prefer occupations that require involvement with others"

On the other hand, they are easily aroused and more attentive to social stimulation.

FI players, on the other hand, show the following characteristics:

1. They "perceive objects as separate from the field"
2. They "can abstract an item from the surrounding field and solve problems that are presented and reorganized in different contexts"

3. They "experience an independence from authority, which leads them to depend on their own standards and values"
4. They "are oriented toward active striving"
5. They "appear to be cold and distant"
6. They "are socially detached but have analytic skills"
7. They "are insensitive to others, lacking social skills"
8. They "prefer occupations that allow them to work by themselves"

The bottom line is that FD children may tend to participate in social play activities, whereas FI children may tend to engage more in nonsocial play activities.

Even though some characteristics attributed to FI individuals, especially No. 5, 6, 7, and 8 may not fit, characteristics 1 through 4 could be conceived as prototypes for CCCC styles, especially when a certain amount of Rationality is necessary to accomplish a task, such as bridge and chess. FD individuals, on the other hand, could be conceived as being represented mostly in reactive games and sports, where immediacy and contextual sensitivity (Emotionality, Activity, Awareness, and Context) may be necessary, as in team games, where players have to react quickly and be sensitive to the playing of teammates and adversaries, as shown in RR styles. Both CC and RR do not include AA styles, which are evident in close-body contact and aggressive sports such as boxing, hockey, certain types of martial arts, and football, as noted above.

The repetitive aspect of emotional reactivity has been researched by Calkins (Calkins & Hill, 2007; Calkins et al., 1999), who related it to caretakers' style and who showed how reactivity does decrease as a function of age and caretakers' influence. As the child matures and becomes more dominated by cognitive (R) rather than solely emotional influences (E), emotional reactivity tends to decrease, even though this style remains perpetuated throughout the life cycle, as present, for instance, in physical rather than emotional reactivity in many team sports and later on in old age in tennis, hunting, or bingo.

Therefore, these play styles are evident in different games and very likely attract different types of players (Eisenberg et al., 2007). Tennis players, for instance, perhaps physically and rationally, may be different from players who like boxing or harsh contact team sports such as football or hockey. All three styles contribute to different levels and types of competence, requiring different skills, interests, and very likely intellectual and emotional personality characteristics (Charles & Carstensen, 2007; Saracho, 1998). Play competence, therefore, is assessed by how successful one is in one or in many games and sports.

Model[10]:

The previous models, Model[8] and Model[9], referred to processes of play without regard to their content. In Model[10] the specific contents of play are added to obtain five types of interactions: multiplicative, additive, static, subtractive, or divisive. Going back again to the model presented in Chapter 6 of this volume, as well as to Model[9], the CCCC style can be differentiated and split between *Conductive/Creative* and *Constructive/Cooperative* play. Conductive/Creative play implies a *Multiplicative* outcome obtained when a player takes the leadership in building a new original structure, toy, or game from existing materials, as in the building of model trains or Lego structures, and the creative stage of the model presented in Chapter 6 of this volume. These interactions show an additional quality of altruism, voluntarism, and helpfulness that make individuals involved in these interactions live with greater satisfaction and even longer (Post, 2007). Vaillant (2007) gives two excellent examples of two individuals who grew up from impoverished and even abusive backgrounds and whose IQs were below normal but who grew up to be "generative," going above and beyond their backgrounds to a constructive life as partners, parents, employees, and leaders in the community, including playing with their own children. Volunteerism in old age (Chapter 13 this volume) is an example of multiplicative interactions that could be interpreted as playing (Post, 2007).

Constructive/Cooperative play, on the other hand, is *Additive* to the extent that there is cooperative construction between a player and play materials with or without cooperation from other players, but the creative element is missing. *Static* interactions could be positive and negative. They occur when the same repetitive toys and games are played without any change in their processes or outcomes. Little if anything is learned. Negative static occurs when the playing becomes an addiction at the expense of other, more constructive activities and other people. The play remains the same, as in pulling the lever in a slot machine. *Subtractive* interactions include games based on adversarial positions, where one wins at the expense of the other, involving an "I win—you lose" process, as in any competitive sport. *Divisive* interactions are found in extreme games where the adversary has to be obliterated from the face of the earth, as in many electronic warlike games, where death or disappearance of the enemy is the outcome, and in the early Mayan and Roman games, where losers lost their lives.

This model can be applied and extended also to how parents, coaches, teachers, or caretakers relate to their children in regard to play. They can assume CC, RR, and AA styles producing different outcomes in their offspring or in players of a team.

Model[11]:

This Selfhood model focuses on how play increases the sense of importance attributed to self and to other players. Selfhood involves attributing importance to something or to somebody that is related to self and to intimate others. In team play, for instance, importance is bestowed when one player passes the cut and is included in a team. The reverse occurs when a potential player is not included in a team; the sense of importance may be shaken if not destroyed. There are four propensities covered by this model: (1) When importance is bestowed or attributed to self and to others, a propensity for *Selfulness* ensues: "We both must win together." (2) When importance is attributed to self but not the other, a propensity for *Selfishness* ensues: "I must win at your expense." (3) When importance is attributed to the other but not to the self, a propensity for *Selflessness* ensure: "You win, I lose." (4) When importance is not bestowed or attributed to both self and other, a propensity for No-self ensues: "We both lose." Neither one of the last two propensities is apparent in most games. However, conceivably, they may occur in specific circumstances.

This model applies to competitive games where there are victories and defeats. In cooperative games, of course, all players win because there are no losers or winners, as in kindergarten sports, representing *Selfulness*. In competitive games winning can vary in intensity (Model[5]). A winner takes all and all the other players are eliminated, as in poker. For every team that wins, there is another one that loses. Who wins may receive recognition in terms of money, possessions, and medals according to a graduated regulation, such as gold, silver, and bronze medals at the Olympic Games. Losers get nothing or are even punished with death (Sutton-Smith, 1971, pp. 306–307). These aspects represent *Selfishness,* but *Selfulness* is also present to the extent that when a single player wins, the other members of the same team (or even the same nation in the Olympics) share in the reflected victory, even if they did not win the first place. All team members share on the reflected importance.

In *Selful-Cooperative* play we both must win, as in paired partners in a bridge game or building castles together in a sandbox as well as volunteerism in old age (Post, 2007). The two dimensions of *Selfishness* and *Selflessness* are represented by competitive games where one party— individuals or members of a team—either win or lose, with nothing in between. When the self is diminished in favor of the other, however, it may lead to depression and early death (Panchanathan & Boyd, 2004; Post, 2007). Importance is a fleeting proposition when one wins at another's expense. The *No-self* propensity, when there are no winners and importance is attributed negatively to self and another, is almost non-existent in play. This is why play might increase the sense of self-importance, perhaps in more lasting and enduring ways than from any other human activity except love (Ghafoori & Hierholzer, 2007; Levin, 2007; Vaillant, 2007).

Model[12]:

Play and Priorities means how playing is considered within other goals, needs, or plans in our lives. If play is important, it is included in one's agenda, as in the case of Australian students reviewed in Chapter 4 of this volume (Dimmock & Grove, 2006) and in the lives of my poker buddies described in Chapter 1. Space and time are allocated in one's life according to how important playing is in comparison to other activities. In this regard, Socio-emotional Selectivity Theory (Charles & Carstensen, 2007) is relevant to this model because of its lifespan perspective "grounded fundamentally in the uniquely human ability to monitor time and to adjust time horizons over the life course . . . When time is perceived as limited, people will forgo knowledge-related goals that are directed for future use and instead focus on more proximal, emotion-related goals" (p. 313). Consequently, as time goes on, we might tend to choose games that are less active and more relational, as shown in the examples given in Chapter 1, switching from tennis to card playing or even to volunteerism in old age (Chapter 13).

Here is where the requirement of redundancy comes into full force, obliging us, consciously or unconsciously, to make choices among the ways to love and to control self and/or others, not only humans but also physical settings. Is the home the safe place to relax and enjoy life, or is work where the most enjoyment is achieved? How about the friendly conviviality of a sports bar, where other lonely individuals meet because they do not have another person or a more important setting to go to? Warren Buffett is reported to have answered the question about how he rated buildings and halls in the possession of his billion-dollar conglomerate:

> I know people who have [lots] of money . . . and they get testimonial dinners and hospital wings named after them. But the truth is that nobody in the world loves them. When you get to my age, you'll measure your success in life by how many of the people you want to have love you do actually love you. That's the ultimate test of how you've lived your life. (Quoted in *Parade Magazine*, 2008.)

Love, in spite of trite Hollywood movies, is indeed a multi-splendored thing, with various meanings and multiple ways to express it, as shown by many models of the theory. As we shall see, we will need one more additional model, Model[15], to arrive at a satisfactory definition of love.

Applications of the Theory

Model[13]:

Play implies *Distance Regulation* with others as in chase games, where there is a Pursuer, a Distancer, and a referee or a judge who serves as Regulator of what can or cannot be done.

Model[14]:

This pathologic *Drama Triangle* is composed of three continuously if not simultaneously rotating or sometimes even fixed roles of Victim, Persecutor, and Rescuer (L'Abate, 2009), as discussed in Chapter 7, this volume, from the work of Fivaz-Depeursinge & Favez, 2006. We need to find whether this triangle is present in some cases of Fantasy Play or only in dysfunctional playing. In playing, the role of Persecutor is found in the bullies, who themselves may have been Victims. When the Victim cannot find Rescuers in parents, teachers, or school administration, this deadly triangle could result in depression, or worse, suicide (Boulton & Underwood, 1992; Pereira, 2004). This triangle may not be found in the imaginative play of functional individuals. However, the possibility of finding it in troubled and traumatized players is very high and needs to be verified further (Horne, Raczynski, & Orpinas, 2008). This triangle seems present in teasing, bullying, and sexual harassment as a revolving process where Victims become Persecutors, Persecutors become Victims, and either could become a Rescuer or leave the rescuing to teachers (Land, 2003). This triangle was already evident in the kindergarten experience of my 5-year-old grandson reported at the outset of Chapter 1 of this volume.

Model[15]:

Intimacy is defined as the sharing of joys and victories as well as the sharing of hurt feelings produced by defeats and losses, as well as the fear of being hurt by being too close emotionally to others, and perhaps the fear of losing control or revealing what may be seen as undesirable or vulnerable parts of oneself (Browne-Miller, 2007; Hutchison, 2005; L'Abate, in press a). It may be temporary, occurring at the end of a game and forgotten over time (Officer & Rosenfeld, 1985) or may last a lifetime when it is not expressed and shared with loved ones. However, sharing these victories or defeats with peers or with teachers and coaches may become grounds for lifelong friendships, requiring forgiveness of one's errors or even transgressions in play as well as in life (Root & McCullough, 2007; Witvliet & McCullough, 2007).

Model[16]:

Negotiation represents the process of bargaining and problem-solving necessary to find a successful outcome to differences in opinions or styles. While the three previous models dealt with dysfunctional play, this model requires a certain level of functionality to achieve a positive outcome. For instance, the two major components of negotiation, structure and process, need to be distinguished. Structure includes who has the *authority* to make decisions, as found in play coaches and referees, and who has the *responsibility* to carry those decisions out, that is, the players. Decisions may be *large,* such as what kind of expensive playground equipment to buy, or *small,* such as which movie should we rent tonight. The process of negotiation depends on the needs for missing functionality *(ill)* that other players may be able to supply, which of those skills are available for successful negotiation *(skill),* and the willingness to negotiate *(will).* Underlying many competitive team games there is a great deal of negotiation about dates, times, rules, and so forth.

DISCUSSION

Now that all the models of the theory have been presented, perhaps the requirement of redundancy may allow us to explain and interpret play and not just describe it. A game—how we play with toys, ranging from a simple stick of wood to an expensive car or yacht—is explained when it becomes part of a hierarchical framework that allows us to understand it from the viewpoints of a variety of models. The relationship of a game to various models of the theory allows us to explain that game. For instance, take a simple chase game, such as tag. It can be seen, described, and videotaped accurately as one player trying to catch another player, a manner of running selectively toward one particular player and by necessity avoiding and running away from other players.

This process implies viewing running (1) as an emotional sequence as present in the component of Emotionality in Model[1], (2) as an Activity in Model[1] occurring within a Context subjectively perceived by the individual players, (3) occurring in a specific place and time, a Setting in Model[3], (4) as an approach on the one hand and an avoidance on the other, as in Model[4] of the theory (Table 19.2), (5) by how fast or slow players are running as described by Model[5], (6) as Performance, that is: Doing in Model[7], (7) from the viewpoint of Model[8], where the choice of pursued player may have been dictated by the degree of resemblance or likeness between the pursuer and the pursued, and (8) in terms of the relationship between Pursuer and Distancer as explained by Model[13]. If there is a referee or judge in the game, that party would serve as Distance Regulator. Other models could be added to refine the explanation of this game. It takes more than one model to explain any game. Here is where a hierarchical theory comes into being with various models explaining and perhaps interpreting the same play behavior from different viewpoints or models.

A possible criticism about this formulation for explanation may note that these models still describe play behavior but do not explain it. If we cannot describe play from various vantage points, then we do not have any other way to "explain" play. The relevant issue here lies in how many models will be necessary to "explain" a game. Will two models be sufficient? The answer to this question lies in explaining a game from as many models as possible that are relevant to that particular play behavior.

CONCLUSION

It takes a fairly functional person to make play an important part of his or her life cycle, to have sufficient time and energy within his or her priorities to consider play an important aspect throughout the life cycle. It is up to education, health promotion, prevention, psychotherapy, and rehabilitation to prepare individuals, couples, and families to learn how to play, to reduce stress, and learn to enjoy life above and beyond mere survival, that is: work. Freud's favored popular quote about functionality being derived from love and work should be expanded to include the abilities to play, including volunteering—to laugh as well as to cry.

REFERENCES

Abbott, G., Cochran, V., & Clair, A. (1997). Innovations in intergenerational programs for persons who are elderly: The role of horticultural therapy in a multidisciplinary approach. *Activities, Adaptation & Aging, 22*, 27-37.

Adatto, C. (1964). On the play and the psychopathology of golf. *Journal of the American Psychoanalytical Association, 12*, 826-841.

Agate, S. T., & Covey, C. D. (2007). Family camps: An overview of benefits and issues of camps and programs for families. *Child and Adolescent Psychiatric Clinics of North America, 16*, 921-937.

Aizen, I., & Driver, B. (1991). Prediction of leisure participation from behavioral, normative, and control beliefs: An application of the theory of planned behavior. *Leisure Sciences, 13*, 185-204.

Alessandri, S. (1991). Play and social behavior in maltreated preschoolers. *Development and Psychopathology, 3*, 191-205.

Allen, K. (2003). Are pets a healthy pleasure? The influence of pets on blood pressure. *Current Directions in Psychological Science, 12*, 236-239.

American Psychological Association (2007). *Dictionary of psychology*. Washington, DC: Author.

Andrews, S. S., Gerhart, K. A., & Hosack, K. R. (2004). Therapeutic recreation in traumatic brain injury rehabilitation. In M. Ashley (Ed.). *Traumatic brain injury: Rehabilitation treatment and case management* 2nd Edition (pp. 539-557). Boca Raton, FL: CRC Press.

Appelman, R. L., & Wilson, J. H. (2006). Games and simulations for training: From group activities to Virtual Reality. In J. A. Pershing (Ed.), *Handbook of human performance technology* (pp. 414-436). San Francisco, CA: Pfeiffer.

Arce, A. (2006). The importance of play in preschool education: Naturalization versus a Marxist analysis. In P. H. Sawchuck, N. Duarte, M. Elhammoumi (Eds.), *Critical perspectives on activity: Explorations across education, work, and everyday life* (pp. 75–88). New York: Cambridge University Press.

Ariel, S. (2002). *Children's imaginative play: A visit to wonderland.* Westport, CT: Praeger.

Aronsson, K., & Thorell, M. (1999). Family politics in children's play directives. *Journal of Pragmatics, 31,* 25–47.

Arya, K., Sharma, S., & Dhaliwal, Y. S. (2001). Television viewing and its effects on the study and playing hours of school going children. *Psycho-Lingua, 31,* 147–149.

Association for Play Therapy (1977). The International Play Association's Declaration of the Child's Right to Play. (Presented at IPA Malta Consultation, 1977.) In R. L. Clements & L. Fiorentino (Eds.), *The child's right to play: A global approach* (pp. 393-397). Westport, CT: Praeger.

Association for Play Therapy (2008). *Play therapy defined.* Retrieved March 20, 2009, from http://www.a4pt.org/ps.playtherapy.cfm?ID=1158

Avedon, E. M., & Sutton-Smith, B. (1971). *The study of games.* New York: Wiley.

Axline, V. M. (1947). *Play therapy.* Boston, MA: Houghton Mifflin.

Aycock, A. (1998). Owning up: Bourdieu and commodified play in the USCF chess catalogue. In M. C. Duncan, G. Chick, & A. Aycock (Eds.), *Play & culture studies: Diversions and divergencies in fields of play. Volume 1* (pp. 253–273). Greenwich, CT: Ablex.

Aydt, H. & Corsaro, W. (2003). Differences in children's construction of gender across culture: An interpretative approach. *American Behavioral Scientist, 46,* 1306–1325.

Aymard, L. L. (1999). Therapeutic applications of computers with children. In C. E. Schaefer (Ed.), *Innovative psychotherapy techniques in child and adolescent therapy.* (pp. 271–314). New York: Wiley.

Bagley. D. M., & Chaille, C. (1996). Transforming play: An analysis of first-, third-, and fifth-graders' play. *Journal of Research in Childhood Education, 10,* 134–142.

Bagley, D. M., & Klass, P. H. (1998). Comparison of the quality of preschoolers' play in housekeeping and thematic sociodramatic play centers. *Journal of Research in Childhood Education, 12,* 71–77.

Bankart. C. P., & Anderson, C. (1979). Short-term effects of prosocial television viewing on play of preschool boys and girls. *Psychological Reports, 44,* 935–941.

Banks. R., & Aveno, A. (1986). Adapted miniature golf: A community leisure program for students with severe physical disabilities. *Journal of the Association for Persons with Severe Handicap, 11,* 209–215.

Barbieri-Weldge, R. L. (1997). Social pretend play in preschool children prenatally exposed to substances. *Dissertation Abstracts International: Section B: The Sciences and Engineering, 57,* 5942.

Barnett, L. A. (1985). Young children's free play and problem-solving ability. *Leisure Sciences, 7,* 25–46.

Barnett, L. A. (1990). Developmental benefits of play for children. *Journal of Leisure Research, 22,* 138–153.

Barnett, L. A. (1998). The adaptive powers of being playful. In M. C. Duncan, G. Chick, & A. Aycock (Eds.), *Play & culture studies: Diversions and divergencies in fields of play. Volume 1* (pp. 97–119). Greenwich, CT: Ablex.

Barnett, L. A., & Kane, M. J. (1985a). Environmental constraints on children's play. In M. G. Wade (Ed.), *Constraints on leisure* (pp. 189–226). Springfield, IL: C. C. Thomas.

Barnett, L. A., & Kane, M. J. (1985b). Individual constraints on children's play. In M. G. Wade (Ed.), *Constraints on leisure* (pp. 43–82). Springfield, IL: C. C. Thomas.

Bar-Sela, G., Atid, L., Danos, S., Gabay, N., & Epelbaum, R. (2007). Art therapy improved depression and influenced fatigue levels in cancer patients on chemotherapy. *Psycho-Oncology, 16,* 980–984.

Bartholow, B. D., & Anderson, C. A. (2002). Effects of violent video games on aggressive behavior: Potential sex differences. *Journal of Experimental Psychology, 38,* 283–290.

Bateson, G. (1982). The message "This is play." In I. E. Herron & B. Sutton-Smith (Eds.), *Child's play* (261–266). Malabar, FL: Robert E. Krieger.

Baumeister, R. F., & Sanders, P. S. (1989). Identity development and the role structure of children's games. *Journal of Genetic Psychology, 150,* 19–37.

Beal, B. (1998). Symbolic inversion in the subculture of skateboarding. In Brown C. C., & Gottfried, A. W. (Eds.). (1985). *Play interactions: The role of toys and parental involvement in children's development.* Skillman, NJ: Johnson & Johnson Baby Care Company.

Beckman, P. J., & Kohl, F. L. (1984). The effects of social and isolate toys on the interaction and play of integrated and nonintegrated groups of preschoolers. *Education & Training of the Mentally Retarded, 19,* 169–174.

Beckwith, L. (1985). Parental-child interaction and socio-emotional development. In C. A. Brown & A. W. Gottfried (Eds.), *Play interactions: The role of toys and parental involvement in children's development* (pp. 152–159). Skillman, NJ: Johnson & Johnson.

Beer, J. S., & Lombardo, M. V. (2007). Insights into emotion regulation from neuropsychology. In J. J. Gross (Ed.), *Handbook of emotion regulation* (pp. 69–109). New York: Guilford.

Belsky, J., Garduque, L., & Hencir, E. (1984). Assessing performance, competence, and executive capacity in infant play: Relations to home environment and security of attachment. *Developmental Psychology, 20,* 406–417.

Bennett, M. G. (1985). Constraints on leisure in middle age. In M. G. Wade (Ed.), *Constraints on leisure* (pp. 319–333). Springfield, IL: C. C. Thomas.

Benson, M. S. (1993). The structure of four- and five-year-olds' narratives in pretend play and storytelling. *First Language, 13,* 203–223.

Benton, L. A. (1999). The agentic and communal motives of boys and girls participating in high school team sports: Implications for adolescent personality development. *Dissertation Abstracts International Section A: Humanities and Social Sciences, 60,* 332.

Bergen, D. (2002). Finding humor in children's play. In J. L. Roopnarine (Ed.), *Conceptual, social-cognitive, and contextual issues in the field of play; Volume 4* (pp. 209–220). Westport, CT: Ablex.

Bergen, D., & Mauer, D. (2000). Symbolic play, phonological awareness, and literacy skills at three age levels. In K.A. Roskos & J. F. Christie (Eds.), *Play and literacy in early childhood: Research from multiple perspectives* (pp. 45–62). Mahwah, NJ: Erlbaum.

Berger, W. B. (2001). Preschool aged girls exposed and non-exposed to domestic violence: Differences in behavior problems, play processes, and pretend play themes. *Dissertation Abstracts International: Section B: Sciences and Engineering, 61,* p. 4390.

Bergman, A. (1993). To be or not to be separate: The meaning of hide-and-seek in forming internal representations. *Psychoanalytic Review, 80,* 361–375.

Bernstein, P. L., Friedman, E., & Malaspina, A. (2000). Animal-assisted therapy enhances resident social interaction and initiation in long-term care facilities. *Anthrozoos, 13,* 213–224.

Bertilson, H. S. (1991). Aggression. In V. J. Derlega, B. A. Winstead, & W. H. Jones. (Eds.), *Personality: Contemporary theory and research* (pp. 457–480). Chicago, IL: Nelson-Hall.

Besevegis, E., Coulacoglou, C., Mitsotakis, P., Arabatzi, E., & Tsitsikas, H. (1988). The development of symbolic maturity in preschool children in relation to chronological age, mental age, sex, and rearing. In E. Hibbs (Ed.), *Children and families: Studies in prevention and intervention* (pp. 193–202). Madison, CT: International University Press.

Best, J. (1998). Too much fun: Toys as social problems and the interpretation of culture. *Symbolic Interaction, 21,* 197–212.

Biben, M., & Champoux, M. (1999). Play and stress: Cortisol as a negative correlate of play in Saimiri. In S. Reifel (Ed.), *Play & culture studies, volume 2* (pp. 191–208). Stanford, CT: Ablex.

Bigelow, N., & Roberts, E. (1968). The state hospital golf course. *Psychiatric Quarterly Supplement, 42,* 327–336.

Bilt, J.V., Dodge, H. H., Panday, E., Shaffer, H. J., & Ganguli, M. (2004). Gambling participation and social support among older adults: A longitudinal community study. *Journal of Gambling Studies, 20,* 373–390.

Birren, J. E., & Shaie, K. W. (1985). *Handbook of the Psychology of Aging,* 2nd ed. New York: Van Nostrand Reinhold.

Bishop, K. (2004). Designing sensory play environments for children with special needs. In R. L. Clements & L. Fiorentino (Eds.), *The child's right to play: a global approach* (pp. 233–242). Westport, CT: Praeger.

Bishop, A., & Clark, J. (1992). "Don't look at us, we're playing": Play in the earliest years of schooling. *Primary Teaching Studies, 6,* 298.

Bishop, A., & Simpson, R. (1995). Strategies for structured play in science in the nursery. *Primary Teaching Studies, 9,* 5–8.

Bishop, A., Swain, J., & Bines, H. (1999). Seizing the moment: Reflections on play opportunities for disabled children in the early years. *British Journal of Educational Studies, 47,* 170–183.

Bishop, M., Hobson, R. P., & Lee, A. (2005). Symbolic play in congenitally blind children. *Development and Psychopathology, 17,* 447–466.

Bjorklund, D. F., & Brown, R. D. (1998). Physical play and cognitive development: Integrating activity, cognition, and education. *Child Development, 69,* 604–606.

Blanche, E. I. (2002). Play and process: Adult play embedded in the daily routine. In J. L. Roopnarine (Ed.), *Conceptual, social-cognitive, and contextual issues in the field of play; Volume 4* (pp. 249–278). Westport, CT: Ablex.

Bloch, M. N., & Adler, S. M. (1994). African children's play and the emergence of the sexual division of labor. In J. L. Roopnarine, J. E. Johnson, & F. H. Hooper (Eds.). *Children's play in diverse cultures* (pp. 148–178). Albany, NY: State University of New York Press.

Blue, G. F. (1986). The value of pets in children's lives. *Childhood Education, 63,* 85–90.

Bock, J. (2005). Farming, foraging, and children's play in the Okavango Delta, Botswana. In Pellegrini, A. D., & Smith, P. K. (Eds.). (Eds.). *The nature of play: Great apes and humans* (pp. 254–281). New York: Guilford.

Bolig, R., Price, C. S., O'Neill-Wagner, P. L., & Suomi, S. J. (1998). Reactivity, and play and exploration behaviors of young rhesus monkeys. In M. C. Duncan, G. Chick, & A. Aycock (Eds.), *Play & culture studies: Volume I* (pp. 164–178). Westport, CT: Ablex.

Bond, M. J., Clark, M. S., Smith, D. S., & Harris, R. D. (1995). Lifestyle activities of the elderly: Composition and determinates. *Disability and Rehabilitation: An International Interdisciplinary Journal, 17,* 63–69.

Bornstein, M. H., Haynes, O. M., Pascual, L., Painter K. M., & Galperin, C. (1999). Play in two societies: Pervasiveness of process, specificity of structure. *Child Development, 70,* 317–331.

Boulton, M. J. (1991). A comparison of structural and contextual features of middle school children's playful and aggressive fighting. *Ethology & Sociobiology, 12,* 119–145.

Boulton, M. J. (1992). Participation in playground activities at middle school. *Educational Research, 34,* 167–182.

Boulton, M. J. (1993). A comparison of adults' and children's abilities to distinguish between aggressive and playful fighting in middle school children: Implications for playground supervision and behavior management. *Educational Studies, 19,* 193–203.

Boulton, M. J., & Smith, P. K. (1992). The social nature of play fighting and play chasing: Mechanisms and strategies underlying cooperation and compromise. In J. H. Barkow, L., Cosmides, L., & J. Tooby (Eds.), *The adapted mind: Evolutionary psychology and the generation of culture* (pp. 429–444). New York: Oxford University Press.

Boulton, M. J., & Underwood, K. (1992). Bully/Victim problems in middle-school children. *British Journal of Educational Psychology, 62,* 73–87.

Bower, E. M., Ilgaz-Carden, A., & Noori, K. (1982). Measurement of play structures: Cross-cultural considerations. *Journal of Cross-Cultural Psychology, 13,* 315–329.

Boyd, A. R., McLearen, A. M., Meyer, R. G., & Denney, R.L. (2007). *Detection of deception.* Sarasota, FL: Professional Resource Press.

Brach, J. S., Simonsick, E. M., Kritchevsky, S., Yaffe, K., & Newman, A. B. (2004). The association between physical function and lifestyle activity and exercise in the health, aging, and body composition study. *Journal of the American Geriatrics Society, 52,* 502–509.

Bradley, R. H. (1985). Play materials and intellectual development. In C. C., Brown & A. W. Gottfried (Eds.), *Play interactions: The role of toys and parental involvement in children's development* (pp. 129–142). Skillman, NJ: Johnson & Johnson Baby Products Company.

Bratton, S. C., Landreth, G. L., Kellam, T., & Blackard, S. R. (2006). *Child parent relationship therapy (CPRT) treatment manual: A 10-session filial therapy model for training parents.* New York: Rutledge.

Bratton, S., Ray, D., Rhine, T., & Jones, L. (2005). The efficacy of play therapy with children: A Meta-analytic review of the outcome research. *Professional Psychology: Research and Practice, 36,* 376–390.

Bratton, S., Ray, D., Rhine, T., & Jones, L. (2001). The effectiveness of play therapy: Responding to the critics. *International Journal of Play Therapy, 10,* 85–108.

Bredekamp, S. (2004). Play and school readiness. In E. Zigler (Ed.), *Children's play: The roots of reading* (pp. 159–174).

Brenner. M., & Omark, L. (1979). The effects of sex, structure, and social interaction on preschoolers' play behaviors in a naturalistic setting. *Instructional Science, 8,* 91–105.

Bretherton, I. (1985). Attachment theory: Retrospect and prospect. *Monographs of the Society for Research in Child Development, 50,* 3–35.

Bretherton, I. (1989). Pretense: The form and function of make-believe play. *Developmental Review, 9,* 383–401.

Bright, M. C., & Stockdale, D. F. (1984). Mothers', fathers', and preschool children's interactions in play settings. *Journal of Genetic Psychology, 144,* 219–232.

Britsch, B. M. (2000). The effect of sport participation on female adolescents' gender-role identity and self-concept: The role of motivation, ability, persistence, and team membership. *Dissertation Abstracts International: Section B: The Sciences and Engineering, 61,* 560.

Brooke, S. L. (2007). *The use of the creative therapies with sexual abuse survivors.* Springfield, IL: Charles C. Thomas.

Brown, C. C., & Gottfried, A. W. (Eds.). (1985). *Play interactions: The role of toys and parental involvement in children's development.* Skillman, NJ: Johnson & Johnson.

Brown, P. S., Thornton, C. D., & Sutterby, J. A. (2004). Kids getting older younger: The adultification of children's play. In R. L. Clements & L. Fiorentino (Eds.), *The child's right to play: A global approach* (pp. 177–183). Westport, CT: Praeger.

Browne-Miller, A. (2007). *To have and to hurt: Recognizing and changing, or escaping, patterns of abuse in intimate relationships.* Westport, CT: Praeger.

Brownell, C. A., & Kopp, C. B. (Eds.). (2007). *Socioemotional development in the toddler years: Transitions and transformations.* New York: Guilford.

Bundy, A. (1989). A comparison of the play skills of normal boys and boys with sensory integrative dysfunction. *Occupational Therapy Journal of Research, 9,* 84–100.

Bundy, A. C., & Clifton, J. L. (1998). Construct validity of the Children's Playfulness Scale. In M. C. Duncan, G. Chick, & A. Aycock (Eds.), *Play & culture studies: Diversions and divergencies in fields of play. Volume 1* (pp. 137-147). Greenwich, CT: Ablex.

Burghardt, G. M. (2004). Play and the brain in comparative perspective. In R. L. Clements & L. Fiorentino (Eds.), *The child's right to play: A global approach* (pp. 293-308). Westport, CT: Praeger.

Burns, S. M., & Brainerd, C. J. (1979). Effects of constructive and dramatic play on perspective taking in very young children. *Developmental Psychology, 15,* 512-521.

Butcher, J. (1991). Development of a playground skills test. *Perceptual and Motor Skills, 72,* 259-266.

Byers, J. A. (1998). Comment/reply to Pellegrini and Smith's paper (1998). *Child Development, 69,* 599-600.

Caldwell, B. M. (1985). Parent-child play: A playful evaluation. In C. C. Brown & A. W. Gottfried (Eds.), *Play interactions: The role of toys and parental involvement in children's development* (pp. 167-178). Skillman, NJ: Johnson & Johnson Baby Products Company.

Calkins, S. D., & Hill, A. (2007). Caregiver influences on emerging emotion regulation: Biological and environmental transactions in early development. In J. J. Gross (Ed.), *Handbook of emotion regulation* (pp. 229-248). New York: Guilford.

Calkins, S. D., Gill, K. L., Johnson, M.C., & Smith, C. L. (1999). Emotional reactivity and emotional regulation strategies as predictors of social behavior with peers during toddlerhood. *Social Development, 8,* 310-334.

Campbell, D. D., & Davis, J. E. (1940). Report of research and experimentation in exercise and recreational therapy. *American Journal of Psychiatry, 96,* 915-933.

Caplan, F., & Caplan, T. (1973). *The power of play.* New York: Anchor Press.

Carmichael, K. D. (2006). *Play therapy: An introduction.* Upper Saddle River, NJ: Pearson Educational Education, Inc.

Carstensen, L. L. (1992). Social and emotional patterns of adulthood: Support for socioemotional selectivity theory. *Psychology & Aging, 7,* 331-338.

Carter, C. S. (2007). Monogamy, motherhood, and health. In S. G. Post (Ed.), *Altruism & health: Perspectives from empirical research* (pp. 371-393). New York: Oxford University Press.

Carvalho, A. M., Smith, P. K., Hunter, T., & Costabile, A. (1990). Playground activities for boys and girls: Developmental and cultural trends in children's perceptions of gender differences. *Play & Culture, 3,* 343-347.

Catley, D., & Duda, J. L. (1997). Psychological antecedents of the frequency and intensity of flow in golfers. *International Journal of Sport Psychology, 28,* 309-322.

Catothers, P., Vaske, J. J., & Donnelly, M. P. (2001). Social values versus interpersonal conflict among hikers and mountain bikers. *Leisure Sciences, 23,* 47-61.

Ghafoori, B., & Hierholzer, R. (2007). The role of love, attachment, and altruism in adjustment to military trauma. In S. G. Post (Ed.), *Altruism & health: Perspectives from empirical research* (pp. 231-245). New York: Oxford University Press.

Champoux, M., Shannon, C., Airoso, W. D., & Suomi, S. J. (1999). Play and attachment behavior of peer-only reared and surrogate/peer-reared rhesus monkey infants in their social group. In S. Reifel (Ed.), *Play & culture studies. Volume 2* (pp. 209–217). Stanford, CT: Ablex.

Chang, S. (2004). *Children's pretend play with television and film-scripted character toys.* Ottawa: National Library of Canada.

Chapman, T., Baron-Cohen, S., Swettenham, J., Baird, G., Cox, A., & Drew, A. (2000). Testing joint attention, imitation, and play as infancy precursors to language and theory of mind. *Cognitive Development, 15,* 481–498.

Charles, S. T., & Carstensen, L. L. (2007). Emotion regulation and aging. In J. J. Gross (Ed.), *Handbook of emotion regulation* (pp. 307–327). New York: Guilford.

Charman, T., Baron-Cohen, S., Swettenham, J., Baird, G. Cox, A., & Drew, A. (2000). Testing joint attention, imitation, and play as infancy precursors to language and theory of mind. *Cognitive Development, 15,* 481–498.

Chen, Y. J. (2001). Beliefs about maternal roles and developmental benefits in parent-infant play contexts: Learning from Taiwanese mothers of children with Down syndrome. *Dissertation Abstracts International: Section A: Humanities and Social Sciences, 62,* pp. 2076.

Chen, D. D., & Rikli, R. E. (2003). Survey of preferences for feedback style in high school athletes. *Perceptual and Motor Skills, 97,* 770–776.

Chethik, M. (2000). *Techniques of child therapy: Psychodynamic strategies.* New York: Guilford.

Cheung, M. (2006). *Therapeutic games and guided imagery.* Chicago, IL: Lyceum Books.

Chick, G., & Barnett, L. A. (1995). Children's play and adult leisure. In A. D. Pellegrini (Ed.), *The future of play theory: A multidisciplinary inquiry into the contributions of Brian Sutton-Smith* (pp. 45–69). Albany, NY: State University of New York Press.

Christie, J. F., & Johnsen, E. P. (1987). Reconceptualizing constructive play: A review of the empirical literature. *Merrill-Palmer Quarterly, 33,* 439–452.

Christie, J. F., Stone, S. J., & Deutscher, R. (2002). Play in same-age and multi-age grouping arrangements. In J. L. Roopnarine (Ed.), *Conceptual, social-cognitive, and contextual issues in the field of play; Volume 4* (pp. 93–110). Westport, CT: Ablex.

Cicchetti, D. (1985). Caregiver-infant interaction: The study of maltreated children. In C. C. Brown & A. W. Gottfried (Eds.), *Play interactions: The role of toys and parental involvement in children's development* (pp. 107–112). Skillman, NJ: Johnson & Johnson Baby Products Company.

Ciofi, R., & Graziano, D. (2003). *Giochi pericolosi? Perche' i giovani passano ore tra videogiuchi online e comunita' virtuali (Dangerous games? Why children spend hours among online videogames and virtual communities?).* Milano, IT: Franco-Angeli.

Clarke, L. J. (1999). Development reflected in chase games. In S. Reifel (Ed.). (1999). *Play & culture studies* (pp. 73–82). Westport, CT: Ablex.

Clawson, M. A. (2002). Play of language-minority children in an early childhood setting. In J. L. Roopnarine (Ed.), *Conceptual, social-cognitive, and contextual issues in the field of play; Volume 4* (pp. 93–121). Westport, CT: Ablex.

Clements, R. L. & Fiorentino, L. (Eds.). (2004). *The child's right to play: A global approach.* Westport, CT: Praeger.

Clendaniel, M. (2008). Fall down, go boom. *Good Magazine, 12,* 84–88.

Clune, C., Paolella, J. M., & Foley, J. M. (1979). Free-play behavior of atypical children: An approach to assessment. *Journal of Autism and Developmental Disorders, 9,* 61–72.

CNN.com (2001). U. S. workers put in most hours. http://archives.cnn. com/2001/ CAREER/trends/08/30/ilo.study/ Retrieved 12/14/2008.

Coan, J. A., & Allen, J. J. B. (Eds.). (2007). *Handbook of emotion elicitation and assessment.* New York: Oxford University Press.

Cohen, D. (1987). *The development of play.* New York: New York University Press.

Colburne, K. A. (2001). The emergence of triadic play in mother-child interactions: Play context and nonverbal communicative behaviors. *Dissertation Abstracts International: Section B. Sciences and Engineering, 61,* p. 6735.

Cole, D. A. (1986). Facilitating play in children's peer relationships: Are we having fun yet? *American Educational Research Journal, 23,* 201–215.

Colotta, V. A. (2006). Controversial treatments in brain injury rehabilitation. *PsycCRITIQUES, 51.* No pagination specified.

Connor, K. (1989). Aggression: Is it in the eye of the beholder? *Play & Culture, 2,* 213–217.

Connor, J. M., & Serbin, L. A. (1977). Behaviorally based masculine- and feminine-activity-preference scales for preschoolers: Correlates with other classroom behaviors and cognitive tests. *Child Development, 48,* 1411–1416.

Constable, A., Genta, M. L., Zucchini, E., Smith, P. K., & Harker, R. (1992). Attitudes of parents toward war play in young children. *Early Education and Development, 3,* 356–369.

Cooney, M. H., Gupta, P., & O'Laughlin, M. (2000). Blurring the lines of play and work to create blended classroom learning experiences. *Early Childhood Education Journal, 27,* 165–171.

Cooper, S. E., & Robinson, D. A. (1989). Childhood play activities of women and men entering engineering and science careers. *School Counselor, 36,* 338–342.

Corrigan, P. W., Liberman, R. P., & Wong, S. E. (1993). Recreational therapy and behavior management on inpatient units: Is recreational therapy therapeutic? *Journal of Nervous and Mental Disease, 181,* 644–646.

Corsaro, W. A. (1993). Interpretive reproduction in children's role play. *Childhood: A Global Journal of Child Research, 1,* 64–74.

Corsaro, W. A. (1998). The sociology of childhood. *British Journal of Educational Studies, 46,* 464–465.

Cotter, M. (2004). A closer look at the ontological role of play. In R. L. Clements & L. Fiorentino (Eds.), *The child's right to play: A global approach* (pp. 329–341). Westport, CT: Praeger.

Cousins. S., & Witcher, C. (2004). Older women living the bingo stereotype: "Well, so what? I play bingo. I'm not out drinking." *International Gambling Studies, 4,* 127–146.

Crain, W. (2003). *Reclaiming childhood: Letting children be children in our achievement-oriented society*. New York: Owl Books, Henry Holt & Co.

Creasey, G. L., Jarvis, P. A., Berk, L. E. (1998). Play and social competence. In O. N. Saracho & B. Spodek, (Eds.), *Multiple perspectives on play in early childhood education* (pp. 116–143). Albany, NY: State University of New York Press.

Crenshaw, D. A., & Hardy, K. V. (2007). The crucial role of empathy in breaking the silence of traumatized children in play therapy. *International Journal of Play Therapy, 16,* 160–175.

Crist, R. W. (1995). The effects of aerobic exercise and free-play time on the self-concept and classroom performance of sixth-grade students. Unpublished Ed. D. dissertation, University of Kentucky, Lexington, KY.

Cusinato, M., & Colesso, W. (2008). Validation of the continuum of likeness in intimate relationships. In L. L'Abate (Ed.), *Toward a science of clinical psychology: Laboratory evaluations and interventions* (pp. 337–352). New York: Nova Science Publishers.

Cusinato, M., Maino, E., Colesso, W., Scilletta, C., & L'Abate, L. (2008). Evidence for a hierarchical theory of relational competence. Manuscript submitted for publication.

Cutler, S. J., & Danigelis, N. L. (1993). Organized contexts of activity. In J. R. Kelly (Ed.), *Activity and aging: Staying involved in later life* (pp. 146–163). Thousand Oaks, CA: Sage.

Danby, S. (1998). The serious and playful work of gender: Talk and social order in a preschool classroom. In N. Yelland (Ed.), *Gender in early childhood* (pp. 175–205). Florence, KY: Taylor & Frances/Routledge.

Danger, S., & Landreth, G. L. (2005). Child-centered group play therapy with children with speech difficulties. *International Journal of Play Therapy, 14,* 81–102.

Darwish, D., Esquinal, G. B., Houtz, J. C., & Alfonso, V. C. (2001). Play and social skills in maltreated and non-maltreated preschoolers during peer interaction. *Child Abuse & Neglect, 25,* 13–31.

Davidson, J. I. F. (1996). *Emergent literacy and dramatic play in early education*. Albany, NY: Delmar Publishers.

Davies, S. L., Glaser, D., & Kossoff, R. (2000). Children's sexual play and behavior in pre-school settings: Staff perceptions, reports, and responses. *Child Abuse & Neglect, 24,* 1329–1343.

Dawkins, M. P. (2003). Race relations and the sport of golf: The African American golf legacy. *Western Journal of Black Studies, 27,* 231–235.

Day, R. C., & Ghandour, M. (1984). The effect of television-mediated aggression and real-life aggression on the behaviour of Lebanese children. *Journal of Experimental Child Psychology, 38,* 7–18.

DeGenova, M. K. (1992). If you had your life to live over again: What would your do differently? *International Journal of Aging & Human Development, 34,* 135–143.

De Giacomo,A. (1999). Giuoco genitori figli. In C. Loriedo, D. Solfaroli Camillocci, & M. Micheli (Eds.). *Genitori: Individui e relazioni intergenerazionali nella famiglia* (pp. 192-195). Milano, IT: Franco Angeli.

DeLong, T. C. (1999). Observations of free-play behavior in captive juvenile bottlenose dolphins (Tursiops truncates). In S. Reifel (Ed.), *Play & culture studies, Volume 2* (pp. 219-236). Stanford, CT: Ablex.

De Long, A. J., Tegano, D. W., Moran, J. D., Brickey, J., et al., (1994). Effects of spatial scale on cognitive play in preschool children. *Early Education and Development, 5*, 237-246.

deMarrais, K. B., Nelson, P. A., & Baker, J. H. (1994). Meaning in mud: Yup'ik Eskimo girls at play. In J. L. Roopnarine, J. E. Johnson, & F. H. Hooper (Eds.), *Children's play in diverse cultures* (pp. 179-209). Albany, NY: State University of New York Press.

DeMasio, A. R. (1994). *Descartes' error: Emotion, reason, and the human brain.* New York: Putman.

Demick, J., & Andreoletti, C. (Eds.). (2003). *Handbook of adult development.* New York: Kluwer Academic.

Densmore, A. E. (2007). *Helping children with autism become more social: 76 ways to use narrative play.* Westport, CT: Praeger.

Dergance, J. M., Calmbach, W. L., Dhada, R., Miles, T. P., Hazuda, H. P., & Moulton, C. P. (2003). Barriers to and benefits of leisure time physical activity in the elderly: Differences across cultures. *Journal of the American Geriatrics Society, 51*, 863-868.

Derrig-Palumbo, K., & Zeine, F. (2005). *Online therapy: A therapist's guide to expanding your practice.* New York: Norton.

Desai, R. A., Maciejewski, P. K., Dause, D. J., Calderone, B. J., & Potenza, M. N. (2004). Health correlates of recreational gambling in older adults. *American Journal of Psychiatry, 161*, 1672-1679.

Dimmock, J. A., & Grove, J. R. (2006). Identifications with sport teams as a function of the search for certainty. *Journal of Sport Sciences, 7*, 1203-1211.

Dixon, W. E., & Shore, C. (1991). Measuring symbolic play style in infancy: A methodological approach. *Journal of Genetic Psychology, 152*, 191-205.

Donder, D., & Nietupski, J. (1981). Nonhandicapped adolescents teaching playground skills to their mentally retarded peers: Toward a less restrictive middle school environment. *Education & Training of the Mentally Retarded, 16*, 270-276.

Doyle, A. B., Ceschin, F., Tessier, O., & Doehring, P. (1991). The relation of age and social class factors in children's social pretend play to cognitive and symbolic ability. *International Journal of Behavioral Development, 14*, 395-410.

Draper, K., Ritter, K. B., & Willingham, E. U. (2003). Sand tray group counseling with adolescents. *Journal for Specialists in Group Work, 28*, 244-260.

Draper, K., White, J., O'Shaughnessy, T., Flynt, M., & Jones, N. (2001). Kinder training: Play-based consultation to improve the school adjustment of discouraged kindergarten and first grade students. *International Journal of Play Therapy, 10*, 1-10.

Drewes, A. A. (2005). *Play in selected cultures: Diversity and universality.* New York: Guilford.

Duarte, G. (2004). The collaborative play of parents, children, and teachers in creating a diverse play space. In R. L. Clements & L. Fiorentino (Eds.), *The child's right to play: A global approach* (pp. 225–232). Westport, CT: Praeger.

Dubrow, L. V., & Howe, N. (1999). Parental play styles and sibling interaction during a problem-solving task. *Infant and Child Development, 8,* 101–115.

Dulicai, D., & Schelly Hill, E. (2007). Expressive movement. In L. L'Abate (Ed.), *Low-cost approaches to promote physical and mental health* (pp. 177–200). New York: Springer.

Duncan, M. C. (1998). The pleasure of resistance: The subversion of the martial arts. In M. C. Duncan, G. Chick, & A. Aycock (Eds.), *Play & culture studies: Diversions and divergencies in fields of play. Volume 1* (pp. 223–230). Greenwich, CT: Ablex

Duncan, M. C., Chick, G., & Aycock, A. (Eds.). (1998). *Play & culture studies: Volume 1.* Greenwich, CT: Ablex.

Dunn, J. (1985). Pretend play in the family. In C. C. Brown & A. W. Gottfried (Eds.), *Play interactions: The role of toys and parental involvement in children's development* (pp. 79–88). Skillman, NJ: Johnson & Johnson Baby Products Company.

Dyer, J., & Stotts, M. L. (2005). *Handbook of remotivation therapy.* Binghamton, NY: Haworth.

Edwards, C. P. (2000). Children's play in cross-cultural perspective: A new look at the 'Six Cultures' study. *Cross-Cultural Research: The Journal of Comparative Social Science, 34,* 318–338.

Eifermann, R. R. (1971). Social play in childhood. In R. E. Herron & B. Sutton-Smith (Eds.), *Child's play* (pp. 270–297). New York: Wiley.

Einlinson, A. R., Austin, M. B., & Pfister, R. (2000). Cooperative games and children's positive behaviors. *Early Child Development and Care, 164,* 29–40.

Eisenberg, N., Tryon, K., & Cameron, E. (1984). The relation of preschoolers' peer interaction to their sex-typed toy choices. *Child Development, 55,* 1044–1050.

Eisenberg, N., Hofer, C., & Vaughan, J. (2007). Effortful control and its socioemotional consequences. In J. J. Gross (Ed.), *Handbook of emotion regulation* (pp. 287–306). New York: Guilford.

Eisenberg-Berg, N., Boothby, R., & Matson, T. (1979). Correlates of preschool girls' feminine and masculine toy preferences. *Developmental Psychology, 15,* 354–355.

Eiss, H. E. (1986). *Dictionary of language games, puzzles, and amusements.* Westport, CT: Greenwood Press.

Elgas, P. M., Klein, E. L., Kantor, R., & Fernie, D. E. (1988). Play and peer culture: Play styles and object use. *Journal of Research in Childhood Education, 3,* 142–153.

Elias, C. L., & Berk, L. E. (2002). Self-regulation in young children: Is there a role for sociodramatic play? *Early Childhood Research Quarterly, 17,* 216–238.

El'konin, D. B. (1976). Problems of the psychology of children's play in the works of L. S Vyotski, his co-workers and followers. *Voprosy Psychologii, 6,* 94–101.

Elkind, D. (2007). *The power of play: How spontaneous imaginative activities lead to happier, healthier, children.* Cambridge, MA: De Capo Press.

Elliott, A. (1993). Effects of gender on preschoolers' play and learning in logo environments. *Journal of Computing in Childhood Education, 4,* 103-124.

Embry, D. D. (2002). The Good Behavior Game: A best practice candidate as a Universal Behavioral vaccine. *Clinical Child and Family Psychology Review, 5,* 273-297.

Epstein, D., Kehily, M., Macan Ghaill, M., & Redman, P. (2001). Boys and girls come out to play: Making masculinities and femininities in school playground. *Men and Masculinity, 4,* 158-172.

Erikson, E. H. (1982). Sex differences in the play configurations of American pre-adolescents. In R. E. Herron & B. Sutton-Smith (1982). *Child's play* (pp. 126-184). Malabar, FL: Robert E. Krieger.

Erikson, E. H. (1972). Play and actuality. In M. W. Piers, M. (Ed.). (1972). *Play and development: A symposium with contributions by Jean Piaget, Peter H. Wolff, Rene A. Spitz, Konrad Lorenz, Lois Barclay and Eric H. Erikson* (pp. 127-167). New York: W. W. Norton.

Escobedo, T. H. (1999). The canvas of play: A study of children's play behaviors while drawing. In S. Reifel (Ed.). *Play & culture studies* (pp. 101-122). Westport, CT: Ablex.

Evaldsson, A. C., & Corsaro, W. A. (1998). Play and games in the peer cultures of preschool and preadolescent children: An interpretative approach. *Childhood: A Global Journal of Child Research, 5,* 377-402.

Ewen, R. B. (1988). *An introduction to theories of personality*. Hillsdale, NJ: Erlbaum.

Fabes, R. A., Shepard, S. A., Guthrie, I. K., & Martin, C. L. (1997). Roles of temperamental arousal and gender-segregated play in young children's social adjustment. *Developmental Psychology, 33,* 693-702.

Factor, D. C., & Frankie, G. H. (1980). Free-play behaviors in socially maladjusted and normal preschool children: A naturalistic study. *Canadian Journal of Behavioral Science, 12,* 272-277.

Fagan, J. (1993). Mother-child play interaction in neglecting and non-neglecting mothers. *Early Child Development and Care, 87,* 59-68.

Fagot, B. I. (1984). Teacher and peer reactions to boys' and girls' play styles. *Sex Roles, 11,* 691-702.

Fagot, B. I., Hagan, R., Youngblade, L. M., & Potter, L. (1989). A comparison of sexually abused, physically abused, and nonabused preschool children. *Topics in Early Childhood Special Education, 9,* 88-100.

Fall, M., Navelski, L. F., & Welch, K. (2002). Outcomes of a play intervention for children identified for special education services. *International Journal of Play Therapy, 11(2),* 91-106.

Fahndrich, D., & Schneider, K. (1987). Emotional reactions of preschool children while exploring and playing with a novel object. *Journal of Genetic Psychology, 148,* 209-217.

Fantuzzo, J., Sekino, Y., & Cohen, H. L. (2004). An examination of the contribution of interactive peer play to salient classroom competencies for urban Head Start children. *Psychology in the Schools, 41,* 323-336.

Farver, J. A. M., & Howes, C. (1993). Cultural differences in American and Mexican mother-child pretend play. *Merrill-Palmer Quarterly, 39,* 344-358.

Farver, J. A. M., & Lee-Shin, Y. (2000). Acculturation and Korean-American children's social and play behavior. *Social Development, 9,* 316-336.

Federlein, A. C., Lessen-Firestone, J., & Elliott, S. (1982). Special education preschoolers: Evaluating their play. *Early Child Development and Care, 9,* 245-254.

Fein, G. G., Campbell, & Schwartz, S. S. (1987). Microcomputers in the preschool: Effects on social participation and cognitive play. *Journal of Applied Developmental Psychology, 8,* 197-208.

Fein, G. G., & Stork, L. (1981). Sociodramatic play: Social class effects in integrated preschool classrooms. *Journal of Applied Developmental Psychology, 2,* 267-279.

Fenson, L. (1985). The developmental progression of exploration and play. In C. C. Brown & A.W. Gottfried (Eds.), *Play interactions: The role of toys and parental involvement in children's development* (pp. 31-38). Skillman, NJ: Johnson & Johnson Baby Products Company.

Fernald, A., & O'Neill, D. K. (1993). Peekaboo across cultures: How mothers and infants play with voices, faces, and expectations. In K. MacDonald (Ed.), *Parent-child play: Descriptions and implications* (pp. 259-285). Albany, NY: State University of New York Press.

Fetter, A. L. (1997). Age and gender differences in social competence during sociodramatic play in preschool. *Dissertation Abstracts International: Section B: The Sciences and Engineering, 58,* 3338.

Field, T. M. (1980). Preschool play: Effects of teacher/child ratios and organization of classroom space. *Child Study Journal, 10,* 191-205.

Field, T. M. (1993). Persistence in play and feeding interaction differences in three Miami cultures. In K. MacDonald (Ed.), *Parent-child play: Descriptions and implications* (pp. 331-347). Albany, NY: State University of New York Press.

Field, T. M., Adler, S., Vega-Lahr, N., Scadifi, F., et al. (1987). Temperament and play interaction behavior across infancy. *Infant Mental Health Journal, 8,* 156-165.

Field, T., Roseman, S., de Stefano, L. J., & Koewler, J. (1982). The play of handicapped preschool children with handicapped and nonhandicapped peers in integrated situations. *Topics in Early Childhood Special Education, 2,* 28-38.

Fine, A. H. (Ed.). (2006). *Handbook of animal-assisted therapy: Theoretical foundations and guidelines for practice.* San Diego, CA: Academic Press.

Fingarette, H. (1969). All work and no play. *Humanitas: Journal of the Institute of Man 5,* 3-19.

Finlinson, A. R., Austin, A. M., & Pfister, R. (2000). Cooperative games and children's positive behaviors. *Early Child Development and Care, 164,* 29-40.

Fiorentino, L. H. (2004). Assessment as an adventure activity. In R. L. Clements & L. Fiorentino (Eds.), *The child's right to play: A global approach* (pp. 171-173). Westport, CT: Praeger.

Fiortoft, I., & Ingunn, L. (2001). The natural environment as a playground for children: The impact of outdoor play activities in pre-primary school children. *Early Childhood Education Journal, 29,* 111-117.

Fishbein, H. D., & Imai, S. (1993). Preschoolers select playmates on the basis of gender and race. *Journal of Applied Developmental Psychology, 14,* 303–316.

Fitzsimmons, P., & McKennzie, B. (2003). Play on words: Humor as the means of developing authentic learning. In D. E. Lytle (Ed.), *Play and educational theory and practice* (pp. 197–211). Westport, CT: Praeger.

Fitzpatrick, T. R., Spiro, A., Kressin, N. R., Greene, E., & Bossé, R. (2001). Leisure activities, stress, and health among bereaved and non-bereaved elderly men: The Normative Aging Study. *Omega: Journal of Death and Dying, 43,* 217–245.

Fivaz-Depeursinge, E., & Favez, N. (2006). Exploring triangulation in infancy: Two contrasted cases. *Family Process, 45,* 3–18.

Flores-Martins, M. (2004). Play initiative in Brazil. In R. L. Clements & L. Fiorentino (Eds.), *The child's right to play: A global approach* (pp. 63–65). Westport, CT: Praeger.

Foley, Y. C., Higdon, L., & White, J. (2006). A qualitative study of filial therapy: Parents' Voices. *International Journal of Play Therapy, 15,* 37–64.

Frances, H. M., Milton, S., & Phelps, P. (2001). Young children's block construction activities: Findings from three years of observations. *Journal of Early Intervention, 24,* 224–237.

Frasher, R. S., Nurss, J. R., & Brogan, D. R. (1980). Children's toy preference revisited: Implications for early childhood education. *Child Care Quarterly, 9,* 26–31.

Fredman, L., Bertrand, R. M., Martire, L. M., Hochberg, M., & Harris, E. L. (2006). Leisure-time exercise and overall physical activity in older women caregivers and non-caregivers from the Caregiver-SOF study. *Preventive Medicine, 43,* 226–229.

Freeman, N. K., & Brown, M. H. (2004). The moral and ethical dimensions of controlling play. In R. L. Clements & L. Fiorentino (Eds.), *The child's right to play: A global approach* (pp. 9–21). Westport, CT: Praeger.

Freie, C. (1999). Rules in children's games and play. In S. Reifel (Ed.). (1999). *Play & culture studies* (pp. 83–100). Westport, CT: Ablex.

Fricchione, G. (2007). Altruistic love, resiliency, health, and the role of medicine. In S. G. Post (Ed.), *Altruism & health: Perspectives from empirical research* (pp. 350–370). New York: Oxford University Press.

Friedrich-Cofer, L. K. (1979). Environmental enhancement of prosocial television content: Effects on interpersonal behavior, imaginative play, and self-regulation in a natural setting. *Developmental Psychology, 15,* 637–646.

Frost, J. L., Shin, D., & Jacobs, P. J. (1998). Physical environments and children's play. In O. N. Saracho & B. Spodek, (Eds.), *Multiple perspectives on play in early childhood education* (pp. 255–294). Albany, NY: State University of New York Press.

Frost, J., & Steele, C. (2004). Play deprivation and juvenile violence: Neuroscience, play, and child development. In R. L. Clements & L. Fiorentino (Eds.), *The child's right to play: A global approach* (pp. 343–346). Westport, CT: Praeger.

Fry, D. P. (1990). Play aggression among Zapotec children: Implications for the practice hypothesis. *Aggressive Behavior, 16,* 321–340.

Fry, D. P. (2005). Rough-and-tumble social play in humans. In A. D. Pellegrini & P. K. Smith (Eds.), *The nature of play: Great apes and humans* (pp. 54–85). New York: Guilford.

Fry, L., Kerr, S., & Lee, C. (1986). Effects of different leader behaviors under different levels of task interdependence. *Human Relations, 39,* 1067–1082.

Galver, K.T., & Evans, I. (2001). Pretend play and the development of emotion regulation in preschool children. *Early Child Development and Care, 166,* 93–106.

Garnier, C., & Latour, A. (1994). Analysis of group process: Cooperation of preschool children. *Canadian Journal of Behavioral Science, 26,* 365–384.

Garvey, C., & Kramer, T. L. (1989). The language of social pretend play. *Developmental Review, 9,* 364–382.

Gaskins, S., Haight, W., Lancy, D. F. (2006). The cultural construction of play. In A. Goncu & S. Gaskins (Eds.), *Play and development: Evolutionary, sociocultural, and functional perspectives.* Mahwah, NJ: Erlbaum.

Gee, J. P. (2008). Video games and embodiment. *Games and Culture, 3,* 253–263.

George, S. W., & Krantz, M. (1981). The effects of preferred play partnership on communication adequacy. *Journal of Psychology: Interdisciplinary and Applied, 109,* 245–253.

Gerdner, L. A. (2000). Music, art, and recreational therapies in the treatment of behavioral and psychological symptoms of dementia. *International Psychogeriatrics, 12,* 359–366.

Getz, S. K., & Berndt, E. (1982). A test of method to quantifying amount, complexity, and arrangement of play resources in the preschool classroom. *Journal of Applied Developmental Psychology, 3,* 295–305.

Ghafoori, B., & Hierholzer, R. (2007). The role of love, attachment, and altruism in the adjustment to military trauma. In S. G. Post (Ed.), *Altruism & health: Perspectives from empirical research* (pp. 231–245). New York: Oxford University Press.

Gil. E., & Drewes, A.A. (2005). *Cultural issues in play therapy.* New York: Guilford.

Gilmore, J. B. (1982). Play: A special behavior. In R. E. Herron & B. Sutton-Smith (Eds.), *Child's play* (pp. 311–325). Malabar, FL: Robert E. Krieger Publishing Company.

Gilmore, J. B., Best, H., & Eakins, S. L. (1980). Coping with test anxiety: Individual differences in seeking complex play materials. *Canadian Journal of Behavioral Science, 12,* 241–254.

Ginsberg, B. G. (1993). Catharsis. In C. E. Schaefer, (Ed.), *The therapeutic power of play* (pp. 107–141). Northvale, NJ: Aronson.

Ginsberg, B. G. (2002). The power of filial relationship enhancement therapy as an intervention in child abuse and neglect. *International Journal of Play Therapy, 11(1),* 65–78.

Ginsburg, H. J., Pollman, V. A. Wauson, M. S., & Hope, M. L. (1977). Variation of aggressive interaction among male elementary school children as a function of changes in spatial density. *Environmental Psychology & Nonverbal Behavior, 2,* 67–75.

Giordano, R. G. (2003). *Fun and games in the twentieth-century America: A historical guide to leisure.* Westport, CT: Greenwood.

Gitlin-Weiner, K., Sandgrund, A., & Schaefer, C. (Eds.). (2000). *Play diagnosis and assessment.* New York: Wiley.

Giuliano, T. A., Popp, K. E., & Knight, J. L. (2000). Footballs versus babies: Child-hood play activities as predictors of sport participation by women. *Sex Roles, 42,* 159–181.

Glasser, William (2001). *Counseling with choice theory.* New York: Harper.

Gmitrova, V., & Gmitrov, J. (2004). The primacy of child-directed pretend play on cognitive competence in a mixed-age environment: Possible interpretations. *Early Child Development and Care, 174,* 267–279.

Gocke-Morey, M. C., Harold, G. T., Cummings, E. M., & Shelton, K. H. (2003). Categories and continua of destructive and constructive marital conflict tactics from the perspective of U.S. and Welsh children. *Journal of Family Psychology, 17,* 327–338.

Goetz, E. M. (1981). The effects of minimal praise on the creative blockbuilding of three-year-olds. *Child Study Journal, 11,* 55–67.

Goldman, L. R. (1998). *Child's play: Myth, mimesis, and make-believe.* New York: Berg.

Goldstein, J. (1995). Aggressive toy play. In A. D. Pellegrini (Ed.), *The future of play theory: A multidisciplinary inquiry into the contributions of Brian Sutton-Smith* (pp. 127–147). Albany, NY: State University of New York Press.

Goldstein, J., Buckingham, D., & Brougere, G. (Eds.). (2004). *Toys, games, and media.* Mahwah, NJ: Erlbaum.

Gomez, J-C., & Martin-Andrade, B. (2005). Fantasy play in apes. In A. D. Pellegrini & P. K. Smith (Eds.), *The nature of play: Great apes and humans* (pp. 139–172). New York: Guilford.

Goodfader, R. A. (1982). Sex differences in the play constructions of preschool children. *Smith College Studies in Social Work, 52,* 129–144.

Goodwin, M. H. (1995). Co-construction in girls' hopscotch. *Research on Language and Social Interaction, 28,* 261–281.

Goodwin, M. H. (2001). Organizing participation in cross-sex jump rope: Situating gender differences within longitudinal studies of activities. *Research on Language and Social Interaction, 34,* 75–106.

Goodwin, M. H., Goodwin, C., & Yaeger-Dror, M. (2002). Multi-modality in girls' game disputes. *Journal of Pragmatics, 34,* 1621–1649.

Goodwin, M. P., Sawyers, J. K., & Bailey, K. (1988). The effects of exploration on preschoolers' problem-solving ability. *Journal of Genetic Psychology, 149,* 317–333.

Gosso, Y., Otta, E., Morais, M., De Lima S., Ribeiro, F. J. L., & Bussad, V. S. (2005). Play in hunter-gatherer society. In A. D. Pellegrini & P. K. Smith (Eds.), *The nature of play: Great apes and humans* (pp. 213–253). New York: Guilford.

Gottfried, A. W. (1985). The relationship of play materials and parental involvement to young children's development. In C. C. Brown & A. W. Gottfried (Eds.), *Play inter-actions: The role of toys and parental involvement in children's development* (pp. 181–185). Skillman, NJ: Johnson & Johnson Baby Products Company.

Graham, D. F., Graham, I., & MacLean, M. J. (1991). Going to the mall: A leisure activity of urban elderly people. *Canadian Journal on Aging, 10,* 345–358.

Gramza, A. F., & Witt, P. A. (1969). Choices of colored blocks in the play of pre-school children. *Perceptual and Motor Skills, 29,* 783–787.

Green, V. P. (1984). Teachers and the play curriculum: Issues and trends. *Early Childhood Development and Care, 17,* 13–21.

Green, V. A., Bigler, R., & Catherwood, D. (2004). The variability and flexibility of gender-typed toy play: A close look at children's behavioral responses to counterstereotypic models. *Sex Roles, 51,* 371–386.

Greenberg, N. (2004). The beast at play: The neuroethology of creativity. In R. L. Clements & L. Fiorentino (Eds.), *The child's right to play: A global approach* (pp. 309–327). Westport, CT: Praeger.

Greenwood, C. R., Walker, H. M., Todd, N. M., & Hops, H. (1981). Normative and descriptive analysis of preschool free play social interaction rates. *Journal of Pediatric Psychology, 6,* 343–367.

Griffin, J., & McKenna, K. (1998). Influences on leisure and life satisfaction of elderly people. *Physical & Occupational Therapy in Geriatrics. 15,* 1–16.

Grinder, E. L. (1995). The influence of toy sex-type on preschoolers' social pretend and interactive behavior in same- and mixed-sex dyads. *Dissertation Abstracts International: Section A: Humanities and Social Sciences, 55,* 2709.

Gross, D. L. (2003). An introduction to research in psychology: Learning to observe children at play. In D. E. Lytle (Ed.), *Play and educational theory and practice* (pp. 34–41). Westport, CT: Praeger.

Grossman, B. D. (2004). Play and cognitive development: A Piagetian Perspective. In R. L. Clements & L. Fiorentino (Eds.), *The child's right to play: A global approach* (pp. 89–94). Westport, CT: Praeger.

Grossman, K., Grossman, K. E., Fremmer-Bombik, E., Kindler, H., Scheuerer-Englisch, H., & Zimmerman, P. (2002). The uniqueness of the father-child attachment relationship: Fathers' sensitive and challenging play as a pivotal variable in a 16-year longitudinal study. *Social Development, 11,* 307–331.

Grugeon, E. (2004). From Pokemon to Potter: Trainee teachers explore children's media-related play, 2000–2003. In J. Goldstein, D. Buckinghams, & G. Brougere (Eds.), *Toys, games, and media* (pp. 73–89). Mahwah, NJ: Erlbaum.

Guerney, B. G. (1964). Filial therapy: Description and rationale. *Journal of Consulting Psychology, 28,* 303–310.

Guerney, L. F. (1976). Training manual for parents: Instruction in filial therapy. In C. E. Schaefer (Ed.), *Therapeutic use of child's play* (pp. 216–227). New York: Jason Aronson.

Guerney, L. F. (2003). Filial play therapy. In C. E. Schaefer (Ed.), *Foundations of play therapy* (pp. 99–142). Hoboken, NJ: Wiley.

Guinn, B., & Vincent, V. (2002). Select physical activity determinants in independent-living elderly. *Activities, Adaptation, & Aging, 26,* 17–26.

Gunnarson, D. F. (1997). Patterns of aggression among preschool children: A naturalistic observation. *Dissertation Abstracts International: Section B. The Sciences and Engineering, 58,* 0407.

Haight, W. I., Black, J. E. (2001). A comparative approach to play: Cross-species and cross-cultural perspectives of play in development. *Human Development, 44,* 228–234.

Haight, W. I., & Sachs, K. (1995). The portrayal of negative emotions during mother child pretend play. In L. L. Sperry & P. A. Smiley (Eds.), *Exploring young children's concepts of self and other through conversation* (pp. 33-46). San Francisco, CA: Jossey-Bass.

Halverson, E. E., & Halverson, R. (2008). Fantasy baseball. *Games and Culture, 3,* 286-308.

Halverson, C. F., & Waldrop, M. F. (1973). The relations of mechanically recorded activity level to varieties of preschool play behavior. *Child Development, 44,* 678-681.

Harkness, A. R. (2007). Personality traits are essential for a complete clinical science. In S. O. Lilienfeld & W. T. O'Donohue (Eds.), *The great ideas of clinical science: 17 principles that every mental health professional should understand* (pp. 263-290). New York: Routledge.

Harrington, R. G. (1987). Creativity in child's play: Verbal elaborations as a facilitator of creative play. *Techniques, 3,* 312-319.

Harris-Strapko, B. E. (2003). A phenomenological study through symbolic interactionism of the leisure lifestyles of Vietnam veterans with post traumatic stress disorder. *Dissertation Abstracts International: Section B: The Sciences and Engineering, 63,* 4636.

Harrison, H., & Kielhofner, G. (1986). Examining reliability and validity of the Preschool Play Scale with handicapped children. *American Journal of Occupational Therapy, 40,* 167-173.

Hart, C. H., & Sheenan, R. (1986). Preschoolers' play behavior in outdoor environments: Effects of traditional and contemporary playgrounds. *American Educational Research Journal, 23,* 668-678.

Hart, C. H., DeWolf, M., & Burts, D. C. (1993). Parental disciplinary strategies and preschoolers' play behavior in playground settings. In C. H. Hart (Ed.), *Children on playgrounds: Research perspectives and applications* (pp. 271-313). Albany, NY: State University of New York Press.

Hartmann, W., & Rollett. B. (1994). Play: Positive intervention in the elementary school curriculum. In J. Hellendoom, R. van der Kooij, & B. Sutton-Smith (Eds.), *Play and intervention* (pp. 195-202). Albany, NY: State University of New York Press.

Harwood, T. M., & L'Abate, L. (2009). *The self-help movement in mental health: A critical evaluation.* New York: Springer.

Hatakeyama, M., & Yamazaki, A. (2002). An observational study of preschoolers' aggressive behavior in free play, in relation to gender and peer group status. *Japanese Journal of Developmental Psychology, 13,* 252-260.

Havitz, M. E., & Howard, D. R. (1995). How enduring is enduring involvement? A seasonal examination of three recreational activities. *Journal of Consumer Psychology, 4,* 255-276.

Hay, D. F. (2007). The gradual emergence of sex differences in aggression: Alternative Hypotheses. *Psychological Medicine, 37,* 1527-1537.

Hayes, E. R., & Games, I. A. (2008). Making computer games and design thinking. *Games and Culture, 3,* 309-331.

Hedenbro, M., Shapiro, A. F., Gottman, J. M. (2006). Play with me at my speed: Describing differences in the tempo of parent-infant interactions in the Lausanne Triadic Play paradigm in two cultures. *Family Process, 45,* 485-498.

Hein, H. (1969). Play as an aesthetic concept. *Humanitas: Journal of the Institute of Man, 5,* 21-28.

Hellendoorn, J., van der Kooij, R., & Sutton-Smith, B. (Eds.). (1994). *Play and intervention.* Albany, NY: State University of New York Press.

Hendrickson, J. M., Strain, P. S., Tremblay, A., & Shores, R. E. (1981). Relationship between toy and material use and the occurrence of social interactive behaviors by normally developing preschool children. *Psychology in the Schools, 18,* 500-504.

Henniger, M. L. (1994). Computers and preschool children's play: Are they compatible? *Journal of Computing in Childhood Education, 5,* 231-239.

Henricks, T. S. (1999). Play as ascending meaning: Implications of a general model of play. In S. Reifel (Ed.). (1999). *Play & culture studies* (pp. 257-277). Westport, CT: Ablex.

Henricks, T. S. (2002). Huinzinga's contributions to play studies: A reappraisal. In J. L. Roopnarine (Ed.), *Conceptual, social-cognitive, and contextual issues in the field of play; Volume 4* (pp. 23-52). Westport, CT: Ablex.

Herron, R. E., & Sutton-Smith, B. (1971, 1982). *Child's play.* New York: Wiley.

Hestenes, L. L., & Carroll, D. E. (2000). The play interactions of young children with and without disabilities: Individual and environmental influence. *Early Childhood Research Quarterly, 15,* 229-246.

Heth, C. D., & Cornell, E. H. (1998). Characteristics of travel by persons lost in Albertan wilderness areas. *Journal of Environmental Psychology, 18,* 223-236.

Heyl, V., Wahl, H., & Mollenkopf, H. (2005). Virtual capacity, out-of-home activities and emotional well-being in old age: Basic relations and contextual variations. *Social Indicators Research, 74,* 159-189.

Higgins, E. T. (2005). Humans as applied motivation scientists: Self-consciousness from "shared reality" and "becoming." In H. S. Terrace, & J. Metcalfe (Eds.), *The missing link in cognition: Origins of self-reflective consciousness* (pp. 157-173). New York: Oxford University Press.

Hill, K. A. (1992). Spatial competences of elderly hunters. *Environment and Behavior, 24,* 779-794.

Hill, O. (1998). Childhood fantasy, creativity, and an internal epistemic style. *Journal of Social Behavior & Personality, 13,* 177-183.

Hirschfelder, A. S., & Reilly, S. L. (2007). Rx: Volunteer: A prescription for healthy aging. In S. G. Post (Ed.), *Altruism & health: Perspectives from empirical research* (pp. 116-140). New York: Oxford University Press.

Ho, Y. C., & Chan, A. S. (2005). Comparing the effects of Mahjong playing and reading on cognitive reserve of the elderly. *Journal of Psychology in Chinese Societies, 6,* 5-26.

Hogg, J., Rogers, S., & Sebba, J. (1988). The effect of classroom provision on object-related social play in an ability-integrated preschool classroom. *Advances in Behavior Research & Therapy, 10,* 25-37.

Hohn, D. (2008). Through the open door: Searching for deadly toys in China's Pearl River Delta. *Harper's,* September Issue, pp. 47-58.

Hold-Cavell, B. C., Attili, G., & Schleidt, M. (1986). A cross-cultural comparison of children's behaviour during their first year in a preschool. *International Journal of Behavioral Development, 9,* 471-483.

Holmes, R. M. (1999). Kindergarten and college students' views of play and work at home and at school. In S. Reifel (Ed.), *Play & culture studies* (pp. 59-72). Westport, CT: Ablex.

Holmes, R. M., & Geiger, C. J. (2002). The relationship between creativity and cognitive abilities in preschoolers. In J. L. Roopnarine (Ed.), *Conceptual, social-cognitive, and contextual issues in the field of play; Volume 4* (pp. 127-148). Westport, CT: Ablex.

Homeyer, L. E., & Sweeney, D. (2005). Sandtray therapy. In C. Malchiodi (Ed.), *Handbook of expressive therapies* (pp. 12-183). New York: Guilford.

Horne, A. M., Raczynski, K., & Orpinas, P. (2008). A clinical laboratory approach to reducing bullying and aggression in schools and families. In L. L'Abate (Ed.), *Toward a science of clinical psychology: Laboratory evaluations and interventions* (pp. 117-131). Hauppauge, NY: Nova Science Publishers.

Howard, A. C. (1986). Developmental play ages of physically abused and nonabused children. *American Journal of Occupational Therapy, 40,* 691-695.

Howe, C. Z. (1987). Selected social gerontology theories and older adult leisure involvement: A review of the literature. *Journal of Applied Gerontology, 6,* 448-463.

Hudson, S., & Thompson, D. (2004). Guidelines for managing playground risks. In R. L. Clements & L. Fiorentino (Eds.), *The child's right to play: A global approach* (pp. 163-169). Westport, CT: Praeger.

Hughes, J. E. (1982). "My daddy's number is C-92760." *Journal of Children in Contemporary Society, 15,* 79-87.

Hughes, F. P. (1998). Play in special populations. In O. N. Saracho & B. Spodek, (Eds.), *Multiple perspectives on play in early childhood education* (pp. 171-193). Albany, NY: State University of New York Press.

Hunnicutt, B. K. (1985). Economic constraints of leisure. In M. G. Wade (Ed.), *Constraints on leisure* (pp. 243-286). Springfield, IL: Thomas.

Huston-Stein, A. U., Friedrich-Cofer, L., & Susman, E. J. (1977). The relation of classroom structure to social behavior, imaginative play, and self-regulation of economically disadvantaged children. *Child Development, 48,* 908-916.

Hutchison, S. S. (2005). *Effects of and interventions for childhood trauma from infancy through adolescence: Pain unspeakable.* Binghamton, NY: Haworth.

Hutt, C. (1971). Exploration and play in children. In R. E. Herron & B. Sutton-Smith (Eds.), *Child's play* (pp. 231-251). New York: Wiley.

Hutt, C. (1982). Exploration and play in children. In R. E. Herron & B. Sutton-Smith (Eds.), *Child's play* (pp. 231-251). Malabar, FL: Robert E. Krieger.

Hyde, J. S., Rosenberg, B. G., & Behrman, J. A. (1977). Tomboyism. *Psychology of Women Quarterly, 2,* 73-75.

Iacoboni, M., Woods, R.P., Brass, M., Bekkering, H., Mazziotta, J.C., & Rizzolatti, G. (1999). Cortical mechanisms of human imitation. *Science, 286,* 2526–2528.

Ilgaz, H., & Aksu-Koc, A. (2005). Episodic development in preschool children's play-prompted and direct-elicited narratives. *Cognitive Development, 20,* 526–544.

International Play Association (2004). Declaration of the child's right to play. In R. L. Clements & L. Fiorentino (Eds.), *The child's right to play: A global approach* (pp. 393–397). Westport, CT: Praeger.

Ireson, J., & Blay, J. (1999). Constructing activity: Participation by adults and children. *Learning and Instruction, 9,* 19–36.

Isambert, F.A. (1969). Feast and celebrations: Some critical reflections on the idea of celebrations. *Humanitas: Journal of the Institute of Man, 5,* 29–41.

Isenberg, J., & Jacob, E. (1983). Literacy and symbolic play: A review of the literature. *Childhood Education, 59,* 272–276.

Isobe, M., Kirk, M., Filho, C., & Maeda, K. (2004). Behavioral orientations and peer-contact patterns of relationally aggressive girls. *Psychological Reports, 94,* 327–334.

Ivory, J. J., & McCullum, J.A. (1999). Effects of social and isolate toys on social play in an inclusive setting. *The Journal of Special Education, 32,* 238–243.

Jackson, E. L. (1986). Outdoor recreation participation and attitudes toward the environment. *Leisure Sciences, 5,* 1–23.

Jackson, E. L. (1987). Outdoor recreation participation and views on resource development and preservation. *Leisure Sciences, 9,* 235–250.

Jackson, S. J. (1998). The 49th paradox: The 1988 Calgary Winter Olympic Games and Canadian identity as contextual terrain. In M. C. Duncan, G. Chick, & A. Aycock (Eds.), *Play & culture studies: Diversions and divergencies in fields of play. Volume 1* (pp. 199–222). Greenwich, CT: Ablex

Jahr, E., & Eldevik, S. (2002). Teaching cooperative play to typical children utilizing a behavior modeling approach: A systematic replication. *Behavioral Interventions, 17,* 145–157.

James, O. O. (1997). *Play therapy: A comprehensive guide.* Northvale, NJ: Aronson.

Jarrett, O. S., & Duckett-Hedgebeth, M. (2003). Recess in middle school: What do the students do? In D. E. Lytle (Ed.), *Play and educational theory and practice* (pp. 227–241). Westport, CT: Praeger.

Jennings, S. (1999). *Introduction to developmental play therapy: Playing and health.* London, UK: Jessica Kingsley Publishers.

Jensen-Arnett, J. (2007). (Ed.). *Encyclopedia of children, adolescents, and the media.* Thousand Oaks, CA: Sage.

Jernberg, A. M., & Booth, S. (1999). *Theraplay: Helping parents and children build better relationships through attachment-based play,* 2nd Edition. San Francisco, CA: Jossey-Bass.

Johansson, E., & Samuelson, I. P. (2006). Play and learning—Inseparable dimensions in preschool practice. *Early Child Development and Care, 176,* 441.

Johnson, P. A. (1972). A comparison of personality traits of superior skilled women athletes in basketball, field hockey, and golf. *Research Quarterly, 43,* 409–415.

Johnson, J. E. (1978). Mother-child interaction and imaginative behavior of pre-school children. *Journal of Psychology: Interdisciplinary and Applied, 100,* 123-129.

Johnson, J. E., & Ershler, J. (1981). Developmental trends in preschool play as a function of classroom program and child gender. *Child Development, 52,* 995-1004.

Johnson, J. E., Ershler, J., & Bell, C. (1980). Play behavior in a discovery-based and a formal education preschool program. *Child Development, 51,* 271-274.

Jones, E. M., & Landreth, G. (2002). The efficacy of intensive play therapy for chronically ill children. *International Journal of Play Therapy, 11(1),* 117-140.

Jones, L., Rhine, T., & Bratton, S. (2002). High school students as therapeutic agents with young children experiencing school adjustment difficulties: The effectiveness of a filial therapy training model. *International Journal of Play Therapy, 11(2),* 43-62.

Juhlin, G. T. (2004). Scandinavian Viking games. In R. L. Clements & L. Fiorentino (Eds.), *The child's right to play: a global approach* (pp. 197-202). Westport, CT: Praeger.

Kaduson, H. G., & Schaefer, C. E. (Eds.) (2000). *Short-term play therapy for children.* New York: Guilford.

Kagan, J. (2007). *What are emotions?* New Haven. CT: Yale University Press.

Kamii, C., & Kato, Y. (2005). Fostering the development of Logical-Mathematical Thinking in a card game at ages 5-6. *Early Education and Development, 16,* 367-383.

Kaplan, F. F. (Ed.). (2007). *Art therapy and social action.* London, UK: Jessica Kindsley.

Karcher, M. J. (2002). The principles and practices of pair counseling: A dyadic developmental play therapy for aggressive, withdrawn, and socially immature youth. *International Journal of Play Therapy, 11,* 121-147.

Karcher, J. M., & Lewis, S. S. (2002). Pair counseling: The effects of a dyadic developmental play therapy on interpersonal understanding and externalizing behaviors. *International Journal of Play Therapy, 11(1),* 19-41.

Karkou, V., & Sanderson, P. (2005). *Art therapies: A research based map of the field.* London, UK: Elsevier.

Karp, A., Paillard-Borg, S., Wang, H. X., Silverstein, M., Winblad, B., Fratiglioni L., et al., (2006). Mental, physical, and social components in leisure activities equally contribute to decreased dementia risk. *Dementia and Geriatric Cognitive Disorders, 21,* 65-73.

Katz, J. R. (2001). Playing at home: The talk of pretend play. In D. K. Dickinson & P. O. Tabors (Eds.), *Beginning literacy with language: Young children learning at home and school* (pp. 53-73). Baltimore, MD: Paul H. Brookes Publishing.

Katz, J. C., & Bucholz, E. S. (1999). "I did it myself": The necessity of solo play for preschoolers. *Early Child Development and Care, 155,* 39-50.

Kavanaugh, R. D. (2006). Pretend play. In B. Spodek & O. N. Saracho (Eds.), *Handbook of Research on the Education of Young Children, 2nd ed.* (pp. 269-278). Mahwah, NJ: Erlbaum.

Kavanaugh, R. D., & Engel, S. (1998). The development of pretense and narrative in early childhood. In O. N. Saracho & B. Spodek, (Eds.), *Multiple perspectives on play in early childhood education* (pp. 80–99). Albany, NY: State University of New York Press.

Kearns, Y. E., Edwards, J., & Carlucci, C. (2004). Play of reconciliation: Play between parent and child. In R. L. Clements & L. Fiorentino (Eds.), *The child's right to play: A global approach* (pp. 71–75). Westport, CT: Praeger.

Kehily, M. J., & Swann, J. (Eds.). (2003). *Children's cultural worlds*. Chichester, UK: Wiley.

Keren, M., Feldman, R., Namdari-Weinbaum, L., Spitzer, S., & Tyano, S. (2005). Relations between parents' interactive style in dyadic and triadic play and toddlers' symbolic capacity. *American Journal of Orthopsychiatry, 75*, 599–607.

Kerns, K. A., & Barth, J. M. (1995). Attachment and play: Convergence across components of parent-child relationships and their relations to peer competence. *Journal of Social and Personal Relationships, 12*, 243–260.

Kidd, A. H., & Kidd, R. M. (1987). Reactions of infants and toddlers to live and toy animals. *Psychological Reports, 61*, 455–464.

Kijima, R. Shirakawa, K., Hirose, M., and Nihei, K. (1994) Virtual sandbox: Development of an application of virtual environment for clinical medicine. *Presence: Teleoperators and Virtual Environments, 3*, 777–784.

King, N. R. (1991). See baby play: Play as depicted in elementary school readers, 1900–1950. *Play & Culture, 4*, 100–107.

Kingsley, R. F., Viggiano, R. A., & Tout, L. (1981). Social perception of friendship, leadership, and game playing among EMR special and regular class boys. *Education & Training of the Mentally Retarded, 16*, 201–206.

Kinsbourne, M. (2005). A continuum of self-consciousness that emerges in phylogeny and ontogeny. In H. S. Terrace, & J. Metcalfe (Eds.), *The missing link in cognition: Origins of self-reflective consciousness* (pp. 142–156). New York: Oxford University Press.

Kittle, K. (2005). *The kindness of strangers*. New York: HarperCollins.

Kleiber, D. A., & Richards, W. H. (1985). Leisure and recreation in adolescence: Limitation and potential. In M. G. Wade (Ed.), *Constraints on leisure* (pp. 289–314). Springfield, IL: C. C. Thomas.

Kleine, S. (1995). The promotion and marketing of toys: Time to rethink the paradox? In A. D. Pellegrini (Ed.), *The future of play theory: A multidisciplinary inquiry into the contributions of Brian Sutton-Smith* (pp. 165–185). Albany, NY: State University of New York Press.

Klitzing, S. W. (2004). Women who are homeless: Leisure and affiliation. *Therapeutic Recreation Journal, 38*, 348–365.

Knox, S. H. (1997). Play and play styles of preschool children. *Dissertation Abstracts International: Section B: The Sciences and Engineering, 58*, 2387.

Koenig, H. G. (2007) Altruistic love and physical health. In S. G. Post (Ed.), *Altruism & health: Perspectives from empirical research* (pp. 422–441). New York: Oxford University Press.

Koenig, L. B., & Bouchard, T. J., Jr. (2006). Genetic and environmental influences on the traditional moral values triad—Authoritarianism, Conservativism, and

Religiousness as assessed by quantitative behavior genetic methods. In P. McNamara (Ed.), *Where God and science meet: How brain and evolution studies alter our understanding or religion; Vol. 1: Evolution, genes, and the religious brain* (pp. 31–60). Westport, CT: Praeger.

Kolanowski, A., Buettner, L., & Moeller, J. (2006). Treatment fidelity plan for and activity intervention designed for persons with dementia. *American Journal of Alzheimer's Disease and Other Dementias, 21*, 326–332.

Kottman, T. (2003). *Partners in play: An Adlerian approach to play therapy.* Alexandra, VA: American Counseling Association.

Kowalski, H. S., Wyer, S. R., Masselos, G., & De Lacey, P. (2004). Toddlers' emerging symbolic play: A first-born advantage? *Early Child Development and Care, 174*, 389–400.

Kyratzis, A. (1999). Narrative identity: Preschoolers' self-construction through narrative in same-sex friendship group dramatic play. *Narrative Inquiry, 9*, 427–455.

L'Abate, L. (1964). Il metodo di laboratorio nella psicodiagnosi (The laboratory method in psychodiagnosis). *Bollettino di Psicologia Applicata, 63–64*, 36–39.

L'Abate, L. (1968a). The laboratory method as an alternative to existing mental health models. *American Journal of Orthopsychiatry, 38*, 296–297.

L'Abate, L. (1968b). Una stanza da giuco automatizzata (An automated playroom). *Bollettino di Psicologia Applicata, 88–90*, 43–54.

L'Abate, L. (1971). Receptive-expressive functions in kindergarten children and adolescents. *Psychology in the Schools, 8*, 253–259.

L'Abate, L. (1973). The laboratory method in clinical child psychology: Three applications. *Journal of Clinical Child Psychology, 2*, 8–10.

L'Abate, L. (1979). Aggression and construction in children's monitored play therapy. *Journal of Counseling and Psychotherapy, 2*, 137–158.

L'Abate, L. (1994). *A theory of personality development.* New York: Wiley.

L'Abate, L. (1997). *The self in the family: A classification of personality, criminality, and psychopathology.* New York: Wiley.

L'Abate, L. (1999). Programmed distance writing in therapy with acting-out adolescents. In Schaefer, C. E. (Ed.). (1999). *Innovative psychotherapy techniques in child and adolescent therapy* (pp. 108–157). New York: Wiley.

L'Abate, L. (2001). Hugging, holding, huddling, and cuddling (3HC): A task prescription in couples and family therapy. *The Journal of Clinical Activities, Assignments, & Handouts in Psychotherapy Practice, 1*, 5–18.

L'Abate, L. (2004). *A guide to self-help workbooks for mental health clinicians and researchers.* Binghamton, NY: Haworth.

L'Abate, L. (2005). *Personality in intimate relationships: Socialization and psycho-pathology.* New York: Springer.

L'Abate, L. (2007). Animal companions. In L. L'Abate (Ed.), *Low-cost approaches to promote physical and mental health* (pp. 473–483). New York: Springer.

L'Abate, L. (2008). *Toward a science of clinical psychology: Laboratory evaluations and interventions.* Hauppauge, NY: Nova Science Publishers.

L'Abate, L. (2009). The Drama Triangle: An attempt to resurrect a neglected pathogenic model in family therapy theory and practice. *American Journal of Family Therapy, 37*, 1–11.

L'Abate, L. (in press a). *Hurt feelings: Theory, research, and applications in inti-mate relationships.* New York: Cambridge University Press.

L'Abate, L. (in press b). Two hierarchical frameworks for epistemological psychology and relational competence theory. In P. De Giacomo, M. Capitelli, L. L'Abate, & S. Longo (Eds.), *Mind, science, and creativity: The Bari sympo-sium.* Hauppauge, NY: Nova Science Publishers.

L'Abate, L., & Cusinato, M. (2007). Linking theory with practice: Theory-derived interventions in prevention and psychotherapy. *The Family Journal: Counsel-ing and Therapy with Couples and Families, 15,* 318-327.

L'Abate, L., Cusinato, M., Maino, E., Colesso, W., & Scilletta, C. (in press). *Relational competence theory: Research and mental health applications.* New York: Springer.

L'Abate, L., & De Giacomo, P. (2003). *Intimate relationships and how to improve them: Integrating theoretical models with preventive and psychotherapeutic applications.* Westport, CT: Praeger.

Lagace-Segui, D. G., & d'Entremont. M.R. L. (2006). The role of child negative affect in the relations between parenting styles and play. *Early Child Development and Care, 176,* 461-477.

Lamb, S., & Coakley, M. (1993). "Normal" childhood sexual play and games: Differ-entiating play from abuse. *Child Abuse & Neglect, 17,* 515-526.

Lambert, S. F., LeBlanc, M., Mullen, J., Ray, D., Baggerly, J., White, J., & Kaplan, D. (2005a). Learning more about those who play in session: The national play therapy in counseling practices project (Phase I). *International Journal of Play Therapy, 14,* 7-23.

Lambert, S. F., LeBlanc, M., Mullen, J.A., Ray, D., Baggerly, J., White, J., & Kaplan, D. (2007b). Learning more about those who play in session: The national play therapy in counseling practices project (phase II). *Journal of Counseling & Development, 85,* 42-46.

Lancy, D. F. (1996). *Playing on the mother-ground: Cultural routines for chil-dren's development.* New York: Guilford.

Lancy, D. F. (2002). Cultural constraints on children's play. In J. L. Roopnarine (Ed.), *Conceptual, social-cognitive, and contextual issues in the field of play; Volume 4* (pp. 53-60). Westport, CT: Ablex.

Lancy, D. F. (2007). Accounting for variability in mother-child play. *American Anthropologist, 109,* 273-284.

Land, D. (2003). Teasing apart secondary students' conceptualizations of peer teasing, bullying, and sexual harassment. *School Psychology International, 24,* 147-165.

Landreth, G. L. (Ed.). (2001). *Innovations in play therapy: Issues, process, and special populations.* Philadelphia, PA: Brunner/Routledge.

Landreth, G. L. (2002). *Play therapy: The art of the relationship* (2nd ed.). New York: Routledge.

Landy, S., & Menna, R. (2001). Play between aggressive young children and their mothers. *Clinical Child Psychology and Psychiatry, 6,* 223-240.

Lang, M., & White, J. (2001). School psychologists and play therapy practice. *Com-muniqué, 30,* 26-28.

Lange, M. A. (2001). "If you do not gamble, check this box": Perceptions of gambling behaviors. *Journal of Gambling Studies, 17,* 247–254.

Laplante, D. P., Zelazo, P. R., Brunet, A., & King, S. (2007). Functional play at 2 years of age: Effects of prenatal maternal stress. *Infancy, 12,* 69–93.

Larder, D. L. (1962). Effect of aggressive story content on nonverbal play behavior. *Psychological Reports, II,* p. 14.

Lauritzen, P. (1992). Facilitating integrating teaching and learning in the preschool setting: A process approach. *Early Childhood Research Quarterly, 7,* 531–550.

Leaper, C., & Friedman, C. K. (2007). The socialization of gender. In J. E. Grusee & P. D. Hastings (Eds.), *Handbook of socialization: Theory and research* (pp. 561–587). New York: Guilford.

Lehman, H. C. (1926). A comparison of the play activities of town and country children. *Pedagogical Seminary, 33,* 455–476.

Leiter, M. P. (1977). A study of reciprocity in preschool play groups. *Child Development, 48,* 1278–1285.

Lejeune, C. W. (1995). The effects of participation in competitive and cooperative games on the free-play behavior of preschoolers. *Dissertation Abstracts International: Section B: The Sciences and Engineering, 55,* 4123.

Lennon, J. L. (2006). Reports and communications: Debriefings of web-based malaria games. *Simulation & Gaming, 37,* 350–346.

Levenstein, P. (1985). Mothers' interactive behavior in play sessions and children's educational achievement. In C. C. Brown & A. W. Gottfried (Eds.), *Play interactions: The role of toys and parental involvement in children's development* (pp. 160–167). Skillman, NJ: Johnson & Johnson Baby Care Products.

Levin, J. (2007). Integrating positive psychology into epidemiologic theory: Reflections on love, salutogenesis, and determinants of population health. In S. G. Post (Ed.), *Altruism & health: Perspectives from empirical research* (pp. 189–218). New York: Oxford University Press.

Levy, D. (1938). Release therapy in young children. *Psychiatry, 1,* 387–389.

Levy, J. (1978). *Play behavior.* New York: Wiley.

Levy, A. K. (1984). The language of play: The role of play in language development: A review of the literature. *Early Child Development and Care, 17,* 49–61.

Levy, A. K., Schaefer, L., & Phelps, P. C. (1986). Increasing preschool effectiveness: Enhancing the language abilities of 3- and 4-year-old children through planned sociodramatic play. *Early Childhood Research Quarterly, 1,* 133–140.

Liang, P. (1999). Playing with computers: Multiple correlates of young children's computer play behaviors. *Dissertation Abstracts International, Section A: Humanities and Social Sciences, 59,* 2844.

Lieberman, J. N. (1977). *Playfulness: Its relationship to imagination and creativity.* New York: Academic Press.

Lillard, A. S. (1998). Playing with a theory of mind. In O. N. Saracho & B. Spodek (Eds.), *Multiple perspectives on play in early childhood education* (pp. 11–33). Albany, NY: State University of New York Press.

Lillard, A. S., Nshida, T, Massaro, D., Valsh, A., Ma, L., McRoberts, G., et al. (2007). Signs of pretense across age and scenario. *Infancy, 11,* 1–30.

Lin, S-H., & Reifel, S. (1999). Context and meaning in Taiwanese kindergarten play. In S. Reifel (Ed.). (1999). *Play & culture studies* (pp. 151–176). Westport, CT: Ablex.

Lin, M-C., Johnson, J. E., & Johnson, K. M. (2004). Dramatic play in Montessori kindergarten in Taiwan and mainland China. In R. L. Clements & L. Fiorentino (Eds.), *The child's right to play: a global approach* (pp. 99-109). Westport, CT: Praeger.

Linder, S. B. (1970). *The hurried leisure class*. New York: Columbia University Press.

Lindley, E. H. (1997). A study of puzzles with special reference to the psychology of mental adaptation. *American Journal of Psychology, 8,* 431–493.

Lindsey, E. W. (2001). Contextual differences in parent-child play: Implications for children' gender role development. *Sex Roles, 44,* 155–176.

Lindsey, E. W., & Colwell, M. J. (2003). Preschooler's emotional competence: Links to pretend and physical play. *Child Study Journal, 32,* 145-156.

Lindsay, E. W., Mize, J., & Pettit, G. S. (1997). Differential play patterns of mothers and fathers of sons and daughters: Implications for children's gender role development. *Sex Roles, 37,* 643–661.

Lisul, I. (2004). Play as a coping strategy during a time of bombing and destruction. In R. L. Clements & L. Fiorentino (Eds.), *The child's right to play: A global approach* (pp. 55–61). Westport, CT: Praeger.

Livod, P., & Fernyhough, C. (Eds.). (1999). *Lev Vygotsky: Critical assessment: Thought and language,* Volume II. Florence, KY: Taylor & Francis/Routledge.

Lloyd, B., & Howe, N. (2003). Solitary play and convergent and divergent thinking skills in preschool children. *Early Childhood Research Quarterly 18,* 22–41.

Loeber, R, et al (2000). Physical fighting in childhood as a risk factor for later mental health problems. *Journal of the American Academy of Child and Adolescent Psychiatry, 39,* 421–428.

Logue P., Penrod J., Zackheim M. (1976). Comparison and partial validation of the Missouri Children's Picture Series on a residential deaf population. *Perceptual and Motor Skills, 42,* 1263-1267.

Long, S., Volk, D., & Gregory, E. (2007). Intentionality and expertise: Learning from observations of children at play in multilingual multicultural contexts. *Anthropology & Education Quarterly, 38,* 239–259.

Loy, J. W., & Hesketh, G.L. (1995). Competitive play on the Plains: An analysis of games and warfare among native American warrior societies, 1800–1850. In A. D. Pellegrini (Ed.), *The future of play theory: A multidisciplinary inquiry into the contributions of Brian Sutton-Smith* (pp. 73–105). Albany, NY: State University of New York Press.

Lozoff, B., Klein, N. K., & Prabucki, K. M. (1986). Iron-deficient anemic infants at play. *Journal of Developmental & Behavioral Pediatrics, 7,* 152-158.

Luszki, M., & Luszki, W. (1985). Advantages of growing older. *Journal of the American Geriatrics Society, 33,* 216-217.

Lyons, M. (2001). In support of a written curriculum based on sport psychology for high school sports teams. *Athletic Insight: Online Journal of Sport Psychology, 3.* Retrieved from http://www.athleticinsight.com/Vol.31ss2/Commentary.htm

Lytle, D. E. (2003). *Play and educational theory and practice*. Westport, CT: Praeger.

Maccoby, E. E. (1989). Gender as a social category. In S. Chess & M. Hetzig (Eds.), *Annual Progress in Child Psychiatry & Child Development*, 22nd Ed. (pp. 127–150). New York: Brunner/Mazel.

MacDonald, K. (Ed.). (1993). *Parent-child play: Descriptions and implications*. Albany, NY: State University of New York Press.

MacDonald, R., Clark, M., Garrigan, E., & Vangala, M. (2005). Using video modeling to teach pretend play to children with autism. *Behavioral Intervention, 20,* 225–238.

MacDonald, K., & Parke, R. D. (1984). Bridging the gap: Parent-child play interaction and peer interactive competence. *Child Development, 55,* 1265–1277.

Mackle, G. L. (1987). No one wants to play with me. *Academic Therapy, 22,* 477–484.

Mactavish, J., & Mahon, M. J. (2005). Leisure education and later-life planning: A conceptual framework. *Journal of Policy and Practice in Intellectual Disabilities, 2,* 29–37.

Maddi, S. (1989). *Personality theories: A comparative analysis*. Chicago, IL: Dorsey.

Madigan, S., Moran, G., Schuengel, C., Pederson, D. R., & Otten, R. (2007). Unresolved maternal attachment representations, disrupted maternal behavior and disorganized attachment in infancy: Links to toddler behavior problems. *Journal of Child Psychology and Psychiatry, 48,* 1042–1050.

Malmberg, J., Miilunpalo, S., Pasanen, M., Vuori, I., & Oja, P. (2005). Characteristics of leisure time physical activity associated with risk of decline in perceived health: A 10-year follow-up of middle-aged and elderly men and women. *Preventive Medicine: An International Journal Devoted to Practice and Theory, 41,* 141–150.

Malone, D. M. (2006). Contextually influenced patterns of play-developmental age associations for preschoolers with and without mental retardation. *Early Childhood Education Journal, 34,* 215–225.

Mancini, J. A., & Sandifer, D. M. (1995). Family dynamics and the leisure experiences of older adults: Theoretical viewpoints. In R. Blieszner & V. Bedford (Eds.), *Handbook of Aging and the Family* (pp. 132–147). Westport, CT: Greenwood Press.

Mann, D. (1996). Serious play. *Teachers College Record, 97,* 446–469.

Marcus, R. F. (1987). The role of affect in children's cooperation. *Child Study Journal, 17,* 153–168.

Marino, L., & Lilienfeld, S. O. (2007). Dolphin-assisted therapy: More flawed data and more flawed conclusions. *Anthropos, 20,* 239–249.

Marino-Schorn, J. A. (1986). Morale, work, and leisure in retirement. *Physical & Occupational Therapy in Geriatrics, 4,* 49–59.

Markman, L. H. (2004). The right to a work-free and playful childhood: A historical perspective. In R. L. Clements & L. Fiorentino (Eds.), *The child's right to play: A global approach* (pp. 3–15). Westport, CT: Praeger.

Martin, P. A. (1963). Play, recreation, and mental health. In A. Deutsch & H. Fishman (Eds.), *The encyclopedia of mental health* (pp. 1511–1522), New York: Franklin Watts.

Martin, A. (2000). The design and evolution of a simulation/game for teaching information systems technology. *Simulation and Gaming, 31,* 445-463.

Martini, M. (1994). Peer interaction in Polynesia: A view from the Marquesas. In J. L. Roopnarine, J. E. Johnson, & F. H. Hooper (Eds.). *Children's play in diverse cultures* (pp. 73-103). Albany, NY: State University of New York Press.

Matsui, M. (2000). Initiation of interactions with peers in play: A longitudinal study of preschoolers. *Japanese Journal of Educational Psychology, 12,* 285-294.

Matsui, M., Muto, T., & Kadoyama, M. (2001). The initiation of peer interaction: Analysis of preschoolers' free play. *Japanese Journal of Educational Psychology, 12,* 195-2005.

Mayer, J. D., Salovey, P., & Caruso, D. R. (2008). Emotional intelligence: New ability or eclectic traits? *American Psychologist, 63,* 503-517.

McCabe, L. A., Rebello-Britto, P., Harnandez, M., & Brooks-Gunn, J. (2004). Games children play: Observing young children's self-regulation across laboratory, home, and school settings. In R. Del Carmen-Wiggins & A. S. Carter (Eds.), *Handbook of infant, toddler, and preschool mental health assessment* (pp. 491-521). Oxford, UK: Oxford University Press.

McCooney, R. (2004). Using audiovisual recording of observe play in preschool settings in Northern Ireland. In R. L. Clements & L. Fiorentino (Eds.), *The child's right to play: A global approach* (pp. 49-54). Westport, CT: Praeger.

McCormick, B. P., & McGuire, F. (1996). Leisure in community life of older rural residents. *Leisure Sciences, 18,* 77-93.

McCune, L. (1998). Immediate and ultimate functions of physical activity play. *Child Development, 69,* 601-603.

McDonald, M.A., Sigman, M., & Ungerer, J.A. (1989). Intelligence and behavior Problems in 5-year-olds in relation to representational abilities in the second year of life. *Journal of Developmental & Behavioral Pediatrics, 10,* 86-91.

McGhee, P. E., Ethridge, L., & Benz, N.A. (1984). Effect of level of toy structure on preschool children's pretend play. *Journal of Genetic Psychology, 144,* 209-217.

McGhee, S. A., Groff, D. G., & Russoniello, C. V. (2005). We care too: Providing community-based therapeutic recreation services for youth with emotional and behavioral disorders. *Therapeutic Recreation Journal, 39,* 32-46.

McGuire, F. A. (1985a). Constraints on later life. In M. G. Wade (Ed.), *Constraints on leisure* (pp. 335-353). Springfield, IL: C. C. Thomas.

McGuire, F. A. (1985b). Leisure co-participant preferences of the elderly: Age-homogeneity versus age-heterogeneity. *Leisure Sciences, 7,* 115-124.

McGuire, F.A., Dottavio, F. D., & O'Leary, J. T. (1987). The relationship of early life experiences to later life leisure involvement. *Leisure Sciences, 9,* 251-257.

McHale, S. M., Crouter, A. C., & Tucker, C. J. (2001). Free-time activities in middle age childhood: Links with adjustment in early adolescence. *Child Development, 72,* 1764-1778.

McIntyre, A., Lounsbury, K. R. Hamilton, M. L., & Mantooth, J. M. (1980). Individual differences in preschool object play: The influence of anxiety proneness and peer affiliation. *Journal of Applied Developmental Psychology, 1,* 149-161.

McLoyd, V. C., & Randolph S.M. (1985). Secular trends in the study of Afro-American children: A review of child development, 1936–1980: *Monographs of the Society for Research in Child Development, 50* (4-5), 4-5.

McMahon, F. F. (1995). Appendix: A list of Brian Sutton-Smith's play-related publications. In A. D. Pellegrini (Ed.), *The future of play theory: A multidisciplinary inquiry into the contributions of Brian Sutton-Smith* (pp. 297–306). Albany, NY: State University of New York Press.

McMahon F. R. (1999). "Play with play": Germany's carnival as aesthetic nonsense. In S. Reifel (Ed.), *Play & culture studies* (pp. 177–187). Westport, CT: Ablex.

Meadows, D. L. (2001). Tools for understanding the limits to growth: Comparing a simulation to a game. *Simulation & Gaming, 32,* 522-536.

Menec, V. H., & Chipperfield, J. G. (1997). Remaining active in later life: The role of locus of control in senior's leisure activity participation, health, and life satisfaction. *Journal of Aging and Health, 9,* 105-125.

Mergen, B. (1995). "Past play": Relics, memory, and history. In A. D. Pellegrini (Ed.), *The future of play theory: A multidisciplinary inquiry into the contributions of Brian Sutton-Smith* (pp. 257–2674). Albany, NY: State University of New York Press.

Mesagno, C. (2006). Review of Sport Psychology Library: Bowling—The handbook of Bowling psychology. *International Journal of Sport and Exercise Psychology, 4,* 484-486.

Midley, B. D., & Morris, E. K. (Eds.). (2006). *Psychology from the standpoint of an interbehaviorist: A review of "Modern perspectives on J. R. Kantor and interbehaviorism."* Reno, NV: Context Press.

Mikulincer, M., & Shaver, P. R. (2007). *Attachment in adulthood: Structure, dynamics, and change.* New York: Guilford.

Millar, S. (1968). *The psychology of play.* Baltimore, MD: Penguin.

Miller, E., & Buys. L., (2007). Predicting older Australian leisure-time physical activity: Impact of residence retirement, village versus community, on walking, swimming, dancing, and lawn bowling. *Activities, Adaptation, & Aging, 31,* 13-30.

Mobily, K. E., Lemke, J. H., & Gisin, G. J. (1991). The idea of leisure repertoire. *Journal of Applied Gerontology, 10,* 208-223.

Mobily, K. E., Lemke, J. H., Ostiguy, L. J., & Woodard, R. J. (1993). Leisure repertoire in a sample of Midwestern elderly: The case for exercise. *Journal of Leisure Research, 25,* 84-99.

Moller, L. C., Hymel, S., & Rubin, K. H. (1992). Sex typing in play and popularity in middle school. *Sex Roles, 26,* 331-353.

Mondell, S., & Tyler, F. B. (1981). Parental competence ad styles in problem solving/play behavior with children. *Developmental Psychology, 17,* 73-78.

Moore, R. C. (1986). The power of nature orientations of girls and boys toward biotic and abiotic play settings on a reconstructed schoolyard. *Children's Environments Quarterly, 3,* 52-69.

Moore, V. A. (2002). The collaborative emergence of race in children's play: A case study of two summer camps. *Social Problems, 49,* 58-78.

Moran, J. D., Sawyers, J. K., Fu, V. R., & Milgram, R. M. (1984). Predicting imaginative play in preschool children. *Gifted Child Quarterly, 28,* 92–94.

Moreno, J. L. (1946). Towards a curriculum of the impromptu play school. *Psychodrama, 1,* 145–149.

Morrison, C. D., Bundy, A., & Fisher, A. (1991). The contribution of motor skills and playfulness to the play performance of preschoolers. *American Journal of Occupational Therapy, 45,* 687–694.

Moufakkir, O. (2006). An analysis of elderly gamers' trip characteristics and gambling behavior: Comparing the elderly with their younger counterparts. *UNLV Gaming Research & Review Journal, 10,* 63–75.

Moustakas, C. F. (1959). *Psychotherapy with children.* New York: Bantam.

Mullen, J. A. (2002). How play therapists understand children through stories of abuse and neglect: A qualitative study. *International Journal of Play Therapy, 11(2),* 107–119.

Murphy, H. A., Hutchinson, J. M., & Bailey, J. S. (1983). Behavioral school psychology goes outdoors: The effect of organized games on playground aggression. *Journal of Applied Behavior Analysis, 16,* 29–35.

Murray, N. P. (2006). The differential effect of team cohesion and leadership behavior in high school sports. *Individual Differences Research, 4,* 216–225.

Musgrove, M. (2008). Game-playing can have more practical purpose. *Atlanta Journal & Constitution,* July 12 issue.

Myers, D. (1998). Playing against the self: Representation and evolution. In M. C. Duncan, G. Chick, & A. Aycock (Eds.), *Play & culture studies: Diversions and divergencies in fields of play, Volume 1* (pp. 31–46). Greenwich, CT: Ablex.

Myers, N. A., Perris, E. E., & Speaker, C. J. (1994). Fifty months of memory: A longitudinal study in early childhood. *Memory: Special Issue, Long-term retention of infant memories, 2,* 383–415.

Nagel, M. (1998). Play in culture and the jargon of primordiality: A critique of Homo Ludens. In M. C. Duncan, G. Chick, & A. Aycock (Eds.), *Play & culture studies: Diversions and divergencies in fields of play. Volume 1* (pp. 19–29). Greenwich, CT: Ablex.

Nelson, K. (2005). Emerging levels of consciousness in early human development. In H. S. Terrace, & J. Metcalfe (Eds.), *The missing link in cognition: Origins of self-reflective consciousness* (pp. 116–141). New York: Oxford University Press.

Neppi, T. K. (1997). Social dominance and cooperative play among preschoolers: Gender comparisons. *Dissertation Abstracts International: Section A: Humanities and Social Science, 58,* 2065.

Neves, P., & Reifel, S. (2002). The play of early writing. In J. Roopnarine (Ed.), *Conceptual, social-cognitive, and contextual issues in the field of play, Volume 4: Play and culture studies* (pp. 149–164). Westport, CT: Ablex.

New, L. D., Cunningham, D. S., & Sughrue, K. (1998). Sexual play and estrous cycle: The relationship between sexual play and estrous cycle in a captive adolescent female chimpanzee (Pan troglodytes). In M. C. Duncan, G. Chick, &

A. Aycock (Eds.), *Play & culture studies: Volume I* (pp.179–188). Westport, CT:Ablex

New, R. S. (1994). Child's play—una cosa naturale:An Italian perspective. In J. L. Roopnarine, J. E. Johnson, & F. H. Hooper (Eds.). *Children's play in diverse cultures* (pp. 123–147).Albany, NY: State University of New York Press.

Newman, J., Brody, P. J., & Beauchamp, H. M. (1996).Teachers' attitudes and policies regarding play in elementary schools. *Psychology in the Schools, 33*, 61-69.

Nicolopoulou, A., McDowell, J., & Brockmeyer, C. (2006). Narrative play and emergent literacy: Storytelling and story-acting meet journal writing. In D. G. Singer, R. M. Golinkoff, & K. Hirsh-Pasek (Eds.), *Play = learning: How play motivates and enhances children's cognitive and social-emotional growth* (pp. 124–144). New York: Oxford University Press.

Noble, G. (1973). Effects of different forms of filmed aggression on children's constructive and destructive play. *Journal of Personality and Social Psychology, 26,* 54-59.

Norbeck, E. (1969). Human play and its cultural expression. *Humanitas: Journal of the Institute of Man, 5,* 43-55.

Norton, C. C., & Norton, B. E. (1997). *Reaching children through play therapy: An experiential approach.* Denver, CO: Publishing Cooperative.

Nwokah, E. E., & Ikekeonwu, C. (1998).A sociocultural comparison of Nigerian and American children's games. In M. C. Duncan, G. Chick, & A. Aycock (Eds.), *Play & culture studies: Diversions and divergencies in fields of play. Volume 1* (pp. 59–77). Greenwich, CT:Ablex

O'Brian-Cousins, S., & Witcher, C. S. (2007). Who plays bingo in later life? The sedentary lifestyles of "little old ladies." *Journal of Gambling Studies, 23,* 95-112.

Ochoa, S. H., & Palmer, D. J. (1991).A sociometric analysis of between-group differences and within-group status variability of Hispanic learning disabled and nonhandicapped pupils in academic and play contexts. *Learning Disability Quarterly, 14,* 208-218.

O'Connor, K. J. (2000). *The play therapy primer.* New York:Wiley.

Officer, S. A., & Rosenfeld, L. B. (1985). Self-disclosure to male and female coaches by female high school athletes. *Journal of Sport Psychology, 7,* 360-370.

Okuda, R. (2004).The status of child's play in Japan. In R. L. Clements & L. Fiorentino (Eds.), *The child's right to play: A global approach* (pp. 67–70). Westport, CT: Praeger.

Oldenburg, R. (1999). *The great good place.* New York: Marlowe.

Orlick, T. (1981). Cooperative play socialization among preschool children. *Journal of Individual Psychology, 37,* 54-63.

Opie, I. A. (1993). *The people in the playground.* Oxford, UK: Oxford University Press.

Orpinas, P. & Horne, A. (2006). *Bullying prevention: Creating a positive school climate and developing social competence.* Washington DC: American Psychological Association.

Orthner, D. K., Barnett-Morris, L., & Mancini, J. A. (1994). Leisure and family over the life cycle. In L. L'Abate (Ed.), *Handbook of developmental family psychology and psychopathology* (pp. 176–201). New York: Wiley.

Ostrov, J. M., & Keating, C. F. (2004). Gender differences in preschool aggression during free play and structured interactions: An observational approach. *Social Development, 13,* 255–277.

Packer, M. (1994). Cultural work on the kindergarten playground: Articulating the ground of play. *Human Development, 37,* 259–276.

Packman, J., & Bratton, S. C. (2003). A school-based play/activity therapy intervention with learning disabled preadolescents exhibiting behavior problems. *International Journal of Play Therapy, 12,* 7–29.

Page, T. & Bretherton, I. (2003). Gender differences on stories of violence and caring by preschool children in post-divorce families: Implications for social competence. *Child & Adolescent Social Work Journal, 20,* 485–508.

Page, R. M., & Zarco, E. P. (2001). Shyness, physical activity, and sports team participation among Philippine high school students. *Child Study Journal, 31,* 193–204.

Pan, H-L. W. (1994). Children's play in Taiwan. In J. L. Roopnarine, J. E. Johnson, & F. H. Hooper (Eds.), *Child's play in diverse cultures* (pp. 31–50). Albany, NY: State University of New York Press.

Panchanathan, K., & Boyd, R. (2004). Indirect reciprocity can stabilize cooperation without the second-order free rider problem. *Nature, 432,* 499–502.

Papastathopoulos, S., & Kugiumutzakis, G. (2007). The intersubjectivity of imagination: The special case of imaginary companions. In S. Braten (Ed.), *From mirrors to neurons* (pp. 219–233). Amsterdam, NE: John Benjamins Publishing Company.

Parmar, P., Harkness, S., & Super, C. M. (2004). Asian and Euro-American parents' ethnotheories of play and learning: Effects on preschool children's home routines and school behavior. *International Journal of Behavioral Development, 28,* 97–104.

Parten, M. B. (1932). Social participation among preschool children. *Journal of Abnormal Psychology, 27,* 243–269.

Patterson, C. M. (2004). Play-based curriculum: A strong foundation for future learning. In R. L. Clements & L. Fiorentino (Eds.), *The child's right to play: A global approach* (pp. 111–117). Westport, CT: Praeger.

Peck, C. A., Apolloni, T., Cooke, T. P., & Raver, S. A. (1978). Teaching retarded preschoolers to imitate the free-play behavior of nonretarded classmates: Trained and generalized effects. *The Journal of Special Education, 12,* 195–207.

Pellegrini, A. D. (1984). Identifying causal elements in the thematic-fantasy play paradigm. *American Educational Research, 21,* 691–701.

Pellegrini, A. D. (1990). Elementary school children's playground behavior: Implications for children's social-cognitive development. *Children's Environments Quarterly, 7,* 8–16.

Pellegrini, A. D. (1993). Boys' rough-and-tumble play, social competence and group composition. *British Journal of Developmental Psychology, 11,* 237–248.

Pellegrini, A. D. (1995a). Boys' rough-and-tumble play and social competence: Contemporaneous and longitudinal relations. In A. D. Pellegrini (Ed.), *The future of play theory: A multidisciplinary inquiry into the contributions of Brian Sutton-Smith* (pp. 107–126). Albany, NY: State University of New York Press.

Pellegrini, A. D. (Ed.) (1995b). *The future of play theory: A multidisciplinary inquiry into the contributions of Brian Sutton-Smith*. Albany, NY: State of New York University Press.

Pellegrini, A. D. (1998). Play and assessment of young children. In O. N. Saracho & B. Spodek (Eds.), *Multiple perspectives on play in early childhood education* (pp. 220–239). Albany, NY: State University of New York Press.

Pellegrini, A. D. (2002). Perceptions of play-fighting and real fighting: Effects of sex and participant status. In J. L. Roopnarine (Ed.), *Conceptual, social-cognitive, and contextual issues in the field of play; Volume 4* (pp. 223–233). Westport, CT: Ablex.

Pellegrini, A, D., & Davis, P. D. (1993). Relations between children's playground and classroom behavior. *British Journal of Educational Psychology, 63,* 88–95.

Pellegrini, A. D., & Gustafson, K. (2005). Boys' and girls' uses of objects for exploration, play, and tools in early childhood. In A. D. Pellegrini, & P. K. Smith (Eds.), *The nature of play: Great apes and humans* (pp. 113–135). New York: Guilford.

Pellegrini, A. D., & Perlmutter, J. C. (1989). Classroom contextual effects on children's play. *Developmental Psychology, 25,* 289–296.

Pellegrini, A D., & Smith, P. K. (1993). School recess: Implications for education and development. *Review of Educational Research, 63,* 51–67.

Pellegrini, A. D., & Smith, P. K. (1998a). Physical activity play: The nature and function of a neglected aspect of play. *Child Development, 69,* 577–598.

Pellegrini, A. D., & Smith, P. K. (1998b). The development of play during childhood: Forms and possible functions. *Child Psychology & Psychiatry Review, 3,* 51–57.

Pellegrini, A. D., & Smith, P. K. (Eds.). (2005). *The nature of play: Great apes and humans*. New York: Guilford.

Pellegrini, A. D., Blatchford, P., Kato, K., & Baines, E. (2004). A short-term longitudinal study of children's playground games in primary school: Implications for adjustment in the USA and in the UK. *Social Development, 13,* 107–123.

Pellegrini, A. D., Huberty, P. D., & Jones, I. (1995). The effects of recess timing on children's playground and classroom behaviors. *American Educational Research Journal, 21,* 845–864.

Pepler, D., & Ross, H. (1981). The effects of play on convergent and divergent problem solving. *Child Development, 52,* 1202–1210.

Percer, J. A. (2002). Exploring the causes of children's gender segregation: Behavioral compatibility versus gender categorization. *Dissertation Abstracts International: Section B, The Sciences and Engineering, 63,* 568.

Pereira, B. (2004). Bullying in schools in the North of Portugal: What we know about children. In R. L. Clements & L. Fiorentino (Eds.), *The child's right to play: A global approach* (pp. 145–152). Westport, CT: Praeger.

Perez, S., & Gauvain, M. (2007). The sociocultural context of transitions in early socioemotional development. In C. A. Brownwell & C. B. Kopp (Eds.), *Socioeconomic development in the toddler years: Transitions and transformations* (pp. 396–419). New York: Guilford.

Pershing, J.A. (Ed.). (2006). *Handbook of human performance technology: Principles, practices, potential.* San Francisco, CA: Pfeiffer.

Peterson E. (2004). Grounding the players: Social play experience reflect school playground policies. In R. L. Clements & L. Fiorentino (Eds.), *The child's right to play: A global approach* (pp. 153–162). Westport, CT: Praeger.

Petrick, J. F., Backman, S. J., Bixler, R., & Norman, W. C. (2001). Analysis of golfer motivation and constraints by experience use history. *Journal of Leisure Research, 33,* 56–70.

Pettit, G. S., & Harrist, A. W. (1993). Children's aggressive and socially unskilled playground behavior with peers: Origins in early family relations. In G. H. Hart (Ed.), *Children in playgrounds: Research perspectives and applications* (pp. 240–270). Albany, NY: State University of New York Press.

Phelps, P. (1984). Creative playgrounds for the preschool children. *Early Child Development and Care, 17,* 23–35.

Phillips, R. D. (1985). Whistling in the dark? A review of play therapy research. *Psychotherapy, 22,* 752–760.

Piaget, J. (1951). *Play: Dreams and imitation in childhood.* London, UK: Routledge & Kegan Paul.

Piaget, J. (1962). *Play, dreams, and imitation in childhood.* New York: W. W. Norton.

Piaget, J. (1972) Some aspects of operations. In M. W. Piers (Ed.), *Play and development: A symposium with contributions by Jean Piaget, Peter H. Wolff, Rene Spitz, Konrad Lorenz, Lois Barclay, and Eric H. Erikson* (pp. 15–27). New York: W. W. Norton.

Piaget, J. (1951). *Play, dreams, and imitation in childhood.* New York: Macmillan.

Piaget, J. (1952). *The origins of intelligence in children.* New York: International University Press.

Piaget, J. (1965). *The moral judgment of the child.* New York: Macmillan.

Piaget, J. (1976). *Structuralism.* New York: Basic Books.

Pierce-Jordan, S., & Lifter, K. (2005). Interaction of social and play behaviors in preschoolers with and without Pervasive Development Disorder. *Topics in Early Childhood Special Education, 25,* 34–47.

Piers, M. W. (Ed.). (1972). *Play and development: A symposium with contributions by Jean Piaget, Peter H. Wolff, Rene Spitz, Konrad Lorenz, Lois Barclay, and Eric H. Erikson.* New York: W. W. Norton.

Pinhey, T. K. (2002). A research note on body mass, physical aggression, and the competitiveness of Asian-Pacific Islander adolescence in Guam. *Social Biology, 49,* 90–98.

Poidevant, J. M., & Spruill, D. A. (1993). Play activities of at-risk and non-risk elementary students: Is there a difference? *Child Study Journal, 23,* 173–186.

Pollio, H. R., & Pollio, M. R. (2004). Nice monsters, sandcastles, and soccer: A thematic analysis of humor and play. In R. L. Clements & L. Fiorentino (Eds.), *The child's right to play: A global approach* (pp. 375–391). Westport, CT: Praeger.

Porter, H. R., & Burlingame, J. (2006). *Recreational therapy handbook of practice: ICF-based diagnosis and treatment.* Enumclaw, WA: Idyll Arbor.

Post, P. (2001). Play therapy with selective mute children. In G. L. Landreth (Ed.), *Innovations in play therapy: Issues, process, and special populations* (pp. 303–322). Philadelphia, PA: Brunner-Routledge.

Post, S. G. (Ed.). (2007). *Altruism & health: Perspectives from empirical research.* New York: Oxford University Press.

Post, P., McCallister, M., Sheely, A., Hess, B., & Flowers, C. (2004). Child-centered kinder training for teachers of preschool children deemed at-risk. *International Journal of Play Therapy, 13,* 53–74.

Poulsen, A. A., Ziviani, J. M., & Cuskelly, M. (2007). Perceived freedom in leisure and physical co-ordination ability: Impact on out-of-school activity participation and life satisfaction. *Child Care, Health, and Development, 33,* 432–440.

Power, M. B. (1993). Early childhood education: Everyone's challenge for the 21st century. *Early Child Development and Care, 86,* 53.

Power, T. J., House, A., & Radcliffe, J. (1989). The relationship of play behavior to cognitive ability in developmentally disabled preschoolers. *Journal of Developmental Disorders, 19,* 97–107.

Purcell, R. Z., & Keller, M. J. (1989). Characteristics of leisure activities which may lead to leisure satisfaction among older adults. *Activities, Adaptation, and Aging, 13,* 17–29.

Rajouria, S. (2002). The natural context of mother-toddler play interactions in a rural Nepali community. *Dissertation Abstracts International, Section A: Humanities and Social Sciences, 63,* 2124.

Ramsey, P. G. (1987). Possession episodes in young children's social interactions. *Journal of Genetic Psychology, 148,* 315–324.

Ray, D., & Bratton, S. (2000). What the research shows about play therapy. *International Journal of Play Therapy, 9,* 47–88.

Ray, D., Bratton, S., Rhine, T., & Jones, L. (2001). The effectiveness of play therapy: Responding to the critics. *International Journal of Play Therapy, 10,* 85–108.

Reddy, L. A., Files-Hall, T. M., & Schaefer, C. E. (2005). *Empirically-based play interventions for children.* Washington, DC: American Psychological Association.

Register, M., & L'Abate, L. (1972). The clinical usefulness of an objective, nonverbal personality test for children. *Psychology in the Schools, 9,* 378–387.

Reifel, S. (Ed.). (1999). *Play & culture studies.* Westport, CT: Ablex.

Reissland, N., Shepherd, J., & Herrera, E. (2005). Teasing play in infancy: Comparing mothers with and without self-reported depression during play with their babies. *European Journal of Developmental Psychology, 2,* 271–283.

Renson, R. (1998). The cultural dilemma of traditional games. In M. C. Duncan, G. Chick, & A. Aycock (Eds.), *Play & culture studies: Diversions and divergencies in fields of play. Volume 1* (pp. 51–58). Greenwich, CT: Ablex.

Reynolds, M. A. (1997). The development of sexuality: The impact of childhood sexual play on adult sexuality. *Dissertation Abstracts International, Section B: The Sciences and Engineering, 58,* 2723.

Richert, G. Z., & Bergland, C. (1992). Treatment choices: Rehabilitation services used by patients with multiple personality disorder. *American Journal of Occupational Therapy, 46,* 634–638.

Richter, L. M., Grieve, K. W., Austin, D. (1988). Scaffolding by Bantu mothers during object play with their infants. *Early Child Development and Care, 34,* 63–75.

Rike, E. (2004). Imaginative play and the neurology of creative growth in infants through adults: Exchanges between Elizabeth Rike and Karl Pribram. In R. L. Clements & L. Fiorentino (Eds.), *The child's right to play: A global approach* (pp. 277–292). Westport, CT: Praeger.

Roberts, C., Pratt, C., & Leach, D. (1991). Classroom and playground interaction in students with and without disabilities. *Exceptional Children, 57,* 212–224.

Roberts, D., & Foehr, U. (2004). *Kids and media in America.* Cambridge, UK: Cambridge University Press.

Roberts, M. A. (1990). A behavioral observation method for differentiating hyperactive and aggressive boys. *Journal of Abnormal Child Psychology, 18,* 131–142.

Rodney, C. (1997). The influence of selected toys on the cooperative behaviors of preschool children. *Dissertation Abstracts International, Section B: The Sciences and Engineering, 57,* 5950.

Rogers, C. S., Impara, J. C., Frary, R. B., Harris, T., Meeks, A., Semanic-Lauth, S., & Reynolds, M. R. (1998). Measuring playfulness: Development of the Child Behaviors Inventory of Playfulness. In M. C. Duncan, G. Chick, & A. Aycock (Eds.), *Play & culture studies: Diversions and divergencies in fields of play. Volume 1* (pp. 121–135). Greenwich, CT: Ablex.

Rogers, C. S., & Sluss, D. J. (1999). Play and invectiveness: Revisiting Erikson's views of Einstein's playfulness. In S. Reifel (Ed.), *Play & culture studies* (pp. 3–24). Westport, CT: Ablex.

Rogers, M. B. (1972). Therapists' statements and outcome in monitored play therapy. Unpublished doctoral dissertation. Atlanta, GA, Georgia State University Library.

Rogers, S., Wheeler, T. J., & McLaughlin, S. P. (1977). Play-groups—their effects on the language and socialization of children. *Child Care, Health, and Development, 3,* 175–180.

Romeo, L., & Young, S. A. (1999). Using literacy play centers to engage middle grade students in content and in learning. In J. A. Dugan, P. E. Linder, W. M. Linek, & E. G. Sturtevant (Eds.), *Advancing the world of literacy: Moving into the 21st century; The twenty-first yearbook of the College Reading Association,* (pp. 122–136). Readyville, TN: College Reading Association.

Roopnarine, J. L. (1981). Peer play interaction in a mixed-age preschool setting. *Journal of General Psychology, 104,* 161–164.

Roopnarine, J. L. (1994). *Children's play in diverse cultures.* Albany, NY: State University of New York Press.

Roopnarine, J. L. (Ed.). (2002*). Conceptual, social-cognitive and contextual issues in the fields of play: Volume 4.* Westport CT: Ablex.

Roopnarine, J. L., Ahmeduzzaman, M., Hossain, Z., & Riegraf, N. B. (1992). Parent-infant rough play: Its cultural specificity. *Early Education and Development, 3,* 298-311.

Roopnarine, J. L., Hossain, Z., Gill, P., & Bropjy, H. (1994). Play in the East Indian context. In J. L. Roopnarine, J. E. Johnson, & F. H. Hooper (Eds.), *Child's play in diverse cultures* (pp. 9-30). Albany, NY: State University of New York Press.

Roopnarine, J. L., Lasker, J., Sacks, M., & Stores, M. (1998). The cultural context of children's play. In O. N. Saracho & B. Spodek, (Eds.), *Multiple perspectives on play in early childhood education* (pp. 194-219). Albany, NY: State University of New York Press.

Root, L. M., & McCullough, M. E. (2007). Low-cost interventions for promoting for-giveness. In L. L'Abate (Ed.), *Low-cost approaches to promote physical and mental health* (pp. 415-434). New York: Springer.

Root-Bernstein, M., & Root-Bernstein, R. (2006). Imaginary worldplay in child-hood and maturity and its impact on adult creativity. *Creativity Research Journal, 18,* 405-425.

Rosenbaum, D. A. (2005). The Cinderella of psychology: The neglect of motor con-trol in the science of mental life and behavior. *American Psychologist, 60,* 308-317.

Rosenbaum, P. (1998). Physical activity play in children and disabilities: A neg-lected opportunity for research? *Child Development, 69,* 607-608.

Roskos, K., & Christie, J. F. (Eds.). (2000). *Play and literacy in early childhood: Research from multiple perspectives.* Mahwah, NJ. Erlbaum.

Roskos, K., & Neuman, S. B. (1998). Play as an opportunity for literacy. In O. N. Saracho & B. Spodek, (Eds.), *Multiple perspectives on play in early childhood education* (pp. 100-115). Albany, NY: State University of New York Press.

Rothbart, M. K., & Sheese, B. E. (2007). Temperament and emotion regulation. In J. J. Gross (Ed.), *Handbook of emotion regulation* (pp. 331-350). New York: Guilford.

Rothlein, L. (1987). Children's, teachers', and parents' perceptions of play. *Early Childhood Research Quarterly, 2,* 45-53.

Rozza, R. A., & Payne-Jones, J. (2004). A brief look at fantasy play. In R. L. Clements & L. Fiorentino (Eds.), *The child's right to play: A global approach* (pp. 23-27). Westport, CT: Praeger.

Rubin, K. H. (1977). The social and cognitive value of preschool toys and activi-ties. *Canadian Journal of Behavioral Science, 9,* 382-385.

Rubin, K. H. (1982). Nonsocial play in preschoolers: Necessary evil? *Child Devel-opment, 53,* 651-657.

Rubin, K. H. (1985). Play, peer interaction, and social development. In C. C. Brown & A. W. Gottfried (Eds.), *Play interactions: The role of toys and parental involvement in children's development* (pp. 88-96). Skillman, NJ: Johnson & Johnson Baby Products Company.

Rubin, J.A. (2004). *Art therapy has many faces.* Pittsburgh, PA: Expressive Media.

Rubin, K. H., & Coplan, R. J. (1998). Social and nonsocial play in childhood: An individual differences perspective. In O. N. Saracho & B. Spodek, (Eds.), *Multiple perspectives on play in early childhood education* (pp. 144–170). Albany, NY: State University of New York Press.

Rubin, K. H., Watson, K. S., & Jambor, T. W. (1978). Free-play behaviors in preschool and kindergarten children. *Child Development, 49,* 534–536.

Russ, S. W. (2004). *Play in child development and psychotherapy: Toward empirically supported practice.* Mahwah, NJ. Erlbaum.

Russell, C. L., & Russnaik, R. N. (1981). Language and symbolic play in infancy: Independent or related abilities. *Canadian Journal of Behavioural Science, 13,* 95–104.

Sacha, T. J., & Russ, S. W. (2006). Effects of pretend imagery on learning dance in preschool children. *Early Childhood Education Journal, 33,* 341–345.

Sadler, W. A. (1969). Creative existence: Play as a pathway to personal freedom and community. *Humanitas: Journal of the Institute of Man, 5,* 57–79.

Sallis, J. F., Patterson, T. L., McKenzie, T. L., & Nader, P. R. (1988). Family variables and physical activity in preschool children. *Journal of Developmental & Behavioral Pediatrics, 9,* 57–61.

Sandberg, A. (2001). Play memories from childhood to adulthood. *Early Child Development and Care, 167,* 13–25.

Sandberg, A. (2003). Play memories and place identity. *Early Child Development and Care, 173,* 207–221.

Saracho, O. (1989). The factorial structure of three- to five-year-old children's social behavior: Cognitive style and play. *Journal of Research & Development in Education, 22,* 21–28.

Saracho, O. M. (1997). Some implications of cognitive styles on young children's play. *Early Child Development and Care, 131,* 19–30.

Saracho, O. N. (1998). What is stylish about play? In O. N. Saracho & B. Spodek (Eds.), *Multiple perspectives on play in early childhood education* (pp. 240–254). Albany, NY: State University of New York Press.

Saracho, O. N. (1999). A factor analysis of preschool children's play strategies and cognitive style. *Educational Psychology, 19,* 165–180.

Saracho, O. N., & Spodek, B. (1998a). A historical overview of theories of play. In O. N. Saracho & B. Spodek (Eds.), *Multiple perspectives on play in early childhood education* (pp. 1–10). Albany, NY: State University of New York Press.

Saracho, O. N., & Spodek, B. (1998b). Introduction: Play in early childhood education. In O. N. Saracho & B. Spodek (Eds.), *Multiple perspectives on play in early childhood education* (pp. ix–xiii). Albany, NY: State University of New York Press.

Sastre, M. T. (1999). Lay conceptions of well-being and rules used in well-being judgments among young, middle-aged, and elderly adults. *Social Indicators Research, 47,* 203–231.

Sauders, I., Saver, M., & Goodale, A. (1999). The relationship between playfulness and coping in preschool children: A pilot study. *American Journal of Occupational Therapy, 53,* 221–226.

Saunders, T. (2005). *Golf: Lower your score with mental training.* Norwalk, CT: Crown House Publishing.

Sawyer, R. K. (1997). *Pretend play as improvisation: Conversation in the preschool classroom.* Mahwah, NJ: Erlbaum.

Sawyer, R. K. (2001). Play as improvisational rehearsal: Multiple levels of analysis in children's play. In A. Goncu & E. L. Klein (Eds.), *Children in play, story, and school* (pp. 19-38). New York: Guilford.

Scarboro, A., & Husain, J. (2006). Trimming the greens, mastering the course. *Sociological Spectrum, 26,* 237-266.

Scarmeas, N., & Stern, Y. (2003). Cognitive reserve and lifestyle. *Journal of Clinical and Experimental Neuropsychology, 25,* 625-633.

Schaefer, C. E. (1979). *Therapeutic use of child's play.* New York: Aronson.

Schaefer, C. E. (Ed.). (1993). *The therapeutic powers of play.* Northvale, NJ: Jason Aronson.

Schaefer, C. E. (Ed.). (1999). *Innovative psychotherapy techniques in child and adolescent therapy.* New York: Wiley.

Schaefer, C. E. (2003). *Foundations of play therapy.* Hoboken, NJ: Wiley.

Schaefer, C. E., & Cangelosi, D. M. (2002). *Play therapy techniques.* 2nd Ed. Northvale, NJ: Jason Aronson.

Schaefer, C. E., McCormick, J., & Ohnogi, A. (2005). *International handbook of play therapy: Advances in assessment, theory, research, and practice.* Lanham, MD: Jason Aronson.

Schaefer, C. E., & Reid, S. E. (2001). *Game play: Therapeutic use of childhood games.* New York: Wiley.

Schafer, M., & Smith, P. K. (1996). Teachers' perceptions of play fighting and real fighting in primary school. *Educational Research, 38,* 173-181.

Schau, C. G., Kahn, L., Diepold, J. H., & Cherry, F. (1980). The relationship of parental expectations and preschool children's verbal sex typing to their sex-typed toy behavior. *Child Development, 51,* 266-270.

Schneider, K. (1983). Exploring a novel object by preschool children: A sequential analysis of perceptual, manipulating and verbal exploration. *International Journal of Behavioral Development, 6,* 477-496.

Schniederwind, K. (1997). Life-long work or well-deserved leisure in old age? Conceptions of old age within the French and German labor movements in the late nineteenth and early twentieth centuries. *International Review of Social History, 42,* 397-418.

Schoppe-Sullivan, S. J., Mangeldorf, S. C., Frosch, C. A., McHale, J. L. (2004). Associations between coparenting and marital behavior from infancy to the preschool years. *Journal of Family Psychology, 18,* 194-207.

Schwartzman, H. B. (1978). *Transformations: The anthropology of children's play.* New York: Plenum.

Schwartzman, H. B. (1985). Child's structured play: A cross-cultural perspective. In C. C. Brown & A. W. Gottfried (Eds.), *Play interactions: The role of toys and parental involvement in children's development* (pp. 11-18). Skillman, NJ: Johnson & Johnson Baby Products Company.

Schwartzman, H.B. (1995). Representing children: Anthropologists at work, children at play. In A. D. Pellegrini (Ed.), *The future of play theory: A multidisciplinary inquiry into the contributions of Brian Sutton-Smith* (pp. 243–255). Albany, NY: State University of New York Press.

Schwebel, D. C., Rosen, C. S., & Singer, J. L. (1999). Preschoolers' pretend play and theory of mind: The role of jointly constructive pretence. *British Journal of Developmental Psychology, 17,* 333–348.

Scott, K. A. (2002). "You want to be a girl and not a friend?": African American/Black girls' play activities with and without boys. *Childhood: A Global Journal of Child Research, 9,* 397–414.

Searle, M. C., Mahon, M. J., Iso-Ahola, S.E., Sdrolias, H. A., & van Dyck, J. (1995). Enhancing a sense of independence and well-being among the elderly: A field experiment. *Journal of Leisure Research, 27,* 107–124.

Searle, M. C., Mahon, M. J. Iso-Ahola, S. E., Sdrolias, H. A., & van Dyck, J. (1998). Examining the long-term effects of leisure education on a sense of independence and psychological well-being among the elderly. *Journal of Leisure Research, 30,* 331–340.

Segal, M., Peck, J., Vega-Lahr, N., & Field, T. M. (1987). A medieval kingdom: Leader-follower styles of preschool play. *Journal of Applied Developmental Psychology, 8,* 79–95.

Sell, M., & Murrey, G. (2006). Recreational therapy program for patients with traumatic brain injury. In G. Murrey (Ed.), *Alternate therapies in the treatment of brain injury and neurobehavioral disorders: A practical guide* (pp. 89–105). New York: Haworth Press.

Serbin, L. A., & Conner, J. M. (1979). Sex-typing of children's play preferences and patterns of cognitive performance. *Journal of Geriatric Psychology, 134,* 315–316.

Serbin, L.A., Marchessault, K., McAffer, V., Peters, P., & Schwartzman, A. E. (1993). Patterns of social behavior on the playground in 9- to 11-year-old girls and boys: Relation to teachers' perceptions and to peer ratings of aggression, withdrawal, and liability. In C. Hart (Ed.), *Children on playgrounds: Research perspectives and applications* (pp. 162–183). Albany, NY: State University of New York Press.

Sheehan, K. J. (1999). Playing with the sacrificial child: Brian Sutton-Smith's boys' story *Our Street.* In S. Reifel (Ed.), *Play & culture studies* (pp. 25–35). Westport, CT: Ablex.

Shea, J. D. (1981). Changes in interpersonal distances and categories of play behavior in the early weeks of preschool. *Developmental Psychology, 17,* 417–425.

Shen, Y-J. (2002). Short-term group play therapy with Chinese earthquake victims: Effects on anxiety, depression, and adjustment. *International Journal of Play Therapy, 11(1),* 43–63.

Sherrod, K. B., Stewert, I. A., & Cavallaro, S. A. (1984). Language and play maturity in preschool children. *Early Child Development and Care, 14,* 147–160.

Shine, S., & Acosta, T. Y. (2000). Parent-child social play in a children's museum. *Family Relations, 49,* 45–52.

Shirk, S. R., & Russell, R. L. (1996). *Change processes in child psychotherapy: Revitalizing treatment and research*. New York: Guilford.

Shmukler, D. (1983). Preschool imaginative play predisposition and its relationship to subsequent third grade assessment. *Imagination, Cognition, and Personality, 2*, 231–240.

Shores, K. A., Scott, D., & Floyd, M. F. (2007). Constraints to outdoor recreation: A multiple hierarchy stratification perspective. *Leisure Sciences, 29*, 227–246.

Sierra Restrepo, Z. L. (1999). "Play for real": Understanding middle school children's dramatic play. *Dissertation Abstracts International, Section A: Humanities and Social Sciences, 60*, 385.

Simon, T. (1985). Play and learning with computers. *Early Child Development and Care. 19*, 69–78.

Singer, J. L. (1977). Imagination and make-believe play in early childhood: Some educational implications. *Journal of Mental Imagery, 1*, 127–143.

Singer, J. L. (1995). Imaginative play in childhood: Precursor of subjunctive thought, daydreaming, and adult pretending games. In A. D. Pellegrini (Ed.), *The future of play theory: A multidisciplinary inquiry into the contributions of Brian Sutton-Smith* (pp. 187–218). Albany, NY: State University of New York Press.

Singer, D. G., Golinkoff, R. M., & Hirsh-Pasek, K. (Eds.). (2006). *Play=learning: How play motivates and enhances children's cognitive and social-emotional growth*. New York: Oxford University Press.

Singer, J. L., & Lythcott, M. A. (2002). Fostering school achievement and creativity through sociodramatic play in the classroom. *Research in the Schools, 9*, 43–52.

Singer, J. L., & Singer, D. G. (2006). Preschoolers' imaginative play as precursor of narrative consciousness. *Imagination, Cognition, and Personality, 25*, 97–117.

Singer, J. L., Singer, D. G., & Schweder, A. E. (2004). Enhancing preschoolers' school readiness through imaginative play with parents and teachers. In R. L. Clements & L. Fiorentino (Eds.), *The child's right to play: A global approach* (pp. 35–47). Westport, CT: Praeger.

Singh, A. J., Moufakkir, O., & Holecek, D. F. (2007). Development of a trip profile for elderly American casino visitors. *Journal of Retail and Leisure Property, 6*, 61–68.

Singh, V. P. (2004). *Education of the slow learners: Sarup special education series, 2*. New Delhi: Sarup & Sons.

Skinner, M. L., Buysse, V., & Bailey, D. B. (2004). Effects of age and developmental status of partners on play of preschoolers with disabilities. *Journal of Early Interventions, 26*, 194–203.

Skrupskelis, A. (2004). Early playful intellectuals. In R. L. Clements & L. Fiorentino (Eds.), *The child's right to play: A global approach* (pp. 251–261). Westport, CT: Praeger.

Slaby, R. G., & Crowley, C. G. (1977). Modification of cooperation and aggression through attention to children's speech. *Journal of Experimental Child Psychology, 23*, 442–458.

Slovenko R., & Knight, J.A. (Eds.), (1967). *Motivations in play, games and sports*. Springfield, IL: C. C.Thomas.

Slowikowski, S., & Kohn, N. (1998). (Un)toward joy: Movement, sport, and (the meaning of) life. In M. C. Duncan, G. Chick, & A.Aycock (Eds.), *Play & culture studies: Diversions and divergencies in fields of play.Volume 1* (pp. 275–287). Greenwich, CT:Ablex.

Sluss, D. J. (2002). Block play complexity in same-sex dyads of preschool children. In J. L. Roopnarine (Ed.), *Conceptual, social-cognitive, and contextual issues in the field of play;Volume 4* (pp. 77–91).Westport, CT:Ablex.

Smetana, J. G., & Letourmeau, K. J. (1984). Development of gender constancy and children's sex-typed free play behavior. *Developmental Psychology, 20,* 691–696.

Smilansky, S. (1968). *The effects of sociodramatic play on disadvantaged preschool children*. New York: Springer-Verlag.

Smith, A. B. (1983). Sex differences in activities in early childhood centres. *New Zealand Journal of Psychology, 12,* 74–81.

Smith, N. R., Kielhofner, G., & Watts, J. H. (1986). The relationship between volition, activity pattern, and life satisfaction in the elderly. *American Journal of Occupational Therapy, 40,* 278–283.

Smith, P. K. (1978). A longitudinal study of social participation of preschool children. *Developmental Psychology, 14,* 517–523.

Smith, P. K. (2005). Social and pretend play in children. In A. D. Pellegrini, & P. K. Smith (Eds.), *The nature of play: Great apes and humans* (pp. 173–209). New York: Guilford.

Smith, P. K., & Dodsworth, C. (1978). Social class differences in the fantasy play of preschool children. *Journal of Genetic Psychology, 133,* 183–190.

Smith, P. K., Smees, R., Pellegrini, A. D., & Menesini, E. (2002). Comparing pupil and teacher perceptions for playful fighting, serious fighting, and positive peer interaction. In J. L. Roopnarine (Ed.), *Conceptual, social-cognitive, and contextual issues in the field of play;Volume 4* (pp. 235–245).Westport, CT:Ablex.

Smith, P. K., & Syddall, S. (1978). Play and non-play tutoring in preschool children: Is it play or is it tutoring that matters? *British Journal of Educational Psychology, 48,* 315–325.

Smolucha, L., & Smolucha, F. (1998).The social origins of mind: Post-Piagetian perspectives on pretend play. In O. N. Saracho & B. Spodek, (Eds.), *Multiple perspectives on play in early childhood education* (pp. 34–58).Albany, NY: State University of New York Press.

Smyth, J. M. (2007). Beyond self-selection in video game play: An experimental examination of the consequences of massively multiplayer online role-playing game play. *CyberPsychology & Behavior, 10,* 717–727.

Solnit, A. J., Cohen, D. J., & Neubauer, P. B. (1993). *The many meanings of play: A psychoanalytic perspective*. New Haven, CT:Yale University Press.

Solomon, J. (1955). Play techniques and the integration process. *American Journal of Orthopsychiatry, 25,* 591–600.

Song, S., & Lee, J. (2007). Key factors of heuristic evaluation for game design: Towards massively multiplayer online role-playing game. *International Journal of Human Computer Studies, 65,* 709–723.

Soto, L. D., & Negron, L. (1994). Mainland Puerto Rican children. In J. L. Roopnarine, J. E. Johnson, & F. H. Hooper (Eds.), *Children's play in diverse cultures* (pp. 104-122). Albany, NY: State University of New York Press.

Sparkes, K. K. (1991). Cooperative and competitive behavior in dyadic game-playing: A comparison of Anglo-American and Chinese children. *Early Child Development and Care, 68,* 37-47.

Spiegel, J. (1971). *Transactions: The interplay between individual, family, and society.* New York: Science House.

Stafford, I., & Stafford, K. (1995). Aggressive playground behavior in children with emotional and/or behavioral difficulties. *Educational Studies, 21,* 277-291.

Stagnitti, K., Rodger, S., & Clarke, J. (1997). Determining gender-neutral toys for assessment of preschool children's imaginative play. *Australian Occupational Therapy Journal, 44,* 119-131.

Stannard, L., Wolfgang, C. H., Jones, I., & Phelps, P. (2001). A longitudinal study of the predictive relations among construction play and mathematical achievement. *Early Child Development and Care, 167,* 115-125.

St. Clair, C., Danon-Boileau, L., & Trevarthen, C. (2007). Signs of autism in infancy: Sensitivity for rhythms of expression in communication. In S. Acquarone (Ed.), *Signs of autism in infants: Recognition and early intervention* (pp. 21-45). London: Karnac Books.

Stegge, H., & Terwogt, M. M. (2007). Awareness and regulation of emotion in typical and atypical development. In J. J. Gross (Ed.), *Handbook of emotion regulation* (pp. 269-286). New York: Guilford.

Sternberg, P. (2004). Dramatic play for healing. In R. L. Clements & L. Fiorentino (Eds.), *The child's right to play: A global approach* (pp. 359-369). Westport, CT: Praeger.

Stevens, P. (1991). Play and liminality in rites of passage: From elder to ancestor in West Africa. *Play & Culture, 4,* 237-257.

Stitt, B. G., Giacopassi, D., & Nichols, M. (2003). Gambling among older adults: A comparative analysis. *Experimental Aging Research, 29,* 189-203.

Stoecklin, V. L., & White, R. (2004). Multicultural dimensions of a children's play and discovery center in Arabia. In R. L. Clements & L. Fiorentino (Eds.), *The child's right to play: A global approach* (pp. 221-224). Westport, CT: Praeger.

Stormont, M., Zentall, S. S., Beyda, S., Javorsky, T., & Belfiore, P. (2000). Playground contexts for aggression for preschoolers with hyperactivity. *Journal of Behavioral Education, 10,* 37-48.

Stover, C. S., Van Horn, P., Lieberman, A. F. (2006). Parental representations in the play of preschool aged witnesses of marital violence. *Journal of Family Violence, 21,* 417-424.

Strauss, M. B. (1999). *No-talk therapy for children and adolescents.* New York: Norton.

Straver, J., & Straver, F. F. (1978). Social aggression and power relations among preschool children. *Aggressive Behavior, 4,* 173-182.

Strudler, A., & Schaefer, C. (1997). Adult perceptions of favorite childhood play experiences: A replication study. *Psychological Reports, 81,* 1017-1018.

Sutton-Smith, B. (1971). A syntax for play and games. In R. E. Herron & B. Sutton-Smith (Eds.), *Child's play* (pp. 298–307). New York: Wiley.

Sutton-Smith, B. (1982). A hundred years of change in play research. *Newsletter of TAASP, 9,* 13–17.

Sutton-Smith, B. (1986). *Toys as culture.* New York: Gardner Press.

Sutton-Smith, B. (1990). School playground as festival. *Children's Environmental Quarterly, 7,* 3–7.

Sutton-Smith, B. (1995). Conclusion: The persuasive rhetorics of play. In A.D. Pellegrini (Ed.), *The future of play theory: A multidisciplinary inquiry into the contributions of Brian Sutton-Smith* (pp. 275–294). Albany, NY: State University of New York Press.

Sutton-Smith, B. (1997). *The ambiguity of play.* Cambridge, MA: Harvard University Press.

Sutton-Smith, B. (1999). Evolving a consilience of play definitions: Playfully. In S. Reifel (Ed.), *Play & culture studies* (pp. 239–26). Westport, CT: Ablex.

Sutton-Smith, B. (2002). Recapitulation redressed. In J. L. Roopnarine (Ed.), *Conceptual, social-cognitive, and contextual issues in the field of play; Volume 4* (pp. 3–21). Westport, CT: Ablex.

Sutton-Smith, B., & Rosenberg, B. G. (1961). Sixty years of historical change in the game preference of American children. *Journal of American Folklore, 74,* 17–46.

Sweeney, D. S. (1997). Counseling children through the world of play. Wheaton, IL: Tyndale House.

Sweeney, D., & Homeyer, L. E. (Eds.). (1999). *The handbook of group play therapy.* San Francisco, CA: Jossey-Bass.

Sweeney, L. (2008). Playfulness in great artists. http://creativitymentor. blogspot.com/

Swindells, D., & Stagnitti K. (2006). Pretend play and parents' view of social competence: The construct validity of the Child-Initiated Pretend Play Assessment. *Australian Occupational Therapy Journal, 53,* 314–324.

Switzky, H. N., Ludwig, L., & Haywood, H. C. (1979). Exploration and play in retarded and nonretarded preschool children: Effects of object complexity and age. *American Journal of Mental Deficiency, 83,* 637–644.

Sylva, K. (1984). A hard-headed look at the fruits of play. *Early Childhood Development and Care, 15,* 171–183.

Szabo, I. T., & Shapiro, M. (1983). Imaginative play and imagery learning. *Bulletin of the Psychonomic Society, 21,* 105–107.

Takeuchi, M. (1994). Children's play in Japan. In J. L. Roopnarine, J. E. Johnson, & F. H. Hooper (Eds.), *Children's play in diverse cultures* (pp. 51–72). Albany, NY: State University of New York Press.

Tamis-LeMonda, C. S., & Bornstein, M. H. (1996). Variation in children's exploratory, nonsymbolic, and symbolic play: An explanatory multidimensional framework. In C. Revee-Collier & L. P. Lipsitt (Eds.), *Advances in infancy research* (pp. 37–78). Westport, CT: Ablex.

Tamis-LeMonda, C. S., Bornstein, M. H., Cyphers, L., Toda, S., et al. (1992). Language and play at one year: A comparison of toddlers and mothers in the United

States and Japan. *International Journal of Behavioral Development, 15,* 19–42.

Tanaka, K. (2005). Development of group consciousness in preschoolers' tag play. *Japanese Journal of Developmental Psychology, 16,* 192–201.

Tanta, K. J., Deitz, J. C., White, O., & Billingsley, F. (2005). The effects of peer play-level on imitation and responses of preschool children with delayed play skills. *American Journal of Occupational Therapy, 59,* 437–445.

Tauber, M. A. (1979). Parental socialization techniques and sex differences in children's play. *Child Development, 50,* 225–234.

Taylor, L. P. S., & McGruder, J. E. (1996). The meaning of sea kayaking for persons with spinal cord injuries. *American Journal of Occupational Therapy, 50,* 39–46.

Taylor, S. I., Rogers, C. S., Dodd, T., Kaneda, T., Nagasaki, I., Watanabe, Y., et al. (2003). The meaning of play: A cross-cultural study of American and Japanese teachers' perspectives on play. *Journal of Early Childhood Teacher Education, 24,* 311–322.

Taylor, S. I., Rogers, C. S., & Kaiser, J. (1999). A comparison of playfulness among American and Japanese preschoolers. In S. Reifel (Ed.), *Play & culture studies* (pp. 143–150). Westport, CT: Ablex.

Tegano, D. W., Lookabaugh, S., May, G. E., & Burdette, M. P. (1991). Constructive play and problem solving: The role of structure and time in classroom. *Early Child Development and Care, 68,* 27–35.

Terrace, H. S., & Metcalfe, J. (Eds.). (2005). *The missing link in cognition: Origins of self-reflective consciousness.* New York: Oxford University Press.

Tew, K., Landreth, G. L., Joiner, K. D., & Solt, M. D. (2002). Filial therapy with parents of chronically ill children. *International Journal of Play Therapy, 11(1),* 79–100.

Thomas, S. (2006). Pervasive learning games: Explorations of hybrid educational gamescapes. *Simulation and Gaming, 37,* 41–55.

Thorpe, B. (1993). *Gender play: Girls and boys in school.* New Brunswick, NJ: Rutgers University Press.

Thu, K. M., Hattman, K., Hutchinson, V., Lueken, S., Davis, N., & Linboom, E. (2002). Keeping the game close: "Fair play" among men's college basketball referees. *Human Organization, 61,* 1–8.

Tietz, J. A. (1998). Gender segregation in early childhood: A test of the play style compatibility hypothesis. *Dissertation Abstracts International, Section B: The Sciences and Engineering, 59,* 1395.

Torres, M., & Macedo, J. (2000). Learning sustainable development with a new simulation game. *Simulation & Gaming, 31,* 119–126.

Trautner, H. M. (1995). Boys' and girls' play behavior in same sex and opposite sex pairs. *Journal of Genetic Psychology, 156,* 5–15.

Tremblay, R. F. (2000). The development of aggressive behavior during childhood: What have we learned in the past? *International Journal of Behavioral Development, 24,* 129–141.

Trevlas, E., Grammatikopoulos, V., Tsigilis, N., & Zachopoulou, E. (2003). Evaluating playfulness: Construct validity of the Children's Playfulness Scale. *Early Childhood Education Journal, 31,* 33–39.

Triebenbacher, S. L. (1998). Pets as transitional objects: Their role in children's emotional development. *Psychological Reports, 82,* 191–200.

Trifonova, E. V. (2006). On the occasion of the 100th anniversary of A. V. Zaporozhets: The problem of self-organized play in the context of A. V. Zaporozhets' concepts. *Cultural-Historical Psychology, 1,* 77–83.

Tsujino, N. (1978). Development of symbolic use in preschool children: Examination of the role of play activity in symbolic use. *Japanese Journal of Educational Psychology, 26,* 114–123.

Tudge, J., Lee, S., & Putman, S. (1998). Young's children's play in socio-cultural context: South Korea and the United States. In M. C. Duncan, G. Chick, & A. Aycock (Eds.), *Play & culture studies: Diversions and divergencies in fields of play. Volume 1* (pp. 77–90). Greenwich, CT: Ablex.

Tulviste, T., & Koor, M. (2005). "Hands off the car, it's mine!" and "The teacher will be angry if we don't play nicely": Gender-related performance in the use of moral rules and social conventions in preschoolers' dyadic play. *Sex Roles, 53,* 57–66.

Turkheimer, M., Bakeman, R., & Adamson, L. B. (1989). Do mothers support and peers inhibit skilled object play in infancy? *Infant Behavior & Development, 12,* 37–44.

Turner, I. F. (1974). Cognitive effects of playgroup attendance. *Irish Journal of Education, 8,* 30–35.

Turner, B. (2005). *The handbook of sandplay therapy.* Coverdale, CA: Temenos Press.

Tyler, F. B., Holliday, M. Y., Tyler, S. L., Echeverry, J. J. (1987). Street children and play. *Children's Environments Quarterly, 4,* 13–17.

Udwin, O. (1983). Imaginative play training as an intervention method with institutionalized preschool children. *British Journal of Educational Psychology, 53,* 32–39.

Udwin, O., & Shmukler, D. (1981). The influence of sociocultural, economic, and home background factors on children's ability to engage in imaginative play. *Developmental Psychology, 17,* 66–72.

Uttal, D. H., Marzolf, D. P., Pierroutsakos, S. L., Smith, C. M., Troseth, G. L., Scudder, K. V., & DeLoache, J. S. (1998). Seeing through symbols: The development of children's understanding of symbolic relations. In O. N. Saracho & B. Spodek, (Eds.), *Multiple perspectives on play in early childhood education* (pp. 59–79). Albany, NY: State University of New York Press.

Vaillant, G. E. (2007). Generativity: A form of unconditional love. In S. G. Post (Ed.), *Altruism & health: Perspectives from empirical research* (pp. 219–229). New York: Oxford University Press.

Van Andel, J. (1985). Effects of the redevelopment of an elementary school playground. *Leisure Studies, 4,* 307–320.

Vandenberg, B. (1981). The role of play in the development of insightful tool-playing strategies. *Merrill-Palmer Quarterly, 27,* 97–109.

Vandenberg, B. (1998). Real and not real: A vital developmental dichotomy. In O. N. Saracho & B. Spodek, (Eds.), *Multiple perspectives on play in early childhood education* (pp. 295–305). Albany, NY: State University of New York Press.

Van der Kolk, B. A. (2003). The neurobiology of childhood trauma and abuse. *Child & Adolescent Psychiatry Clinics of North America, 12,* 293–317.

Vandermaas-Peeler, M., King, K., Clayton, A., Holt, M., Kurtz, K., Maestri, L., Morris, E., & Woody, E. (2002). Parental scaffolding during joint play with preschoolers. In J. L. Roopnarine (Ed.), *Conceptual, social-cognitive, and contextual issues in the field of play; Volume 4* (pp. 165–181). Westport, CT: Ablex.

Van Fleet, R. (2005). Filial therapy: *Strengthening parent-child relationships through play.* 2nd Ed. Sarasota, FL: Professional Resource Press.

Van Lue, E. M. (2004). Integration of traditional play and games to enhance learning, In R. L. Clements & L. Fiorentino (Eds.), *The child's right to play: A global approach* (pp. 185–196). Westport, CT: Praeger.

Van Rossum, J. H. A. (1998). Why children play: American versus Dutch boys and girls. In G. Hofstede (Ed.), *Masculinity and femininity: The taboo dimension of national cultures.* Thousand Oaks, CA: Sage.

Varner, M., & Knottnerus, J. D. (2002). Civility, rituals, and exclusion: The emergence of American golf during the late 19th and early 20th centuries. *Sociological Inquiry, 72,* 426–441.

Vaughter, R. M., Sadh, D., & Vozzola, E. (1994). Sex similarities and differences in types of play in games and sports. *Psychology of Women Quarterly, 18,* 85–104.

Verghese, J., LaValley, A., Derby, C., Kuslansky, G., Katz, M., Hall, C., Buschke, H., Lipton, R. B., et al., (2006). Leisure activities and the risk of amnestic mild cognitive impairment in the elderly. *Neurology, 66,* 821–827.

Vidoni, C., & Ward, P. (2006). Effects of dependent group-oriented contingency on middle school physical education students' fair play behavior. *Journal of Behavioral Education, 15,* 81–92.

Vlietstra, A. G. (1978). Exploration and play in preschool children and young adults. *Child Development, 49,* 235–238.

Von Zuben, M. V., Crist, P. A., & Mayberry, W. (1991). A pilot study of differences in play behavior between children of low and middle socioeconomic status. *American Journal of Occupational Therapy, 45,* 113–118.

Voss, L. S. (1997). Teasing, disputing, and playing: Cross-gender interactions and space utilization among first and third graders. *Gender and Society, 11,* 238–256.

Wachs, T. D. (1985). Home stimulation and cognitive development. In C. A. Brown & A. W. Gottfried (Eds.), *Play interactions: The role of toys and parental involvement in children's development* (pp. 142–152). Skillman, NJ: Johnson & Johnson.

Wade, M. G. (Ed.), (1985). *Constraints on leisure.* Springfield, IL: C. C. Thomas.

Wade, M. G., & Hoover, J. H. (1985). Mental retardation as a constraint on leisure. In M. G. Wade (Ed.), *Constraints on leisure* (pp. 83–110). Springfield, IL: C. C. Thomas.

Wagner, B. J. (2004). Educational drama and learning. In R. L. Clements & L. Fiorentino (Eds.), *The child's right to play: A global approach* (pp. 347–358). Westport, CT: Praeger.

Wall, S. M., & Pickert, S. M. (1982). Language and play of preschool children learning English as a second language and native English speakers. *Psychological Reports, 50,* 119–124.

Waller, D., & Sibbett, C. (Eds.). (2005). *Art therapy and cancer care.* Maidenhead, UK: Open University Press.

Wardell, J. (2008). Feels like gaming, but it's no toy. *Atlanta Journal-Constitution,* Sunday, July 20, p. F9.

Wasserstein, S. B. (1997). Empirically derived subtypes of social withdrawal: Association with behavioral and cognitive functioning in a naturalistic preschool setting. Ph.D. dissertation, University of Miami, Florida.

Watkinson, E. J. Dunn, J. C., Cavaliere, N., Calzonetti, K., Wilhelm, L., & Dwyer, S. (2001). Engagement in playground activities as a criterion for diagnosing developmental coordination disorder. *Adapted Physical Activity Quarterly, 18,* 18–34.

Weisler, A., & McCall, R. R. (1976). Exploration and play: Résumé and redirection. *American Psychologist, 31,* 492–508.

Welteroth, S. J. (2002). Increasing play competence for very young children: How two early Head Start home visitors conceptualize and actualize their roles. *Play and Culture Studies, 4,* 183–208.

Western Psychological Services (2004). Creative Therapy Store. 12031 Wilshire Boulevard, Los Angeles, CA 90025-1251; 1-800-648-8857; fax 310-478-7838; www.creativetherapystore.com, www.wpspublish.com.

White, B. A. (1999). Development of a multidisciplinary cognitive rehabilitation program to maximize functional independence in geriatric stroke patients. *Dissertation Abstracts International, Section B: The Sciences and Engineering, 60,* 1875.

White, J., & Flynt, M. (1999). Play groups in elementary school. In D. S. Sweeney & L. Homeyer (Eds.), *Group play therapy: How to do it, how it works, whom it's best for* (pp. 336–358). San Francisco: Jossey-Bass.

White, J., & Wynne, L. S. (in press). Kinder training: A play based model for helping teachers build positive relationships with their students. In A. Drewes (Ed.), *The effective blending of play therapy and cognitive behavior therapy: A convergent approach.* Hoboken, NJ: Wiley.

White, J., Draper, K., & Flynt, M. (2003). Kinder training: A school counselor and teacher consultation model utilizing an integration of Filial Therapy and Adlerian theory. In R. VanFleet, & L. Guerney (Eds.), *Casebook of filial play therapy* (pp. 331–350). Boiling Springs, PA: Play Therapy Press.

White, J., Draper, K., Flynt, M., & Jones, N. (2000). *Kinder training: Play-based teacher consultation to promote the adjustment and achievement of discouraged students.* Norcross, GA: KdChoice.

White, J., Draper, K., & Jones, N. P. (2001). Play behaviors of physically abused children. In G.L. Landreth (Ed.), *Innovations in play therapy: Issues, process, and special populations* (pp. 99–118). Philadelphia: Brunner-Routledge.

White, J., Flynt, M., & Draper, K. (1997). Kinder therapy: Teachers as therapeutic agents. *International Journal of Play Therapy, 6,* 33–49.

White, J., Flynt, M., & Jones, N. P. (1999). Kinder Therapy: An Adlerian approach for training teachers to be therapeutic agents. *Journal of Individual Psychology, 55,* 365–382.

White, J., O'Shaughnessy, T., Flynt, M., & Jones, N. P. (2001). Kinder training: Play-based consultation to improve the school adjustment of discouraged kindergarten and first grade students. *International Journal of Play Therapy, 10,* 1–30.

Wilburn, R. E. (1998). Prosocial entry behaviors used by preschoolers to enter play groups in the natural setting of the playroom. *Dissertation Abstracts International, Section A: Humanities and Social Sciences, 58,* 3411.

Wilkinson, J. A. (2004). Rike's guided dramatic play system, the brain, and language. In R. L. Clements & L. Fiorentino (Eds.), *The child's right to play: A global approach* (pp. 263–210). Westport, CT: Praeger.

Williams, L. E., & Bargh, J. A. (2008). Keeping one's distance: The influence of spatial distance clues on affect and evaluation. *Psychological Science, 19,* 302–308.

Wing, L. A. (1995). Play is not the work of the child: Young children's perceptions of work and play. *Early Childhood Research Quarterly, 19,* 223–247.

Witt, P. A., & Goodale, T. L. (1985). Barriers to leisure across family stages. In M. G. Wade (Ed.), *Constraints on leisure* (pp. 227–242). Springfield, IL: C. C. Thomas.

Witvliet, C. V. O., & McCullough, M. E. (2007). Forgiveness and health: A review and theoretical exploration of emotion pathways. In S. G. Post (Ed.), *Altruism & health: Perspectives from empirical research* (pp. 259–276). New York: Oxford University Press.

Wolfgang, C. H., & Sanders, T. (1982). Teacher's role: A construct for supporting the play of young children. *Early Child Development and Care, 8,* 107–120.

Wolfgang, C. H., Stannard, L. L., & Jones, I. (2003). Advanced constructional play with LEGOs among preschoolers as a predictor of later school achievement in mathematics. *Early Child Development and Care, 173,* 467–475.

Woolgar, M. (1999). Projective doll play methodologies for preschool children. *Child Psychology & Psychiatry Review, 4,* 126–134.

Wynne, L. S., & White, J. (in press). Relationship skills for educators. In R. P. Colarusso & C. M. O'Rourke (Eds.), *Special education for all teachers* (5th ed). Dubuque, IA: Kendall/Hunt.

Wyver, S. R., & Spence, S. H. (1999). Play and divergent problem solving: Evidence supporting a reciprocal relationship. *Early Education and Development, 10,* 419–444.

Yang, L., Zou, X., & Bergen, D. (1995). The development of social and cognitive complexity in preschoolers' play: A cross-cultural comparison. *Acta Psychological Sinica, 27,* 84–90.

Yawkey, T. D. (1986). Creative dialogue through sociodramatic play and its uses. *Journal of Creative Behavior, 20,* 52–60.

Yawkey, T. D., & Hrncir, E. J. 1983). Pretend play tools for oral language growth in the preschool. *Journal of Creative Behavior, 16,* 265–271.

Yogman, M. W. (1981). Games fathers and mothers play with their infants. *Infant Mental Health Journal, 2,* 241–248.

Young, J. C. (1985). The cultural significance of (male) children's playground activities. *Alberta Journal of Educational Research, 31,* 125–138.

Young, B. A. (1995). A comparison of the play of aggressive and non-aggressive kindergarteners. *Dissertation Abstracts International, Section B: The Sciences and Engineering, 56,* 2908.

Young, S. (2003). Time-space structuring in spontaneous play on educational percussion instruments among three- and four-year-olds. *British Journal of Music Education, 20,* 45–59.

Youngblade, L. M., & Dunn, J. (1995). Social pretend with mothers and siblings: Individual differences and social understanding. In A. D. Pellegrini (Ed.), *The future of play theory: A multidisciplinary inquiry into the contributions of Brian Sutton-Smith* (pp. 221–240). Albany, NY: State University of New York Press.

Yuen, T., Landreth, G., & Baggerly, J. (2002). Filial therapy with immigrant Chinese families. *International Journal of Play Therapy, 11(2),* 63–90.

Zacharatos, A., Barling, J., & Kelloway, E. K. (2000). Development and effects of transformational leadership in adolescents. *Leadership Quarterly, 11,* 211–226.

Zahn-Waxler, C., Shirtcliff, E. A., & Marceau, K. (2008). Disorders of childhood and adolescence: Gender and psychopathology. In S. Nolen-Hoeksema, T. D. Cannon, & T. Widiger (Eds.), *Annual Review of Clinical Psychology* (pp. 275–303). Palo Alto, CA: Annual Reviews.

Zeiliger, E. O., & Levina, M. A. (1995). Structural analysis and the internal mechanisms of play activity, in preschoolers. *Journal of Russian & East European Psychology,* 33, 6–49.

Ziangdong, G., & Zheng, R. (1998). Role play for assessment of social skills of middle school students: A three-factor experiment research. *Acta Psychologica Sinica, 30,* 70–77.

Zucker, K. J., & Corter, C. M. (1980). Sex-stereotyping in adult-infant interaction: Some negative evidence. *American Journal of Orthopsychiatry, 50,* 160–164.

RESOURCES

Toy and game resources included in this appendix are mentioned for information purposes only and not for any other purposes. These resources are neither endorsed nor recommended because of their mention here. Consequently, Praeger cannot and will not be held responsible for their inclusion in this book. It will be up to readers to determine their relevant usefulness and appropriate application to children, youth, and later stages of play development.

Now chain toy stores like Toys'R'Us in major cities of the United States make it easy to obtain toys and games of almost any kind, even those made in China. Moreover, people living in smaller cities where such a chain is not available can obtain any toy or game they want on the Internet. For an interesting background story about the early beginnings of toy makers and commercial in Europe and United States, the interested reader may want to consult Caplan and Caplan (1973).

American companies that still produce toys and games, not necessarily in the United States, include giants such as Mattel and Hasbro (owner of Tonka, Playskool, and Parker Brothers, famous for the adult-level Trivial Pursuit game and Monopoly), smaller firms such as HandsOnToys, and of course Lego among many others. Many toys can be found in the catalogues of Western Psychological Services and other companies listed below. The choices are immense for any child, youth, and adult.

HARD COPY RESOURCES: BOOKS

Ariel, S. (2002). *Children's imaginative play: A visit to wonderland.* Westport, CT: Praeger.

This resource contains extensive, up-to-date, classified bibliographies of references that cover pretend, make-believe, and fantasy play from a variety of disciplines, including language, symbiotic, and symbolic systems, componential and textual analyses, and theoretical orientations in anthropology, specifically in the anthropology of play.

Arnett, J. J. (Ed.). (2007). *Encyclopedia of Children and Adolescents and the Media: Volumes 1 and 2.* Thousand Oaks, CA: Sage.

The Greek term from which we get the word "encyclopedia" means all the available knowledge about a topic or field of study. These two volumes, then, admirably fulfill the meaning of that term. The editor relied on an Editorial Board of acknowledged experts in their respective disciplines and on literally hundreds of contributors to as many entries in alphabetical order from A to Z. Entries are divided into sections, such as from "advertising" and "advocacy groups" to "theories" and "violence and aggression." Almost every entry is cross-indexed and documented by a list of further readings relevant to that entry. Two concepts dear to my heart as a former play therapist (Chapter 6, this volume), "exploration" and " creativity," strangely are not included in the plethora of entries, even though a great deal of socialization in children and adolescents consists of trial-and-error exploration, and exploration is part of creativity. Readers will have to find information about both terms indirectly, between the lines and among possibly related entries.

Yet, the crucial question to ask of any encyclopedia, but especially of this one, is "Who will read it and who will profit by reading it?" Parents on Main Street or any street in America will probably not know about the existence of this two-volume set and, even if they knew it existed, they will probably not be able to afford it. Even then, it would be difficult to find ways to consult entries relevant to their needs.

Of course, every public and academic library should have this encyclopedia on its shelves. Developmental psychologists, personality theorists, social psychologists, and even play therapists would benefit by consulting entries that are particular to their practice, teaching, and research interests. Whether these professionals should own a copy remains open to their interests and pocketbooks. If they cannot afford this encyclopedia, however, they must make sure that libraries in their respective institutions or even in their close-by public libraries order it as a reference text. In it they will find the base for almost any conceivable topic they need to consult and use in practice, research, and teaching. What more can one ask for?

(Adapted from a book review originally printed in *PsycCRITIQUES* (2007) with permission of the American Psychological Association.)

Bellin, H. F., & Singer, D. G. (2006). My Magic Story Car: Video-based play intervention to strengthen emergent literacy in at-risk preschoolers. In D. G. Singer, R. M. Golinkoff, & K. Hirsh-Pasek (Eds.), *Play = learning: How play motivates and enhances children's cognitive and social-emotional growth* (pp. 101–123). New York: Oxford University Press.

"My Magic Story Car" is a video-based program that strengthens emergent literacy skills of at-risk preschoolers from low-income families through one of the most effective available modalities: make-believe play. The program addresses its objective by interweaving three elements: (1) make-believe play as an intrinsically motivating modality for engaging preschoolers in learning activities, (2) empirical studies of the requisite skills of emergent literacy, and (3) video-based programs as an effective medium for empowering parents and caregivers of poor children with easily replicable, reliable interventions for implementation in any childcare setting. The approaches at the heart of the program have proven effective in democratizing and leveling the emergent literacy playing field for at-risk, disadvantaged preschoolers.

Berggren, L. A. (2004). Community mural: A visual history of Field's Corner in Dorchester, Massachusetts. In R. L. Clements & L. Fiorentino (Eds.), *The child's right to play: a global approach* (pp. 243–248). Westport, CT: Praeger.
An illustration of how creation of a large 9' × 17' clay mural can become a focal playful point of community participation.

Bishop, K. (2004). Designing sensory play environments for children with special needs. In R. L. Clements & L. Fiorentino (Eds.), *The child's right to play: a global approach* (pp. 233–242). Westport, CT: Praeger.
This chapter discusses the role of the environment and the meaning of the sensory quality, including issues of what should be excluded and why layout and placement and scaling of activities is very important, including emphasis on sensory details such as color, texture, smell, sound, and lightning. A case study of a sight impaired individual illustrates a specific application of these qualities.

Children's Book of the Month Club. P. O. Box 916461. Indianapolis, IN: 46291-6461.

Davis, L. C. (2004). Using intergenerational puppets to convey play and recreational principles. In R. L. Clements & L. Fiorentino (Eds.), *The child's right to play: a global approach* (pp. 209–210). Westport, CT: Praeger.
The title says it all.

Densmore, A. E. (2007). *Helping children with autism become more social: 76 ways to use narrative play.* Westport, CT: Praeger.
An extremely detailed manual for helping autistic children become more socially attuned. The rationale for each step or strategies necessary to achieve this goal are well illustrated with case examples.

Eiss, H. E. (1986). *Dictionary of language games, puzzles, and amusements.* Westport, CT: Greenwood Press.
This excellent dictionary includes as many (some completely unknown) language games as there can be in existence, at least in the United States, starting alphabetically with ABC language (where words are substituted with similar sounding letters), Acromania, Across-Tic, anagrams, black box, charades, codes, jump rope rhymes, oxymorons, Sotadic Palindrome, and ending at Word Hunt. It

might be worth looking for this book with all the games included in it on *http://www.amazon.com*. However, I doubt whether they can be found anywhere else.

Eiss, H. E. (1988). *Dictionary of mathematical games, puzzles, and amusements.* Westport, CT: Greenwood Press.

Starting with ABC and ACE words, Achi Board game, and Achilles and the Tortoise and ending with Zeno's paradoxes, this is a veritable encyclopedia of games covered by the title. Each game's history and bibliographical references are thoroughly included to make this a valuable resource for play therapists, educators, and researchers to apply in ways that would be extremely useful in helping children as well as adults, including senior citizens keep their minds alive and working.

Gemeinhardt, M. (2004). Imaginative play as a component of a multisensory art experience. In R. L. Clements & L. Fiorentino (Eds.), *The child's right to play: a global approach* (pp. 211–215). Westport, CT: Praeger.

This resource contains (p. 214) an extensive list of activity expansions and links.

Giordano, R. G. (2003). *Fun and games in twentieth-century America: A historical guide to leisure.* Westport, CT: Greenwood.

This is a fascinating must-read historical guide about play in its multifarious manifestations, starting from the beginning of the last century (1900–1914) and progressing to World War I (1914–1918); the epidemic influenza (1918), to the stock market crash (1929); the Great Depression and the New Deal (1929–1939); World War II and its aftermath (1940–1946); the age of television, teenagers, and rock and roll (1947–1964); the jet age and political and lifestyle turbulence (1964–1979); yuppies, *Star Wars,* and MTV (1980–1992); and ending with Generation X, the Internet, and virtual reality (1992–2000).

Gitlin-Weiner, K., Sandgrund, A., & Schaefer, C. (Eds.). (2002). *Play diagnosis and assessment.* New York: Wiley.

This resource includes any conceivable instrument to evaluate development, diagnosis, parent–child interaction, family play, peer play interactions, and projective play techniques to evaluate play at various stages and contexts of play. This volume is crucial for any professional who might want to research play in its various contexts and stages.

Gratton, C. (1969). Summaries of selected works on personality and play. *Humanitas: Journal of the Institute of Man, 1,* 101–108.

An excellent but by now outdated commentary that could serve as the basis for future commentaries.

Gratton, C. (1969). Selected subject bibliography (on play) (covering the past ten years). *Humanitas: Journal of the Institute of Man, 1,* 111–119.

An excellent but by now outdated bibliography that could serve as the basis for future bibliographies.

Harwood, T. M., & L'Abate, L. (2009). *Self-help in mental health: A critical appraisal*. New York: Springer.
This book covers all possible and imaginable methods to allow people in need of help to help themselves and also to help themselves with the help of paraprofessionals and professionals.

Heynes-Dussel, J. (2004). Creating homemade play equipment. In R. L. Clements & L. Fiorentino (Eds.), *The child's right to play: A global approach* (pp. 191–196). Westport, CT: Praeger.
This resource contains instructions on how to make balls, foxtails, and puppets and to set boundaries, goals, and markers for sporting equipment, games, and activities.

International Play Association (2004). Declaration of the child's right to play. In R. L. Clements & L. Fiorentino (Eds.), *The child's right to play: a global approach* (pp. 393–397). Westport, CT: Praeger.

Juhlin, G. T. (2004). Scandinavian Viking games. In R. L. Clements & L. Fiorentino (Eds.), *The child's right to play: a global approach* (pp. 197–201). Westport, CT: Praeger.
This unusual resource shows game pieces and examples to follow of training games for combat and hunting, including a Viking chess board and a burnball field.

Kaduson, H. G., & Schaefer, C. E. (Eds.). (2000). *Short-term play therapy for children*. New York: Guilford.
Here child therapists will find specific ways to address specific developmental disorders, with chapters about childhood fears and phobias, grieving children, disruptive school students, traumatized children, attention-deficit/hyperactivity disorder, children of divorced parents, families with chronic illness, enhancing attachment in adopted children, involving and empowering parents with disruptive children, child psychiatric problems, group treatment of sexually abused children, play group therapy for social skills deficits with separate modules with homework for children and parents, complete with a structured interview to assess social skills in children (pp. 342–343), and a play-based parenting program to facilitate parent-child attachment.

Kelly-Vance, L., & Ryalls, B. O. (2005). A systematic, reliable approach to play assessment in preschoolers. *School Psychology International, 26,* 398–412.
Play assessment is gaining attention as a measure of the developing skills of young children. However, procedures and methods of coding child behaviors vary considerably across researchers and practitioners. Because of this gap between researchers and practitioners, definitive statements about the use of

play assessment cannot be made without further research. This article includes an attempt to report on a set of standardized procedures for play assessment along with an empirically based coding scheme. High inter-observer reliability was found along with moderate test–retest correlations for both the typically developing and exceptional children. Thus, this version of play assessment holds promise as an observation system to evaluate interventions and monitoring progress in early childhood play. More research is needed in this area before play assessment can either be used in early childhood or discarded as an inappropriate approach.

Linder, T. W. (1993). *Transdisciplinary play-based assessment: A functional approach to working with young children.* Baltimore, MD: Paul H. Brookes Publishing.

This volume provides a model for conducting holistically accurate assessments of children from infancy to age 6 using natural play interactions. Grounded in a team approach that includes the child's parents as vital team members, this easy-to-use book contains observation guidelines and worksheets for assessing a child's development in cognitive, socioemotional, communication and language, and sensorimotor domains. Team members will be able to identify the child's strength, needs, and areas of concern in these areas of development. Comprehensive and user friendly, observation and summary worksheets are linked to this book's companion volume. Used together, both books will enable professionals and parents to complete the assessment–intervention–evaluation process and design an individualized family service plan or an individualized education program quickly and effectively.

Masman, K. (Ed.). (2003). *Mates Traits Cards.* Bendigo, Victoria, Australia: St. Luke Innovative Resources.

Mates Traits is a set of colored activity cards about friendship developed after 9/11 and the Bali bombings as an antidote to hatred, terrorism, and war. It consists of a deck of thirty-two 12×12 centimeter cards labeled with one aspect of friendship illustrated with humorous cartoons of Australian animal characters. These cards are designed to appeal to primary school children, but the appeal may extend to adolescents and even parents.

McHale-Small, M., & Uhrich, T. A. (2004). Simon says . . . "Reading is Fun!" In R. L. Clements & L. Fiorentino (Eds.), *The child's right to play: a global approach* (pp. 119–123). Westport, CT: Praeger.

This resource contains specific instructions (p. 120) for Movement Activity: "Jumping Jellybeans and Elephants," and "Mystery Writer" (pp. 121).

Moyles, J. (Ed.). (2005). *The excellence of play* (2nd edition). Maidenhead, Berkshire, UK: Open University Press.

The longest part of this book links play with specific curriculum areas in the United Kingdom, including outdoor and physical play, science, mathematics, art, and music.

Patterson, C. M. (2004). Play-based curriculum: A strong foundation for future learning. In R. L. Clements & L. Fiorentino (Eds.), *The child's right to play: a global approach* (pp. 111–117). Westport, CT: Praeger.

Instructions for play activities (pp. 115–116) for "What's the Password?," "What is Missing?," "Friendship Match," and "Flower and Seed Match Game."

Singer, D. G., & Singer, J. L. (2001). *Make-believe: games and activities for imaginative play: a book for parents, teachers, and the young children in their lives.* Washington, DC: Magination Press/American Psychological Association.

This how-to-guide contains more than 100 activities and games that parents, teachers, and other adults can use to stimulate the imagination and sense of play in 2- to 5-year-olds. These activities are based on evidence gathered from years of testing these materials and games with children in this age range. There is also a list of appropriate preschool materials for parents and teachers interested in increasing children's imagination.

Sori, C. F., & Hecker, L. L. (2003). *The therapist's notebook for children and adolescents: homework, handouts, and activities for use in psychotherapy.* New York: Haworth.

This source is sprinkled with make-believe, constructive, mock, pretense, and symbolic activities, includes also Play Genograms (pp. 49–55), an original way to construct a possible play therapy plan—a detail that is missing in many play therapy treatises. There is also a Play Interaction Checklist Form (pp. 132–140) useful in clinical, nonclinical, and research applications. This source is highly recommended not only for play therapists but also for teachers, school psychologists, and school counselors.

Stagnitti, K., & Unsworth, C. (2004). The test–retest reliability of the Child-Initiated Pretend Play Assessment. *American Journal of Occupational Therapy, 58,* 93–99.

This research supports the reliability of the Child-Initiated Pretend Play Assessment (ChIPPA).

Sutton-Smith, B. (1986). *Toys as culture.* New York: Gardner Press.

This resource contains all you need or want to know about toys during the first two years of life.

Van Lue, E. M. (2004). Integration of traditional play and games to enhance learning. In R. L. Clements & L. Fiorentino (Eds.), *The child's right to play: a global approach* (pp. 185–190). Westport, CT: Praeger.

This recommended resource gives a complete list of "The best toys in life are free" from A to Z.

White, C. (2006). *The social play record: A toolkit for assessing and developing social play from infancy to adolescence.* London, UK: Jessica Kingsley Publishers.

This practical resource for parents and teachers is designed to evaluate as well as help children develop social skills through play, especially for children within autistic spectrum disorders, from 1 to 13 years of age.

JOURNALS

Games and Culture. Sage Publications, 2455 Teller Road, Thousand Oaks, CA, 91320.

International Journal of Play Therapy, Published by the Association for Play Therapy, Suite 101, 2050 North Winery, Fresno, CA 93703.

KIDS Enabled:A Publication for Parents of Children with Learning Differences. 5579 B Chamblee Dunwoody Rd., Suite 318, Atlanta, GA 30338. *http://www.kidsenabled.com*

Simulation & Gaming. Sage Publications, 2455, Teller Road, Thousand Oaks, CA, 91320.

INTERNET RESOURCES

Source	Gender(s)	Age	Contents & Comments
aarp.org.books	M/F	Seniors	Games of all kinds for senior citizens.
aarp.org.games	M/F	Seniors	
apple.com	M/F	Adolescents	Most of the games on this source are very aggressive.
amazon.com	M/F	All ages	Playtime online superstore. You name it, they've got it. Immense.
americanboy.com	M		Not worthy of access— sells only caps and T-shirts. Not comparable to *americangirl.com.*
americangirl.com	F	5+	Huge variety of games and puzzles.
barbie.com	F		Activities and competitive games for girls only.
bbc.co.uk/cbeebies/ teletubbies	M/F	3+	Animated games featuring Teletubbies. Reward for success and no penalty for failure
bulletin.aarp.org	M/F	All ages	Play an interactive Sudoku.
cartoonnetwork.com		All ages	190+ free games. Build your own game. Videos of favorite shows to shop.

INTERNET RESOURCES *(continued)*

Source	Gender(s)	Age	Contents & Comments
discoverystore.com	M/F	Teens to adults	All kinds, mostly for adults.
disney.go.com		All ages	"The Official Home Page For All Things Disney." They have "For You" pre-set applications based on choices between boy and girl; preschool, kids, and teens; families; and Disney fans. Very user friendly. Movies, music, games, live events, TV, travel, shop; mobile; characters; DxD = interactive live stream applications including music, trailers, games, etc.
disneychannel.com		All ages	Disney Channel TV Network (4 channels). Watch full length episodes, Radio Disney, make your own music mix. Gamer.
epets.com		Adults	"Where Pet Lovers Meet." Blog about your pet. Tips and Pet of the Day. Music and videos not very interactive for children. Not appropriate for all ages with the unlimited access to blog.
everythinggirl.com	F	Adolescent	Run by Mattel Company, includes *barbie.com, barbiegirls.com, pollypocket.com, mymeebas.com, highschoolmusical.com,* and *myscene.com.*
fatworld.org		Teens and adults	Gamelike approach to help combat obesity.[a]
freeverse.com/2bbg25		Teens and adults	Memory training games.

INTERNET RESOURCES *(continued)*

Source	Gender(s)	Age	Contents & Comments
gamepuzzles.com		All ages	Easy-to-find games, but this is mainly for advertisement of products. Puzzle Parlor (*gamepuzzle.com/pparlor/puzzleparlmm.html*) is the interactive site. Visual representation of physical puzzle fit. Jigsaw-like puzzles. Hard, Harder, and Hardest.
games.com	M/F	Tweens	All genres. You can play games against other online users. *Most download automatically.* AOL games.
happyneuron.com	M/F	Seniors	All kinds of games.
itoons.com		4+	"The Game and Animation Studio." Games and Applications for many different companies that appeal to children including: Nickelodeon, General Mills, Lego, and Sesame Street. Cartoons to watch requiring QuickTime.
lego.com	M/F	2+	Here is where, in addition to plastic blocks, small and large, the famous (or infamous depending on your viewpoint) Bionicles are sold.
mindware.com	M/F	5+	Brainy toys for kids of all ages.
miniclip.com	M/F	Parental guidance suggested	Many genres including action, sports, shoot 'em up, puzzles.
noggin.com		"Baby things"	Printables, videos of favorite TV shows (Nickelodeon), games, arts and craft ideas, favorite character cutouts.
mylittlepony.com			All variations on the theme of My Little Pony toys; no punishment for failure.

INTERNET RESOURCES *(continued)*

Source	Gender(s)	Age	Contents & Comments
nickatnite.com		Nostalgic ages	Access to old shows (i.e., from the 1980s and 1990s), message boards, and games.
nick.com	M/F	5–15	Games, access to all shows by Nickelodeon, Neopets, shopping. Make your own video.
pbskids.org			Simple game starting with Sesame Street gang, Barney, and others. Bright friendly site with lost of options that are loved by children 5+ years.
playattention.com		From childhood to adulthood	Computer-connected games to treat attention-deficit/hyperactivity disorders.
play.com		Late elementary school children and adolescents	Computer games of an aggressive, warlike nature as well as more peaceful games.
playmobil.com		Variety of age-appropriate settings	3D imagination building, interactive games with numerous themes to choose.
playtherapy.org		For professionals and parents	International information about various types of play therapy, including filial therapy.
poissonrouge.com	M/F	Whole family	Quirky, elegant, dreamlike. Coloring, learn music, optical illusions! Surprising and unconventional amusement without advertisements. "You will LOVE IT!"
pollypocket.com	F	Elementary school	Interactive gaming: all things having to do with Polly's world.
positscience.com		Children to adults	Memory training games for the whole family.
schoolbox.com		0–17+ years	All sorts of toys and games.

INTERNET RESOURCES *(continued)*

Source	Gender(s)	Age	Contents & Comments
ty.com	M/F	3+	Interactive Beanie Babies 2.0 website with homemade videos, shop, games, chat, Tyfolio for Beanie information. Ty Talk: Daily newsletter for the Beanies. BBOT: Ty trader (postings as in *craigslist.com*). Questions for Ty Info Beanie: all the info you need about your Beanie Babies. Fun-O-Rama (AWESOME!) puzzles, coloring, matching, Most wanted list
webkinz.com		6–13+, but some games for younger children	Virtual pets, which require the child to become responsible for the well-being of the pet. Feeding, walking, playing, health are all monitored online once child registers toy pet online.
wii.com	M/F	pre pubescent+	Website doesn't have much interaction but advertises the Wii product through videos and demos.
youngexplorers.com	M/F	Infancy to elementary age	Great variety of electronic toys.
zanybrainy.com		Preschool to high school	Toys to foster thinking and skills. "Kids learn best when they're having fun!"

   *a*Jacobs, T. (2008)/Policy-heavy play: "Fatworld" shows video games can tackle (urp) weighty issues. *Miller-McCune, 1,* 72–73.
   Authoritative source: 8-year-old Alessandra L'Abate

TOY AND GAME SUPPLIERS AND CATALOGUES

In these catalogues one can find every imaginable toy, game, or gamelike product available on the market for entertainment, education, therapy, and rehabilitation purposes.

Back to Basics Toys: Games & Hobbies. P. O. Box 9300, Pueblo, CO 8100-9300.

Boys Town Press: Resources for youth-serving professionals, educators, and parents.

Bright Apple, P. O. Box 14554, Scottsdale, AZ 85267, 1-800-728-9783; fax 1-800-728-8891; *www.brightapple.com.*

Childswork/Childsplay. P.O. Box 1246, Wilkes-Barre, PA 18703-1246; 1-800-962-1141; *www.childswork.com.*

Courage-To-Change. CTC Publishing, 10431 Lawyers Rd., Vienna, VA 22181; or P.O. Box 486, Wilkes-Barre, PA 18702-0486, 1-800-440-4003; *www.couragetochange. com.*

Creative Therapy Store. 12031 Wilshire Boulevard, Los Angeles, CA 90025-1261; 1-800-648-8857, fax 310-478-7838; *www.creativetherapystore.com.* E-mail: *info@creativetherapystore.com.*

Discovery Store. P.O. Box 869011, Plano, TX 75086-911.

Father Flanagan's Boys' Home. 14100 Crawford Street, Boys Town, NE 68010, 1-800-282-6657; *www.girlsandboystown.org/btpress.*

Free Spirit Publishing, Inc. Suite 200, 217 Fifth Avenue North, Minneapolis, MN 55401-1299; 1-800-735-7323 or fax 1-612-337-5050; *www.help4kinds@ freespirit.com.*

Highlights: Fun with a Purpose. 1800 Watermark Drive, P.O. Box 182112, Columbus, OH, 43218-2112; 1-800-422-6202; *www.shophighlights.com.*

ImagiPlay, Inc. Boulder, Colorado, produces some 150 toys tested for safety using recycled or sustainable materials, such as compressed sawdust and rubberwood from Southeast Asia, with prices ranging from $12 to $37 (see Whole Foods for distribution of these toys).

MindWare. 2100 County Road C West, Roseville, MN, 55113.

Museum Tour. 2517 SE Mailwell Drive, Milwaukie, OR 97222; *www.museumtour. com.*

NRCYS. The University of Oklahoma OUTREACH National Resource Center for Youth Services. Schusterman Center, Building 4W, 4502 East 41st Street, Tulsa, OK 74135-2512.

PlastWood Corporation. Room 953, 2000 Fifth Avenue, The International Toy Center, New York, NY 10010, USA. E-mail: *info@plastwood.de.* For parents who are concerned about plastic toys made in China, the very inventive magnetic games sold by this company all over the world are made of wood or a wood composite with magnets inserted inside to connect various pieces of the game. Games from this resource are very ingenious and worthy of consideration.

Pro-ed. 8700 Shoal Creek Boulevard Austin, TX 78757-6897; 1-800-897-3202; fax 1-800-397-7633; *www.proedinc.com.*

Slosson Educational Publications, Inc. P.O. Box 544, East Aurora, NY 14052-0544; 1-888-Slosson; fax 1-800-655-3850; *www.slosson.com.* E-mail: *slosson@ slosson.com.*

Sunburst. Suite 201, 101 Castleton Street, Pleasantville, NY 10570; 1-800-431-1934; *www.sunburst.com.*

Western Psychological Services (2004). Creative Therapy Store. 12031 Wilshire Boulevard, Los Angeles, CA 90025-1251; 1-800-648-8857; fax 310-478-7838; *www.creativetherapystore.com, www.wpspublish.com.*

Whole Foods, Inc. This grocery store sells ImagiPlay's originating earth-friendly wooden African Safari set with 18 hand-painted animals.

Young Explorers. P. O. Box 3338, Chelmsford, MA 01824-0938; *www. YoungExplorers.com.*

PROFESSIONAL AND SCIENTIFIC ORGANIZATIONS FOCUSED ON PLAY

Association for Play Therapy, Inc. Suite 101, 2050 N. Vinery, Fresno, CA 93703.

Association of Childhood Education International. 17904 Georgia Avenue Suite 215, Olney, MD 20832. Phone: (301) 570-2111, (800) 423-3563

MONITORED PLAY THERAPY

Pessimistic conclusions about the inadequacy of research about the process and outcome of play therapy were reached 40 years ago, as reported in a recent publication (L'Abate, 2008a). Results reported in Chapter 15 of this volume do give a much more positive picture of play therapy than was present at the time the experiment was performed (1966–1974). Under the assumption that aggression and constructions were the two major aspects of play and play therapy, a pair of connecting playrooms was used. One room was full of aggressive games and toys, including three electric shooting galleries (common in those days) plus a chest of nine drawers with a variety of aggressive materials, such as hammers, toy guns, and water pistols as well as competitive board games. The other room contained constructive games, toys, and materials, such as shuffleboard, plaster of Paris, Lego, and Lincoln Logs to build and create something new.

Automatic counters and timers recorded how much time the child spent in either room (according to the light switch) and how much time was spent with each toy or game, according to timers connected to drawers in the chest, the guns in the shooting galleries, and the machines in the construction playroom. Once a child pulled out a drawer to fetch a toy, its timer would be engaged and would continue running until the child finished playing and closed the drawer. Gun shooting was monitored not only by how much time was spent on each gun but also by how many shots were fired. All counters and timers were contained in master boards in an observation room with one-way mirrors through which observers and a supervisor could also follow the process in both playrooms.

The information gathered on the master boards was input to a computer (in those days, a mainframe that occupied an entire room!) via punch cards. Children, mostly boys, were evaluated with a battery of tests before and after a constant number of play therapy sessions, most of them with a therapist present. Two nonclinical boys volunteered to follow the same process for experimental purposes without a therapist. Their process of playing was found to be identical to the majority of the process for clinical (i.e., referred) boys. Only a few girls were referred to this process, and they were not considered in the final analysis of the data obtained over a period of five years.

Children referred for this playroom were drawn from the writer's Family Study Center as well as a Children's Center between the ages of 5 and 14 years. Their IQ scores ranged from defective (70) to distinctly superior (150). They were all evaluated with the Wechsler Intelligence Scale for Children (WISC), the Peabody Picture Vocabulary Test (PPVT), the Wechsler Range Achievement Test (WRAT), the Missouri Children Picture Series (MCPS; Register & L'Abate, 1972), and Rorschach ink blots.

For the purposes of brevity a great deal of the literature background specific to the rationale for this study must be eliminated to concentrate on the methodological details of this study (L'Abate, 1964, 1971).

Essentially the two major dimensions of interest and relevance to the present study were: (a) aggression and (b) construction.

METHOD

Playroom

Children were monitored during fifteen sessions of play therapy by means of a special type of playroom. The child faced three doors. The central door led to the control room, the left door led to the aggressive room (room A), and the right door led to the constructive room (room C). Rooms A and C were interconnected. In each room there was a large institutional clock right above each toy chest on the far wall. Microphones were placed in the ceiling to collect as much of the child–therapist sounds as possible.

The control room (6 × 6 feet), between the two playrooms, contained one panel for each room, timers and counters, tape recorders, an amplifier, two earphones, and one-way mirrors covering both playrooms. Playroom A contained three automatic, electrically operated guns, each connected to a counter in the control panel monitoring the number of shots and timers to measure how much time was spent on the gun. Against the end wall there was a chest of nine drawers, each containing a wire mesh basket for each toy. As the child pulled a basket out of its drawer, a microswitch against the wall activated a timer, as did the light switches beside the entrance doors and the door interconnecting the two playrooms. The drawers contained a Pound-a-Peg for younger children and a heavy piece of wood into which older children could hammer nails; boxing gloves, one pair for the child and the other pair for the therapist; plastic play soldiers, cowboys, and Indians; dart guns; and three boxed War Games (Dogfight, Hit-the-Beach, and naval war games).

Thus, six types of measures for aggressive behaviors were obtained here: (1) time spent in the A playroom, (2) three frequencies of shots for the three guns,

(3) total frequency of shots, and (4) time spent with toys in the A-drawers; (5) time spent on each of the three guns; and (6) total time on guns.

In the C room there were three constructive play machines. One was a simple "skill game" consisting of levers that spring a light coin through three series of animal shapes. If the child could move the coin through the same animals from one series to the next, the board would light up and the child would receive points. Actually this was as much a game of chance as skill and was the simplest of the electrical games in this room. The next toy machine was a baseball game where two people would play, one to pitch and the other to bat. The third was a Shuffle Alley geared also for two players. All three machines were connected to timers in the control panel.

In the drawers against the end wall, there were a collection of plastic models and molds for plaster construction to suit all levels of skills and interest; blocks of various dimensions; motorized Tinkertoys; two-player games such as dominoes and Scrabble; painting equipment (paper and soft-tipped pens); and plaster of Paris. A wall table on the right side of the room was used for this constructive activity. (There was no such table in the A room, because only a minimum of facilitation and encouragement was to be given for aggressive activities; if they occurred, both the child and the therapist would need to use the floor.)

The C room, then, yielded four types of measures of constructive behaviors: (1) time spent in the room; (2) time spent with each electric machine (three measures); (3) total time with machines and (4) time spent with toys from the drawers. A comparison of ratios of measures from one room to the other (A/C) could become the major dependent variable studied as a function of (a) age; (b) type of problematic behavior prior to entrance in play therapy; (c) family composition and handling; (d) socioeconomic background; (e) intelligence; and (f) child–therapist interaction. In this report the data on intellectual and personality functioning were the main independent variables.

Participants

Children were referred to the Child Development Laboratory for a variety of reasons (underachievement, behavior problems, etc.). The total number of children who completed the procedure was 26. For the nineteen clinical children, typically, after a complete psychodiagnostic evaluation, a conference was held with the child and his parents where the results were discussed and various recommendations would include play therapy when appropriate. If the parents were willing to follow this course, it was agreed that the child would be assigned an available therapist (actually a graduate student) at the discretion of the writer and that he would come for monitored play therapy for at least fifteen consecutive sessions. After the fifteenth therapy session, parents agreed to retesting and a follow-up conference to discuss the results of therapy and progress, if any. During play therapy, parents were also seen separately if the need arose.

In addition to the clinical children referred for help to the Child Development Laboratory, an effort was made to obtain a contrast sample of seven nonclinical children to serve as controls and comparisons. Two groups of children were used for comparison of baseline measures: one heterogeneous group of children who completed fifteen sessions (stayers) and another dropout group who were unsuccessful in completing the program (quitters). This group stayed from one to ten sessions. The successful completion group was made up of five nonclinical children with a therapist constantly with them in the playroom, two nonclinical children who were without therapists and were left alone to play by themselves but observed continuously by an observer in the central control booth. The average age of these children was 9 years with a range from 5 to 14 years. Intellectually these boys came from a very heterogeneous background. Although their mean IQ score reached normality, IQ scores ranged from the defective (70) to the distinctly superior (150).

Baseline and Outcome Measures

The measurement of outcome in monitored play therapy was achieved through the laboratory method of psychodiagnosis developed by this writer (L'Abate, 2008a). This method consists of standard test batteries for three age levels: from 3 years to 5 years 11 months; from 6 years to 8 years 11 months; and from 9 years to 14 years and 11 months. The test administration and scoring were done by graduate students who were not familiar with the child on the pre-test and who not only were unfamiliar with the child on post-testing but had no knowledge of test results from pre-therapy testing. The rationale and reasons and results for this method can be found in the sources already cited.

The measures of outcome common to all three test batteries that were analyzed in the present study were as follows:

(a) Wechsler Intelligence Scale for Children (WISC)

Intellectual functioning in children who have not undergone therapy has been shown to be markedly stable. The WISC Full Scale IQ is reported to have a high coefficient of reliability over periods of months and years.

(b) Peabody Picture Vocabulary (PPVT)

Another measure of intellectual functioning, the PPVT is reported to have alternate form correlation of 0.77 and to have a correlation coefficient of 0.88 when re-administered after an interval of 1 year. Since intellectual functioning is normally stable, it seems reasonable to use IQ test scores after therapy as a measure of improvement.

(c) Wide Range Achievement Test (WRAT)

The measure of academic achievement used in this study, the WRAT, is reported to have a statistically average reliability coefficient of .93. Of the three scales of the WRAT, the reading scale has the highest clinical reliability coefficient .91 and was the most reliable of fifteen tests used in repeat examinations during a study of 100 juvenile delinquents. In view of the evidence of this test's stability, increase in standard scores should indicate improvement.

(d) Missouri Children Pictures Series (MCPS)

One of the personality measures used in this study is the MCPS, an objective, nonverbal test of personality for children. Reliability coefficients ranged from .26 to .70, with most of these coefficients being significant at the .01 level (Register & L'Abate, 1972). None of the reliability coefficients matches those for intelligence tests, but most of them compare favorably with those for personality tests such as the Minnesota Multiphasic Personality Inventory. Movement toward the norm would seem indicative of improvement. This test was partially validated with a residential deaf population (Logue, Penrod, & Zackheim, 1976).

(e) Rorschach Ink Blots

Form level ratings of the Rorschach are important in evaluating intellectual capacity and efficiency. They have been widely used as indicators of personality function. The form level refers to the subject's regard for and adherence to the perceptual reality of the ink blot and is therefore taken to reflect his ability to meet reality's demands by formal reasoning. Several different desirable personality factors are thought to be reflected on the Rorschach form level. Mature ego functioning involves a capacity for undistorted perception and the degree to which the subject is attentive to or departs from "reality" if the blots become a measure of ego strength. The achievement of adequate form results from the individual's capacity to delay discharge of impulse. High percentage of F+ responses depends on the ability to concentrate and on the effective functioning of the highest levels of cerebral organization. Because with clinical improvement there should be a general rise in F+%, increase in form level after therapy will be considered evidence of improvement. In addition to Beck's scoring system, content responses were also scored according to size (large, medium, or small) and type of animal (aggressive, unpleasant, or timid). There were a total of twenty-two different scoring categories used with a combination of both methods.

Time Limits in Monitored Play Therapy

Time-limited psychotherapy has been used with adults, and there is no obvious or evident reason why it should not be used with children. Different rates of treatment would add an additional uncontrolled factor that would make data analysis more difficult. Consequently, it was decided beforehand that the process of monitored play therapy should last fifteen sessions. Each child would be evaluated with each test battery before and after fifteen sessions of monitored play therapy.

Gender Limitations

Not all the children seen in the monitored play therapy were boys, but the number of girls in this study was too small to allow significant generalizations. Two girls were followed up in the monitored play therapy room, but these results will not be presented here. Consequently, the results of the present study have been based on boys, and the implications from possible results should be limited to boys.

Nonverbal Measures of Process with Baseline and Post-Evaluation Scores

This analysis is the most inclusive and, it is hoped, more conclusive than the next ones. It deals with the relationships among nonverbal process measures (time spent in either of the two rooms, aggressive, or constructive), time spent on either of two drawers, aggressive or constructive, and time spent on either guns (aggressive) or machines (constructive) with the test scores achieved by each child before and after fifteen sessions of play.

Limitations of the Study

The most obvious limitation of this study, in addition to the exclusion of girls, was the small number of children in the control group, which at the time was difficult to obtain for logistic and institutional reasons. Most children in schools could not come during the week, and there was no way to transport them to the laboratory without parental consent. School authorities could not allow transportation of children from their schools without parental consent.

QUANTITATIVE RESULTS

Intercorrelations among Process Measures

Time in A-Room for all children ($N = 26$) correlated positively with Time on Guns ($r = .73, p < .01$), Number of Shots ($r = .54, p < .05$), and Time on Aggressive Drawer ($r = .96, p < .01$). Obviously, because of their separate nature, Time in A-Room correlated negatively with Time in C-Room ($r = -.98, p < .0001$), as could be expected. Time on Guns correlated positively with Number of Shots ($r = .86, p < .001$) and negatively with Time in C-Room ($r = -.68; p < .01$) and with Time on C-Drawers ($r = -.71, p < .01$). Number of Shots correlated with three measures on construction: negatively with Time in C-Room ($r = -.51, p < .05$), positively with Time on Machines ($r = .47, p < .05$), and negatively with Time on C-Drawers ($r = -.62, p < .01$). Time on A-Drawers correlated negatively with Time in C-Room ($r = -.77, p < .01$) and with Time on C-Machines ($r = -.62, p < .05$). Time in C-Room correlated positively with Time on C-Drawer ($r = .44, p < .05$). Time on C-Machines correlated negatively with Time on C-Drawer ($r = -.59, p < .05$). These patterns of correlations appear in line with possible expectations that, as a whole, time spent in one of the two rooms should correlate negatively with the other, while some of the activities within a room may not be necessarily correlated positively. The more time the child spends on one activity, regardless of whether it was aggressive or constructive, the less time he could spend on the other activity. This generalization applies between rooms as well as within each room, guns vs. A-drawers (Time on Guns was not correlated with Time on Drawers), while Time on C-Drawers correlated negatively with Time on C-Machines.

Correlations between Pre-Test Baseline and Process Measures

Among the 350 intercorrelations between the fifty pre-therapy baseline measures and the eight process measures, there were no significant correlations among the PPVT, Rorschach, and the process measures. On the WRAT, spelling correlated negatively with Time on Guns ($r = -.46, p < .05$), and with Number of Shots ($r = -.49, p < .05$). WRAT Arithmetic correlated negatively with Number of Shots ($r = -.05, p < .05$).

On the WISC, comprehension correlated negatively with Time on Guns ($r = -.51, p < .05$) and Number of Shots ($r = -.53, p < .05$). Similarities correlated negatively ($r = -.45, p < .05$) with Number of Shots. Vocabulary correlated negatively with Time on Guns ($r = -.46, p < .05$) and positively with Time on C-Drawer ($r = .50, p < .05$). Block Design correlated negatively with Time on Guns ($r = -.49; p < .05$). Picture Arrangement correlated negatively with Time on Guns ($r = -.63, p < .01$) and Number of Shots ($r = -.54, p < .05$). Object Assembly correlated positively with Time on A-Drawers ($r = .54, p < .05$). Verbal IQ correlated negatively with Time on Guns ($r = -.44, p < .05$) and positively with Time on C-Drawer ($r = .44, p < .05$). Performance IQ correlated negatively with Time on Guns ($r = -.62, p < .01$) and Number of Shots ($r = -.55, p < .05$) and positively with Time on C-Drawer ($r = .47; p < .05$). Full IQ, correlated negatively with Time on Guns ($r = -.52, p < .05$), and positively with Time on C-Drawer ($r = .48, p < .05$).

Among these intercorrelations, Time on Guns had the highest number (nine) of significant correlations, all negative, with WISC baseline scores, followed by Number of Shots (seven significantly negative correlations), and Time on C-Drawer (seven significantly positive correlations). It follows from these results then that intellectual functioning is one of the best predictions not only of aggressive but also of constructive activities.

On the MCPS, the only three and possibly random correlations occurred positively between the Aggression Scale and Time Spent on the A Drawer ($r = .60, p < .01$), and negatively between the Aggression Scale and Time Spent in C-Room ($r = .60, p < .01$), and negatively between the Aggression Scale and Time Spent in C-Room ($r = -.61, p < .01$), and positively with Time in A-Room ($r = .60, p < .01$). These correlations tend to lend a certain degree of predictive validity to this scale.

Process Measures with Post-Therapy Results

Among the 350 correlations between eight process measures and fifty- eight pre- and post-therapy measures, the only significant ($p < .05$ or better) pattern of correlations clearly shown was Time Spent on Guns. This measure correlated negatively and significantly with PPVTIQ ($r = -.45, p < .05$), with WRAT-Spelling ($r = -.53, p < .05$), and with WRAT-Arithmetic ($r = -.52, p < .05$).

On the WISC, Time on Guns correlated negatively and significantly with the following subscales: Comprehension ($r = -.46, p < .05$), Similarities($r = -.63, p < .01$), Vocabulary ($r = -.53, p < .05$), Vocabulary IQ ($r = -.53, p < .05$), Verbal IQ ($r = -.52, p < .05$), Performance IQ ($r = -.52, p < .05$), and full IQ ($r = -.55, p < .05$).

Correlations between Pre- and Post-Therapy Measures

All correlations among PPVT, WRAT, and WISC were significantly ($p < .01$) correlated with each other on the pre–post- therapy basis. None of the inter-correlations between intellectual (PPVT, WISC), educational (WRAT), and person-ality (MCPS, Rorschach) correlated with each other to a significant extent. If there were any significant correlations between MCPS and Rorschach, they were too few to be nonrandom.

Reliability within Pre- and Post Measures

All of the correlations within each pre- and post measure were highly signifi-cant ($p < .01$) for the PPVT, WRAT, and WISC. For the MCPS, the scales that showed a significant correlation on a before–after basis were Maturity ($r = .37$), Aggression ($r = .35$), Hyperactivity ($r = .32$), Sleep Disturbance ($r = .37$), except for Somatization ($r = -.02$). The other three scales showed acceptable levels of reliability: Conformism ($r = .69, p < .01$) Masculinity–Femininity ($r = -.62$, $p < .01$). Hyperactivity was somewhere in the middle ($r = .43, p < .01$).

Among the Rorschach measures significant reliability scores were found for Number of Responses ($r = .72, p < .01$), Affective ratio ($r = .72, p < .01$), Monitor responses ($r = .77, p < .01$), Animal Percentages ($r = .48, p < .05$, Anatomy Percentages ($r = .65, p < .01$), Number of Aggressive Responses ($r = .51$, $p < .05$), Large responses ($r = .54, p < .01$), Small responses ($r = .61, p < .01$), and Unpleasant responses ($r = .69, p < .01$).

Comparison of Pre- and Post-Measures

The pre-therapy baseline measures were compared with the same measures taken on a post-therapy basis after 15 sessions of monitored play therapy. For all the boys as a whole (both clinical and nonclinical), the only significant differ-ences occurred in the WISC and Performance IQ scores ($t = 2.13, p < .05$), on the MCPS Conformism Scale ($t = 2.38, p < .01$), on the Rorschach Popular responses ($t = 2.05, p < .05$), and Unpleasantness Scores ($t = 2.51, p < .05$). For the clinical group as a whole ($N = 15$), significant differences occurred in the MCPS conformism Scale ($t = 2.34, p < .05$) and on the Rorschach Unpleasant-ness score ($t = 2.91, p < .05$). The nonclinical group was too small to allow a reliable statistical analysis of their pre- and post-measures.

A Note on Reliability

The weak reliability of some measures may not necessarily represent a shortcoming in the measuring instrument. The weak correlation between before- and after-treatment measures may also represent a change in the behavior intervening between the two testings. If a high correlation means high reliability and no change in scores, a low correlation could mean low reliability and consequently a change in scores. Hence what is considered as a shortcoming could actually represent a sensitivity in the instrument that is not available in other, more objective tests. The issue, then, may not be one of reliability as much as what are these scores related to. This is an issue of validity.

Process Measures and Spurious Correlations

Out of a large number of correlations (350), any significant correlation outside of the clear pattern described between Time on Guns and intellectual (PPVT and WISC) and educational measures (WRAT Spelling and Arithmetic), one needs to accept that the remainder of significant correlations may be random or spurious. They are reported more for the sake of possibly accidental findings than for their isolated significance. Significant correlations in such a large matrix can be meaningful mostly as a pattern rather than as isolated and accidental findings: Time on A-Drawers, for instance, correlated positively with Block Design on the WISC ($r = .44, p < .05$), positively with Hyperactivity Scale of MCPS ($r = .49, p < .05$), and negatively with the Timid Score on the Rorschach ($r = -.50, p < .05$). Time on A-Room correlated negatively only with the Timid Score on the Rorschach ($r = -.48, p < .05$), while Time on C-Room correlated positively with the same Rorschach Timid Score ($r = .45, p < .05$). Thus, of all the Rorschach measures the only one that seemed vaguely and remotely correlated with post-therapy results was Timidity. Time on C-Machines correlated negatively ($r = -.53, p < .05$) with the Hyperactivity scale of the MCPS. This is the only measure in the MCPS that correlated with post-therapy results, positively with Time on A-Drawer, and negatively with Time on C-Machines. Time on C-Drawer correlated positively with Object Assembly on the WISC ($r = .45, p < .05$).

Thus, the main significant pattern of correlation between process measures and post-therapy results is the negative correlations between Time on Guns and intellectual and educational measures (PPVT, WISC, and WRAT).

Pre- and Post-Measures

When both clinical ($N = 19$) and control ($N = 7$) children were lumped together for analysis, only four measures showed a statistical significance (at the .05 level). There was a statistically significant ($t = 2.41$) increase in WISC Performance IQ Score, in the Masculinity–Femininity Scale of the MCPS ($t = 2.19$), in the Rorschach Total F+% ($t = 2.35$), and on the number of "Unpleasant" responses on the Rorschach ($t = 2.19$).

Clinical Boys (N = 19)

For the clinical boys there was a significant increase ($t = 3.05, p < .01$) in the Masculinity–Femininity scores of the MCPS, while on the Rorschach there was a significant increase in the number of F+ responses ($t = 2.75, p < .05$), and consequently an increase in the F+% ($t = 2.39, p < .05$) and Total F+% ($t = 2.19, p < .05$).

Control Boys (*N* = 7)

For the control boys there were some significant decreases on the WRT Arithmetic ($t = 3.09, p < .05$) and on the WISC Comprehension Test ($t = 3.31$, $p < .05$). There was a noticeable increase on the WISC Performance IQ score. However, the small number of children in this group makes the use of parametric statistical tests questionable. These results are presented more for the sake of completeness and accuracy than for their statistical value. They may suggest future areas of interest and allow comparisons with other results.

Verbal Measures and Outcome

These results are summarized from Rogers's (1972) dissertation concerning the relationship between therapist's statements and outcome in monitored play therapy. Her analysis dealt with the therapy tapes of nine clinical boys. Her content analysis covered the following categories: (1) questions, (2) negative, (3) positive, (4) suggestions, (5) direct praise, (6) agreements, (7) disagreements, (8) reflections, and (9) miscellaneous. Scoring reliabilities were in the 90s except for reflections and praise, which were between the .30 and .50 levels of probability.

The outcomes for those variables that were predicted to be significantly associated with post-therapy test score improvement were as follows:

Praise was significantly related to WISC Performance IQ (Mann-Whitney $U = 1.00$, $p < .016$); WRAT Spelling ($U = 2.50, p < .004$); MCPS ($U = .05\ p < .012$) and ($U = 2.00, p < .032$). The relationship between Praise and WISC Full Scale IQ approached significance ($U = 3.00, p < .056$).

Agreement was not significantly related to any outcome measure; however, the relationships between *Agreement* and WISC Performance IQ and between Agreement and the MCPS approached significance ($U = 3.00, p < .056$).

Positives were not significantly related to any outcome measure. These results were the same for absolute frequency and percentage frequency and are summarized in Rogers's original manuscript (1972). The outcome for the seven types of therapists' verbalizations about which no directional outcome was predicted was as follows:

Absolute frequency of therapists' verbalization per session question was significantly related to WRAT Reading ($U = 0, p < .016$, two-tailed). When percentage frequency of therapists' verbalization per session was considered, question was significantly related to WISC Verbal IQ ($U = 1.00, p < .032$, two-tailed) and WRAT Spelling ($U = 1.50, p < .048$, two-tailed).

There were no significant relationships between *Reflection, Suggestion, Negative, Disagreement, Miscellaneous Statement* or *Total* and any of the outcome measures.

THE PROCESS OF MONITORED PLAY THERAPY: QUALITATIVE OBSERVATIONS

Usually the first hour was exploratory. The child could not believe that he would be allowed to play, seemingly without limits, with such a vast array of games and toys. Consequently, he went from one game to another and from one toy to another to check out that indeed he could play with them without restrictions from the therapist, who was following him. Subsequently, after this exploratory introduction, most children went to play with either one of the three shooting galleries, which were their first choices for at least the first couple of sessions. Eventually, after staying in the A-room anywhere from 3 to 7 sessions (with individual differences in how long they were staying there), most children progressed to the C-room, and a few even reached the last stage: creative construction.

Since aggression and construction in this physical setup were mutually exclusive, their graphic expression (see Figure 6.2) shows one line being the reverse reflection of the other. As this figure shows, time spent on constructive behavior increases as, of course, time spent on aggressive behavior decreased accordingly. The decrease and increase were fairly straightforward up to the ninth session, when there was a sudden spurt of time on aggressive behavior followed by another spurt on the fourteenth session, when there was another increase.

The use of guns and machines showed a parallel decrease for both as monitored play therapy progressed. On the average, more time was spent on baseball and Shuffle Alley than on guns for all sessions except the first one, when their respective use is about even.

The use of aggressive and constructive drawers shows an increase over sessions for the constructive drawers while aggressive drawers were used each session for an average of 8 to 10 minutes. Peaks in the usage of the constructive drawer were on the ninth, thirteenth, and fifteenth sessions. Peaks on constructive machines were on the second and sixth sessions. Peaks for aggressive drawer were on the fourth, eleventh, and fourteenth sessions. The use of constructive machines was greatest during the first six sessions, after which constructive drawers were increasingly used. As the guns were used decreasingly over sessions, the use of the aggressive drawers peaked on the fourth, ninth, and fourteenth sessions, the eleventh session having the highest peak. Essentially, these trends show that with each activity, aggressive or constructive, guns and machines were most used at the beginning, while toys in drawers were used most toward the end of each major phase of monitored play therapy.

This recorded process, using thousands of data, produced a model of aggression and construction with three successive but very distinctive stages for each room. Each stage was easily discernible from how children progressed from one stage to another. Both rooms produced a predictable sequence of stages that was followed by most children (Figure 6.2), as discussed in Chapter 6 of this volume.

Aggression was expressed in three sequential stages: (1) *displaced,* in the sense that the child took to the shooting galleries and shot to his heart's content until he was tired of concentrating on just one toy; (2) *kinesthetic,* consisting of using toy guns, hammers, water pistols, and toy soldiers and Indians, and (3) *competitive,* when the child finally engaged the therapist in aggressive board games that depicted battle scenes or in aggressive touch games like football.

Once the child was satisfied about having expressed most if not all his aggressive tendencies, which, of course, varied from one child to another, he eventually entered the constructive playroom. The three stages in this room consisted of (a) continuing to play with nonaggressive but *competitive* games, such as shuffleboard by himself first, then with the therapist, and then baseball with the therapist, then (b) switching to a *productive* stage, such as using plaster of Paris to make various objects that he could take home as trophies (after they were photographed for the records); (c) for some children, a *creative* stage, where they used Lego and Lincoln Logs to construct houses or forts. The most creative example of creative play consisted of a child building an entire fort, complete with houses and storerooms, with Lincoln Logs and Lego pieces and then going into the aggressive room to retrieve toy soldiers to occupy and defend the fort and toy Indians to attack it!

The foregoing stages are somewhat more detailed and more empirically based than those proposed by Piaget (1951) more than half a century ago: (1) practice, (2) construction, (3) symbolic, and (4) rule-controlled games. As noted repeatedly, reviews of developmental stages in the play and play therapy literature fail to mention any stages except in very general and abstract vagaries, with the sole exception to references to Piaget's work (Piers, 1972). As far as this writer knows, no detailed and specific model of stages of play therapy or play development has been available in the extant literature to this date.

Because accepting the child as an identified patient allowed and even reinforced the family's externalization on him, with the family avoiding taking responsibility for change in the family, this approach was eventually discontinued. The two rooms were changed for use in couple and family enrichment and therapy.

DISCUSSION

The results of this investigation indicate, among other implications, that (1) there is a significant inverse relationship between intellectual level and use of aggressive toys, especially guns, and that (2) given sufficient time and availability of materials, any child, regardless of intellectual level, can learn to work with constructive materials. Consequently, these findings have far-reaching educational and therapeutic implications that cannot be considered here for reasons of space.

The research by Noble (1973) validated the importance of the two dimensions of aggression and construction of monitored play therapy. Noble videotaped children exposed to aggressive films to evaluate their effects on constructive or destructive play. He found that significant amounts of destructive play were apparent (to observers) only after realistically filmed aggression had been viewed. Children played more constructively after seeing stylistic aggression filmed at a distance than after exposure to any other film.

Since the creation of the playrooms described above, a great many strides in technology and computers would allow a virtual therapeutic playroom to be assembled in one single computer (Kijima, Shirakawa, Hirose, & Nihei, 1994).

RECOMMENDATIONS

From the incredibly large number of toys and games commercially available on the Internet (Appendix A), it is now possible to select those that will fit into the six stages outlined above, as shown in Table 6.1 this volume.

Selection of toys and games would not only follow the stages of this model but also consider relevant variables such as age, sex, and possibly disabilities. Length of play session would be based on the child's age and developmental level, from at least 30 to at most 60 minutes per child. Major independent variables would be (1) mental age computed in intellectual rather than chronological criteria; and (2) gender. Whether it is possible to find games and toys that are more gender appropriate remains to be seen. Perhaps three different virtual playrooms could be built (in the same computer) according to developmental stages: (1) below 8 years, (2) between 9 and 13 years, and (3) between 14 and 17 years of age.

An important implication of this technology lies in supplanting the therapist with automatic feedback built in the computer. For instance, were a child to remain stuck in the aggressive displacement stage, feedback would be built in to inform the child that there is not time left to play. However, if the child were to play with other (more advanced!) games and toys, play time could be extended. Furthermore, in addition to keeping time and recording the child's performance, the computer can be programmed to provide feedback information on the quality of performance, quantity of production, and nature of problem-solving.

CONCLUSION

Virtual playrooms of the type proposed here could be used in clinics and hospitals to aid in the medical and psychological treatment of sick or troubled children, by themselves or in conjunction with other modalities of intervention (medication, family therapy, etc.).

An Experimental Theory-Derived Structured Play Interview

METATHEORETICAL ASSUMPTIONS

This interview is strictly experimental and has not been validated. It will need modifications and evaluations by anyone interested in applying it for research before using it for clinical purposes.

Note that not all questions in this interview need to be asked. The questions included in this interview are suggestive rather than absolute. The language needs to be adapted to the gender and age of the participant, and left to the sensitivity, flexibility, and experience of the interviewer.

Model 1: Width of Play Relationships

Emotionality: How do you feel when you play? Can you tell me a little more about how you feel while you play? How do you feel before you are going to play? How do you feel after you have played? What happens to you if you win or lose in a game? How do you feel when you win? How do you feel when you lose? Can you remember when you laughed while playing? Did you ever cry when you play? What is it about your play that makes you cry or laugh? Do you remember anybody laughing or crying when playing? Who? When? Why?

Rationality: What do you think while you are playing? Do you ever think before playing? How much thinking do you do while playing? A great deal, some, or none? Could you please tell me more about your thinking while you are playing? What about after you have played? Any thoughts after you are finished with playing? What do you think about winning or losing a game? Do you plan how you are going to play or do you play without thinking?

Activity: How much time do you spend playing in one day? How many hours? Do you keep track of time while you are playing? How much time would you like to spend playing in one day? How do you do when you are playing?

Awareness: What are you aware of while playing? What are you not aware of? Why should anyone be aware while you are playing? Aware of what? Are you aware of anything after you have finished playing?

Contest: Do you ever worry about yourself when you play? Do you ever worry about other players? Do you ever worry about other people (children, parents, siblings, adults, friends, teachers) while you are playing? Who do you worry the most about? Do you worry about your family? Do you worry about teachers? Do you worry about whoever is watching you play?

Model 2: Depth of Play Relationships

Do you even think about what impression your play will make on others? Do you care to make as good impression on others while you play? How about your appearance when you play? Does appearance mean anything to you while you play? Do you like to impress other people with your play? How does your family feel about your play? How do you feel inside when you play? Were there games played in your family? Are you playing any games that were played by either one of your parents or your grandparents?

Model 3: Play   Settings

How much of your time in spent playing at home, at school/work, or free time? How different is when you play at home from your playing anywhere else? Same, different, or the opposite? Where do you like to play the most? At home, on the playground, on the computer? At friends' homes? Where do you like to play the most? Why?

THEORETICAL ASSUMPTIONS OF THE THEORY

Model 4: Ability to Love

What kinds of toys do you like the most? What kind of games do you like best? With whom do you like to play the most? What are your favorite toys? What are your favorite games? What kind of toy do you like to use when you are playing? What kind of game do you like to play the most? What kind of toy you do no like to play with? What kind of game you do not like to play? Which game are you good at? Which game are you not very good at? Who are your favorite friends you like to play with? Who you do not like to play with? How do you avoid playing with people you do not like? How do you go to friends you would like to play with? How do you feel when you are accepted in a team? How do you feel when you are rejected from a team?

Model 5: Ability to Control Self

How fast or slow are you while playing? Can you tell when you are slow or fast at which game? When? With whom? With what toy or game? What is the fastest game you like the most? What is the slowest game you like the most? What or who do you controls your playing? Do your parents control your play? How? How much? Do you control your playing? How do you control it? Is there any game you cannot control?

Model 6: Both Abilities

How good are you as a player? Excellent, good, middle, poor, or very poor? How do your friends see you as a player? Excellent, good, middle, poor, or very poor? How do your parents see you as a player? Excellent, good, middle, poor, or very poor? What kind of games are you good at? What kind of games are you poor at? What toys and games do you like the best? What kind of games you do not like?

Model 7: Contents of Play Relationships

What kind of play are you allowed in the house? Who allows you to play? Who likes your playing? If you could choose, would you prefer to play by yourself or play with others? If you could choose, would like to play or to be close to those you love and who love you without having to do anything, not even playing? Do you prefer to have money and things rather than being close to those you love? Who loves you without conditions regardless of how and what you play? Does anyone you know want you to play perfectly, perform perfectly, and win at all costs? Do you feel loved regardless of what and how you play? How? When? Why?

NORMATIVE MODELS OF THE THEORY

Model 8: Likeness Continuum in Playing

How much do you resemble people you love in your playing? Do any of your parents (caretakers), brothers and sisters, relatives, and other people play the same games you play? Do they like the same toys you play with? How strong is this resemblance? Very close, close enough, not close at all, different from someone, the opposite of someone, or completely without any resemblance to anyone? Who in your family plays or has played the same games you play? Who plays completely different games from games you play? Who plays games that are completely opposite from the games you play? Who plays games that are completely outside of what you or your family feels are the most popular games?

Model 9: Styles In Play Relationships

What is your preferred style while playing? Do you think and plan before dealing? Do you like to be on your own and build something new, or do you prefer to play by the rules that players should follow? Do you play immediately without thinking about the consequences of your playing? Do you become abusive and foul-mouthed when playing with others? How? When? Why? Do you like rough games, with close body contact or do you like to play without close body contact?

Model 10: Functionality in Play Interactions

How much do you play above and beyond home chores, school, or work responsibilities? Do you leave time to play by yourself and with others? How do you have and use extra free time? Do you belong and are you active in any play organization or team? Do you have any hobbies or other play interests outside of home, family, school or work? How? Why?

Model 11: Selfhood

How important are your toys and games to you? How important is your playing to your family? How important are your playmates to you? Are your playmates more important than your family? Is your importance more important than your toys and games? Is any toy or game unimportant to you? Are others more important than playing? How? When? Why? Does your play make you feel important? Good, bad, or indifferent? How did you learn to feel that way about yourself while playing?

Model 12: Play and Priorities

In play what toys are most important to you? What kind of toys and games do you like best? Are these toys and games more important than other people? What other toy or game is more important than other toys or games? What play activities are more important than other play activities? How is playing more or less important than other things?

APPLICATIONS OF THE THEORY

Model 13: Distance Regulation

When you play, who pursues you and whom do you pursue? When? Who keeps away from you while you are playing? When? Why? Whom do you go to when you need or want something or help with your play? Whom do you keep away from while playing? When? Why? Who sends you away when you need or want something about playing? While playing, who wants something from you on one hand and then sends you away because whatever you do or say was not good enough? Do coaches, judges, referees, or teachers ever get you out from a nasty player or play situation?

Model 14: Drama Triangle

In your play fantasy, pretend play, imagination, or made-up stories, does anyone ever play the part of the Victim? Does anyone ever play the part of the Persecutor? Does anyone ever play the part of the Rescuer? Do you ever switch parts, the Victim may become the Persecutor and the Rescuer becomes the Victim? When? How? Why? Does anybody ever rescue you from a nasty play situation and a rough, mean game? Who rescues you when you play the Victim or the Persecutor? Do you ever persecute anybody? Is there any bullying in your experience with play? When? Where? With whom? Why?

Model 15: Intimacy

How do you feel after you have won a game? How do you celebrate after you have won a game? How do you feel after you have lost a game? Do you ever share past and present hurt feelings about or after losing a game? With whom? Have you ever cried after you lost a game? When? How? Where? Why? Have you ever seen any player cry? When? How? Why? If you have cried for a loss, do you share your hurt feelings with anyone? Why not? Do you ever forgive yourself for past or present games lost? Do you ever forgive anybody else for past or present game losses? How? When? Why? Why not? Do you ever forgive others who may have been responsible for game losses? How? When? Why? Why not?

Model 16: Negotiation

Who makes decisions about when, with whom, and with what do you play? How do you make those decisions? Who makes big decisions and who makes small decisions about your playing? Who carries those decisions out? How do you solve disagreements about your playing? How do you solve problems about playing with your family? With your playmates? With your teachers? Do you ever sit down to talk things over with anyone who is involved in playing with you?

INDEX

About the Author

Luciano L'Abate, PhD, is a professor emeritus of psychology at Georgia State University at Atlanta. He is a diplomate and former examiner of the American Board of Professional Psychology, and a fellow and approved supervisor of the American Association of Marriage and Family Therapy. Author or co-author of more than three hundred papers, chapters, and book reviews in professional and scientific journals, he is also author, co-author, editor, or co-editor of forty-three books. His work has been translated in Argentina, China, Denmark, Finland, French Canada, Germany, Italy, Japan, Korea, and Poland. He is also the 2009 recipient of the Award for Distinguished Professional Contribution in Applied Research by the American Psychological Association.